Ram Publications

Hal Dawson, Editor

Detector Owner's Field Manual
Explains total capabilities and HOW TO USE procedures of all types of metal detectors.

Electronic Prospecting
Learn how to find gold and silver veins, pockets and nuggets using easy electronic metal detector methods.

Gold Panning Is Easy
This excellent field guide shows you how to FIND and PAN gold as quickly and easily as a professional.

Modern Metal Detectors
This advanced handbook for home, field, and classroom study gives the expertise you need for success in any metal detecting situation, hobby or professional, and increases your understanding of all fields of metal detector use.

Successful Coin Hunting
The world's most authoritative guide to FINDING VALUABLE COINS with all types of metal detectors. The name speaks for itself!

Treasure Hunter's Manual #6
Quickly guides the inexperienced beginner through the mysteries of FULL TIME TREASURE HUNTING.

Treasure Hunter's Manual #7
The classic! THE book on professional methods of RESEARCH, RECOVERY, and DISPOSITION of treasures found.

Treasure Hunting Pays Off!
An excellent introduction to all facets of treasure hunting.

Buried Treasure of the United States
Complete field guide for finding treasure with state-by-state listing of sites where treasure can be found.

Weekend Prospecting!
Written for the person who wants to know exactly how to get started in the fascinating and rewarding hobby of weekend prospecting with metal detectors and gold panning equipment.

TREASURE RECOVERY
from
SAND and SEA

CHARLES GARRETT

ISBN 0-915920-51-4
Library of Congress Catalog Card No. 87-063128
Treasure Recovery From Sand and Sea
© Copyright 1988.
Charles L. Garrett.

First Edition Printing, January 1988

88 89 90 10 9 8 7 6 5 4 3 2 1

For FREE listing of related treasure hunting books write
Ram Publishing Company • P.O. Box 38649 • Dallas, Texas 75238

DEDICATION

To all those over the world who seek treasure with Garrett equipment...may the close of every day in the field and surf find you returning home with a pouch overflowing with newfound treasure. It is my fondest hope that techniques and ideas presented in this book will add to that overflowing pouch.

By CHARLES GARRETT
Treasure Recovery from Sand and Sea
Modern Metal Detectors
Successful Coin Hunting
Treasure Hunting Pays Off!
Treasure Hunting Secrets
Electronic Prospecting (with Lagal)
Complete VLF-TR Metal Detector Handbook (with Lagal)

CONTENTS

About the Author
Author's Note
Introduction

ABOUT THE AUTHOR

The year 1988 marked the Silver Jubilee of Garrett Electronics, Inc., the company founded by Charles Garrett to manufacture metal detectors he had designed. Chief among these designs has been the legendary Master Hunter.

Over the past quarter century this name has come to describe Charles Garrett himself. In fact, the affable Texan is now accepted among dedicated treasure hunters as the Grand Master of all Hunters. He has earned this title by searching for and finding treasure with a metal detector on five continents—from gold fields of the remote Australian outback to waters of South America which conceal shipwrecked treasures bound for Seville and Madrid four centuries ago.

Charles was reared in the piney woods of Deep East Texas where he enjoyed the normal outdoor adventures of a growing boy in the rural South. His first real interest in buried treasure or lost wealth came at about age 12 when he discovered a "cache" of old National Geographic magazines in the attic of his aunt's home. He read about the discovery of King Tut's tomb, and the treasure-hunting spark was ignited. Furthermore, World War II brought faraway places even closer to the young lad as he heard tales of Americans in distant lands.

After graduation from high school in Lufkin, TX, in 1950, he served four years in the U.S. Navy during the Korean conflict. He spent more than three years as an electrician's mate aboard the USS Bottineau APA235, a World War II Liberty ship. The treasure-hunting flame spread to include electronics.

After marriage to Miss Eleanor Smith, a school teacher from Pennington, TX, he further enlarged his knowledge of electronics with a Bachelor of Science degree in electrical engineering from what is now Lamar University in Beaumont, TX.

He then worked several years in the young but booming electronics industry as America boisterously entered the space age. As an engineer at Texas Instruments and Teledyne Geotech in the Dallas area, he participated in a number of important developments in military, space and earth science electronics. These included design of a power supply and amplifier for the Mariner II space probe; electronic radar terrain-scanning displays for the U.S. Air Force F-111 fighter-bomber (a design concept now used on the F-16); an electronically stabilized earth platform used in testing seismographs; various earth seismograph components; and a seismograph amplifer that was "planted" on the moon by Neil A. Armstrong, Apollo 11 astronaut.

Treasure hunting was never far from the thoughts of the young electronics engineer. Charles used his spare time to design metal detectors and explore Texas ghost towns and early day settlements with them. The treasures he was finding soon made it obvious that his equipment was superior to that being sold to the public by commercial manufacturers.

The result was Garrett Electronics, which he and his wife founded in 1963. The company's products were quickly accepted by treasure hunters, first in the United States, then all over the world. The Master Hunter was setting a standard of excellence by which all treasure hunting metal detectors were to be judged. This standard has steadily been raised. Today the Garrett line is the most extensive in the industry, and its detectors have been associated recently with three of the greatest discoveries in treasure hunting history.

These great finds include the fabulous million-dollar Hand of Faith gold nugget in Australia, and the magnificent Middleham Jewel, a gold pendant said to have been owned by England's King Richard III in the 15th century, which were found with Garrett detectors. Garrett underwater instruments were used by Mel Fisher's team in their successful search for a Spanish King's multi-million-dollar treasure off the Florida Keys.

From his earliest days as a commercial manufacturer of metal detecting equipment, the Grand Master of Treasure Hunters vowed to "practice what I preach." Before any new Garrett equipment is offered to customers, he tests it personally to insure that it works regardless of ground conditions or environment. In this effort he has traveled extensively throughout the United States, Australia, Canada, islands in the Caribbean, Colombia, Mexico, England and seven other Western European countries.

In Australia he and Peter Bridge, the "Father of Australia's Electronic Gold Rush," held electronic prospecting seminars in every major city. Australia's electronic gold rush blossomed, and millions of dollars of nuggets were discovered with Garrett detectors.

He has been involved — on land and in the water — in every area of treasure hunting with a metal detector, including coin hunting, relic hunting, ghost towning and prospecting. He has generously shared with others the knowledge he has gained. He has written countless articles, books and films and participated in literally hundreds of lectures, seminars and panel discussions.

He has already produced 10 treasure-hunting and adventure videos and faces an ambitious shooting schedule. The most recent production, GOLD PANNING IS EASY, is already considered to be the "primer" of the prospectors' art. A new video, WEEKEND PROSPECTING, explains all areas of gold-hunting for the novice and professional alike and appears destined for equal acclaim. For 15 years his highly regarded books SUCCESSFUL COIN HUNTING and the more recent MODERN METAL DETECTORS have served as basic texts for all treasure hunters.

He organized the American Metal Detectors Manufacturers Association and served as its first president. In 1983 he was again elected president. He sponsored and founded the International Treasure Hunting Society (Search International).

The name Garrett has come to be synonymous with metal detecting just as the name Cousteau is synonymous with underwater exploration.

In this book Charles Garrett enters the water himself with various types of metal detectors to disclose secrets of finding treasure on the beach as well as in surf, oceans, rivers and lakes. This is a "how to" book indeed, but it is filled with exciting stories of treasures found in or near the water. In this volume he shares knowledge gained over decades of experience; it is an absolute must for anyone who seeks hidden wealth.

The Editor
RAM Publishing
Dallas, Texas

AUTHOR'S NOTE

To many people I owe a debt of gratitude and thanks...

A very special "thank you" to my wife, Eleanor, and my children, Charles Lewis, Jr., Deirdre Lynne and Vaughan Lamar.

Virgil Hutton reviewed my chapter on Cleaning and suggested several changes. Monty Moncrief with his experience contributed to the section on Aerial Photography; plus, he supplied many fine photographs taken at Galveston. Walter E. "Rip" Parker, Dallas attorney, reviewed the chapter on Laws and made excellent suggestions and additions. George Sullivan freely provided excerpts from his forthcoming book on Mel Fisher and the *Atocha* for the chapter on the Archaeologist and the Treasure Hunter. Robert Marx graciously offered research reference data from several of his superb books on underwater salvage and archaeology.

I especially thank Hal Dawson for his many days spent improving my manuscript and making sure "every last thing" was correct prior to printing. Marie England spent countless and uncomplaining hours typing and retyping the manuscript. Special thanks also to Ken Durham, Elaine Campbell and Mary Penson for their endeavors.

Thanks to Tom Edds, Jack Lowry, Ed Morris and others who read portions or all of the manuscript and suggested improvements in treasure locating and recovery techniques.

Concerning illustrations and photography, I am grateful to so many it would be impossible to list them all. Mel Climer's professional contributions are to be found throughout the book. His wife, Lisa, assisted during several photography expeditions on the Texas coast. Many photographs in this book were supplied by friends and fellow treasure hunters whose names are included in captions. Other photos were taken by my "delayed shutter" camera.

To all, my profound thanks.

INTRODUCTION

I recently presented a slide talk to some 500 treasure hunters. It covered this book's basic outline, and I explained a few of the techniques that beach and surf hunters use in locating lost treasure. Following that talk, a crowd gathered around the Garrett Metal Detector exhibit, eagerly seeking to purchase copies of this book and to learn more about water-related treasure recovery. It was because of experiences such as these that I began writing *Treasure Recovery from Sand and Sea* several years ago. It was obvious to me that a good percentage of the tens of thousands of land hunters also wanted to pursue and find treasures in the water. I set about to apply knowledge and experience gained over a lifetime of treasure hunting on land to every aspect of successful searching for all types of treasure that could be found in and around water.

As you will discover from reading this book, I left very few stones unturned in my quest. And, let me emphasize that I enjoyed every minute of every field trip I made to learn, first hand, what water hunting was all about. I learned also that there are many professional water hunters who have filled bank vaults with their discovered treasure. I learned something else, though...something very important to YOU.

While many fortunes in treasure have been taken from beaches, the surf and under the water, only the "surface" has been scratched, so to speak. The amount of treasure left to be discovered cannot be comprehended. Believe me.

Let me leave you to the reading and study of this book with what I consider the wisest course of action, my belief in an eight-letter word that must begin all treasure hunts. That word is RESEARCH! Do your homework, find the best places to search and you'll find more treasure than you every dreamed or imagined possible.

You can also count on something else; I practice what I preach. See you in the water.

Charles Garrett

CHAPTER 1

The Lure of Instant Riches—
What Treasure Hunting is About

The lure of instant riches...that's what treasure hunting is all about. The discovery of a single coin, a ten-thousand-dollar ring, or a chest of gold...each is thrilling. And, when treasure is found, the search for more begins immediately. The lure of lost, buried or sunken riches beckons people from all walks of life. Treasure hunters range from the armchair adventurer to the seasoned professional. Some only dream of finding treasure while others set about with determination born from the belief that the next turn of the shovel will unearth instant riches.

No one has enough wealth. No one, it seems, ever loses the desire or the dream of finding treasure. Sales of treasure hunting equipment reflect this yearning. When the value of gold reached nearly $800 an ounce in 1980, sales of metal detectors jumped nearly 400% in a single year. Garrett Electronics' metal detector production lagged nearly two months behind orders during that period of high gold value. The company simply could not keep up with the demand.

After *P.M. Magazine,* Figure 1-1, presented on network television a story about treasure hunters finding coins and jewelry in a California surf, metal detector dealers were swamped the next day with purchasers. When Mel Fisher announced he found the location of a $400-million treasure from a sunken Spanish treasure galleon and that he was hauling gold and silver on board in buckets, adventurers beat a path to metal detector and treasure hunting equipment shops.

When stories are reported locally about treasure being found, sales of detector equipment take a noticeable leap. Even though the desire for instant riches may be depressed into the subconscious, only a small spark often brings it to life. The fever hits! When it does, there is no cooling down until the person tries his or her hand at treasure recovery. Whether doctor, lawyer, movie star, teacher, plumber, electrician, librarian or whatever, you are a prime candidate to respond to the lure of treasure hunting. Whether you have a grade school education, a high school diploma or a doctor's degree, the reward of instant riches probably appeals to you.

As a manufacturer of metal detectors, I meet many of our customers. What I have just related, I have witnessed firsthand. People of all ages find the prospect of discovering riches irresistible. There is nothing wrong with finding lost wealth. The Bible speaks of a man who found a treasure hidden in a field and sold all he had to get money to buy that field. Treasure hunting is recognized by many as an activity with merit beyond greed. They accept it as a lifetime hobby. Granted, many people do not understand treasure hunting or know what metal detecting is all about. Others have read fabulous stories, yet refuse to believe that lost treasure exists, much less that a man-made device can find it. Manufacturers continually devise programs to teach how metal detectors work and can find treasure.

Lest I lead you astray, let me emphasize that treasure hunting is *not* easy. In fact, more often than not, it is downright hard work. The actual truth is that success is measured in direct proportion to time and effort spent selecting the right equipment, learning how to use it, then carrying out research that leads to successful recovery.

When I was young I repeated the old maxim, "Practice makes perfect." My mother quickly corrected me, saying, "Perfect practice makes perfect." How right she was. When you learn the correct way to use your detector, when you learn the proper way to research and locate potentially rich treasure sites, and when you correctly and persistently apply this acquired knowledge, you will be successful. You'll never be satisfied, however, because you'll always know of a better place to search for treasure, and you'll always be ready to improve your skills.

Figure 1-1: The television show, P.M. MAGAZINE, has aired several documentaries on both land and water treasure hunting. Each time, a flurry of activity is created and treasure hunting picks up briskly. George Mroczkowski, center back row, is the host for a brief P.M. MAGAZINE inquiry into treasure hunting in Southern California.

The earth is an enormous treasure bank. Because it offers wealth to be found, treasure hunters will always search for their share. When YOU join the ranks of the beach, surf and underwater searchers, you'll be thrilled when you find your first coin. Then, when nickels, dimes and quarters cease to excite, you'll begin searching for rare and more valuable coins and rings, jewelry, relics and sunken treasure. Your determination will stimulate more research and literally force you to discover history and experience its fascination. Whether young or old, male or female, when you find your first treasure, there will be no turning back. This book is designed to guide you along that path. Believe me: start right and you'll finish successfully.

CHAPTER 2

There is Treasure to be Found

"The surest antidote to failure in treasure hunting is correct knowledge."
Karl von Mueller

If all lost treasure and items of value could be recovered from Davy Jones' locker (which includes all beaches, lakes, streams and rivers) and if this wealth could be evenly distributed, I believe every man, woman and child on earth could live comfortably for the rest of their lives on this wealth.

Seventy percent or nearly 200 million square miles of the earth's surface is water. Since the dawn of mankind, man has lived on or near water. Warfare, commerce, recreation, exploration and the search for food have lured men and women to water since mankind began. And when man makes contact with water, he generally brings wealth with him.

Such wealth takes many forms: it may be a single coin, a diamond ring or a ship laden with millions of dollars in cargo. Countless possessions of man have been lost and will continue to be lost in the world's water—if not today, then tomorrow.

What is mankind doing to retrieve this wealth? Comparatively speaking, practically nothing, even though men each day execute elaborate plans to search for sunken wealth. Recovery teams attempt to locate and retrieve planes, ships and lost cargo. Archaeologists and historians meticulously locate and recover artifacts from sunken historical sites and shipwrecks.

Treasure hunters scan beaches and surf and dive under water to recover lost treasure worth millions yearly. In reality, however, the amount of wealth currently being lost each day exceeds the amount being recovered.

All lost wealth can never be recovered. Man's best efforts will locate only a small percentage of lost treasure and recover just part of this. The purpose of this book is to help you learn how to search for, and find, your share of this lost wealth. Much of the "how-to" material explains the use of the modern metal detector. Since most wealth that can be recovered is metal, a detector is the perfect tool for finding it. We all dream of discovering a rich Spanish treasure ship laden with thousands of silver pieces of eight and gold escudo coins. But, on a more practical note, the typical treasure hunter would gladly settle for just the coins and rings lost daily by those who use the water for recreation and commerce.

This book gives basic instruction on locating sunken ships and underwater treasure of all kinds. Its main purpose, however, is to teach you how to find and recover coins and jewelry from the earth's recreational beaches, surf areas and accessible waterways. Diligent effort will leave you extremely pleased with newfound wealth. Beachcombing, surf searching and shallow water recovery techniques are quick to master, yet long on rewards. Surf searching begins where beachcombing ends. Shallow underwater searching begins where surfing ends.

Found treasure delights the mind and puts a sparkle in the eyes. There's nothing like the thrill of instant wealth in your hand. You'll experience it when you master simple research methods, metal detector skills and recovery techniques. The amount of wealth recovered daily by men and women like yourself is staggering to contemplate. It's not necessary to be a soldier of fortune trekking off to a distant country or a Caribbean island in search of a lost pirate chest. The wealth that can probably be recovered within your hometown city limits — most likely, within your county — and absolutely within your state totals thousands upon thousands of dollars.

In the next chapter I'll introduce several people just like you who ventured forth, followed the rules of the game and won. Countless volumes would be required to present all those who have been successful in treasure hunting. You may know some of them. I wish this book could be large enough to list them all. But, that's not our purpose. We want to help you get on a beach or in the water, and we want you to be equipped to wrest from Davy Jones some of the wealth stored in his treasure vaults.

THE FIRST STEP

This book is for everyone who dreams of discovering lost and sunken treasure. Whether you seek treasure from the beach, the surf or the depths of the sea, you'll need an earnest desire, a lively imagination and a keen interest in finding riches.

Besides offering wealth, treasure recovery is a delightful activity. You'll enjoy the smell of springtime and the warmth of summer; even the crisp winds of autumn and the chill of winter can bring pleasure. Treasure hunting is one of the safest and most enjoyable hobbies in the world; depending upon an individual's skill, it can be one of the most rewarding.

For the beginner, this book is the first step toward successful treasure recovery. "How-to" knowledge presented here results from more than 40 years of study and experience. Metal detector and treasure hunting instruction might not, at first, seem important. Take this opportunity for a proper beginning to your knowledge, however, and you'll become more successful as a treasure finder later.

For the seasoned treasure hunter, this book has assembled the latest information in metal detectors and detecting techniques to help you sharpen your skills. Even a lifetime of treasure hunting is not sufficient to learn all there is to know about this fascinating hobby and its primary tool, the metal detector. I know because I learn more each time I use one. A metal detector is perfectly obedient and will do exactly what it is told to do—either find a ton of trash or locate the treasure you are seeking. Its performance depends upon the knowledge and skill of the user.

Very little educational material is available on the use of metal detectors for recovery in beach, surf and water locations. Available advice is often in the form of first-person accounts that include a generally unorganized assortment of suggestions. Unfortunately, some of the information and advice has proven to be inaccurate and can limit your opportunities to find treasure.

You can search the right way or the wrong way. If you are fully prepared, if you understand your equipment and know how to use it, treasure hunting will be thrilling and profitable. You'll finish with more wealth to show for your efforts than you ever imagined.

CHAPTER 3

You Can Find Lost Treasure-- Meet Others Who Have

Recently, I passed the forty-year "anniversary" of the day I found my first treasure. By eyesight I found a walking Liberty half-dollar and a watch lying partly concealed in grass near the front entrance of the Lufkin, TX, High School building, Since that time I have found more than my share of lost wealth, but the amount of treasure that I have seen others discover exceeds mine many thousands of times.

It would be easy to fill this chapter with nothing but names of people who have shown me their discoveries or who sent photographs of the wealth they found. Occasionally, I encounter so much treasure that I am left speechless when I realize the vast amount that waits to be found!

FULL-TIME TREASURE HUNTER

In a sense, I am a full-time professional treasure hunter. Much of my time, however, is spent directing Garrett Electronics, a company that my wife and I founded in the early 1960s. Often I work alone in my quest for treasure, but I also join forces with other treasure hunters. During all my treasure hunting activities I put many "miles" on my metal detection equipment.

Often, I help others search for valuables they have lost or for treasure they expect to find. I spend a good percentage of my time testing new Garrett equipment and accessories. Whenever possible, I test equipment at treasure sites seeking "double-barrel" success. I test and prove Garrett equipment while finding lost, buried and sunken treasure, Figure 3-1.

The majority of my hunting has been done on land, which includes beaches. More recently, I have begun to search for treasure in the surf. And, since I have been a scuba diver since the early 60s, my searches often lead under water. Consequently, the amount of treasure I have found, or have witnessed, bestows upon me real authority to state that if you sincerely want to "strike it rich," you should become a beachcomber, surfer or a shallow water treasure hunter.

If you are not yet convinced that beachcombing or water hunting is for you, read on.

JAMES "MONTY" MONCRIEF

James "Monty" Moncrief, Figure 3-2, resides near one of the world's greatest treasure vaults, the Texas coast. It was this coast that "converted" him from land hunting to beach and surf hunting. Monty

Figure 3-1: The author holds a 17th Century Spanish icon which he has just detected and dug from the beach sands of Guadeloupe. In almost every instance whenever Mr. Garrett tests new Garrett instrumentation, he tries to select good treasure locations.

served several years in United States Naval Intelligence before accepting a position with the National Aeronautics and Space Administration. He and his wife, Becky, now reside in Nassau Bay near Galveston, TX. Monty and I often talked about the need for a combination land/underwater metal detector. As a result of these discussions, he became instrumental in the mechanical design and development of the Garrett Sea Hunter detector. While testing it on Galveston beaches, he began to find lost coins and jewelry, These early successes whetted his appetite for further discoveries. Consequently, he now spends much of his free time searching productive coastal sites. His finds are measured not in items but rather in pounds of coins and jewelry. At

8

a recent South Texas treasure hunter's gathering he showed me a beautiful 18-karat ladies bracelet he had recently added to his collection of found jewelry. While his beach and surf finds are spectacular, he continues in other phases of treasure hunting, especially electronic prospecting.

JACK LOWRY

Jack Lowry, Figure 3-3, began his treasure hunting career looking for coins in recreation areas and homesites. He amassed buckets filled with coins of all descriptions. While he found an occasional piece of lost jewelry, he was not satisfied. He decided to try his luck on a Texas recreational beach. Since that first day, he has become an avowed beach/surf hunter. Even though he lives in Garland, TX, about 300 miles from Galveston, he makes the trek to the beach every chance he gets. He still finds coins, but his ring and jewelry collection has sharply increased in size and value. To improve his beach and surf hunting efficiency, he keeps track of storms and tides. Whenever there is an exceptionally low Texas tide, you can expect to see Jack in the surf, regardless of weather conditions. He occasionally travels to New Mexico and Arizona to electronic prospect and cache hunt, but he will quickly tell you that his first love is water hunting. As this was being written, Jack showed the author a 14-karat man's ring he had recently found. The ring with a large ruby and two diamonds mounted in the crown is worth more than $800.

T.R. (TOM) EDDS AND WALTER STARK

Tom Edds, Figure 3-4, and Walter Stark are ordinary folks like me and perhaps like you. If you happen to meet them, they probably will have beach sand in their cuffs and a beautiful tan — instant clues that they like the great outdoors. Beyond that, you might never know they are two of the world's most successful metal-detecting beachcombers.

Their Florida residence gives them instant access to countless miles of recreational beaches that might better be described as storehouses of lost treasure. Should you be lucky enough to see them display some of their finds at a treasure meet, you won't believe your eyes. The gold, silver and platinum rings, diamond rings, high school rings, gold and silver bracelets, religious medals and other jewelry they have found would put a well-equipped jewelry store to shame. You'll listen spellbound as they describe these various treasures and as they tell you exactly when and where each object was found. You may be equally surprised at the tremendous quantity of lesser-valued items they have recovered from the sand: toys, locks, keys, sunglasses and an endless list of ordinary metal items.

Listening to these men and watching them search is an education. They're never in a hurry. They methodically pursue their hobby with precision and deliberate slowness and they know what they're doing.

Figure 3-2: James "Monty" Moncrief helps test a Sea Hunter underwater metal detector on the salty beaches of Galveston, TX. While testing equipment on Galveston beaches he began to find lost coins and jewelry. Since then, he now spends much of his free time searching these productive coastal sites.

Figure 3-3: That's right, Jack, smile! And, who wouldn't smile if they could claim for themselves this vast horde of treasure that Jack Lowry has found during his past few years searching local parks and the surf along Texas' coastline.

They have developed beach treasure recovery into a fine art, perhaps, even a science. Should you meet them on the beach, they may take a few minutes from their scanning to give you tips on how you can find your share of beach treasure. "There's plenty to go 'round, join us and let's find some treasure," they'll tell you.

Figure 3-4: Tom Edds (in photo) and Walter Stark are quite possibly the world's most successful beach hunters. These men started searching Florida's endless recreational beaches many years ago, long before beach hunting became a popular sport.

ELEANOR HUBE

Eleanor Hube's eyes are always sparkling and she never loses her smile, Figure 3-5. Perhaps she's thinking of what tomorrow may bring when she'll again seek lost treasure. Eleanor is a surf hunter. She used to search the land and has spent many thousands of hours in local parks, playgrounds and ghost towns. But since the day she ventured forth at a local swimming beach and found her first gold ring, she's never gone back to dry land hunting.

She has spent so much time enjoying the rewards of surf searching that she's as much at home in the water as out. Because she rarely removes it from the bank vault, you'll never see much of Eleanor's found treasure. Occasionally, however, she'll bring out a few choice pieces for a talk before some local treasure hunting club. She has, on occasion, let me photograph a few of her valuable finds. I assure you, if you could see the rewards that have come from this dedicated surfer's persistence, you would quickly follow in her footsteps.

Of course, those footsteps don't end at the local beach. She, her husband and friends travel throughout the United States, the Caribbean and to England. The first thing she packs is her underwater Garrett Sea Hunter metal detector. Usually the results of her first day of surf hunting on the Caribbean beaches more than pay for the entire trip.

"It's not work," she once told me. "It's pure vacation. I love every minute of it. I'm hooked—but who wouldn't be if they could spend the rest of their life enjoying a rewarding hobby like the one I pursue."

Figure 3-5: Eleanor Hube of Connecticut is most likely the world's most traveled surf hunter and quite possibly the world's most successful lady surf hunter. During her early days of treasure hunting she spent many thousands of hours in local parks, playgrounds and ghost towns. But since the day she ventured forth at a local swimming beach and found her first gold ring, she has never gone back to dry land hunting.

12

ED MORRIS

Ed Morris is a retired Air Force officer who lives in Santa Maria, CA. Upon retirement he began spending his leisure time treasure hunting. Over the years he developed a knack for beach hunting because he lives immediately adjacent to miles of prime swimming and recreational beaches. He gained mastery over his first detector and as new instruments came along he quickly became proficient in their operation. Over the years he amassed a large quantity of rings, coins, jewelry and other valuable items discovered by his metal detector in the sands of the beach. Since he was heavily involved in journalism in the Air Force, he began writing articles about his hobby and published them in the various treasure hunting magazines. You probably have read several of Ed's helpful articles. "There has never been any need for me to search for another hobby," says Ed. "The activity of metal detecting on local beaches is all I need. It's solid fun. I enjoy it, and it's very rewarding. It's one of the most healthful activities I can think of. I'm hooked on the great outdoors and the sunshine and, of course, the rewards of treasure hunting."

DON CYR

Don Cyr, of Burlington, Ontario, Canada, Figure 9-2, Chapter 9, has been a water hunter for many years. In spite of the cold weather and frozen lakes during a good portion of the year, he and many other Canadians continue their quest wearing hip waders and wet suits. He likes water hunting, because many of his best treasure finds come from the water.

His activities often take him throughout Canada as well as into the United States. Because of his dedication to the hobby, he was voted President of the Canadian Metal Detecting Association. He worked diligently to help form a coalition between CMDA and FMDA (United States Federation of Metal Detectors and Archaeological Clubs. In other chapters in this book you will see photographs of many of Cyr's finds.

SHERRILL WILLIAMS AND BOB DARNELL

Sherrill Williams and Bob Darnell are lake hunters. The story of their adventures and finds is so interesting, they were featured in the *Lake Country Banner* of Tiptonville, TN. During the "good old days," thousands of sun lovers frolicked on the beaches and swam in the warm water at several nearby recreational areas. Until Sherrill and Bob began their underwater recovery work, no one thought much about or believed that those early day fun seekers lost their wealth. There were a few remembered instances of missing rings, but that was about it. The newspaper article tells their true story, and readers are awed by the treasure they have found.

Many of the found class rings have been returned to their owners who lost the jewelry as far back as 1931. Much of the treasure, however, is on display at Sherrill Williams' True Value Hardware in Hornbeak,

TN. At last count the treasure included more than 3300 coins, 334 of which are silver. There are 28 buffalo nickels, 118 mercury dimes, 108 Roosevelt dimes, 84 silver quarters and 24 silver half dollars. The oldest coin dates 1894. Other items included 5 gold rings with stones, 30 silver rings, 14 class rings, 8 gold bands and 2 diamond rings. There are 19 religious items, a 5-gram gold piece and a large assortment of knives, lighters, buckles, keys, bathing suit pins, chains, bracelets, watches, lifeguard whistles, pendants and sunglasses.

HARRY AND LUCILLE BOWEN

Harry and Lucille Bowen, of Spokane, WA, have been active metal detector enthusiasts for three decades. Harry is a retired Spokane police officer. Years ago they began to think about life after Harry's retirement and they decided to open a treasure hunting specialty shop. They believed many people in Spokane would be interested in treasure hunting, With the experience they had gained in the past, plus the experience they would gain in the next few years, they could teach their customers about this great hobby.

As the years progressed, Harry continued to concentrate mostly on land hunting. However, Lucille began to search local beaches. It soon became obvious that her rewards were great. Whenever the opportunity presents itself, Lucille and some of her friends head for swimming areas. Though she hasn't given up her love for searching ghost towns and other promising sites, the lure of treasure in the sands and shallow water is very strong. She has found thousands of coins, rings, religious medallions, bracelets, necklaces and other forms of jewelry. Lucille has never claimed to be a professional water hunter; her success simply proves it.

KEN SCHAFFER

You could never tell by looking at Ken Schaffer, Virginia Beach, VA, that he often spends eight hours a day treasure hunting in the Chesapeake Bay area surf. One look at his showcases, however, would convince you immediately. After a few minutes of conversation with Ken, you'll be satisfied that he knows his business and that he has learned how the hobby of shallow water metal detecting can. pay off.

He won't tell you how many gold, silver and platinum rings he's found in the past two decades, nor will he tell you how many diamond rings he's added to his collection since January this year. But, he will tell you why he often searches eight hours a day. "Because it pays off!" he'll quickly explain. No one spends that much time searching the cold water of Chesapeake Bay unless it pays dividends. Ken admits that most of his hunting is done in the winter. The tides run in two directions along these beaches, he says. During the warm, summer months the tides cause the sand to pile up. During the colder months, however, a reverse tide removes the accumulation of sand. That's when he goes to work: when the gold rings and other valuables are at their shallowest depth. If you are lucky enough to meet Ken, ask him about surf hunting and he'll give you quick, straight answers.

BOB TREVILLIAN AND FRANK CARTER

Bob Trevillian and Frank Carter need no introduction. They discussed their sucess in DIAMONDS IN THE SURF and FIRST AND SECOND ADVENTURE. Bob and Frank's early finds were so spectacular that the men retired and now devote their energies searching recreational beaches and surfs for treasures lost by sun lovers. They have discovered an amazing quantity of wealth others left behind. The treasure hunters began their activities mainly in the water, but research kept turning up promising land sites such as abandoned beaches and ghost towns. Curious, they searched these places and their results were so spectacular, they wrote a third book, THE POOR MAN'S TREASURE HUNTER. Bob and Frank's success story is remarkable but, as they point out, it is within the reach of anyone with the time, desire and determination to succeed.

WALLACE CHANDLER

I first met Wallace Chandler, Figure 3-6, in 1972 at a prospector's meeting in Southern California while he was on vacation. Though his home base is in Michigan, he travels around the United States searching beaches. Not a water man, he's content to make his living — a quite acceptable living — searching for treasure that sun worshipers leave behind. He's been a full-time beachcomber going on two decades and he says he wouldn't give it up for anything. He's come by the Garrett Metal Detector factory several times to show me his latest treasures. The accompanying photograph includes some of these finds that establish him as a man who knows what he is doing.

It's easy to understand why he searches the beaches full-time. It would be difficult to make that kind of money working at a regular job. He drives a Volkswagen Rabbit equipped with a diesel engine and at this writing he has driven the car one-quarter-million miles. Wallace told me one day he could afford to drive a larger, more expensive car, but why should he? He gets 50 miles to the gallon out of that Rabbit, and it's never yet failed to take him to a place he wanted to search.

Wallace plans well into the future. Each spring he knows where he's going to be the next springtime. Research is one of the key reasons for his success and it seems obvious that Wallace has built a pretty good life for himself. He goes where he wants to go and stays as long as he likes when he gets there. As he finds more treasure than he needs, most of his most valuable rings are transferred to a bank safe deposit box. Should he need a little extra cash for gas or other expenses, he sells a few rings and keeps going to his next job — or rather his next vacation spot.

THE WORLD OF THE DIVERS

You've probably heard or read about men known the world over for the vast amounts of sunken treasure, relics and artifacts they've found. ROBERT MARX, MEL FISHER, BURT WEBBER, the famed JACQUES COSTEAU and others have become household words. They have so many kings' treasures consisting of mountains of silver, Spanish pieces of eight and gold escudo coins and other treasures that they have lost count. Of course, these men are notable exceptions to the rule. They have gone well beyond finding their share and have found hundreds and perhaps even thousands of other persons' shares as well! The wealth they found didn't fall into their laps. They worked long, hard hours and spent countless months researching locations of treasures they knew existed. And, do you know what? They probably enjoyed every minute of it! Successes like theirs don't come very often, but when they come, the rewards make the effort worthwhile.

Figure 3-6: Wallace Chandler retired many years ago from a regular job. He travels around the United States searching lucrative recreational beaches. He has been a full-time beach hunter going on nearly two decades and he says he wouldn't give it up for anything. It is easy to understand why he searches the beaches full-time.

ROBERT MARX

Robert Marx, Figure 3-7, is an adventurer, a historian, a marine archaeologist and a treasure hunter. He has written more than 30 books and has published hundreds of scientific articles and reports. He has been an editor for *Argosy* and *The Saturday Evening Post*. Since the age of ten, Marx has been an active deep sea diver.

During his early days he was a treasure hunter, but he has abandoned most of these adventures to become a serious archaeologist. Marx now focuses his attention on educating governments on the importance of not only protecting archaeological areas, but also actively supporting qualified projects. His numerous books are astonishing in their descriptions of various projects in which he has participated.

Marx is known as one of the most successful and well-known specialists in the fields of marine archaeology and he has an equally strong reputation for his work in naval and maritime history. He studied at UCLA and the University of Maryland and served in the U.S. Marine Corps where he worked in diving and salvage operations. Among his more popular writings are: SHIPWRECKS OF THE WESTERN HEMISPHERE, INTO THE DEEP, THE UNDERWATER DIG, TREASURE FLEETS OF THE SPANISH MAIN, FOLLOWING COLUMBUS; VOYAGE OF THE NINA II, ROBERT MARX: QUEST FOR TREASURE and BURIED TREASURE IN THE UNITED STATES.

In QUEST FOR TREASURE, Marx discovers the remains of the Spanish treasure ship *Nuestra Senora de la Maravilla* which sank in 1656 off the Bahamas. Marx vividly describes the find and recovery of a vast fortune in gold and silver coins and ingots, jewelry, ship's cannon and relics. He and his crew battled the sea, sharks, corrupt government officials and modern-day pirates who wanted to take the treasure for themselves. To read this book is to learn the true life of a modern-day adventurer who searches for and finds fabled wealth we all dream of finding.

Though he has spent a lifetime in an exciting field, his discoveries and recoveries represent only a miniscule fraction of the lost wealth awaiting the underwater explorer. Marx's books contain a wealth of information. Anyone interested in this fascinating and rewarding hobby is encouraged to read his material and learn from a true professional. Marx's wife, Jennifer, is a professional as well. She is a diver, historian, author and lecturer. One of her best known books, THE MAGIC OF GOLD, is a fascinating story you'll be unable to put down.

MEL FISHER

"Today is the day!" Mel Fisher, Figure 3-8, has lived by this positive statement every day for more than two decades.

It became Treasure Salvors' marching cry as the group searched the Florida Keys for the Spanish treasure galleon *Nuestra Senora de*

Atocha which went down in 1622 with a cargo of valuables. When the *Atocha* sank in a hurricane it nearly caused a depression in Europe and almost threw the Spanish Court into bankruptcy. The ship's manifest listed more than 600 pounds of gold, 1,200 silver bars weighing upwards of 70 pounds each and 250,000 silver coins and rare art objects of extreme value. Precious cargo totaled nearly 40 tons of treasure, valued at almost four hundred million dollars! What's more, it often has been said that most Spanish treasure ships carried from three to four times the amount of treasure listed on the manifest. Smuggling apparently was rampant in those days and tremendous quantities of unregistered treasure have been found on most Spanish shipwreck sites.

Fisher's first big treasure find came in the mid-1960s when he and his partners discovered part of the 1715 Spanish Plate Fleet of 10 treasure galleons between Vero Beach and Fort Pierce, FL. After discovering more than two million dollars worth of gold and silver, he decided to go after the *Atocha*.

Even though he has witnessed tragedy and has found himself in many legal battles, most of which were decided in his favor, Mel's faith remains firm. One July morning in 1985 he came into his office and once more said, "Today is the day!" Little did he know that 41 miles

Figure 3-7: Robert Marx (right) points out to the author the markings on a Spanish silver bar that he located during one of his many thousands of sea explorations. Bob, at age 10, dedicated his life to the great outdoors and the equally great underwater world. He has, probably, spent more time searching underwater treasure sites and documenting historical locations then any other individual.

west of Key West, in what has been described as an underwater desert, his team members would dive 55 feet to check out a strong electronic reading. While scanning over ballast stones, Garrett underwater metal detectors screamed an alert. With a mass of solid silver bars stacked all about them on the sea floor, they had found the Mother Lode. In the first week the crew recovered nearly 500 silver bars, each one weighing 70 pounds. Treasure chests, similar to those you would visualize, some complete with hinges, were located. Seven contained up to 2,000 pieces of silver. Each treasure chest was worth about two million dollars. The eighth chest was filled with gold bars.

This find placed him at the pinnacle of success. Through many trials and discoveries, Mel Fisher and his wife, Dolores, have carved for themselves a niche in the annals of treasure hunting history.

Figure 3-8: Mel Fisher, left, and the author, right, descuss the merits of the large "sled" metal detector searchcoil. constructed of white PVC tubing and leaning against the ship's railing. Note also the two twin blasters. The black set is attached to the boat on which the men are standing, and the white set visible at the rear is mounted on a smaller boat tied alongside.

BURT WEBBER, JR.

Burt Webber made a name for himself when he searched for and discovered the famous ship, *Nuestra Senora de la Concepcion*. His quest for treasure, described in John Grissim's THE LOST TREASURE OF THE CONCEPCION, is an exciting adventure to read. He brought up millions of dollars in treasure, proving once again that the oceans contain treasures beyond imagination.

BARRY CLIFFORD

While diving off the Massachusetts town of Wellfleet, a modern-day adventurer named Barry Clifford located the ship—with its remains still containing cargo—of the notorious 18th century buccaneer, Samuel "Black Sam" Bellamy. When it sank in 1717 in sight of the beach, the *Whidah* was carrying a treasure valued today at hundreds of millions of dollars. Among the recovered *treasure* were gold and silver coins, ingots, jewelry, weapons and artifacts. Shipboard booty, captured from 22 ships, includes 180 canvas bags that each held 50 pounds of jewels.

The ship is also of great historical value since it is the first pirate ship discovered. "Black Sam" Bellamy roamed the Caribbean and left a legacy of misadventures as spectacular as those of Blackbeard and Captain William Kidd. Clifford's plans are to keep the recovered treasure intact and establish a museum to exhibit his findings.

JACK KELLEY

Tulsa architect and oil man Jack Kelley is basking in the glow of a crowning achievement—the discovery of a cargo ship that sank off Turkey about 1400 B.C. This discovery and excavation has been called the most exciting event in the decades-long search for ancient artifacts in the Mediterranean Sea. Cargo from the merchant ship totals an estimated 20 tons. Kelley believes the shipwreck to be the next most significant archaeological find since the discovery by Howard Carter of King Tut's tomb.

KEVIN McCORMICK

Kevin McCormick, project manager for Sub-Sal, Inc., reported the salvaging of the sunken sailing vessel *HMS deBraak* from Delaware Bay. The 18th century British brig sank nearly two centuries ago and carried a cargo valued at several million dollars.

MIKE HATCHER

Explorer and treasure hunter Mike Hatcher achieved fame when he discovered a sunken Chinese junk containing millions of dollars worth of Ming procelain. More recently, he located the remarkable rich sunken cargo of the Dutch East Indiaman merchant vessel *Gelder-malsen* which went down in the South China Sea in 1752 with 270 men on board. The gold and porcelain cargo brought over 10 million pounds at a Christie's auction in Amsterdam. Should you have the opportunity to view the documentary THE NANKING CARGO don't miss it.

OTHERS YOU'VE HEARD ABOUT

In various books, magazines and trade publications, treasure hunters regularly reveal their successes, some of which are phenomenal. I wish space in this book would let me include more stories. Among the successful beach, surf and water hunters (and this acknowledgment is by no means complete) are Richard and Heather Ambrose, Keith Hetherington, Australian author of BEACHCOMBING WITH A METAL DETECTOR, Bill and Sherie Kasselman, Rene LeNeve, Don Littlejohn, Joe Maenner, Kay Moduling, George Mroczkowski, Ettore and Diana Nannetti, Mike Numann, Roy Volker, Betty Weeks and Ken Wherry.

OTHER SUCCESS STORIES

Louisiana state officials released information that an 18th century shipwreck found off its coast yielded nearly a half million dollars in gold and silver. The Spanish vessel *El Constante* was lost in a hurricane in 1766. This ship was one of six in a fleet bound from Veracruz, Mexico, to Spain. A hurricane drove it into shallow water and smashed it to bits. This find could lead to a total recovery of several hundred million dollars; records indicate the entire fleet carried over 50 million pesos worth of gold, silver, copper and pottery.

The *U.S.S. Hatteras,* a 210-foot iron ship, was a Union vessel used during the Civil War. It was sunk by a Confederate ship in 1863. Using sophisticated equipment, JEFF BURKE and CHARLES ROSE found the ship near Galveston in 20 feet of water. The men have plans to raise the *Hatteras* and convert her into a floating museum.

A World War II Wellington bomber was found resting on the bottom 230 feet deep in Scotland's Loch Ness.

A few miles off the coast of Egypt, French and Egyptian divers discovered the wreck of the *Orient,* flag ship of the ill-fated fleet that convoyed Napoleon Bonaparte and his army to Egypt. The fleet was destroyed and sunk in 1798 by the British.

After 73 years of solitude, the mighty *Titanic* was found at a depth of two and one-half miles. Using sophisticated underwater photography equipment, a group of professional marine explorers located the ship. It was mostly intact and covered by only a light silt sediment.

You have already read my belief that more treasure is being lost than is being recovered. People continue to lose valuable items on the beach and in the surf. Ships continue taking their precious cargo to the bottom. And, old treasure continues to be redistributed as storms arise and literally churn up the beaches and shallow waters. Treasure from ships that have sunk recently as well as riches that disappeared centuries ago is picked up by storms and hurled into the shallow surfs and even onto land. Pounding surf, changing tides and relentless winds deposit untold amounts of treasure in troughs, washes and other sites along the beaches.

Travel to any popular beach and watch people at play. They engage in horseplay or, perhaps, play ball. Without knowing it, they lose coins, rings and other valuables. Gold and silver chains break and fall to the ground to be lost. Sunbathing on towels is a popular activity. All too often, sunbathers remove jewelry which they promptly forget about. When they leave, they grab their towel and swing it to shake off the sand. I have discovered "pockets" of coins and jewelry on the beach, and I believe this is why these hordes are so often lost.

Swimming draws people into the surf. All too often swimmers forget about their gold and silver rings, even diamond rings. They just don't realize how easy it is to lose rings off fingers made slippery by suntan lotions and oils. Plus, the hot summer sun expands metal, making rings slightly larger than normal. Swimmers dash into the surf, not realizing that they are about to add more treasure to Davy Jones' locker as rings slide off their fingers and into the water. By the time they discover their jewelry is missing, they have no idea where to look. Many scratch through the sand, but more often than not, the search is futile.

Only the modern day treasure hunter, equipped with sophisticated metal detection equipment, can locate lost treasure. When found, it is no longer "lost wealth", but more properly, *SUDDEN WEALTH!*

CHAPTER 4

Find More than Your Share of
Treasure—through Proper Research

"We inherited these lost fortunes but we must seek them out."
Roy Lagal

Treasure is where you find it. You may diligently seek it or you may stumble upon it—the choice is yours. You can increase your chances of finding treasure one thousand fold if you will learn how to research projects through to successful conclusion. Without research, treasure discovery comes only by chance and luck—and the booty is most often far less valuable.

Treasure found by accident represents only a very small percentage of that found by persons using good, acceptable research practices. Research can consume up to 99% of a successful search and recovery undertaking. Without proper research you'll be as lost as a driver without a map in a strange city. You need a waybill—directions to guide you to the best locations. These waybills, these directions, come from many sources, both public and private.

I never advise buying a treasure map or taking anyone's word as gospel. You must always find the primary source. To begin at the beginning involves a study of basic research material and sources. You must know WHAT you are looking for and that it EXISTS. Certain forms of treasure hunting require a knowledge about where specific types of treasure, of the type you are searching for, can be found. You don't search for Spanish doubloons in a city park or lost gold rings in a child's sand box. (Even though tiny children's rings and mother's rings are occasionally found there!)

Since failure to prepare groundwork generally results in wasted time, effort and money, I have included this chapter to give you a headstart. Also, other chapters contain specific research information. Unfortunately, there is no one-two-three-step procedure I can give you. One hundred people reading this book may begin looking for one hundred different treasures. The main thing is to get started by defining your goals. What are you looking for? Does it exist? Where is it? Will you have clear title to it if you find it? Have others looked for it? How do you know they didn't find it? What will it cost you to find it? Is it worth what it will cost you to find it?

Certainly, these questions are rudimentary, but yet very important. Don't go searching for the will-o-the-wisp. Spend your time wisely and efficiently. Don't waste time looking for treasure unless you are sure, based upon your research, it exists. Use the following sources

23

and others to discover how to track down the information about the treasure you seek. Establish your goal, believe in it and your ability to achieve it; then work like the dickens to make it come true.

To repeat a truth, successful treasure hunting can be 99% research and 1% recovery. Do not think of research as though it were an uninteresting stint in the back room of some dusty, ill-lighted library where you must read volumes of scarcely legible books, articles and newspapers. Research can be fun. It can become something you do as naturally as eat breakfast. When you become obsessed with beach and surf hunting, you'll continually think about it. You'll scan newspapers and magazines for stories and data about local sites. When you talk with people, especially oldtimers, you'll ask them about such-and-such a place. You'll ask them if they remember whether the present swimming beach is in the same location as it was decades ago. You'll ask them if they remember incidents when sunbathers lost jewelry and other valuables.

Just yesterday I was walking around the lake where I have spent time writing protions of this book. I came upon three elderly walkers who had stopped to rest and were sitting on a bench. After a brief discussion about the weather, I asked them if sunbathers used to swim anywhere other than at the presently designated swimming site. They replied that the present swimming area is the only one ever used. I asked if they recalled anyone ever losing rings or other valuable jewelry. They said they didn't remember any such incidents, but one lady quickly added that, yes, there was a person, back in the 1960s who lost a watch. The reason the lady remembered the story and when it happened was that her father was caretaker at the time. She said that this swimmer told her father that she had dropped a watch through the floorboards of the bathhouse. She asked the caretaker if he would keep his eyes open and watch for the watch. Sure enough, sometime later, the man spotted the watch gleaming in the sun as it lay a few inches deep in the water slightly back under the edge of the bathhouse. Then one of the oldtimers looked at me and said, "You do know that there used to be changing booths built on the present pier?" I told him I didn't know that. "Yes, there was," the oldtimer replied, "and I'll bet that they lost a lot of coins and valuables as they changed clothes."

In that brief conversation, I fairly well had the history of the beach and swimming area plus I now had even more reason to don my dive suit and work beneath the pier.

When you read the newspapers, be alert for leads. In a recent issue of the *Dallas Morning News,* there was a large, front page, color photo of a mass of teenagers playing on an ocean beach. The photo was captioned, "Where the Joys are!" The article described thousands of teenagers taking spring break frolicking on a South Padre Island beach. When school spring break comes for a week, students from far and wide flock to the beaches where they release pent-up frustrations; these

24

treks to the beaches have been going on for a quarter of a century. Even some students who formerly spent their break at a popular Fort Lauderdale, FL, beach have come over to South Padre. One lass who was an Indiana University senior and a "survior" of two Florida spring breaks, said "Florida is getting boring and the boys are nicer here. They're not animals."

I talked with my son, Vaughan, who spent two of his high school spring breaks on North Padre Island. He said that spring break is the time when students like to show off. "They do their best to impress everyone else; they give it everything they've got." He continued, "They wear their best clothes and swim suits and certainly their best jewelry. Many of the girls are husband-looking and they really put on the dog. Things often get so wild, I don't see how they can keep from losing lots of money, jewelry and other valuables".

The moral to that story is for the beachcomber and surfer metal detectorist to work those beaches immediately after the parties have ended, if not during.

Be alert to news reports of modern day heists and robberies. When a safe, for instance, is stolen, the thieves must do something with it. Usually, "hot" items are discarded in nearby water areas. A fellow who was repairing the roof on one of the Garrett buildings told me an interesting story. His friend had stolen a private coin collection. Realizing that the property could be traced, the thief hastily threw the collection into a nearby creek. The roofer said he would show me the exact spot. Well, embarrassing as it is "to tell the rest of the story," I delayed too long. A few months later when I tried to locate the roofer, I could not. The fellow had moved to Houston and no one knew his whereabouts. So the moral to that story is, when you hear of a "good one," GO IMMEDIATELY. DON'T DELAY. CHECK THE STORY TO A SATISFACTORY CONCLUSION!

Robert Podhrasky, a Garrett Electronics' engineer, and I taught an underwater metal detector seminar for the local Garland police. Following classroom instruction, we drove to a North Texas rock quarry that had filled with water. During our training activities, we located a safe, two coin changers and, believe it or not, an automobile. Proof enough that thieves do discard stolen property.

There's an unlimited amount of research information available to you. The only limits will be those you impose upon yourself. Knowing that everyone has shortcomings, never rely wholly upon the work of others. When someone writes about a treasure project, you can be sure that person has abandoned it for one reason or another. You must analyze the data with a cautious eye. Failure of the person to complete research and recovery could be due to lack of funds, time or simply interest. But, if a person took the time to travel to and investigate a site, it means that the person BELIEVES in his story.

Do not become discouraged if in early stages of your treasure hunting activities, you cannot achieve expected success. You'll notice I said, "expected" success. I could have used the word, "satisfactory," but I want to stress that you must set goals—realistic ones, to be sure. Only when you establish goals will you have a target at which to shoot. Set goals for your success and strive to achieve them. Do not become discouraged in the early stages. Success will come if you persist.

You must never doubt that you will be successful. Dogged patience, perseverance, continued study and research and field practice are necessary ingredients in the formula of success in this fascinating and rewarding hobby. If you are skeptical and do not continue unswervingly in your quest, you will achieve mediocre results. But, when you one day "round the corner" and begin filling your pouch with coins, jewelry and treasure, you will know you have "made it" and can look forward to successes of which you may never have dreamed or envisioned.

RESEARCH SOURCES

MODERN DAY PHOTOGRAPHS:

The undisputed value in photography lies in the fact that photographs will reveal objects and features you normally do not see when scanning hurriedly. You can do your own photography or obtain photographs from many public and private sources. The U.S. Forestry Service maintains an extensive photo library through which you can obtain aerial photos of Forest Service and soil conservation sites. For information on this service contact your local U.S..Forestry Department or you can write the Engineering Staff Unit, Forest Service-U.S.D.A., Washington, D.C. 20250 or the Cartographic Division, Soil Conservation Service, U.S.D.A., Federal Building, Hyattsville, MD 20748. From your local forester or the Engineering Staff in Washington D.C. (address above) you can obtain the address of the various regional Forest Service field offices.

Two additional aerial mapping photo sources are the Tennessee Valley Authority, Map Files and Records Section, 200 Haney Building, Chattanooga, TN 37401 and the U.S. Geological Survey, EROS Data Center, Sioux Falls, S.D 57198. Refer also to Eugene Avery's book, INTERPRETATION OF AERIAL PHOTOGRAPHS.

OLD PHOTOGRAPHS:

Photographs capture forever the activities of man. Sooner or later a photographer is bound to show up at every recreation and swimming site. The old time photographer seemed to enjoy photographing swimmers of the day in their funny-looking (to us) costumes. Old time photographs offer a world of information and in many cases the exact spot where swimming took place. Unfortunately, most old photographs are not identified. No one took the time to write, on the reverse side, the site location. But a little research can lead to an oldtimer.

OLDTIMERS:

The oldtimer is one source of information that you must never pass up. In fact, these storage vaults of treasure locations should be actively sought out and quizzed for every last scrap of information that can guide you to a fruitful location. When talking with oldtimers about old locations, quiz them concerning jewelry items that they may know of being lost years ago. Oftentimes they'll tell you of valuable rings and other jewelry items that were lost by their companions. If they'll take you to these treasure sites, all the better.

INSURANCE AGENTS:

Your insurance agent is likely to be a warehouse of information. If he has paid claims on lost jewelry, he'll have records specifying the objects, the value and the probable location of the loss.

BEACH MANAGER OR PROPRIETORS:

Oftentimes lost items are reported to managers or proprietors in the hopes the lost article will be found. One fellow I struck up a conversation with at an abandoned swimming site described the probable location of a safe that was stolen by two men approximately 15 years earlier. One of the men was this man's friend who told him that they stole the safe and hauled it part way across the dam. During their attempt to open the safe they were fearful of being caught by the police so they rolled the safe down the dam's slope into the water. I investigated the area and determined that the dam was soft earth and, in all probability, the safe quickly sank several feet into the earthen dam below water level. I earmarked that one for future investigation.

Figure 4-1: The Australian Garrett Metal Detector Club is a dedicated group of metel detectorists and gold hunters who are not only very active in their hobby, but meet on a regular basis to discuss members' successes in the gold fields, to view film, video and slide presentations and to examine recent finds. Photo courtesy Ted Sheehan.

LIBRARIES:

Here's where you can spend lots of time that can pay off. Unless you're familiar with library cataloging, ask the librarian to give you a short course. Tell her you're looking for history books, periodicals, maps and other sources that will list early day swimming sites and beaches. Take your time and look through every reference you find. Either use the copier to gather the information you need or take along some 3 × 5 cards and list each site on a card. The more specific you can be with the librarian as to what you're looking for, the more help you will get.

NEWSPAPERS:

When you have free time, go down to your local newspaper office and ask to browse through their old newspapers or microfilm of past editions. Scan the lost and found column for items lost by persons visiting local beaches and swimming areas. Study the travel sections for information about beach resort sites. Read articles that describe severe storms, especially hurricanes, in which beach homes were flooded or destroyed. These areas could be a true treasure vault of many types of lost valuables. Especially be on the lookout for photographs of people swimming and enjoying the beaches of bygone years.

CHAMBERS OF COMMERCE:

Contact chambers for maps and literature they have regarding swimming and recreation beaches. Often chambers of commerce promote special programs to encourage locals and tourists to participate.

DEPARTMENT OF PARKS AND RECREATION:

Write, call or go by and request lists of all recreational facilities that include a swimming area. Ask them to send you all promotional literature describing the type of sites you're searchng for. Don't forget aerial photographs, especially the old ones that show the locations of lakes, ponds and other swimming sites, many of which may have been completely forgotten and no longer be in use. When you study these photographs, watch for piers, landing docks, bath houses and other promising sites.

OLD ATLASES:

Your library or historical society may have old community issues you can review. From these you can learn the location of long-gone communities, railway and stage stations, fords, Indian encampments and the like. Old city maps will show the location of the oldest recreational parks where you can find, perhaps, the oldest coins.

DEPARTMENT OF PERMITS:

If there is one in your area, they may have a list of swimming spots for which, in order to swim, a permit is required.

YEARBOOKS:

School and college yearbooks often abound with photographs

taken by young, enterprising photographers. These yearbooks can be a valuable source of swimming sites that could keep you busy for years to come.

HISTORICAL BOOKS:

Historical books are written about practically every town, city and county in the United States. The editors all seem to try to outdo each other by placing more and more extremely valuable photographs and data in the yearbooks regarding early day activities. These early day recreational sites are the true bonanza locations where you'll want to work and scan for lost treasure of yesteryear. When you scan through these yearbooks, be on the lookout for millponds and other water areas that could have been used for swimming.

MAPS:

Never pass up the opportunity to scan both new and old maps for locations of swimming beaches. United States topographical maps show remarkable detail of all bodies of water in any given area. Deeds and surveyors' notes describe or include maps showing bodies of water.

MUSEUMS:

Don't be content just to browse through your local museum. Tell the curator what you're looking for; they can dig back into dusty files and come up with some true treasure vault locations you might not find down any other avenues. Be sure to browse photograph and old book departments since valuable relics such as these are often donated to museums. Your local museum can be as good as the library in providing good research material. You are more likely to meet resistance when it comes to trying to work with museum curators and other personnel, so a good idea is to develop a historical RESEARCH thesis of the local area. You may get lots more assistance.

GHOST TOWN BOOKS:

Be on the lookout for books written about ghost towns and old sites of your area. Many towns of bygone days have their own swimming tank, blue hole or whatever they might have called it. Certainly you'll want to locate these treasure vaults and clean them out.

HOTEL AND MOTEL LOBBIES:

They'll almost always have a literature rack containing free brochures that describe various vacation and tourist spots.

HISTORICAL SOCIETIES:

If the town or city is large enough, there'll be a "home" where the historical society has its headquarters. Not only will the persons on duty probably be well versed in local sites of interest, there may be a library of invaluable maps and books that contain the locations of more places than you can search in a year.

U.S. FOREST SERVICE:
The U.S. Forest Service maintains an excellent photo and map library that may contain photos of areas that are of interest to you. Check with your local Forest Service office or write the Chief, Forest Service, U.S.D.A., South Building, 12th and Independence Avenue, S.W., Washington, D.C. 20013, for information.

PAPER AND TIMBER COMPANIES:
These companies have millions of acres accessible to vacationers. Contact them to obtain information on swimming and recreational sites.

NATIONAL FORESTS:
Write to them and request information and locations of swimming and recreational areas open to metal detectors.

NATIONAL PARK SERVICE RECREATION AREAS:
For specific information write to the Regional Office, National Park Service, Room 3043, Interior Building, Washington, D.C., 20240.

BUREAU OF RECLAMATION:
The Federal Reclamation office assists all levels of government with the management of water and related land resources. Current reclamation maps and data available from older maps have locations of many interesting sites. Write to the Bureau of Reclamation, U.S. Department of the Interior, Washington, D.C., 20240.

NATIONAL CARTOGRAPHIC INFORMATION CENTER:
Available to you are 1.5 million maps and charts, 25 million aerial and space photographs and 1.5 million geodetic control points. Write to the National Cartographic Information Center, U.S. Geological Survey, 507 National Center, Reston, VA 22092.

U.S. GOVERNMENT PRINTING OFFICE:
The U.S. Government Printing Office offers more than 25,000 books and pamphlets through a centralized mail order office and 24 bookstores throughout our nation. To have your name added to this free descriptive booklet distribution list, write the Superintendent of Documents, U.S. Government Printing Office, Attention: Mail List, Washington, D.C. 20401.

NATIONAL WEATHER SERVICE:
Climate data and flooding information will be of interest to every beach and surf hunter. For information about general information offered, write to the National Weather Service, National Oceanic and Atmospheric Administration, 8060 13th Street, Department of Commerce, Silver Spring, MD 20910.

BUREAU OF OUTDOOR RECREATION:
For information on outdoor recreation programs, write to the Bureau of Outdoor Recreation, Department of the Interior, Washington, D.C. 20240.

STATE ARCHIVES:

During normal working hours, you can search through historical documents, maps, charts and prints relating to the history of your specific state. The archives are funded by your tax dollars, so put this source to work.

STATE TOURIST BUREAU:

Write to the appropriate bureau and request specific information related to your investigation.

MUNICIPAL GOVERNMENT INFORMATION SOURCES:

Cities and towns change with time. Study available maps and look for defunct parks and other gathering places.

MAPS:

Various state and federal agencies make available to the public maps of practically all types. Here are a few for your consideration as you research a given locale. Treasure Maps and Charts (Superintendent of Documents), River Charts (Corps of Engineers), Historical/Military Maps (National Archives), Selected Civil War Maps (Supt. of Documents) and Township Plats (National Archives).

RIVER AUTHORITIES:

A good source of information for old boat landings, river ports, forts and long-past ghost towns.

CORPS OF ENGINEERS:

Contact the Corps of Engineers in your area to learn where salvage contract records are kept. These records may contain lake and river information about a shipwreck you are researching.

LIFE GUARDS:

These lifesavers often know where valuables have been lost; for sure, they will know where activities take place. Strike up a conversation and tell them what you have in mind.

LOCAL TREASURE HUNTING CLUBS:

If you are not a member, sign up now! Active members will know where the hot spots are. Don't miss out on the rewards that can come from being an active member of your local and/or state clubs. See Figure 4-1. Join national clubs devoted to helping members find treasure.

AND BOOKS:

This is one of the best sources for finding swimming and recreational beaches. Check with your local library and bookstores to learn what has been printed. For instance, the books, THE MID-ATLANTIC TREASURE COAST, WEST COAST BEACHES and THE NEW ENGLAND BEACH BOOK, all listed in the bibliography, contain the location of beaches in their respective areas where you can search for coins, rings and jewelry to your heart's content.

AND MAGAZINES:

Treasure and other magazines can be a source of good information, but be cautious. Articles contained in these publications make interesting reading and many contain factual information. But, use common sense when spending time and money seeking out "hot spots" that authors boast about. If hunting is that good, would YOU write an article and tell the world about its location? You know that when you talk about your treasure finds, you probably paint a more glowing picture than actually exists. And, probably, the person listening to your story sees it as even more romantic and rewarding than you intended to describe it. Always, if possible, obtain two or three credible references about a subject before striking out on the treasure trail.

RESEARCH SOURCES AND OTHER INFORMATION TO HELP YOU LOCATE SHIPWRECK AND OTHER SUNKEN TREASURE LOCATIONS:

THE UNITED STATES NATIONAL ARCHIVES:

Located in Washington, D.C., the archives is the largest source of information available concerning shipwrecks.

THE UNITED STATES COAST GUARD:

Reports of thousands of marine disasters since 1915 are available from the Public Information Division of the U.S.C.G.

THE UNITED STATES LIFE SAVING SERVICE:

From 1872 until 1915 when it became the United States Coast Guard, it maintained records of all United States Life Saving Service Districts.

THE UNITED STATES LIGHTHOUSE SERVICE:

You'll find reports of maritime disasters in the records of the Lighthouse Service. These records contain information on shipwrecks that took place within the jurisdiction of any given lighthouse.

UNITED STATES MARITIME COMMISSION:

Located in Washington, D.C., this is another valuable source of maritime shipwreck disasters.

THE UNITED STATES WEATHER BUREAU:

Shipwreck charts and much other valuable information can be obtained from the Weather Bureau.

THE UNITED STATES COAST AND GEODETIC SURVEY:

Since 1900 wreck charts have been published covering the area from Newfoundland to the Gulf of Mexico.

THE UNITED STATES STEAMBOAT INSPECTION SERVICE:

Since the Steamboat Inspection Service was founded to insure steamboats were sound and safely equipped, careful records for analysis were kept of steamboat disasters.

LIBRARY OF CONGRESS:

The LC is the nation's library that serves researchers throughout the world. Its current holdings exceed 75 million items with more than seven thousand new items added each work day. When you need additional information or have exhausted all research sources, write to the Library of Congress, Information Office, Washington, D.C. 20540.

THE SITE SEARCH

There are two areas of approach to site research, one is to explore probable area sites and then concentrate your research on a particular site that you have located. The second is to select one or more area sites as objectives, then conduct in-depth research before any attempt is made to locate and excavate. In every country in the world there are many research sources. As stated before, you must know what you are looking for and then doggedly go after the research information. A good filing or computer system will be necessary for you to keep track of the voluminous material that you will encounter. Several books, including THE UNDERWATER DIG by John S. Potter, Jr, are recommended sources for those who are just entering the realm of shipwreck research. These men gained vast knowledge and experience and have presented it in fascinating form in the above publications. You would do well to learn from them.

Sources of information and research data include books, archives, newspaper reports, maps and charts, marine insurance companies of which Lloyd's of London is probably the largest, ships' manifests, ships' logs, official reports, letters, eyewitness reports, testimony, court martial records, interviews and many other sources.

THE ENCYLOPEDIA OF AMERICAN SHIPWRECKS by Bruce D. Berman includes information on ships wrecked in the United States waters. As a result of eight years of intensive research, the author collected data on more than 50,000 wrecks in American waters. He wrote about some 13,000, excluding all vessels of less than 50 gross tons. Some of these wrecks are pre-Revolutionary and his list includes ships lost prior to 1971. Included in the information about each wreck is the name and tonnage of each vessel, the year of construction, the date, loss and locations.

A GUIDE TO SUNKEN SHIPS IN AMERICAN WATERS by Adrian. L. Lonsdale and H.R. Kaplan lists 11,000 wrecks off the coasts of the United States as well as many in rivers and the Great Lakes. Although most of the wrecks mentioned in this book are also listed in Berman's Encyclopedia, they are covered in somewhat greater detail. Dozens of other books deal with shipwrecks in particular areas or describe ships lost at specific times. For the Great Lakes you can read MEMORIES OF THE LAKES and SHIPWRECKS OF THE LAKES, both by Dana Thomas Bowen. New England wrecks are dealt with in WRECKS AROUND NANTUCKET by Arthur H. Gardner and another book, SHIPWRECKS OF CAPE COD by Isaac M. Small.

A good book on West Coast ships is SHIPWRECKS OF THE PACIFIC COAST, by James A. Gibbs, Jr. An excellent book about river wrecks is STEAMBOAT DISASTERS AND RAILROAD ACCIDENTS, by S.A. Howland. For information on almost every military and merchant ship lost during the Civil War there is the 42-volume work entitled RECORDS OF THE NAVIES OF THE CIVIL WAR, published by the U.S. Government.

For Spanish ships there are two major works: LA ARMADA ESPANOLA, in nine volumes, and DISQUISICIONES NAUTICAS, in six volumes, both by Fernandez Cesareo de Duro. For French ship losses you should consult THE HISTOIRE DES NAUFRAGES, by Gene L. Desperthes. The best work on British warships is the ROYAL NAVY, in three volumes, by William L. Clowes.

Shipwrecks source book information falls into two categories, descriptions written at the time of the disaster and data compiled at a later date, perhaps in modern times. Books written at the time of the disaster may be more reliable, as they often contain firsthand information and eyewitness reports. Books written at a later date contain the best information the author was able to obtain. Books published in recent years can be quite helpful in selecting and locating a site, but it is still wise to go back to the primary source whenever possible. Every state in the United States has many books about its history, and it is good idea to acquire and read the ones of interest. Try to obtain the oldest and those written soon after a particular ship loss.

Books written before 1800 are generally difficult to locate. Check with your local library and, perhaps, with large city libraries through inter-library loans. Your librarian can suggest book titles:

NEWSPAPERS

Newspaper accounts are a valuable source of information, and they may be the best source relating to the exact location of the vesel for which you are seeking. Newspapers were first printed in the Colonies in 1690. In addition to listing the movements of all ships in and out of port and their cargos, the papers printed a great deal of information on shipwrecks, not only in America but throughout the world. To determine which newspapers were being published or were published nearest to the site of the wreck, it is helpful to consult the following excellent works, HISTORY AND BIBLIOGRAPHY OF AMERICAN NEWSPAPERS 1690 to 1820, 2 volumes, by Clarence S. Brigham, and THE DICTIONARY OF NEWSPAPERS PERIODICALS, Ein W. Ayer and Sons, which covers the period until 1880. The New York Times was founded in 1851 and is a comprehensive source of information on later shipwrecks.

You probably know that you should read newspaper accounts carefully in order to obtain and separate the factual information from the excitement of the times. You may find it difficult to gather sufficient factual information from newspaper reports alone.

Original research undertaken in archives may be far the most rewarding as well as the most challenging and time consuming method of learning about underwater sites. The greatest collection of Spanish Colonial documents is stored in the Archivo de las Indias in Seville. There are many other depositories of information in Spain as well.

Documents describing shipwreck locations can be vague. In the very early days (which would apply primarily to Spanish shipwrecks) there were few fixed place names on charts used by navigators. In Florida, for example, on most 16th century charts only two places are named: Martires (spelled a number of ways) in the Florida Keys and Cabo de Canveral or Cape Canaveral. By the mid 17th century a few more places names had been added to charts including Las Tortugas (the Dry Tortugas), Vivoras and Matacumbe (two islands in the Florida Keys), Rio de Ais (Fort Pierce Inlet on the East Coast) and La Florida (St. Augustine). By the beginning of the 18th century many other names were on charts rendering them more accurate.

Another important factor to keep in mind when working with primary source material is that there was no standardized calendar system followed by all countries. In 1582 Pope Gregory XIII ordered that 10 days of the year be omitted to bring the calendar and the sun once again into alignment, thus creating the Gregorian Calendar which we use today. All the Protestant countries stuck to the old calendar, however, for many years. Until England adopted the Gregorian Calendar in 1752, her new year began March 25th; so a date of February 11, 1733, to the English was February 21, 1734, to the other European nations.

In England primary sources of shipwreck research are the British Museum, the Public Records Office, the Admiralty Library, the National Maritime Museum and the Archives of Lloyd's of London. Because of the great fire of London in 1666, there are virtually no available documents on British shipwrecks in the New World before the mid-seventeenth century.

In 1740 a newspaper called *LLOYD'S LIST* was founded and is still published. It charts the movement of British shipping around the world and gives brief accounts of ship losses and the movement of important foreign shipping, such as the Spanish fleets or ships engaged in the East Indies trade. *LLOYD'S LIST* also has published information regarding salvaging of ships. Until recently it was necessary to go to England to consult these lists. Now, however, all the lists dating from 1740 to 1900 have been republished in a multi-volume work which is found in a number of large United States libraries including the Library of Congress in Washington, D.C. and the New York Public Library.

Before attempting any research in United States depositories, either on American or foreign ship losses, one should consult the GUIDE TO ARCHIVES AND MANUSCRIPTS IN THE UNITED STATES by Philip M. Hamer to determine which archives or library contain relevant materials. The National Archives in Washington, D.C. is the most important source of shipwreck data postdating the American Revolution, but there are many others with original documents also. Each state has archives which should be consulted for information about a wreck off the coast of, or in a river or lake in a particular state. In some cases many of the most important documents in the state archives have been published, as have indexes of what the archives contain. If you are interested in shipwrecks off Virginia, for instance, the first step in researching them would be to consult the CALENDAR OF VIRGINIA STATE PAPERS AND OTHER MANUSCRIPTS, preserved in the capitol in Richmond, an eleven-volume edition edited by Kraus Reprint Corporation of New York.

In addition to the state archives, many state and private universities have large manuscript collections. Some contain a wealth of information from foreign archives. At the University of Florida, for instance, there is a collection of documents on microfilm obtained from the Archivo de las Indias and other depositories abroad, dealing with early Florida history. Thus, when seeking primary source material about Spanish shipwrecks off the coast of Florida, one should first consult this source to make a trip to Spain unnecessary. The Bancroft Library of the University of California at Berkely has a good collection of documents and microfilm gathered from many archives. These are relevant to ships lost not only off the California coast, but throughout the Pacific.

A number of maritime museums also have original documents and microfilm. All countries of the Western Hemisphere and many of the Caribbean Islands have national archives worth consulting. Archives of the countries bordering the Mediterranean have a great amount of original documentation on ship losses after the year 1400.

Museums are another good source for the dedicated researcher. The Peabody Museum in Salem, MA, has some of the finest information obtainable and will allow a researcher to use its facility. The Mystic Seaport in Mystic, CT, is another institution available to the researcher. They have photographic files and research libraries. They have lifesaving and service records and even records of early wrecking companies. Another museum claimed to be the finest source of information relating to government owned vessels in the United States is the Mariner's Museum of Newport News, VA.

Maps and charts are often valuable sources for locating underwater sites. Some will reflect astonishing accuracy and others equally astonishing inaccuracy. A number of important facts should be considered in referring to old maps and charts. Over the century, shorelines have receded in some places and extended farther out to sea in others. Many small islands that existed years ago have disappeared. Others have built up; new ones made by man. The mouths of rivers and streams have in some cases meandered considerable distances. The present Fort Pierce Inlet is now two miles south of where it was about 1750.

Most depositories of primary source material have a good collection of maps and charts. The most extensive, covering the entire world, is the map room of the British Museum. In the United States, the two best sources are the New York Library and the Library of Congress. Many books containing fine reproductions of old maps are available. An excellent guide to colonial maps and charts of Florida and several adjacent states is THE SOUTHEAST IN EARLY MAPS by William Cummings which lists locations of hundreds of old maps and charts covering these areas.

A number of charts showing locations of ships lost during the last 20 years of the 19th century are available. In 1893 the U.S. Hydrographic Office produced a "Wreck Chart of the North Atlantic Coast of America," covering the area from Newfoundland to the mouth of the Orinoco River in South America. It shows the locations and gives pertinent information on 965 vessels lost between 1887 and 1891. The U.S. Weather Bureau published two charts about the same time, the "Wreck Chart of The Great Lakes," which lists 147 ship losses between 1886 and 1891.

Modern navigational charts are sometimes useful in shipwreck sites; many list place names associated with wrecked ships. Throughout the world are many places named "Wreck Point" or "Wreck Bay" or other names indicative of past shipwrecks. In the Caribbean there are at least two dozen places with such evocative names as "Money Cay" or "Treasure Cay," implying ships sank with treasure or that treasure was hidden ashore.

Research should not overlook historical societies from whom much general information can be obtained. The United States Army Corps of Engineers destroys obstructions to navigation and ships sunk in shallow harbors that pose a problem to other vessels entering the port. Data from the Corps of Engineers pinpoints these sites.

Another approach to gathering information is to start with anyone who might have accidentally found an underwater site. Fishermen, sponge divers and others may know where shipwrecks lie. Commercial salvage divers and operators of dredging barges are also good sources of information. Fishermen and shrimpers must know the surrounding sea bottom to avoid snagging their nets on shipwrecks and other obstructions. They also know that fish are around wreck sites, and many have their own "wreck charts" to locate choice fishing grounds or avoid areas where they might lose valuable nets.

Each location chapter in this book contains its own research information. Review this material to obtain additional, specific information that will further guide you toward your specific treasure site.

CHAPTER 5

Metal Detectors Find Treasure-- The Easy Way

GETTING STARTED

Some detectors will find a coin one inch deep; others will detect that same coin when extremely deep. A most important factor, however, is the expertise and ability of the operator. You must learn how to use your detector correctly. Success will come in direct proportion to the amount of time and study you devote to learning how to use your instrument.

Purchasing equipment through the mail, or from someone who won't or can't instruct you, can cause you to miss treasure that could have been found with proper training. Your goal should be to find treasure, not to find a metal detector bargain! Getting hands-on instructions from the dealer from whom you purchase your new detector is the first step. Learn from your dealer, then go into the field and practice. Then, return to your dealer for additional instructions if you have questions or if you cannot master basic techniques. LEARN YOUR METAL DETECTOR and don't worry, at least at first, about what you are finding! You will soon find yourself getting better and better. You will become more at ease, and there will be fewer and fewer "problems" that bother you. The quantity of found items will be growing at an accelerated rate. All though your learning and training period and even on down through the years, you must develop persistence. Never give up!

Read your instruction manual, not once, but several times. The first time through, read it as you would a story — from front to back. Pay no attention to the metal detector or its controls; simply read the instruction manual. If you have an audio instruction tape, listen to it several times. Then, assemble your instrument; take the time to do it correctly. The next step is to become familiar with the various controls. The instruction manual should explain each switch and each control, describing to you its function and basic operation.

When you have adjusted each control and understand how it works, begin to test the instrument with various metal targets. After you have become familiar with the sounds of your instrument, the meter functions, how the detector works and its response to targets in various modes, it is time to go out into the field.

Your metal detector may have "set and forget" controls. Controls like TONE, AUDIO, MANUAL, AUTOMATIC are just that; once you set them, you rarely have to change or reset them. If you set them when you followed preliminary instructions, you don't have to worry about them now. The beginner should initially consider the Target Elimination (Discrimination) control as a "set and forget" control. Set it to zero elimination (all-metal detection) and leave it there until you have operated your detector for at least 10 hours. In other words, dig all detected targets.

Work smarter, not harder. Each time you receive a signal, try to guess what the target is before you dig. Try to guess its size, shape and depth. Analyze the audio and/or meter signals. Say to yourself, "This is a coin, or this is a bottlecap. It is approximately three inches deep." Then, pay attention when you dig the object. Did you guess right? Great! If not, try to determine why not. The more you do this, the greater your success will be. Use the straight-line sweep method recommended later in this chapter. Hold the searchcoil slightly above the ground and scan at a rate of about one foot per sound. Don't get in a hurry; don't try to cover an acre in 10 minutes. What you are looking for is buried just below the searchcoil scanning sweep you are now making, not across the field.

After 10 operating hours, begin using your Target Elimination mode. At first don't use too much Target Elimination, just enough to eliminate from detection the junk you have been digging. After you become comfortable with your detector, it's time to go back over those areas you searched before you learned how to use your machine. You'll be suprised how many coins and other objects you missed. Come back six months and then a year later. Each time you'll find more things, especially at greater depths.

Learn about other forms of treasure hunting such as ghost towning, relic and cache hunting and prospecting. Learn the various optional accessories and searchcoils available for your detector. Keep in mind at all times the idea that detectors are not complicated nor difficult to use. The first time you tried to operate a car it was difficult, but now you drive without thinking about it. The same will be true with your detector. Keep working with the instrument, restudy your manual, contact your dealer or manufacturer and ask for more information. Often, problems are cleared up with one simple demonstration by your dealer or someone who knows how to use detectors. During your learning period, keep the Detection Depth control turned to minimum or to the "Initial" set point. Scan with the searchcoil about two inches above the ground and scan at a moderate speed. Even in high junk areas which are very difficult to work, the reduced detection depth and moderate scanning speed improve your chances of hearing individual target signals rather than a jumbled sound.

Treasure is being found right now in your community and a lot of treasure is waiting for you. Detectors are not magic wands, but when used correctly, they will locate buried and concealed treasure. Maintain faith in your detector and have patience until you have it mastered. Success will be yours!

MAKE YOUR OWN TEST PLOT

One of the first things a new detector owner does is bury a few coins to see how deeply he can detect them. This test usually results in disappointment. The longer an object has been buried, the easier it can be detected. Not only is a "barrier" to electromagnetic field penetration created when a coin is first buried, but no "halo" effect has been developed. As time passes, coins become more closely associated, electrically, with surrounding earth materials, and the molecules of metal begin to move out into the surrounding soil. Also, it is theorized that in some cases (especially in salt water) the coin's surface becomes a better conductor. All of these phenomena result in the "detectability" of coins increasing the longer they are buried. It is estimated that coins and other buried metals can be detected at twice the depth or deeper, after a period of time in the soil, compared with the same object freshly buried.

Select an area where you can make your own test plot. Scan the area thoroughly in the all-metal mode and remove all metal from the ground. Select targets such as coins, a bottlecap, a nail and a pulltab. Select also a pint jar filled with scrap metal, a long object such as a foot-long pipe and a large object such as a gallon can. Bury the objects about three feet apart, in rows, and make a map showing items buried, location and depth.

Bury pennies at varying depths, beginning at one inch. Continue, with the deepest buried about six to eight inches. Bury one at about two inches, but stand it on edge. Bury a penny at about two inches with a bottlecap about four inches off to one side. Bury the bottlecap, nail and pulltab separately at about two inches deep. Bury the jar at 12 inches to the top of the jar lid. Bury the pipe horizontally, three or four inches deep. Bury the gallon can with the lid two feet below the surface.

The purpose of the buried coins is to familiarize you with the sound of money. If you can't detect the deeper coins, don't worry. After a while, you'll be able to detect them. After you have been able to detect them all, rebury some out of detection range. The penny buried next to the bottlecap will give you experience in "super-sniping" and will help you learn to distinguish individual objects. It will also be a good test to help you understand "detuning." The jar and gallon can will help you learn to recognize "dull" sounds of large, deeply buried objects. Check the targets with and without headphones; you'll be amazed at the difference headphones make.

The test plot is important. Don't neglect it; from time to time expand it and rebury the targets deeper and add new ones. This will be a measure of how well you are progressing and how well you have learned your equipment. Remember to make an ACCURATE map showing location and depth of all objects.

MISCELLANEOUS TIPS

When searching near wire fences, metal buildings, swing sets, etc., reduce detection depth and scan the searchcoil parallel to the structure. You may also try detuning and operating in the "silent" tuning zone, especially if the manufacturer recommends "silent" operation.

Learn to use a probe to locate the exact point where coins are buried. This will help you retrieve coins with minimum damage to grass and the target.

MORE TIPS

Coins lying in the ground at an angle may be missed on one searchcoil pass but detected when the searchcoil comes in from another direction. If your detector has a volume control, keep it set at maximum. Don't confuse volume control with Audio (Threshold) control. You can use earphones that have individual earpiece volume adjustment and set each one to suit yourself.

Never dial in more Target Elimination (Discrimination) than you need; too much may reduce detector efficiency.

If you are working on the beach, set target elimination at about bottlecap rejection. Slight adjustment may be necessary but you can set the detector to ignore salt water. Pulse Induction and automated VLF detectors, however, ignore salt water automatically.

Use common sense. THINK your way through perplexing situations. Remember that success will come from your expertise, research, patience, enthusiasm and use of common sense.

Don't expect to find tons of treasure every time you go metal detecting. There may be times when you don't find anything. But the fun and reward of our hobby is never knowing what you'll dig up next!

Be sure to check your batteries before you venture out, and check them often. Carry spare batteries every time you go searching.

Keep the searchcoil level as you scan and always scan slowly and methodically. Scan the searchcoil from side to side in a straight line in front of you.

Do not scan the searchcoil in an arc unless you are scanning extremely slowly. The straight-line scan method allows you to cover more ground in each sweep, helps keep the searchcoil level, reduces skipping and helps maintain uniform overlapping. You should overlap by advancing the searchcoil as much as 50% of its diameter. When the searchcoil reaches the extremes of each sweep, rotate your upper body to stretch out for an even wider sweep. This gives the double benefit of scanning a wider sweep while you get additional exercise. To insure a complete scan of any given area, use string or cord to mark scan paths. The width of your paths can be from three to six feet wide.

When you dig a target, scan back over the hole to make sure you recovered everything in and around it.

FILL YOUR HOLES,
PICK UP AND CARRY OFF ALL TRASH.
DON'T DESTROY PROPERTY!

SHORT COURSES FOR THE BEGINNER

These exercises will help you learn to use your detector and gain confidence in its abilities. This short course is, however, no substitute for study, application and practice. These instructions are for the popular manually adjusted VLF detectors.

1. Assemble your detector according to the Manual, using the smallest diameter searchcoil (three-inch to four-inch minimum) you have.

2. Hold the detector with the searchcoil about four feet in the air.

3. Turn the detector on and reduce detection depth to minimum.

4. Adjust the audio (tuner) to achieve a very low sound. This is your threshold level. Depending upon your detector, you may have to hold a switch in the depressed position while you make this adjustment.

5. If your detector has a Tuning Selector, select the MANUAL mode.

6. Select the All Metal Detection (no trash elimination) mode.

7. Adjust the Ground Elimination (Cancel) control knob (if your detector has one) to the "center" position.

   a. If it is a one-turn control, rotate the knob to the half-way point or the initial preset arrow.

   b. If it is a ten-turn control, rotate the knob either direction ten turns. Turn the knob five turns in the opposite direction. This will be the center point.

8. Momentarily press your Retune switch. If there is no retune button or switch, rotate the tuning control, if necessary, to regain a minimum audio threshold level.

9. Lower the searchcoil to a height of about two inches above the ground. If you continue to hear the faint threshold sound, begin slowly scanning the searchcoil over the ground, keeping a constant height. (See NOTES, below.)

10. Where the audio increases, a target is buried in the ground.

NOTES

If the ground is extremely mineralized, the mid-point ground elimination adjustment (Number 7, above) may not permit operation. The audio threshold level may change as you lower the searchcoil to the two-inch height. If that occurs, you must adjust the Ground Elimination control. Refer to your manual. Remember that each time you make an adjustment to the Ground Elimination control, or whenever the threshold sound level changes because of minerals, temperatures etc., you must press your Retune button or switch.

INITIAL "PRESET" SETTINGS

If your detector control panel has initial "preset" points, it will be easier for you to learn to use the instrument. Set all knobs and switches to the preset points. These adjustments are for average soil and operating conditions. Any controls without initial preset points should be set according to the instructions given above.

HEALTH SAFEGUARDS

Within the past three decades, metal detecting has become a very popular activity. People of all ages roam parks, ghost towns, beaches and gold mining areas in search of treasure. Some individuals occasionally complain of pains after they have used metal detectors for long periods of time. Such complaints usually come from those who are just beginning the hobby and swing their detector some 10 to 12 hours the first day out. On the next morning they naturally wake up with a good case of sore muscles. After a few days, the soreness disappears and off they go again.

Although the instances are rare, some hobbyists suffer from what is known as "tennis elbow." This is a perfectly real condition—an injury to the tendons of the elbow—whose medical name is epicondylitis. The condition is characterized by mild to sharp pain at the side of the elbow. It is believed to be caused by a gradual weakening of muscle tissue. Repeated muscle strain without time in-between for the muscles to repair themselves causes the problem.

I have been using metal detectors for more than 40 years and I have never had tennis elbow or any serious problem. I develop more problems from using my gym equipment. The following recommendations are aimed at further lessening the dangers of strained muscles:

1. Select the proper equipment, including accessories.
2. Strengthen your hand, arm, back and shoulder muscles through an exercise program.
3. Before beginning each day's detecting activity, spend a few minutes doing warmup exercises.
4. During your metal detecting activities, use the correct scanning techniques and take an occasional break. Stopping to dig a target is usually sufficient "break" time, however.

Let's expand each of these four preventive procedures. First, adjust the stem to the proper, though not necessarily shortest, length. If it is too long, you will have a balance problem and your swing will be awkward. If it is too short, you'll have to stoop over to search. If large searchcoils do not give proper balance, use a hipmount kit or armrest.

Select an excercise program that will strengthen your fingers, hand, arm, shoulder and back muscles. You don't need much strengthening, not even bar bell and dumbell workouts. Toning up is of primary importance. As you use your metal detector you'll develop the correct muscles. It's just that at the beginning, and after periods of inactivity, you should protect against strained muscles and ligaments. And, that brings us to the third preventive measure.

43

Warmup exercises should precede each day's metal detecting activity. A few minutes of stretching and other activity are needed to loosen muscles and joints and prepare you for a day's work. Begin by observing how cats stretch themselves; then, try to imitate these graceful animals. A brisk walk, a few toe touches, a few arm and wrist curls holding a one or two-pound weight, a few body twists at the waist while standing erect and perhaps a minute or two running in place will get the job done. You can develop your own warmup exercises.

Now, to the proper scanning methods. First, keep a firm footing; don't try to scan while balancing on one foot. This can cause your muscles to make unnatural movements. Keep all movements as natural as possible. If you find yourself scanning on steep hills, in gullies and other unlevel places, keep good balance, take shorter swings and don't place yourself in awkward positions.

Grasp the metal detector handle lightly. Slight wrist and arm movements are O.K. if your searchcoil swing, from side-to-side, is short. But, when you swing the detector widely from side to side, use a method that is natural and one that causes a minimum amount of unnecessary wrist movement. Let the entire arm "swing" with the detector. Occasionally, change hands and use the other arm to swing the detector. If you feel yourself tightening up, stop and rest. Most likely, however, each time you stop to dig a target, you can rest. Then, you can think of your next detected target as a blessing. You'll get to stop, stoop down and dig. This activity gives other muscles a workout, which will help prevent sore muscles that come from long periods of continuous metal detector swinging without a break.

HOW METAL DETECTORS WORK

NOTE: This chapter's illustrations are reproduced from the author's book, MODERN METAL DETECTORS; see Appendix I.

Electronic metal detector development had its beginning at least as early as 1881, when Alexander Graham Bell developed a metal detector circuit. Records describe an attempt he made to locate a bullet in the body of President John A. Garfield. There have since been many references to metal detectors being developed for prospecting and industrial applications. It was not until the 1920s that the "consumer" began using detectors to locate precious metals and lost treasure. Technology improved considerably during World War II when the U.S. and other governments developed military equipment essentially for mine detection. Following the war, much of this equipment came on the surplus market where it was welcomed by treasure hunters and prospectors.

Beginning in the 1950s, transistorized metal detector designs began replacing vacuum tube designs. By the 1960s, integrated circuits were being used. Today, exotic electronic components and microprocessors are available to enhance detector capabilities. A better understanding of ground mineralization has allowed engineers to develop circuitry specifically designed to eliminate this problem.

Over the years various types of detectors have been produced. Garrett and other advanced manufacturers began to develop all-purpose or universal type detectors that could, to a great extent, "do everything." In other words, one detector with a wide assortment of searchcoils could perform just about every detecting task with a great degree of efficiency.

Basic theory and component function are presented in following pages. To expand even more your knowledge of electronic theory and field application as it applies to metal detecting, I refer you to MODERN METAL DETECTORS.

RADIO WAVE TRANSMISSION AND RECEPTION

Metal detection is achieved by the transmission and "reception" of a radio wave signal. The signal circulates in the searchcoil antenna wire. An electromagnetic field, Figure 5-2, is generated that flows out into the surrounding medium, i.e.: air, wood, rock, earth, water or any other material. When the electromagnetic field lines pass through metal the pheonomena of eddy current generation and electromagnetic field distortion take place. The searchcoil antenna array senses these disturbances. Electronic circuits produce audio and other signals that alert the operator to the presence of a metal "target."

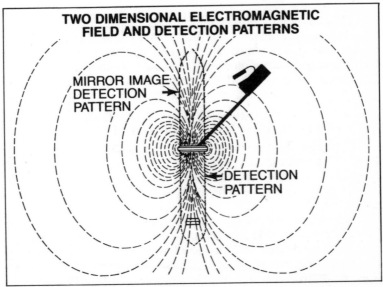

Figure 5-2: TWO DIMENSIONAL ELECTROMAGNETIC FIELD AND DETECTION PATTERN. The transmitter current flowing in the antenna generates the electromagnetic field. The detection pattern, shown by the heavy dashed lines, is the area within which metal detection takes place. A mirror-image detection pattern is formed on the opposite side of the searchcoil (the top), but it is not utilized.

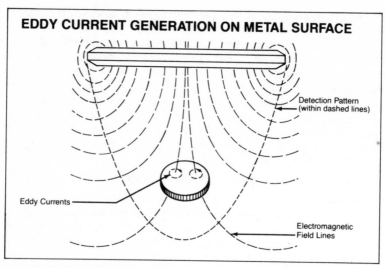

EDDY CURRENT GENERATION ON METAL SURFACE

Detection Pattern (within dashed lines)

Eddy Currents

Electromagnetic Field Lines

Figure 5-3: EDDY CURRENT GENERATION ON METAL SURFACE. When metal comes within the detection pattern, electromagnetic field lines penetrate the metal. Tiny circulating currents called "eddy currents" are caused to flow on the metal's surface. The resulting power loss by the electromagnetic field (the power used up generating the eddy currents) is sensed by the detector's circuits. The detector alerts the operator to the presence of the metal.

The detection of earthen minerals occasionally occurs. The two most troublesome minerals are iron, often called magnetite (black magnetic sand), and wetted salt. Not only do these minerals produce audible and visual detection signals, they also inhibit the ability of metal detectors to detect metal. Modern metal detectors, however, are able to ignore these minerals to a great extent.

EDDY CURRENTS AND SECONDARY ELECTROMAGNETIC FIELD GENERATION

Depending upon the metal detector type, one or both of the above described phenomena cause target detection to take place. A simplified explanation of these characteristics is presented to help you understand why your metal detector reacts as it does to metals and detectable minerals.

Whenever metal comes within the detection pattern, Figure 5-3, the electromagnetic field lines penetrate the metal. Tiny circulating currents called "eddy currents" are caused to flow on the metal's surface. The power, or motivating force, that causes eddy currents to flow comes from the electromagnetic field. The power loss (the power used up in generating the eddy currents) is sensed by the detector's circuits. A secondary electromagnetic field generated by the eddy currents flows into the surrounding medium. A portion of the field intersects the searchcoil's receiver winding, causing a detection signal current to occur in that winding. The power loss and the receiver winding current are sensed by the receiver circuitry. A signal then alerts the operator to the metal's presence.

ELECTROMAGNETIC FIELD DISTORTION

The detection of non-conductive iron (ferrous) minerals takes place in another manner. The searchcoil's receiver winding is positioned with respect to the transmitter winding so that minimum transmitted power is induced into the receiver winding. In other words, the windings are "balanced."

When iron mineral comes near and within the detection pattern, as illustrated in Figure 5-4, the electromagnetic field lines are redistributed. This redistribution upsets the winding "balance," resulting in power being induced into the receiver winding. Such induced power is sensed by the detector's receiver circuits. A signal then alerts the operator to the presence of the mineral. The detection of iron mineral is desired in some cases; for example, an electronic prospector might seek black magnetic sand that could contain gold or silver.

These explanations of eddy current, secondary electromagnetic field generation and field distortion are obviously simplified. Actually, all three effects generally occur upon detection of most targets.

SEARCH MATRIX

The ground (or material) over which a metal detector scans is called the "search matrix." Any substance penetrated by the electromagnetic field is "illuminated," as illustrated in Figure 5-5. Many elements and minerals are within the soil, including moisture, iron, salt and various

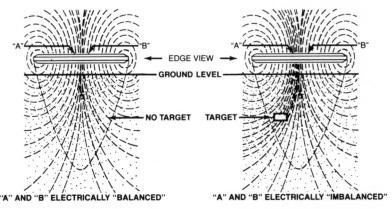

"A" AND "B" ELECTRICALLY "BALANCED"   "A" AND "B" ELECTRICALLY "IMBALANCED"

Figure 5-4: SEARCHCOIL TRANSMITTER/RECEIVER WINDINGS BALANCED (LEFT) AND IMBALANCED (RIGHT). Metal detection (or searchcoil imbalance) takes place, for instance, when iron comes near and within the detection pattern. Electromagnetic field lines are redistributed as illustrated. This redistribution upsets the winding "balance" at points A and B resulting in power being induced into the receiver winding.

47

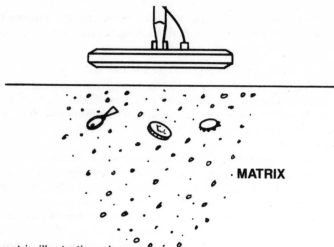

MATRIX

This matrix illustration shows
the main (detection) area illuminated
by the electromagnetic field.

Figure 5-5: TYPICAL MATRIX AREA ILLUMINATED BY ELECTROMAGNETIC FIELD. This illustration shows a searchcoil hovering above the ground (called, in metal detection terminology, the search matrix). There are various elements including soil and rocks in the matrix that are being illuminated by the electromagnetic field. The metal detector's response at any given moment is caused by all conductive metals and minerals and ferrous non-conductive minerals that are illuminated by the electromagnetic field.

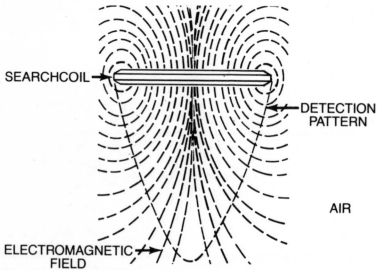

SEARCHCOIL

DETECTION
PATTERN

AIR

ELECTROMAGNETIC
FIELD

Figure 5-6: NORMAL DETECTION PATTERN IN AIR (PERFECT COUPLING WITH AIR MATRIX). "Coupling" describes the penetration of the electromagnetic field into any object near the transmitter antenna. As shown in this illustration, there is perfect coupling into the air matrix. Generally, perfect coupling is achieved in objects such as wood, fresh water, air, glass and certain non-mineralized earth materials.

48

other minerals — some detectable and some not. You hope that treasure is also present. A metal detector senses, at any given moment, all conductive metals and minerals and ferrous non-conductive minerals that are illuminated by the electromagnetic field.

ELECTROMAGNETIC FIELD COUPLING

"Coupling" describes the penetration of the electromagnetic field into the search matrix. There is perfect coupling, Figure 5-6, into some objects such as wood, fresh water, air, glass and certain non-mineralized earth materials. Coupling is inhibited (distorted), Figure 5-7, when the electromagnetic field attempts to penetrate iron mineralization, wetted salt and other substances. This inhibiting decreases the detection capability of the metal detector. Even though some instruments, such as the VLF, can eliminate the detection effects of iron minerals, the electromagnetic field is still inhibited to reduce detection capability and performance.

SALT WATER DETECTION

Perhaps in some science class you inserted two electrodes into a glass of fresh water and learned that no electrical current flowed when you attached a battery to the electrodes. You then added salt to the water and discovered that the salt water takes on conductive properties. In effect, salt ocean water looks like conductive "metal" to some detectors. Manufacturers are, however, able to design detectors capable of "ignoring" salt water.

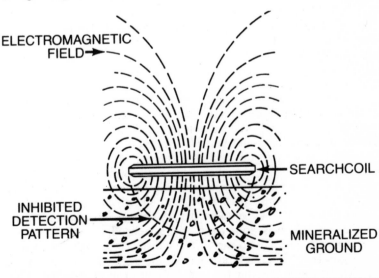

Figure 5-7: DISTORTED DETECTION PATTERN IN MINERALS (COUPLING INHIBITED BY MINERALS). In some elements such as iron mineralization and wetted salt, coupling is inhibited when the electromagnetic field attempts penetration. This inhibiting of the electromagnetic field decreases detection depth capability.

49

DEPTH OF DETECTION

Several factors influence depth detection. The transmitted electromagnetic field flows into the search matrix generating eddy currents on the surface of conductive substances. Detectable targets that sufficiently disturb the field are detected. Three factors determine whether the disturbance is sufficient for detection: electromagnetic field strength, target size and surface area.

ELECTROMAGNETIC FIELD STRENGTH

Even though the electromagnetic field theoretically extends to infinity, a few feet away from the searchcoil it is considerably reduced in strength. Both distance and absorption by the search matrix materials reduce the field strength. A detector has several thousand times less detection capability at six feet than at one foot.

TARGET SIZE

The larger a metal target, the better and more deeply it can be detected. You know how eddy current generation causes metal detection to take place. The more eddy currents that are generated, the larger will be the detector signal produced. An object with double the surface area of another will produce detection signal strength twice that of the smaller object, but it will not be detected twice as far. A large target will produce the same detection signal strength as a small target positioned closer to the searchcoil.

SURFACE AREA DETECTION

For the most part metal detectors are SURFACE AREA detectors. They are not metallic volume (mass) detectors. The larger the surface area of a metal target that is "looking at" the bottom of the searchcoil, the better that target will be detected. The actual volume or mass of the target has very little to do with most forms of detection. Prove this for yourself.

Turn your detector on and tune it to threshold. Move a large coin in toward the searchcoil with the face of the coin "looking at" the bottom of the searchcoil. Make a note of the distance at which the coin is first detected. It should be, let's say, eight inches.

Now, move the coin back and rotate it so that the edge of the coin "looks at" the bottom of the searchcoil. Bring the coin in toward the searchcoil. You will see that the coin cannot be detected at eight inches. In fact, it probably will be detected only at a distance of four inches or less. The mass of metal did not change, only the surface area of the coin that was "looking at" the searchcoil.

Another proof is to measure the distance a single coin can be detected. Then, stack several coins on the back side of the test coin and check to see how far the stack of coins can be detected. You'll find the stack can be detected at only a slightly greater distance, illustrating that the greater volume of metal has very little effect on detection distance.

FRINGE AREA DETECTION

Fringe area detection, Figure 5-8, is a characteristic whose understanding will enable you to detect metal targets to the maximum depth capability of any instrument. To review, the detection pattern is the area below the searchcoil where metal detection takes place. The size of this pattern depends upon the size of the target.

The detection pattern for a coin may extend, say, one foot below the searchcoil. The detection pattern for a small jar of coins may extend, perhaps, two feet below the searchcoil. Within the area of the detection pattern, an unmistakable detector signal is produced.

Does detection take place outside the detection pattern? Yes, but the signals are too weak to be discerned by the operator EXCEPT in the fringe area around the outer edges of the detection pattern.

If you desire fringe area signals, a good set of headphones is a must along with training in the art of discerning those faint whispers of sound that occur in the fringe area. Skill in fringe area detection can be developed with practice, training, concentration and faith in your ability. Those of you who develop fringe area detection ability to a fine art will make treasure discoveries that many other detector operators will miss. The ability to hear fringe area signals improves metal detection efficiency and success.

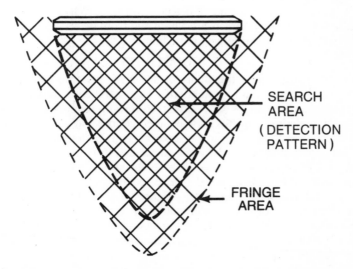

SEARCH
AREA
(DETECTION
PATTERN)

FRINGE
AREA

Figure 5-8: SEARCHCOIL DETECTION PATTERN AND FRINGE AREA. Detection takes place outside the detection pattern, but the signals are too weak to be discerned by the operator EXCEPT in the fringe area around the outer edges of the detection pattern. This illustration shows that location and approximate proportional size of a detection pattern. See the text for an explanation of how to detect objects within the fringe area.

CONDUCTIVE MATRIXES

Most ground matrixes contain minerals that will conduct eddy currents. Conductive minerals tend to "mask" targets. Since the metal detector sees the ground beneath the searchcoil (the matrix) as a single target, a smaller target, say a coin, is not as easily "seen" by the detector in a conductive matrix compared with its detection in a low-conductive matrix. Ocean (salt) water or wetted beach sands are examples of low-conductive matrixes. A Trash Elimination control (sometimes called the "Discriminator") lets the operator "dial out" materials that have low conductivity. Consequently, the control can be set to ignore salt water. Most desirable metals will be detected, however, because they have a higher conductivity.

TARGET ELIMINATION (DISCRIMINATING) METAL DETECTORS

A Trash Elimination (Discrimination) metal detector "tells" the operator whether detected metal is desirable or not, depending on what the operator seeks. The detector gives the operator this information by meter deflections and increases or decreases in speaker or headphone volume. Good (or desirable) objects cause the audio or visual indicators to increase in amplitude; junk (undesirable) objects cause the indicators to decrease. Target identification indicators give additional "value quality" information to the operator.

The terms "Elimination" and "Discrimination" mean the same thing. The term "Elimination" is more easily understood because it more accurately describes the metal detector function. When the control is set to zero, no metal targets are eliminated from detection. The higher the setting, the more targets are eliminated.

CONDUCTIVITY

"Conductivity" is the ability of any given metal to conduct electricity compared with a standard. The searchcoil's radiated electromagnetic field causes eddy currents to flow on the surface of metals. The more desirable metals such as silver, copper and gold have higher conductivities (and more flow of eddy current) than iron, foil, tin and other less desirable metals. Since metal detectors can "measure" the amount of power that is used to generate eddy currents, the detector can "tell" which metals are the better coductors.

Most detectors have controls, Figure 5-9, that let the operator "dial in" the amount of desired elimination. The metal detector measures the conductivity of each detected target and compares it with the control setting made by the operator. All targets positioned "below" the pointer are eliminated from detection. All targets positioned "above" are accepted.

The accompanying chart represents the conductivity positioning of one particular metal detector. Since conductivity is a function of the frequency of the transmitted signal and other factors, the exact posi-

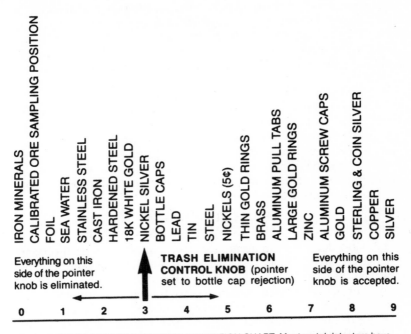

Figure 5-9: METAL DETECTOR TARGET ELIMINATION CHART. Most metal detectors have a control that allows the operator to "dial in" the amount of desired target elimination (discrimination). This is an illustration of a metal detector target elimination control with various targets placed in the order of their conductivity. The arrow is the knob's pointer. The metal detector measures the conductivity of each target and "compares" it to the setting the operator has "dialed in" with the control. All targets to the left of the pointer are eliminated from detection. All targets to the right of the pointer are accepted.

tion on the chart may vary from detector to detector. You can develop a chart for your detector by testing various small targets and determining where, on your Trash Elimination control, each target is eliminated. The lowest control setting at which any given target can no longer be detected, is that target's position on the conductivity chart.

To determine where salt water should be positioned on your chart, dissolve one-half cup of salt in a gallon plastic container filled with water. Move the container toward the bottom of the searchcoil with the trash eliminator dial set at zero. If the instrument can detect the salt water, rotate its control to "1," retune the detector and test again. The point on the control at which salt water is no longer detected is its "position" on the conductivity chart.

TRASH (TARGET) ELIMINATORS

BFO trash elimination circuitry is primarily of the metered type. All metals are indicated as "good" by the audio circuits. Only meter circuits can analyze targets. BFOs do not ignore iron mineralization

53

nor can salt water be eliminated. Metered BFO trash elimination is satisfactory, but requires an experienced operator.

TRs are very accurate trash eliminators. Salt water interference can be eliminated, but iron earth minerals cannot. When iron earth minerals are present, TR operation (and trash elimination) becomes difficult.

VLF audio and meter trash eliminator circuitry works very well. Salt water and iron earth minerals can be eliminated. VLFs can reject foil, nails, pulltabs and screw caps quite well, but some models eliminate bottlecaps and pulltabs better than others.

Pulse induction eliminator circuits perform well in rejecting junk targets. Iron nails, however, tend to be accepted. Pulse detectors ignore iron earth minerals and salt water automatically; no operator control adjustments are necessary.

TRASH ELIMINATION—
CIRCUITRY IS NOT 100% ACCURATE

Most detectors can accurately classify small, coin-sized objects, but larger targets cannot be accurately classified. Objects such as cans, buckets and sheet metal may be read as "good." An experienced operator, however, using certain detector models, can distinguish between the desirability of large targets by elevating the detector searchcoil and/or detuning the detector. These methods prevent "saturating" target I.D. meters and allowing them to give readings in the linear (normal) range.

The intrinsic value of a target is not a consideration. For instance, an extremely valuable platinum diamond ring may read "poor" because platinum is a relatively poor conductor compared with copper, silver and gold. Most rings and jewelry items are a mixture (alloy) of several metals. A gold alloy ring may be rejected if the metal alloyed with gold is a poor conductor.

Small jewelry items such as gold and silver chains, fine wire bracelets and thin rings may be rejected because there is minimal flat surface where eddy current generation can take place. Since aluminum pulltabs "read" about the same as rings, some rings may be rejected when a detector's controls are set at pulltab rejection. United States pennies dated prior to 1983 will read "better" on classifier meters than 1983 and newer pennies because more copper was used in manufacturing the earlier pennies.

Because the conductivity of United States nickels is relatively poor, they will often be rejected when pulltab elimination is used. An exception to this is World War II-era nickels which contain about one-third silver. Some tinfoil, when crumpled, has a large volume in relation to its surface area. These crumpled tinfoil balls may then read "good." Small steel pieces, when bright and shiny, may read good because the surface tends to be a good conductor. Rust causes the surface to resist current, resulting in rejection.

At many coin sites along the United States/Canadian border, coins of both countries may be in the ground. Some Canadian coins have poorer conductivity than United States coins. In ghost towns "tokens" are often plentiful. Since some tokens were made of metals with lower levels of conductivity, they will classify as "poor" on the conductivity chart. In areas where old coins are waiting to be found, you will learn that their conductivity is relatively poorer than that of modern coins. Also, patina may decrease a coin's conductivity. You should remain alert to these situations and adjust elimination control so that no desirable objects are rejected.

A masking effect causes some good targets to escape detection because negative signals from trash targets cancel positive signals from desirable targets. Dialing more elimination increases the problem of target masking. In other words, the more elimination you use, the more good targets you will miss. So, use target elimination sparingly! The earth's minerals can upset a detector's "air" settings, causing good targets in the ground to be missed.

TRASH ELIMINATION

How much trash elimination should you use? It's up to you. I recommend the following method to determine the correct amount of discrimination: Scan the area without eliminating anything. After you have dug a few targets you'll be able to decide the amount and kind of junk present in the ground. Then, adjust the control to reject targets you don't want to dig.

METERS

There are two types of meters in use: signal strength indicators and classifiers. Lights, bargraphs and other visual means are also provided, but they serve the two basic functions of signal strength indication and/or target classification.

SIGNAL STRENGTH INDICATORS

A meter permits the operator to observe detection functions visually. The indicator pointer generally operates in synchronism with speaker sounds. When the audio increases in volume, the meter pointer deflects upward; when the speaker sound decreases, the meter pointer drops downward.

Aside from noting the presence of a detected target, the meter has two other important functions. First, it can be used for precise pinpointing of buried objects. As you scan the searchcoil across a buried object, note where maximum deflection of the meter pointer occurs and indicates target center. If the target is large, or shallowly buried, it may be necessary to elevate the searchcoil several inches and scan over the target so that the meter pointer stays on scale. Otherwise, you will not be able to determine the point of maximum signal. Also, you can detune the metal detector to keep the meter pointer on scale.

A second important meter function is parallel indication. You may hear a sound so weak that you are not sure you detected a target. Scan back over the spot, paying careful attention to the meter pointer. If you see the pointer deflect upward as you pass the spot where you hear the weak audio sound, then you are doubly assured that a target has been detected.

Of course, parallel indication on deep targets is not always possible for all detectors under all conditions, because meters on some detectors are less sensitive than the speaker.

Some people have developed what is called a "musical ear" which is the ability to hear sounds that are either extremely weak or composed of harmonic frequencies that occur when metal is detected. People with this exceptional ability can hear detection signals that do not show on the meter.

TARGET CLASSIFIERS

All targets fall into one of three categories: POOR, FAIR or GOOD. "Poor" targets are usually bottlecaps, iron and some foil. "Fair" targets are usually nickels, pulltabs, some rings and other medium conductivity metals.

"Good" targets are usually silver, coins and other high conductivity metals. Certain objects like tiny platinum rings and some alloy jewelry, are difficult to categorize, but most targets likely to be found fit accurately into one of the three categories. Since Target I.D. meters do not identify targets as deeply as audio circuits can detect them, some targets won't read on the meter. The meter reading remains the same as the previous target.

All things considered, accurate indicators can be built to improve the operator's efficiency by properly classifying detected targets before they are dug.

AUDIO INDICATORS

Speakers are the easiest audio indicators to use; there is no fuss with headphones or dangling cords. Speakers will drain batteries more quickly because they use more power than headphones, meters or indicator lights. As a rule of thumb, speakers use five times as much battery power as headphones.

BFO tuning threshold is generally a frequency about 50 to 60 cycles per second. When the searchcoil passes over a conductive metal target, the frequency increases. When you pass it over non-conductive iron minerals, the frequency decreases.

TR and VLF systems operate on fixed audio frequencies, usually of approximately 800 to 1,000 cycles. Threshold tuning is set so that you can barely hear the sound. Some detectors can be operated silently. As you pass over a metal target, there is a loudness change (increase); the frequency does not change as in a BFO.

Pulse induction detector audio is a "bell" tone sound that increases in loudness when a target is detected.

TONE INDICATIONS

Several audio systems are available. One system measures the "quality" or conductivity of the target. The audio tone varies in pitch: low-range pitch indications occur when targets are "poor" conductors; mid-range pitch indications occur when targets are "fair" conductors; high-range pitch indications occur when targets are "good" conductors. This tonal identification method, or some variation of it, when coupled with an accurate indicator meter, improves operator efficiency.

A problem with this system is the operator's difficulty in analyzing tones as the audio varies constantly up and down the scale. The sounds are somewhat like a horn on the old Ford Model "A" — Ahhhhhhh...Oooooooo...Gaaaaaaa! After several scans over the target, the sound usually levels out; with experience the operator can decide with reasonable accuracy which category the tonal system is indicating. Targets with conductivities that fall between ranges, however, are difficult to interpret. Also, the constantly rising and falling tone is annoying. Another drawback of this type tonal system is that reject targets, which should not be dug, do not have a fixed or definite "no" sound.

AN IMPROVED TONAL SYSTEM

The ideal system is one that alerts the operator instantly—with one searchcoil scan—to the type target detected. But, the "ideal system" then depends on the operator and the goal of his or her search. Cache hunters search for money caches; prospectors search for gold, silver, nuggets, veins, etc.; relic hunters search for relics; coin hunters search for coins. Can there be distinct tonal sounds for each category? No. It would not be practical—nor possible, for that matter.

One solution that helps the majority of searches is a system for coin hunters. Since 95% of all detectorists search for coins, a "coin" circuit is the most practical.

The accompanying illustration, Figure 5-10, describes Garrett's new circuit response. Each time the instrument detects a coin, the operator hears a bell-like ringing. The sound is unmistakable. There is no need to look at the classifier meter to know that a coin (an upper range target) has been detected. The operator simply digs at the point where the bell sound is the loudest.

But what about targets that are not coins? How are they distinguishable? The answer is simple. All other category sounds are exactly those that metal detector operators have heard for years. Reject targets cause the audio level to decrease. Mid-range targets cause the audio level to increase in loudness (not a bell ringing sound but a normal VLF audio sound). Reject and mid-range targets are determined by where the operator sets the trash elimination control. So,

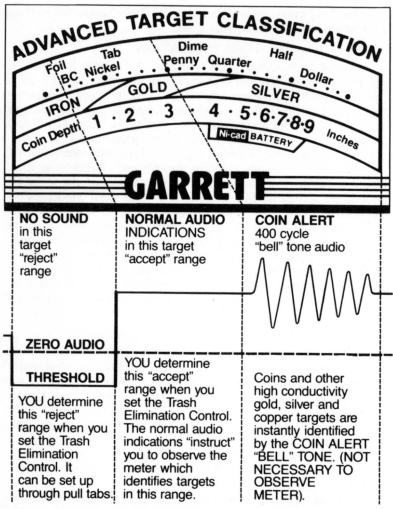

NO SOUND in this target "reject" range	NORMAL AUDIO INDICATIONS in this target "accept" range	COIN ALERT 400 cycle "bell" tone audio
ZERO AUDIO		
THRESHOLD YOU determine this "reject" range when you set the Trash Elimination Control. It can be set up through pull tabs.	YOU determine this "accept" range when you set the Trash Elimination Control. The normal audio indications "instruct" you to observe the meter which identifies targets in this range.	Coins and other high conductivity gold, silver and copper targets are instantly identified by the COIN ALERT "BELL" TONE. (NOT NECESSARY TO OBSERVE METER).

Figure 5-10. BELL TONE COIN ALERT/AUDIO/VISUAL TARGET CLASSIFICATION SYSTEM. This composite drawing illustrates a unique meter/audio target classification system. A coin-alert audio "bell tone," indicates the presence of coins and upper-range, high-conductivity targets. A standard audio tone alerts the operator to the presence of mid-range targets that are then identified by the meter. Lower range reject targets do not produce an audio tone but cause the audio threshold to decrease to silent. The coin-alert range is set by the operator, generally at "coins." All coins that have conductivities of United States one-cent copper and higher cause the bell tone to sound. With a single adjustment of the discrimination control knob, the operator sets the mid and lower ranges. In the illustration, the point between these two ranges is set at foil (bottlecaps). This system allows the operator to adjust the detector's computer circuitry to achieve maximum efficiency regardless of the nature of the targets in the ground.

in effect, the operator has complete control over the detector's trash elimination circuitry. The audio tells, instantly, with one searchcoil sweep, the type target detected.

The bell tone is caused by targets that have conductivity within the silver or higher range. All targets (including silver, clad and copper coins) with a conductivity higher than United States zinc pennies, activate the bell tone sound. Since some valuable targets (nickels, rings, high patina coins, etc.) may fall in the mid-range category, the operator must check the classifier meter whenever the mid-range sound is heard in order to indentify the detected target.

CLASSIFIER INDICATOR/TONAL SYSTEM ADVANTAGES

There are many advantages to this system. The operator's efficiency improves. One argument against these new audio/visual systems is that since good targets will be dug anyway, why identify them? That's a good argument, but with the proper audio/visual system, valuable targets can be located and recovered more quickly. For instance, good targets buried close to trash may be rejected by the detector. The classifier meter and/or a tonal system, however, operates even though "zero" trash elimination is dialed in. The bell tone is heard regardless of where the trash elimination circuit is set. Thus, a far better probability of not rejecting these good targets is possible. Operators can find coins in high trash areas that less capable detectors would probably miss.

Just knowing what a target is, prior to digging, has a certain psychological value that stimulates a treasure hunter's interest. Detectors that feature only a classifier meter are not as efficient as the combination audio/visual system because operators must visually observe the meter each time a target is detected if they wish to know its identity. This reduces speed and efficiency. If the detector has an accurate tonal system, the operator knows instantly that, if it is a coin, it is to be dug. It is not necessary to view the meter to learn target identity.

TUNING/RE-TUNING

Tuning is one of the most misunderstood of all metal detector adjustments. Tuning is nothing more than adjusting a knob to achieve the optimum audio threshold level. On most detectors this optimum level is the lowest possible sound that the operator can hear. If the threshold is set down in the silent zone or, conversely, set too loud, detection depth can suffer.

On most models, audio threshold is set when the operator first uses his detector. With one exception, this level is never manually readjusted on a detector equipped with a flip switch or push button "retune" switch. These "retune" switches instantly reset the audio to the operator's present threshold whenever it needs resetting. This may occur during temperature changes and battery drift.

The exception to this "set-and-forget" rule occurs when the speaker or headphones are used interchangeably. Headphones generally require a lower threshold.

MANUAL VERSUS AUTOMATIC TUNING

Tuning can be further confusing, especially considering the difference between MANUAL and AUTOMATIC tuning. Some detectors have a switch that can be placed in either the MANUAL or AUTOMATIC tuning position. When the MANUAL position is selected, this handle-mounted retune switch (or push button) must be MANUALLY PRESSED momentarily to return the audio to threshold. When AUTOMATIC tuning is selected, the retune switch does not have to be pressed; the detector AUTOMATICALLY and ELECTRONICALLY keeps the audio level at the preset threshold. When a detected target, drift or some other occurrence causes the audio threshold to change, the automatic circuit "pulls" the audio back to preset threshold. That is why the detector searchcoil must be kept in continuous motion, and why the searchcoil cannot "hover" or be held stationary over a target. Also, when automatic tuning is used, detection depth capability and sensitivity may be reduced.

TARGET PINPOINTING

Detector operators should strive to develop accurate pinpointing methods. The target will be recovered more rapidly with less damage to sod and grass when it is located precisely before digging. It is especially important for coin hunters working in parks and recreational areas to learn good pinpointing and recovery methods. Laws have been enacted to keep coin hunters out of city-owned parks because of some hunters who have left gaping holes. The future well-being of the coin hunting hobby depends upon YOU!

DETUNING

By noticing where maximum sounds occur and drawing an imaginary "X" with the searchcoil, you can precisely pinpoint buried targets. One method that makes pinpointing more precise is DETUNING, Figure 5-11. First, locate maximum sound as precisely as you can by drawing the imaginary "X". Then, place the searchcoil on the ground at that point. Press the retune switch momentarily and release. This operation tunes the detector TO THE TARGET.

Now, slide the searchcoil back and forth keeping it in contact with the ground. Each time the target center of your searchcoil is directly over the target, you will hear a slight "blip" audio sound. This method is performed most easily in the VLF Ground Eliminating all-metal manual mode.

Target center of a searchcoil may be at its exact physical center, or it may be slightly forward of center toward the "toe" of the searchcoil. Determine your instrument's target center by placing a small coin directly on the searchcoil bottom near the center. Press the retune button momentarily, then slide the coin around on the bottom of the searchcoil. The point where audio is loudest will be your target center.

ELECTRONIC PINPOINTING

Electronic pinpointing is a noteworthy metal detector circuit development that enhances the ability of the detector to pinpoint targets. When the electronic pinpointing switch is pressed, circuits come into play that narrow the audio response. The audio "blip" becomes more noticeable and discernible whenever the searchcoil is directly above a target.

BACK-READING

Back-reading produces a "good" signal when a "reject" target is brought closer than one inch from the bottom of the searchcoil. This occurs in the discrimination mode only. The signal, even though positive, is easily recognizable as back-reading. If you suspect you have a back-reading signal, raise the searchcoil one inch above the ground, press the retune button and scan back over the spot. You will hear a positive indication only if the target is "good."

OVERSHOOT

Overshoot is a phenomenon that occurs only when the automatic mode is used. It occurs when a reject target is detected in trash

Figure 5-11: AUDIO RESPONSE CURVES ILLUSTRATING DE-TUNING OVER TARGET. This illustration compares normal audio response to de-tuned audio response. You will notice the detection pattern is reduced in size when the detector is de-tuned.

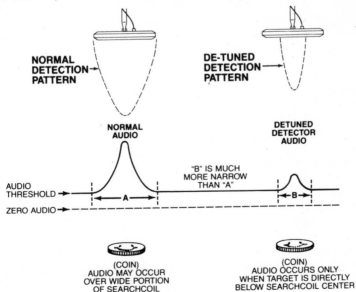

61

elimination or when a mineralized (non-conductive iron) rock is detected in the VLF mode. As the searchcoil moves clear of such a target, the audio suddenly increases to a loud sound. This also occurs when the searchcoil is scanned in the opposite direction. Thus, a loud audio "overshoot" occurs on both sides of the detected target.

COIN DEPTH MEASUREMENT

Coin depth measurement circuitry is very accurate on Garrett and other quality-built detectors. When a switch is pressed as the object is scanned over, the meter pointer indicates approximate coin depth. Meter scales are usually calibrated in inches and millimeters with circuitry operating for coin-sized objects only.

Objects larger than coins cause the meter to read more shallow than the true depth. Smaller objects cause the meter to read deeper. Some detectors must be hovered above a target while the meter is read. Other meter circuits "lock in" on the reading with just one pass over the coin; the reading holds steady until a handle-mounted switch is released. Other detectors require several passes over the target before an accurate reading is obtained.

Circuitry for measuring coin depth is a desirable feature and supplies the coin hunter with valuable data. Coin retrieval is simplified when approximate depth is known. Depth-measuring circuits are calibrated for a given size searchcoil, usually seven to eight inches in diameter. The searchcoil must be in contact with the ground for the most accurate reading.

MODE SWITCHING

Some detectors feature electronic mode switching. Pressing a switch causes modes to change instantly. As many as six modes can be controlled by a single switch. Usually, whenever a mode switch is pressed, the detector "returns" to audio threshold.

Often, I receive questions such as, "Which mode do I use?" and "How do I know when to change modes?" As a response to these common questions, listed below are descriptions of modes presently in use. I have not listed any trademarked mode designations.

AUTOMATIC (TUNING): For use when drift becomes a problem or when you prefer to use it. Compare MANUAL and AUTOMATIC operating characteristics (detection depth, discrimination, etc.) before using.

AUTOMATED VLF TYPE DETECTOR: For use primarily in coin hunting, but this type detector can perform other tasks.

BFO DISCRIMINATION: For use when coin hunting or ghost towning for coins, tokens, etc. Do not use when searching for caches, relics, nuggets or veins.

BFO METAL ZONE: For use when searching for metal and when ore sampling.

62

BFO MINERAL ZONE: For use when searching for black magnetic sand (magnetite).

COIN DEPTH MEASURING: For use when you wish to know coin depth.

DE-TUNING: For use when you wish the most precise pinpointing, and when you are searching only for very shallow targets.

ELECTRONIC PINPOINTING: For use in fast, quick pinpointing that is more accurate than regular pinpointing.

PULSE INDUCTION-ALL METAL: For use when you wish to dig every target.

PULSE INDUCTION-TRASH ELIMINATION: Use when you do not wish to dig every target.

RETUNING: For use any time the audio drifts away from your preset threshold; simply push a button or flip a switch to restore threshold. Retune as often as necessary to maintain threshold.

REVERSE DISCRIMINATION: For use primarily when scanning a TR over heavy ground mineralization and identifying targets, hot rocks, etc.

SILENT (NO AUDIO) TUNING: For use only when you do not wish to hear the steady tone of audio threshold. You will lose some detection depth and sensitivity. The newer, Automatic VLF Ground Elimination detectors can be operated silently, but some detection depth and sensitivity will be lost.

THRESHOLD (AUDIO) TUNING: For use when you desire the greatest detection depth, sensitivity and detector efficiency; use slight audio sound (threshold).

TR ALL-METAL: For use when you wish to dig every target. Mineralized ground may necessitate VLF ALL-METAL mode (detector).

TR DISCRIMINATION: For use when coin hunting and "trash" targets are not to be dug. Mineralized ground may require VLF TRASH ELIMINATION mode (detector).

VLF ALL-METAL: For use when you wish to dig every target; when gold (precious metal) searching; when cache and relic hunting and at all other times for detecting to maximum depth. For use over mineralized or non-mineralized ground.

VLF CALIBRATED: For use when ore sampling (high grading mine dumps, etc.) or identifying hot rocks.

VLF TRASH ELIMINATION (DISCRIMINATION): For use when you do not wish to dig every target. Do not use when cache and precious metal searching. Use over mineralized or non-mineralized ground.

CHAPTER 6

Metal Detectors:
Equipment Types and Searchcoils

This chapter contains discussions about metal detector configurations available for beach, surf and underwater hunting. These configurations include standard models, pistol-grip types, hip mounts and chest mounts, as well as models designed to be convertible or used only under water, Figure 6-1. The various types of searchcoils, headphones and other accessories are also discussed. This material should help you select the configuration best suited to your personal requirements.

STANDARD METAL DETECTOR CONFIGURATION: These are standard configuration metal detectors. They have the control housing attached to the handle and stem. Serveral sizes of searchcoil are available. This style is restricted to land or very shallow water hunting. The Garrett Master Hunter configuration is often called the "wrist action" model. Lightweight models can be used for long periods without causing much fatigue.

PISTOL-GRIP CONFIGURATION: The pistol-grip configuration with built-in arm rest is shown in Figures 6-4 and 6-5. This style is used for land and shallow water hunting. Lightweight, properly balanced models can be used for long periods without causing much fatigue. Some models such as the Garrett AT3, shown in Figure 9-1, are designed for use in rain and in the surf.

When non-submersible models are used in shallow water, the control housing must be flotation or high body mounted. Either mounting keeps the detector housing above water and lessens the risk of the detector circuitry and other components being damaged by a sudden wave or other mishap. The chest mount configuration gives good protection when the control housing is mounted high up on the chest just under the chin.

HIP-MOUNT CONFIGURATIONS: A few hip-mount configuration models are produced. The control housing, mounted on a belt, can be slung around the waist (hip-mounted) or slung over the shoulder. Most hip-mounted configurations are non-convertible because they cannot be assembled into the standard detector configuration. An adjustable-length stem and an armrest are supplied. Belt clips are attached to the control housing. Some hip-mount styles permit use of more than one searchcoil. Ideally, the meter is protected and all controls are readily accessible. This configuration is not as popular as the standard configuration.

Figure 6-1: The author tests various detector models on a Galveston beach. The adverse effect that salt water has on man-made materials, plus the conductive nature of salt water must be considered in all aspects of metal detector design. The detectors must be able to withstand the elements as well as perform flawlessly over the conductive salt water.

HIP-MOUNT ACCESSORY KITS: A hip-mount accessory kit permits you to convert your standard configuration into hip-mount. Generally, the control housing is mounted on a belt and slung around your waist or across one shoulder. Equipping your detector with hip-mount components may require minor fabrication such as hole-drilling and/or mounting one or more strap clips. If you are hesitant to put a tool to your detector, ask your dealer for instructions. Some dealers are factory-trained in this procedure.

The use of the hip-mount configuration requires searchcoil cable that is longer than normal. Ninety inches is the normal length. Using a standard-length cable on a hip-mount unit necessitates the use of an extension cable two or three feet long with mating conductors. If the unit is to be used under water, the connectors must be waterproof. Hardware kits are available that allow you to waterproof such connections; see Chapter 24. Also, you can cut off the closed end of a balloon, slip the balloon over the connector, use silicone grease under the ends before tightly binding them with rubber bands.

CHEST-MOUNT CONFIGURATIONS: The chest-mount configuration while quite functional, has never enjoyed popularity. Usually, the control housing is suspended with an X cross-shoulder strap that holds the housing flat against the upper part of the chest. The control housing should be as slim as possible to permit an unrestricted view of the ground. If a meter is provided it must be mounted either on top of the control housing or on the lower part protruding away from the body so that it can be readily viewed. The knobs should be readily accessible, but should not interfere with clothing.

CONVERTIBLE CONFIGURATION: Convertible configuration detectors are designed to permit the control housing to be attached to the stem (standard operation) or worn on the body. The body-mount configuration requires a cable length of about 90 inches. The extra weight of the cable is noticeable when the detector is used in the standard configuration.

FLOTATION MOUNTING: Flotation mounting locates the control housing on a flotation device when the detector is used for surf searching. Almost any type of detector is suitable for flotation mounting if extra searchcoil cable is available. Flotation mounting is satisfactory for lakes and ponds with calm water but is risky when operating in ocean surf. Some floats are made from inflatable articles; others are made of syrofoam. Most surfers build their own flotation devices.

They can be built with a wire mesh sifter, preferably one that is hinged to facilitate quick dumping of accumulated rock and debris. Of course, metal trash should not be dumped but brought in for proper disposal. Compartments on the float are designed to hold treasure finds and trash. Hook arrangements can support digging equipment,

Figure 6-4: This is a Freedom model that features arm extension design, excellent balance and ultra lightweight operation. Electronically, it is designed primarily for coin and jewelry hunting, but serves also very well as a general purpose metal detector.

and some THers carry food and drink to permit a snack without leaving the water. The float can also be used as a "life raft" when flotation support is needed. In Chapter 24, recovery tools and flotation devices are discussed in greater detail.

OPERATING CONSIDERATIONS: If you have never worked in water, the first time you get a detector signal and start to dig an object, you will immediately encounter a problem: "What do I do with the detector?" Holding it with one hand while operating the scoop with the other is usually best. If you find this awkward, there are several other methods. Secure the detector to your body with a short cord and, if necessary, attach a buoyancy device (styrofoam or a plastic bottle) to the housing. Try to keep it floating in the correct position with the searchcoil down to make it easier for you to start scanning again.

UNDERWATER DETECTOR CONFIGURATION: In this section, we will discuss submersible detector configurations that can be used to depths of 200 feet. The detector shown in Figure 6-6 is a Garrett Sea Hunter XL500 Pulse Induction detector. It is designed for efficient land, surf and underwater hunting. It is built in the hip-mount configuration but the control housing can also be mounted on an arm, leg or the upper chest.

When searching underwater (not surfing), I have found it awkward to have a long stem attached to the searchcoil because it is difficult to dig and retrieve discoveries. With the searchcoil several feet in front of you it is inconvenient to swim to the point of detection. Also, it is difficult to search your hole thoroughly because the long stem keeps the searchcoil far in front of you. A short (12-inch) stem keeps the searchcoil at arm's length. When you detect a target, you simply extend your free hand to the point of detection, dig or fan the sand away. To check the hole, you scan the searchcoil back over the spot.

The XL500 Sea Hunter is convertible into the stem mount. An accessory, the Scubamate, as pictured assembled in Figure 6-6, allows conversion from hip-mount to the "short arm" "standard" configuration. The searchcoil is attached to the lower stem; the cable is wound around the stem or criss-crossed below the control housing support. An arm rest and grip then keeps the detector firmly "locked" to your arm.

METAL DETECTOR SEARCHCOILS

Think of detector searchcoils as having the same function as wheels on an automobile. Wheels take power from the motor and interface between the automobile and the ground. They roll along, take the bumps, grinds and shocks to get you to your destination. Searchcoils take power from the oscillator via the searchcoil cable. They are the interface between the metal detector and the ground. They scan along and take the bumps, grinds and shocks. They get you to your destination... the target.

Most searchcoils have electromagnetic transmitter and receiver antennas. These antennas are embedded within the searchcoil. The searchcoil is mounted on the lower end of the metal detector stem to be scanned over bare ground or a specific object. An invisible electromagnetic field generated by the transmitter winding flows out into the surrounding medium, whether it be air, wood, rock or whatever.

Without searchcoils the metal detector would not function. The searchcoils, therefore, constitute an important element. There are many sizes and shapes, Figure 6-7, ranging in size from about four inches in diameter to the very large, deep seeking depth multiplier, Figure 6-8. Roughly speaking, the smaller the searchcoil, the smaller the object that can be detected. The larger the searchcoil, the deeper the detection, but the larger the object must be, Figure 6-9.

Figure 6-5: The author uses a Freedom III in a park in England. This detector as you will notice features the arm extension design. The excellent balance and light weight make it an instrument that a hobbyist can use for days on end with minimal tiring. You will notice that the detector is an "extension" of the arm; its searchcoil stem lies along the same line as the forearm. Motion is accomplished almost without thinking since its operation is very close to the simple "pointing of a finger." Photo by Ken Durham.

For hunting large objects at great depths, large searchcoils are needed. The most popular cache hunting searchcoils are the 12 inch to 14 inch sizes. These are large enough to give excellent depth, small enough to be reasonably lightweight. Larger searchcoils obviously make it more difficult to maneuver around obstacles. Under water, however, the extra weight is no problem.

WATERPROOFING DESIGNATIONS

Searchcoils are built with varying degrees of waterproofing. SPLASHPROOF indicates that operation will not be affected if a small amount of water gets on the searchcoil, such as moisture from wet grass. WATERPROOF means the searchcoil can be operated in a heavy rain and operation will not be affected. SUBMERSIBLE means the searchcoil can be submerged as deep as the cable connector without affecting the detector's operation. Standard configuration metal detectors, generally, have searchcoils that can be submerged about 30 inches under water (to the connector). Hip-mount models have searchcoils that can be submerged about five to six feet. UNDERWATER metal detectors have searchcoils designed to withstand great depths, even down to 200 feet.

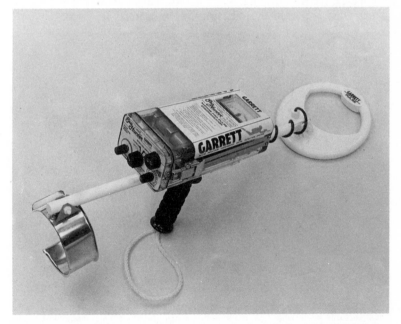

Figure 6-6: This is the Sea Hunter detector designed not only for land operation but also to be submerged to water depths of 200 feet. It is a Pulse Induction type instrument and features meter and headphone operations. The model shown here features a Scubamate accessory configuration. The housing is mounted on the Scubamate stem handle and arm bracket assembly. The housing and searchcoil can be removed and utilized in land hunting with a long stem and the housing carried on a body belt.

ELECTRONIC SHIELDING

There are two types of electronic field potential, electromagnetic and electrostatic. Electromagnetic field potentials are the radiated power fields that illuminate the matrix being scanned. When the electromagnetic field penetrates metal, eddy currents are generated on the metal's surface. Power is drawn from the electromagnetic field, thus alerting the operator to the presence of the metal.

An electrostatic field potential is of a constant voltage nature. This electrical phenomenon occurs when two objects come in close proximity to one another. When wet grass, for instance, comes close to the searchcoil, a "false" detector signal may occur. Fortunately, well engineered detectors have solved the electrostatic potential problem. Manufacturers construct what is called a Faraday Shield that "shields" the windings from nearby objects.

You are advised not to purchase a detector without an electrostatic shield on each searchcoil. To test a searchcoil, pull a handful of weeds and wet them with water. Turn the detector on and adjust the threshold. When you drag the weeds across the bottom of the searchcoil, if very noticeable changes occur in the threshold sound, the searchcoil does not have effective shielding. Slight audio changes are not objectionable when grass is passed over the top of the searchcoil.

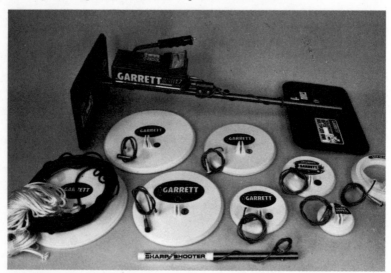

Figure 6-7: The VLF ground canceling detector such as the Garrett Master Hunter is the most versatile all-purpose type metal detector manufactured. This capability is made possible by numerous searchcoils that are available. The various sizes and shapes of searchcoils shown in this photograph allow the user to search for all types of both land and underwater treasures. The searchcoil to the left is submersible with a cable that permits it to be lowered to water depths of 50 feet. The upper configuration with the two black searchcoil halves mounted on the center rod is the Bloodhound attachment. It multiplies the depth capability of the instrument on large objects by a factor up to 300%

Generally, the standard searchcoil accompanying most metal detectors is the type that gives the best general purpose results. Figure 6-10 will guide you in your understanding and selection of characteristics and capabilities of the various sizes of searchcoils. For more information on searchcoils and the operational characteristics of metal detectors, I refer you to my book, MODERN METAL DETECTORS.

Generally speaking, for most beach and surf hunting, you should select a searchcoil that ranges in diameter from about seven to ten inches. Searchcoils this size will scan a wide swath and give good detection depth. As searchcoils increase in size, however, it becomes more difficult for them to pinpoint detected objects.

When working in high trash areas, you should consider using the smaller three-inch to four-inch diameter searchcoil sizes. These Super Sniper class searchcoils offer an extra measure of success by "helping" the detector to read individual targets, Figure 6-11. This increased capability is especially valuable when the discrimination mode is being

Figure 6-8: The author is shown using the Master Hunter detector with the Bloodhound Depth Multiplier accessory. This accessory is used when the operator is looking for objects quart size and larger at great depths. Maximum obtainable depths are in the range of 20 feet on large objects.

71

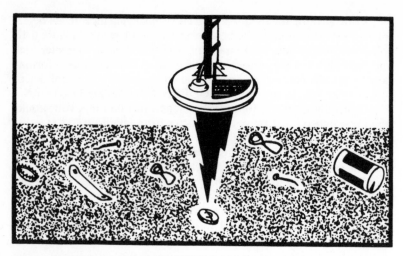

Figure 6-11. SUPER-SNIPING IN HIGH JUNK AREAS. Super-sniping is an effective way to cover the maximum number of coins in high junk areas. The Super-Sniper penetrates below junk targets to detect individual coins and other high conductivity targets. The negative response of nearby junk targets is reduced or eliminated. The Super-Sniper searchcoil operates effectively near large metal objects, playground equipment and sidewalks, in parks and at shipwreck sites.

used. Larger searchcoils obviously can have more objects under them at any given time. Consequently, the detector circuitry has greater difficulty identifying objects beneath the searchcoil when it is trying to read several of them simultaneously. The small Super Sniper searchcoils eliminate this problem for the most part. They won't detect as deeply as larger coils, but can often be far more efficient, especially in trashy areas.

SHIPWRECK SEARCHING

When searching shipwrecks, there are several situations to consider. In loose sand an initial search should use a larger searchcoil for good detection depth. This is important because soft sand permits digging to such depths. When there are many small targets, however, you should consider a smaller searchcoil, especially if you are using discrimination. For such precise pinpointing as that required when you are digging coins from coral, the smaller searchcoil will be best. Since digging in clay or coral is generally difficult and time consuming, pinpointing and target identification are vital.

DETERMINING TARGET CENTER

Any given searchcoil may or may not produce maximum audio when small coin-size targets are directly beneath its exact PHYSICAL center. To determine TARGET center of detection, retune the instrument to threshold with a small coin directly on the bottom near the center. Slide this coin around on the bottom. The target center is the spot where you hear maximum audio sound. Place an "X" with a felt tip pen at this point on the searchcoil both bottom and top. Knowing the target center enables you to pinpoint targets precisely. Pulse in-

Figure 6-9: RECOMMENDED SEARCHCOIL SIZES FOR OPTIMUM RESULTS. This table suggests the optimum searchcoil sizes for various types of searching. Note the overlapping capability of all the searchcoils. The wide dynamic range of several is obvious.

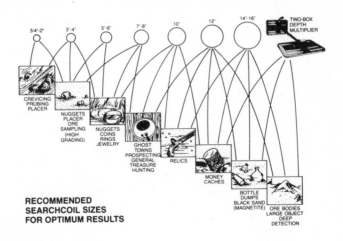

73

duction searchcoils are generally constructed with an open center. It is not necessary (nor possible) to mark the center of these coils because target center is the exact center of the searchcoil.

DYNAMIC DETECTION RANGE

The Dynamic Detection Range of a searchcoil reflects the various target sizes it can detect to a practical depth. These examples illustrate dynamic detection range: A 12-inch VLF searchcoil can detect objects from BB shot size to very large targets and detect this wide range of targets to practical depths. This searchcoil can be considered to have a wide dynamic detection range. On the other hand, a 12-inch BFO searchcoil can detect a very large target to a practical depth, but the smallest target it can detect to a practical depth is a coin. Thus, the BFO searchcoil has less dynamic detection range than does a comparable size VLF searchcoil.

BFO searchcoils have the smallest dynamic detection range of all metal detectors; VLF searchcoils have the widest dynamic detection range. In between are TR and Pulse Induction searchcoils. For all practical purposes, the dynamic detection range of TR, Pulse Induction and VLF searchcoils are acceptable. A few minutes study of the searchcoil charts in this chapter will reveal the relative dynamic detection ranges of the various types and sizes of searchcoils.

SEARCHCOIL SPECIFIC GRAVITY CONSIDERATION

When manufacturers produce searchcoils for use both on land and under water, they must achieve a happy medium. The searchcoil must be light enough for practical land use yet have neutral or slightly negative buoyancy for use under water.

Buoyant searchcoils require the use of added weights. Sand bags placed on top of the searchcoil or lead weights attached to the stem are satisfactory solutions.

While searchcoil weight and buoyancy may seem to be minor considerations, they can be very important. Neutral or slightly negative buoyancy searchcoils require considerably less underwater scanning effort than searchcoils with positive buoyancy. When in doubt about equipment for surfing or underwater use, always contact your dealer and/or factory for specific information.

THREE-INCH TO FOUR-INCH DIAMETER SEARCHCOILS

The three-inch to four-inch diameter searchcoils are generally referred to as Super Sniper-type searchcoils. They have an intense electromagnetic field which gives good detection of small objects. The narrow detection pattern permits excellent target isolation and precise pinpointing. They scan a more narrow width than do larger searchcoils and they do not detect as deeply. Close proximity scanning to fences, sidewalks with rebar and other metal objects is an added plus.

Treasure hunters rate these searchcoils highly, but not all detectors are capable of using them nor do all manufacturers provide them. The purchase and use of one is suggested, especially if you hunt in worked-out or high junk areas.

SEVEN-INCH TO EIGHT-INCH DIAMETER SEARCHCOILS

Most detector types and brands are sold with seven-inch to eight-inch diameter searchcoils as standard equipment. These are the best general purpose sizes because they generally are lightweight, have good scanning width and are sensitive to a wide range of target sizes. Objects as small as BB shot can be detected. Good ground coverage can be obtained with shallow scanning width equal to the approximate diameter of the searchcoil. Scanning width becomes less toward the bottom of the detection pattern, Figure 5-6. Since the detection pattern of all searchcoils is somewhat coneshaped, overlapping of each detector sweep is necessary to lessen the possibility of missing targets. Pinpointing is good but can be made even better by electronic pinpointing and detuning to target center.

10-INCH TO 12-INCH DIAMETER SEARCHCOILS

Searchcoils of this size while still able to detect small coin-size objects at great depths are classified as the smallest searchcoils to be used for cache and relic hunting. Precise pinpointing is more difficult with these larger sizes and the extra weight necessitates use of an arm rest or hip-mounted control housing, especially when the detector is used for long periods of time.

SEARCHCOIL SELECTION CHART

COIL SIZES	BEGINNER	GENERAL COIN HUNTING	SUPER SNIPING	EXTRA DEPTH (COINS)	BEACH HUNTING	RELIC HUNTING	BUILDING SEARCHING	GHOST TOWNING	BOTTLE DUMPS	CACHE (MONEY) HUNTING (OUTHOUSES)	MAXIMUM DEPTH LARGE OBJECTS	PLACER SNIPING (CREVICING)	ORE SAMPLING	NUGGET HUNTING	BLACK SAND	MINE DUMPS (DREDGE PILES)	ORE BODIES (VEINS)
3/4"-2"												✱		✱			
3"-4"	✱		✱									✱	✱				
5"-6"	✱	✱			✱	✱							✱				
7"-8"	✱	✱			✱	✱	✱					✱	✱	✱			
10"			✱	✱	✱	✱	✱	✱						✱			
12"			✱	✱	✱			✱	✱			✱	✱	✱	✱	✱	
14" (and larger)					✱				✱	✱					✱		✱
BLOODHOUND DEPTH MULTIPLIER					✱				✱	✱	✱						✱

Figure 6-10: SEARCHCOIL SELECTION TABLE. The various sizes of searchcoils and their recommended applications are shown in this chart. You will note that most of the searchcoils can be used in more than one application. In the beach hunting category four different searchcoil sizes are recommended.

More accurate pinpointing can be achieved by using the detuning method.

When coin and nugget hunting, how do you know when to use a 10-inch or 12-inch size? Just try a little reasoning. Suppose, when using an eight-inch searchcoil, you find a target in the fringe area of detection, Figure 5-8. Weak audio signals indicate you're reaching the outer detection limits of the searchcoil. By using the next larger size, you will detect deeper. Of course, as explained under Dynamic Range in this chapter, there are limitations. You may not find BB shot size targets with a 12-inch searchcoil. You stand a better chance of finding very small objects with the Super Snipers. Practically speaking, a 10-inch searchcoil is the largest size to use when coin hunting. If you're relic hunting, if the targets are deeply buried, or if you are searching for money caches, use the larger searchcoils.

Figures 6-9 and 6-10 illustrate recommended searchcoil sizes for optimum results. Note the overlapping capability of all searchcoils. The wide dynamic range of several searchcoils is obvious.

DEPTH MULTIPLIER ATTACHMENT

Last in our searchcoil discussion, but certainly not least, is the Depth Multiplier attachment. The Depth Multiplier attachment performs just as the name implies: it multiplies the depth that VLF detectors can detect. Larger objects can be detected at proportionally greater depths. Larger searchcoil sizes can increase depth multiplication factors on the order of two to three times. For instance, if a large cannon or safe can be detected to a depth of seven feet with a 12-inch searchcoil, the Depth Multiplier can locate it to perhaps twice that depth.

Two examples will help explain Depth Multiplier capabilities. A battlefield searcher, using a Depth Multiplier, found a three and one-half inch-diameter, seven inch-long iron projectile at a depth of four feet. A treasure hunter found a pint jar of pre-1930 pennies to a measured depth of 27½ inches. While a 12-inch searchcoil would have found this jar, no junk items like nails were found with the Depth Multiplier. These finds show that Depth Multiplier attachments can find small targets, even though, to be on the safe side, they are not recommended if the sought-for target is less than approximately quart size.

A large, round corrugated culvert was easily detected at a depth of 12 feet to the top of the culvert. A law enforcement agency located several automobile engines in a ravine at depths of better than 10 feet. The engines were removed from stolen automobiles and buried because they were too "hot" to sell.

The Depth Multiplier, as shown in Figure 6-8, is easy to use. It can be attached to the control housing in a matter of minutes. No Tuning or Ground Elimination adjustments are required. Simply turn the detector on and select the VLF Ground Elimination mode. Do not use the Automatic Tuning mode. Press the retune switch to achieve threshold sound and begin searching. Walk straight ahead with the "nose" of the Depth Multiplier held at an approximate height of one foot above the ground.

Operation of the Depth Multiplier is very simple. When a signal is first heard, mark its location on the ground. Walk across the target, then walk back. When a signal is heard, make another mark on the ground. The target will lie directly below the centerpoint of the two marks.

The Depth Multiplier is recommended when searching for money caches, large relics, safes, cannons, ore veins and mineral structures. The Depth Multiplier takes no more battery power than smaller searchcoils, but the depth multiplication capability is one that no detector owner should be without.

HEADPHONES

You should use headphones whenever you search with a detector. They are especially useful in noisy areas, such as the beach and near traffic lanes. Headphones enhance audio perception by bringing the sound directly into your ears while masking "outside" noise interference.

There is no question that most persons can hear weaker sounds and detect deeper targets when quality Garrett headphones are used. As proof, bury a coin at a depth that produces a faint speaker signal. Then, use headphones and scan over the spot. You'll be amazed at how much better you can hear the detector signals with headphones than you can with the speakers.

Headphones come in many sizes, shapes and configurations, the most popular being stereo types that cover the ears, see Chapter 24. Many detectors do not have volume controls, but headphones equipped with volume controls allow a wide degree of loudness adjustment while not degrading detector sounds.

Manufacturers know that reducing sound volume of the detector's signals is accompanied by loss of detection depth and sensitivity. Reducing circuit gain reduces the sharp, quick audio turn-on necessary for good operation. Even on detectors with volume control, the manufacturer usually recommends that volume be set to maximum. Most detectors are operated at full volume with the tuning (audio) control adjusted so that a faint sound (threshold) is coming from the speaker. When a target is detected, the sound rises quickly from threshold to maximum loudness. Headphones allow this threshold to be set even lower, giving improved performance. Automatic VLF Ground Elimination detectors can be operated "silent" or with slight threshold sound.

A mono/stereo switch on the headphone set is desirable. If you want to use both headphone pieces, flip the switch to mono to let sound come through both earpieces. If you want to use only one headpiece, perhaps to leave the unused headpiece resting off your ear to enable you to hear sounds around you, flip the switch to stereo and only one headpiece will be operative. Some detectors have an internal connection, however, that sends audio into both headpieces.

In that case, a mono/stereo headphone switch would be non-functional.

Dual, miniature headphone types, as shown in Chapter 24, are commonly used. They are good, but do not block as much external sound as the large padded kind. They are, however, lightweight and comfortable and a quality pair will produce good sound. A coiled extension cord is desirable to keep the cord out of the way.

Headphones help you keep others from knowing what you are doing. In most cases, a person standing within a few feet will not be able to hear the headphone signals unless the sound is very loud.

Headphone plug sizes range from one-eighth inch to one-fourth inch in diameter. Make sure of the size you need before purchasing headphones. Right angle plugs may be desirable because they lessen the possibility of plugs being broken, which often occurs with plugs that extend straight out.

THAT SECOND DETECTOR

Probably two thirds of active treasure hunters own more than one metal detector. Usually, they have a main instrument—the one they search with most often. The keep on "standby" one or two additional detectors which are usually older models. Should their primary instrument fail, or get stolen, the hunter always has a backup unit.

Many THers have several detectors because they enjoy more than one type of hunting. They may be both land and surf or underwater searchers. In that case, they need a dry land model and one that can get wet. Other hunters have several models, perhaps a specialized coin hunting type, a deep seeking cache hunting type and a model for electronic prospecting.

Many hunters purchase a new detector almost every year as newer, deeper-seeking and more capable detectors are introduced. They know how just a slight bit of extra detection depth can pay dividends.

Some detectors are all purpose; they can perform many treasure hunting and prospecting tasks. All purpose detectors eliminate need for more than a single detector unless the hunter is concerned with primary detector failure. Also, there is no all purpose detector built that can be submerged for surf hunting.

Should you obtain a second detector? In the event of primary detector failure—which, by the way, is not likely to occur—a backup detector is necessary. If you don't travel far from home and rental instruments are available, your need for a second instrument is reduced. After you have purchased a surfing model, when you decide to cache hunt or go prospecting as well, you may wish to purchase another model for more effective performance in those other fields.

A second detector is especially beneficial when there is someone to use it. Perhaps your spouse or other family member could hunt with the second detector, yet be willing to temporarily give it up (or maybe do the digging...) if the primary detector fails or is stolen. Let me urge, however, that you purchase wisely any and all instruments you buy. Choose quality and reliability no matter how many instruments you need and you may never have to purchase again.

In the following five chapters, BFO, TR, VLF, Automated VLF (motion), Pulse Induction and Microprocessor Technology metal detectors are described and compared. To help you understand the relative merits all these types of instruments, the following subject discussions are made for each type: CIRCUITS, AUDIO RESPONSE, SENSITIVITY, DETECTION DEPTH, GROUND ELIMINATION, DISCRIMINATION (TRASH ELIMINATION), AUDIO RESPONSE, SEARCHCOILS, PINPOINTING, CAPABILITIES, APPLICATIONS AND LIMITATIONS.

CHAPTER 7

Beat Frequency Oscillator (BFO) Transmitter/Receiver (TR) Metal Detectors

THE BFO

For four decades the Beat Frequency Oscillator Metal Detector, better known as the BFO, was used by amateur and professional treasure hunters and electronic prospectors and established as the work horse of the industry.

Quality built BFOs were dependable, stable, highly efficient and versatile instruments. They could perform all major metal detector tasks, including coin and relic hunting, prospecting and underwater searching. The BFO never was as sensitive and deep-seeking as other types of instruments, which is why they are obsolete and not manufactured today.

On a scale of one to ten the BFO rates six or seven in detection depth and sensitivity. Even though the BFO does not have ground canceling capabilities, thousands of BFO users learned to manipulate the detector despite the worst mineralized ground conditions. BFO production ceased during the mid 1980s. Thousands remain in use, however, and most owners would not part with their BFO except for a great deal of money.

CIRCUITRY

BFO circuitry is the simplest of all detector types. Two radio frequency oscillators, the reference oscillator and the other coupled to the search antenna are mixed together. This mixing causes an audio frequency to be produced. When conductive metal and non-conductive mineral are detected, the audio frequency changes. There are no exotic circuits, just simple designs to produce usable information for the operator. One of the main features of the BFO is its true metal-mineral null tuning point. This null is the true point between detection of conductive metals and non-conductive iron minerals. It is the only detector with this inherent feature, even though other types can be designed to have it. When the instrument is adjusted to the metal side of null, conductive metal targets cause the audio frequency to increase. Non-conductive iron mineral causes the audio to decrease. Conversely, when the detector is tuned to the mineral side of null, non-conductive iron minerals cause the audio frequency to increase and conductive metal targets cause the audio to decrease. This feature is widely used in electronic prospecting.

SENSITIVITY

Sensitivity is a term used to define the capability of a metal dectector to detect small pieces of metal. While the BFO rates only fair in this category, only about six or seven out of a possible ten, it nevertheless is a capable metal detector, especially in the field of prospecting or ore sampling. For beach, surf and underwater hunting, sensitivity of the BFO is adequate because most targets are coin-sized or larger. A main problem, as previously stated, is lack of depth capability.

DETECTION DEPTH

The detection depth capability of the BFO rates six to seven on a scale of one to ten. The BFO has excellent fringe area detection (See Chapter 6). Still, operators who have mastered the BFO can achieve detection depth greater than persons with VLF instruments who have not mastered their equipment. Targets as small as a button can be detected. Accurate tuning, proper selection of searchcoils and reliance upon fringe area detection (using headphones) are important for good BFO performance.

GROUND ELIMINATION

BFOs do not have adjustable or automatic ground elimination circuitry. The two most worrisome minerals are wetted salt and nonconductive iron. There are several "tricks" that can be used to lessen the disturbing effects of these minerals. The instrument can be operated in the null (quiet) zone, which reduces detection depth and sensitivity. BFO operators seek to achieve improved performance over minerals by tuning the instrument at a higher than normal audio tone. Normally, the BFO is adjusted to operate at approximately 50 to 60 hertz per second. Tuning the instrument to a higher frequency, 100 hertz per second and higher, somewhat smooths out the disturbing effects of minerals. The searchcoil can also be held at an increased operating height and scanned at a faster rate. While a normal searchcoil scanning rate is from one to two feet per second, rates of three to four feet per second are acceptable. Also, scrubbing of the searchcoil, keeping it in contact with the ground while scanning, helps to eliminate or smooth out signals from minerals. These techniques, when properly deployed, improve BFO operation over heavily mineralized ground.

DISCRIMINATION (TRASH ELIMINATION)

Since the early 1950s engineers have observed that amplitude variations in BFO oscillator voltages were either positive or negative, depending upon the type of metal detected. This characteristic led to development of discriminating circuitry that controlled visual indicators. Audio discrimination was never achieved in BFO detectors except by skilled operators who understood the detector's audio characteristics and could recognize its inherent audio discriminating signals. Visual discrimination, however, is very good. In use, the operator observes meter pointer deflection to learn what the detector is reporting with regard to target identification. Undersirable targets cause the meter pointer to deflect downward. Desirable targets cause the meter pointer to point upwards. No target analysis or coin depth circuitry was ever incorporated in BFO detectors.

SEARCHCOILS

The BFO has as wide a range of searchcoils as any detector manufactured; sizes range from three-quarter inches up to 24 inches in diameter. In the early 1960s, searchcoils three feet in diameter were manufactured. BFO searchcoils do not have as wide a dynamic range as other detector types. The most popular searchcoils are the five to six-inch diameter and 12 to 13-inch diameter sizes. Larger searchcoils do not detect small coins as deeply as the smaller sizes.

For coin, ring and jewelry hunting the five to eight-inch sizes are recommended. Three to four-inch diameter searchcoils are good for "super sniping."

Underwater searchcoils are available with connecting cables 50 feet in length. Searchcoils can be lowered into the water to locate sunken boats, motors, tool boxes and other metal objects. The control housing must be kept above water.

CAPABILITIES

The BFO is capable of good performance in all phases of treasure hunting and electronic prospecting. Even though salt water and iron minerals interfere with BFO operation, most interference can be eliminated by using the techniques described earlier.

APPLICATIONS

BFO detectors are especially recommended for electronic prospecting, particularly for ore sampling and locating black sand. Cache hunting with large searchcoils rates high. Coin and ring hunting rates seven on our scale of ten.

For beach and surf hunting with a BFO, use a five to eight-inch diameter searchcoil to achieve maximum depth. The searchcoil should be scrubbed on the ground with audio frequency at 50 to 60 hertz per second. If black magnetic sand is present, it may be necessary to tune the audio to a higher frequency.

LIMITATIONS

BFO performance is limited by its lack of ground canceling, target classification, maximum depth detection and extreme sensitivity. Despite these reduced capabilities, the BFO detector can be used effectively in all treasure hunting and electronic prospecting situations.

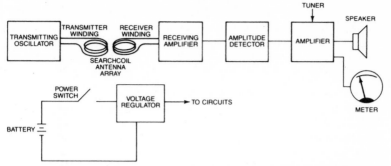

Figure 7-1. ELECTRONIC BLOCK DIAGRAM OF TRANSMITTER-RECEIVER METAL DETECTOR. This block diagram illustrates basic metal detector components. The electronic transmitter oscillator generates a signal current which travels through the searchcoil cable to the transmitter winding (antenna). As the current circulates in the antenna, an invisible electromagnetic field is generated that flows out into the air or other surrounding medium. When conductive metal and certain minerals interrupt the electromagnetic field, metal detection occurs.

THE TR

CIRCUITRY

TR circuitry, Figure 7-1, is comprised of a transmitter signal generation circuit and a receiver circuit. Transmitter and receiver windings embedded in the searchcoil are mechanically and electronically positioned (balanced) with respect to each other to induce minimal r.f. signals in the receiver winding. When metal comes into the searchcoil's electromagnetic field radiation pattern, antenna balance is upset, causing current flow in the receiver winding. Also, detecting metal targets causes r.f. power loss. These two factors combine to produce a detector response. More information on these principles is available in my book, MODERN METAL DETECTORS. The book describes TR circuitry and operation as well as other characteristics of major types of metal detectors.

The transmitter/receiver detection characteristics of TRs, manual VLFs and automated VLF detectors are nearly identical.

AUDIO RESPONSE

If one feature of TRs could be designated as "most desirable," it would be audio response, which is sharp and quick. This audio response is largely responsible for the excellent depth and precise pinpointing for which TRs are famous. The audio operating threshold of TRs should be set optimally to the lowest audible level. Whenever a metal target is detected, the audio response increases. This quick "turn on" of sound that occurs when targets are detected is one reason for the TRs' popularity. Even deeply buried targets produce large, sharp audio responses. Quality-built TRs have high gain circuitry and excellent stability. Manual-adjust VLF Ground Canceling detectors offer the same type audio respose as TRs.

83

SENSITIVITY

TRs are also well known for their super sensitivity. They are able to detect very small objects at extreme depths. TR searchcoils have a wide dynamic range and sensitivity does not suffer even when large searchcoils are used.

DETECTION DEPTH

The detection depth of TRs is excellent on almost all metal targets. While the TR cannot reach as deep as VLF detectors, they give better depth than BFOs. TR detectors do not feature ground elimination circuitry.

DISCRIMINATION (TRASH ELIMINATION)

TRs have always featured excellent target discrimination, which does an efficient job of rejecting most metal trash. Signals on accepted targets such as coins and rings are always sharp and pronounced. There is no mistaking good target and bad target TR response. Synchronized audio and meter discrimination circuits are found on most TRs. Signals are positive for good targets and negative for reject targets. No TRs are manufactured that feature target analyzing and coin depth measuring.

SEARCHCOILS

There has never been a wide range of searchcoils available for TRs. Most TR searchcoils range in size from about six inches to twelve inches. Since the TR has never been recommended for prospecting, small nugget-type searchcoils and probing searchcoils were never manufactured. Also, since TRs were never recommended for cache hunting because of iron mineral disturbance, very large searchcoils were never needed. The most pupular sizes of searchcoils are seven to eight-inch diameter sizes. These have wide dynamic range and can be used for most general purpose applications: beach hunting to surfing, ghost towning and the like.

CAPABILITIES

When TRs are correctly used, their capabilities are very good, especially for coin hunting. While they don't feature the capabilities of the VLF instrument, the TR can be counted upon to produce favorable results. For various reasons, TRs do not perform well in the fields of cache hunting and electronic prospecting. In salt water applications, unless adjustable discrimination is available TR capabilities are limited.

APPLICATIONS

TRs have always been good general purpose instruments. Since most who use detectors search for coins, rings and jewelry, the TR throughout its popular lifetime was a desirable instrument. TRs were not favored, as I have stated, for prospecting and cache hunting. Sure,

TRs may have found lots of gold nuggets but I have often wondered how many gold nuggets were missed by those who tried to use the TR for electronic prospecting.

LIMITATIONS

The severest limitation of TRs is lack of ground canceling capabilities; they cannot be adjusted to ignore iron earth minerals. The presence of iron within the search matrix of their searchcoil causes an imbalance to occur between the transmitter and the receiver winding which results in "false" signals. The greater the concentration of iron minerals, the worse the problem. During the popular years of the TR, operators managed some sort of iron mineral detection. We adjusted the audio threshold down to null, scrubbed the searchcoil directly on the ground and scanned at a slightly faster than normal rate.

Wetted salt can be eliminated from detection if the detector features discrimination. The discrimination circuitry control is adjusted to the approximate bottlecap rejection point. Here, the conductivity of wetted salt and other similar metals will be ignored. Deviation from this adjustment, either positive or negative, results in salt detection. At this operating point, detection depth and sensitivity is reduced because, generally speaking, as discrimination control is rotated to a higher number (for a greater amount the target rejection) detection depth and sensitivity worsens. While also true of other types of detectors, this characteristic is particularly evident in TRs. Limited availability of searchcoils is also a negative factor for TRs. In addition, they lack target identification and coin depth measuring circuitry.

CONCULSIONS:

TRs are rated at level seven on our ten scale for most phases of coin, ring and jewelry hunting, as long as iron mineral conditions are satisfactory. This includes beach hunting, especially in dry sand. Some beach hunters can use TRs if they feature target discrimination adjustable to achieve wetted salt cancellation.

Only token numbers of TRs are manufactured today since production generally features lower cost instruments. Even so, quality TR instruments of today are better than TRs of the past decade.

CHAPTER 8

The Manual-Adjust
Very Low Frequency (VLF)
Ground Canceling Metal Detector

CIRCUITS

The VLF's primary detection circuits are similar in construction to TR detection circuits. Searchcoil construction is also similar. Target detection signals are "split" into what electronic jargon terms "vectors." Ground mineral signals and metal target signals are individualistic, especially in their phase (angular time) displacement. This time displacement allows engineers to construct adjustable ground canceling circuitry, and signals received from iron earth minerals can be "nullified." Without interference from minerals, signals can then alert the operator to the presence of metal targets. We are fortunate to have this capability because it eliminates a major problem. With iron mineral detection eliminated, metal target signals are not masked, and greater circuit gain can be utilized. As a result, greater detection depth and target analysis can be achieved.

VLF detectors, Figures 8-1 and 8-2, feature iron mineral elimination, coin depth measuring, target identification and metal trash rejection. This type of detector is the deepest seeking and the most sensitive manufactured. The VLF with its greater range of capabilities and performance is used by more metal detector buffs than, perhaps, all the other types combined.

AUDIO RESPONSE

Manual-adjust VLF audio response characteristics are almost identical to those of TR detectors. Most operators cannot tell the difference. Adjusted for minimum audio, a VLF audio increase signals the presence of a detected target. A decrease signifies reduced mineral beneath the searchcoil. These instruments can be operated silently (the null zone), with only a slight performance loss.

SENSITIVITY

VLFs are noted for their super sensitivity. Metal targets as small as a pin head can be detected, especially with higher frequency instruments. One reason the 15-kilohertz Groundhog instruments have achieved wide popularity in the gold fields is their ability to detect tiny nuggets. Lower frequency (5-kilohertz) detectors like the Garrett Master Hunter series, however, will detect larger and deeper nuggets than the higher frequency models.

DETECTION DEPTH

No other type instrument can equal the superior detection depth performance of manual-adjust VLFs. In all phases of coin hunting and electronic prospecting these detectors excel — even when general purpose-size searchcoils are used. Seven to eight-inch diameter searchcoils can detect objects to depths below six feet. With the use of a depth multiplier attachment as shown in Figure 6-8 depths of 15 to 20 feet on large targets are possible. Since VLF searchcoils have wide dynamic range, searchcoils of seven to eight-inch diameter can be used with confidence in beach, surf and underwater hunting. Detection depth and pinpointing here can be relied upon.

Smaller searchcoils such as the three to four-inch diameter Super Sniper variety give excellent depth and should be used in high junk and "worked out" areas.

GROUND ELIMINATION

Most VLF metal detectors feature fully adjustable ground elimination. The availability of wide range tuning allows cancellation of the greatest concentration of iron minerals anyone is likely to encounter.

Figure 8-1: At this beach site on Guadeloupe, the author used a Master Hunter all-purpose metal detector that features iron mineral and salt water elimination, coin depth measuring, target identification and metal trash rejection to locate an icon buried at a depth of approximately 12 inches.

87

The 10-turn ground adjustment control is very precise, offering elimination of unwanted mineral disturbance.

DISCRIMINATION (TARGET ELIMINATION)

Manual-adjust VLF detectors feature superb metal trash rejection (discrimination). The terms trash elimination, trash rejection and discrimination mean essentially the same thing. The term target elimination, however, more clearly defines the function of this circuit, meaning that unwanted targets are ELIMINATED from detection. Other circuitry such as target identification goes an additional step to provide greater accuracy in target categorizing and identifying individual targets.

TARGET ANALYZING: INDICATORS

Target analyzing circuitry helps identify detected targets. These circuits are called "probability" circuits since they are not 100% accurate. Yet, they indicate the probable identity of most targets. Less than 100% accuracy is achieved, not through the fault of the circuitry, but because many metal targets are composites or alloys. Also, errors may occur when several targets are close together. Metal detectors simultaneously read all metal targets that are beneath the searchcoil.

Figure 8-2: Ted Sheehan of Australia detects for coins and jewelry on a Western Australia beach. Australia has, perhaps, a thousand miles of lovely sandy beaches where over the past 100 or so years vacationers and sunworshippers have lost coins and jewelry.

No metal detector can identify several different targets that appear beneath it at the same time.

Target identification is achieved by both audio and visual target identifiers. Visual identifiers feature the D'arsenal-type meters and bar graphs. Whenever a target is detected, the pointer or "bar" moves a certain distance to mark probable identity. These indicators are generally calibrated in three ranges: iron, gold and silver, with copper coins classified as silver. Gold coins and nickels are classified as gold, and almost no coins are classifed as iron.

Manual-adjust VLF detectors rate a superior nine-plus on a ten scale.

TARGET ANALYZING: AUDIO

There are two types of audio target analyzers: variable pitch and "bell tone." The variable pitch system alerts the operator to the characteristics and nature of detected targets by producing a tone that varies in pitch depending upon the conductivity of the detected target

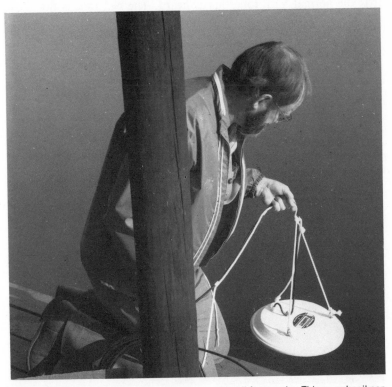

Figure 8-3: The author lowers an underwater searchcoil from a pier. This searchcoil can locate sunken weapons, tool boxes, motors, boats and other lost metal objects in water depths of 50 feet. The searchcoil attaches to the Garrett Master Hunter detector. The searchcoil will detect an object as small as an individual coin. Photo by Eleanor Garrett.

in three categories: iron, gold and silver. As a searchcoil is scanned across the target, the audio tone will change frequency until it has achieved the pitch that identifies the target in one of the three categories. The lower the category, the lower the pitch. Generally, several scans of the searchcoil are required before the metal detector reaches a constant tone. As a result, the audio tone sometimes continually varies in pitch, creating a situation where the operator is not sure what he is hearing. At best, this is somewhat disturbing until the operator has learned, by memory, the various pitches. Also, since there are no distinct audio levels to set apart the three main categories, the operator has even more difficulty in learning the nature of targets.

An improved method is the "bell tone" system that produces a distinct, unique bell tone alert whenever highest range coins are detected. Coins that have conductivity equal to or greater than United States copper pennies produce this tone. One sweep across such a detected object causes the bell tone to sound loud and clear. Objects that have conductivity in the mid-range produce an increase in audio tone but it is the normal VLF tone that is heard. The bell tone is not heard in the middle range. When reject targets are "detected," no audio is produced. Figure 5-10 illustrates the three detection ramges.

Figure 8-4: Don Littlejohn of Fort Worth, TX, is a successful water hunter. One of the instruments he uses is a Master Hunter with a special stem extension and searchcoil with nine feet of searchcoil cable. He uses a short-handle digger to retrieve his finds.

CHAPTER 9

Very Low Frequency (VLF) Ground Canceling Metal Detector

CIRCUITS

Automated, very low frequency ground canceling metal detectors, Figure 9-1, often referred to as "motion" detectors, utilize the basic circuitry of manual-adjust VLF ground canceling metal detectors. The primary difference is that automated VLFs ignore iron earth minerals without manipulation of a ground elimination control knob. Various versions of this type detector are marketed. In one type, the manufacturer pre-selects an average ground cancel control setting with plus and minus parameters adequate for a given range of ground mineral situations. The second type of circuit monitors iron earth minerals beneath the searchcoil and automatically adjusts internal ground canceling circuitry.

These circuits are automatic because a searchcoil cannot be hovered over a target like a manual-adjust VLF detector. When the searchcoil is hovered above a metal target, the audio automatically returns to the audio threshold setting within one to three seconds.

Other characteristics, features and searchcoils are the same as those of manual-adjust instruments. Automated VLFs, however, are not as versatile as manual-adjust VLFs. Automated VLFs are intended primarily to hunt coins, rings and jewelry, Figure 9-2. They are not as efficient when used for prospecting and for other forms of treasure hunting.

AUDIO RESPONSE

The audio response is non-linear, which means the detector's audio signal is not proportional to that of target size and depth. As the searchcoil approaches a target, the audio response in a manual-adjust VLF gradually increases in loudness, peaking when the searchcoil is directly above the target. This peaking, however, can occur before the center of the searchcoil reaches the target if it is large and not buried deeply. As the searchcoil moves past the target, audio response follows a mirror image curve, decreasing in amplitude until it returns to threshold level.

The audio of an automated VLF similarly increases in amplitude as the target is approached. But, at some distance from target center it surges to full audio peak. The audio remains at peak until the searchcoil center has cleared the target, then it returns abruptly to threshold. This sudden, FULLY ON signal occurs so rapidly that the slight in-

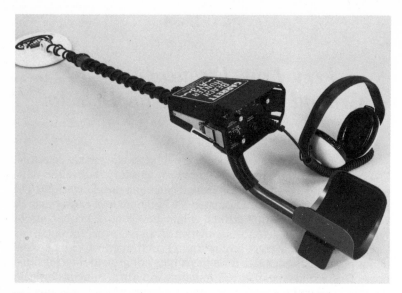

Figure 9-1: Automated very low frequency ground canceling metal detectors such as the Garrett AT3 shown here are motion detectors. Automated VLFs ignore iron earth minerals without manipulation of the ground elimination control. This model is an all-terrain, all-weather detector. It can be used in rain, blowing dust and in shallow water.

crease in audio as the searchcoil begins to detect a target is generally not heard. Through practice, however, an operator can learn to hear these small amplitude signals when targets are small or buried deeply.

Audio signals are enhanced when headphones are used since they direct the sound into the ears and mask most outside interference.

When target elimination is used, no audio is produced by detection of reject targets. There is an exception to this, however, and it varies depending upon the detector manufacturer. In addition, junk targets cause the audio to "break up" or become erratic. With experience, however, the operator can identify most of these.

Many persons prefer the automated VLF's non-linear circuitry. Because the sudden sharp increase in audio is easily distinguished, they prefer it to non-linear audio circuits of the manual-adjust VLF. Many people, however, use both types of detectors and have no difficulty interpreting the two different audio responses.

SILENT OPERATION OR THRESHOLD?

There are two operational audio settings: silent and threshold. Silent audio operation means that there is no audible sound except when a target is detected. The silent point is achieved by adjusting the audio control (sometimes designated, "Tuning") to achieve sound, and then backing the control just down far enough to permit silent operation. Threshold operation is achieved by adjusting audio control to the faintest possible level that can be heard.

Is sensitivity and detection depth lost during silent operation? Yes, there is a loss, but it occurs primarily in the fringe area of detection as illustrated in Figure 5-8. Audio signals generated by very small or deeply buried targets produce a slight sound increase. These signals occur in the fringe area. Operators who have mastered their detectors can hear these and recover valuable coins and other treasures. When operating a detector in the silent mode, however, it is difficult, if not impossible, to hear fringe area signals. Some percentage of detection signals are lost and not heard by the operator; thus, some discoveries are overlooked.

SENSITIVITY

Sensitivity is the ability of a detector to detect small objects. The smaller the object that can be detected, the greater the sensitivity of a detector. Sensitivity and detection depth are inseparable. The greater the sensitivity of a detector, the greater will be the depth at which it can detect small targets. Extreme sensitivity in automated VLF type detectors is not as important as in manual-adjust VLF detectors that are utilized for prospecting. Since automated VLF detectors are used primarily for coin hunting, sensitivity is not particularly important. Coins are, relatively speaking, large targets.

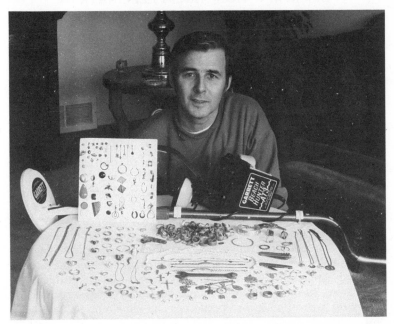

Figure 9-2: Don Cyr of Burlington, Ontario, President of the Canadian Metal Detecting Association, is obviously a successful metal detectorist. Shown in the photograph are a few of the items he has found working the water. He has been a water hunter for many years and prefers it over most other forms of metal detecting.

DETECTION DEPTH

Detection depth aptly describes that ability of any given detector. Detection depth is measured by how deeply a metal detector will detect a given target.

GROUND ELIMINATION

Ground elimination is the ability of a metal detector to ignore iron earth minerals either automatically or by manipulation of a control knob. Do not confuse ground elimination of iron earth minerals with the ability of a detector to ignore salt water (wetted salt). In manual-adjust VLF detectors iron earth minerals are eliminated from detection in the ground canceling mode; salt water is eliminated from detection in the trash elimination or discrimination mode. Automated VLF detectors, however, eliminate both iron earth mineral and wetted salt simultaneously. Under certain conditions, however, the effects of salt water on the detection ability of automated VLF detectors can become apparent. When an operator digs a hole in wetted sands on an ocean beach, and the searchcoil is scanned over the hole, a slight signal will be produced.

DISCRIMINATION (TRASH ELIMINATION)

The trash elimination ability of automated VLFs varies from brand to brand. Some are better than others. Audio of some models "breaks up" over reject targets while other models ignore these same targets unless they are close to the searchcoil. Ground mineral content, however, affects this ability to some extent. Full range trash rejection is possible with most detectors, eliminating nails, foil, bottle caps and pulltabs from detection. A control knob is provided that allows the operator to dial out a range of undesirable metal targets. Detection depth decreases slightly as more targets are eliminated. Consequently, a minimum amount of target elimination is desired. Also, good targets will be lost in direct proportion to the amount of trash elimination that is used. Junk targets lying adjacent to good targets cause the good target to be lost. Since rings appear similar in characteristics to aluminum pulltabs, some rings will not be detected when pulltabs are eliminated.

A new type circuit, however, has been developed to allow the operator a greater measure of ring acceptance during pulltab elimination. Until recently the only type of trash elimination available was that just described. A control knob was provided for the operator to dial trash elimination from zero through pulltabs. This adjustment was cumulative. As the control was rotated "upwards" from zero, foil and nails were first rejected, then bottlecaps and aluminum pulltabs came next. When the aluminum pulltab setting was elected, all "reject" targets, including those just described, were also eliminated. Various circuits are now available that allow the operator to select certain categories of targets to be accepted or eliminated, Figure 9-3. For instance, a "ring

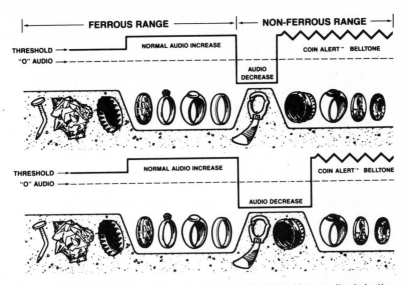

Figure 9-3: These illustrations show just two of the Garrett multi-range discrimination circuit capability. You will notice there are four ranges—two in the ferrous range and two in the non-ferrous range. Two control knobs permit the operator to virtually reject and/or accept targets at will. You will note in the upper illustration that junk targets such as nails, foil, bottlecaps and pulltabs are rejected, while rings of various sizes and coins are accepted. If aluminum screw-caps are numerous in the search area, the upper range control knob can be turned slightly counter-clockwise to a position that includes the rejection of aluminum screw-caps.

only" category can be selected that permits the detector to detect rings while ignoring most, if not all, aluminum pulltabs. The multi-control circuit allows the operator to select several ranges of targets to be detected while ignoring all other targets. Width of these ranges can be adjusted.

SEARCHCOILS

Since automated VLFs are not "all purpose" or "universal" detectors, fewer searchcoils are available than for manual-adjust VLF detectors. Popular searchcoils for automated VLFs range from three inches in diameter to 12 inches. The most popular, however, are coin hunting searchcoils from three inches in diameter up through about eight inches. The larger searchcoils are also used by some relic and cache hunters.

SUPER SNIPER SEARCHCOIL

Three to four-inch diameter searchcoils give the operator an ability to recover coins and other treasures from high junk and worked-out areas and areas adjacent to playground equipment, fences and metal buildings. Since these Super Sniper searchcoils have a small diameter, they more readily detect individual targets; thus, to a good extent, they eliminate the masking effect of junk targets.

SEVEN-INCH TO EIGHT-INCH-PLUS DIAMETER SEARCHCOILS

Searchcoils with diameters of seven to more than eight inches are the most popular sizes used by coin hunters. These sizes provide excellent depth and good scanning width. For an area known to produce valuable coins, rings and jewelry, I recommend that both sizes of searchcoils be used. One size searchcoil should be used to scan the area first, then the Super Sniper can ferret out targets "hidden" among trash.

10-INCH TO 12-INCH DIAMETER SEARCHCOILS

Ten-inch to 12-inch diameter searchcoils have limited use with VLF automated detectors. Coins can be found to good depths, but these larger searchcoils are heavier and pinpointing is more difficult. If searchcoils this size are available, they should be used in areas where numerous targets are expected.

PINPOINTING

Electronic pinpointing is available on some detector models. It sharpens detector signals, giving an extra measure of pinpointing ability. Improved pinpointing speeds recovery and minimizes damage to manicured lawns.

Figure 9-4: Nadine Terry searches for coins, rings and jewelry in the shallow surf of a North Texas lake. She is using a Garrett Beach Hunter AT3 detector, which is very popular with those who search recreational sites. The detector has a "ring only" category that can be selected that permits the detector to detect rings while ignoring most, if not all, aluminum pulltabs. Photo by Mel Climer.

CAPABILITIES

The capabilities of automated VLFs must be rated excellent. They are not as deep seeking as manual-adjust VLFs. They, nevertheless, do an excellent job of locating coins, rings and jewelry. On a scale of one to ten, automated VLFs would rate eight or nine.

APPLICATIONS

Since no knob manipulations are required to achieve ground canceling, many persons have selected this type of instrument as their choice for coin hunting. I recommend it be used primarily for coin, ring and jewelry hunting and to a lesser extent in cache and relic hunting and prospecting. The forms of hunting described in this book, including beach and surf hunting, Figure 9-4, can be readily performed with good results when the recommended searchcoil sizes are used. There are, of course, limitations as explained next.

LIMITATIONS

Most limitations of automated VLFs have already been described in this chapter. Since these instruments are automatic, hovering above the target is not possible; this reduces pinpointing precision. Electronic pinpointing helps the operator overcome this shortcoming. Actually, however, adequate pinpointing can be easily accomplished with all types of detectors. Simply stated, target pinpointing is just not a problem. Detection depth and sensitivity are good and very acceptable, but not as good as manual-adjust VLF types. The range of optional searchcoils is somewhat restricted but several are available for coin, ring and jewelry hunting.

They have many plus factors, however, such as excellent audio response and automatic ground cancellation. Many instruments of this type are constructed in the pistol grip configuration, which reduces fatigue.

PISTOL GRIP CONFIGURATION

The pistol grip configuration provides handling comfort, balance and ease of operation not achieved with other detector designs. Operators can scan this type of instrument for hours, experiencing only minimum fatigue. This configuration has been called the "natural arm-extension" design. Maneuvering the searchcoil is something like pointing your finger; you do it without thinking.

CONCLUSIONS

Automated VLF metal detectors are recommended for coin, ring and jewelry hunting. They are recommended for all types of land and beach hunting, and when constructed with submersible control housing and searchcoils, they are recommended for surfing. They are not as efficient for cache, relic hunting and prospecting, because they do not possess the sensitivity and detection depth of manual-adjust VLF detectors.

CHAPTER 10

The Pulse Induction Metal Detector

Pulse Induction Metal Detectors, Figure 10-1, differ from VLF detectors. You'll remember that VLF circuitry included transmitter and receiver windings that are electrically balanced. Metal is detected with a VLF instrument when eddy current generation draws power from the electromagnetic field and a metal target causes an imbalance between the windings. Pulse Induction circuitry, as you will see, is different.

A Pulse Induction metal detector utilizes only one antenna in its searchcoil, Figure 10-2, serving as both transmitter and receiver. The transmitter signal causes a current to flow in the antenna, and an electromagnetic field is generated that flows out into the matrix surrounding the searchcoil. When this electromagnetic field penetrates metal, eddy currents are caused to flow within the metal and generate their own electromagnetic field which is called the secondary field. The transmitter delivers only a short burst of energy. Then the detector becomes a passive instrument awaiting signals from the secondary electromagnetic field of the target.

When this secondary field flows out into the surrounding matrix, a portion flows upward and intersects the searchcoil antenna. Receiver and amplifier circuitry alert the operator to the presence of the metal. One important characteristic of this type operation is that most ground minerals are ignored. Because only minimal eddy currents are generated in earth materials, these minerals are not detected. Their eddy currents die out prematurely and are not received by circuitry of the antenna. Consequently, there is no need to provide the Pulse Induction detector with ground cancellation capability.

AUDIO RESPONSE

Because of the nature of Pulse Induction circuitry, the audio response is considered slower, with a slight delay discernible between the time the target is detected and an audio signal is produced. This characteristic makes pinpointing slightly more difficult. Most Pulse Induction circuits feature an audible bell tone. The audio is adjustable for slight threshold, but what the operator hears is the faint ringing of a bell. This was first developed for use in underwater detectors to enable scuba divers to hear the detector's sounds over the noise of air bubbles created by their scuba gear. This bell tone sound is very pleasing, however, and many operators prefer it.

Operation of the Pulse Induction detector requires only tuning for faint threshold sound. Since the circuitry ignores earth minerals,

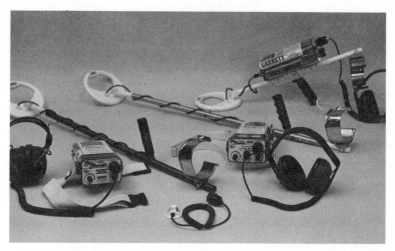

Figure 10-1: Garrett Sea Hunter underwater detector models can be used in two configurations. The long stem, or land configuration, are the two models on the left. The short stem configuration (right) is made possible by the use of the Scubamate accessory. The housing attaches to the short handle. The cable is wrapped around the stem. Pulse Induction detectors need no ground canceling because they automatically ignore iron earth minerals and salt water.

Figure 10-2: This photo shows a closeup of the Sea Hunter attached to the Scubamate accessory. The control housing is attached to the short stem and the searchcoil cable is wrapped around the lower part of the stem. The unit is carried by slipping the arm into the rear stainless steel cradle. The operator grips the black handle that protrudes from the bottom beneath the housing.

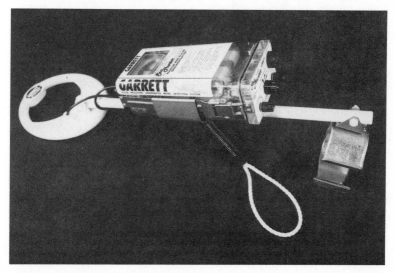

there is no ground canceling control. There is, however, a trash elimination control that the operator can adjust.

Whenever a target is detected, the bell sound increases in loudness.

SENSITIVITY

Sensitivity (the ability to detect very small objects) of most Pulse Induction metal detectors is excellent. Earlier models of this detector experienced difficulty in detecting tiny platinum and white gold rings. Later versions, however, have overcome this problem.

DETECTION DEPTH

The detection depth of Pulse Induction detectors is excellent; in fact, in some cases it is truly remarkable. Unexplained phenomena occur in some models. Targets can often be detected deeper in salt water environments than in air. To some extent detection depth is proportional to the amount of power pumped into the transmitter winding. Consequently, larger and heavier batteries are often installed in these instruments.

For greater detection depth, searchcoils larger than the standard sizes are available. When greater depth is achieved, however, pinpointing becomes slightly more difficult.

GROUND ELIMINATION

Because Pulse Induction detectors ignore most earth minerals, including iron and salt, ground elimination controls are not needed. Extremely dense minerals may slightly affect operation but this effect is minimal.

DISCRIMINATION (TRASH ELIMINATION)

Some Pulse Induction detectors are manufactured with an adjustable trash elimination control to permit the amount of trash elimination desired. Some small iron objects such as ladies' hairpins and very small nails may not be rejected.

Trash elimination depends on the conductivity of metal targets. Whenever transmitter power is shut off, eddy currents from targets begin to die out. Those from metals with high conductivity last longer. Eddy currents flowing in elements like conductive salt die out almost immediately when the primary electromagnetic field shuts off. Currents flowing in silver and gold have a longer lifetime. This phenomenon is the "key" to Pulse Induction operation. Generally speaking, when the transmission of the electromagnetic field ceases, the detector "waits" for the secondary electromagnetic field to arrive at its searchcoil antenna winding. Actually, receiver circuitry is not turned ON immediately after the primary electromagnetic field is shut off. There is a delay of a fraction of a second which provides the "dead" time needed for eddy current generation in wetted salt and other minerals to die. This delay is too brief, however, to permit eddy current generation from desirable metals to die. Thus, the receiver circuits turn on after eddy current ceases flowing from targets with poor conductivity. A trash elimination control permits operators to shorten or lengthen this delay. The amount of undesirable targets not detected will increase as this time before "turn on" is lengthened.

PINPOINTING

Pinpointing becomes slightly more difficult with this detector because peak audio signals are not generated at normal scanning speeds until the searchcoil center has passed across the target. Pinpointing can be improved, however, by rotating the searchcoil as it hovers above the target. After a little practice with this technique, operators generally are able to pinpoint with ease.

Figure 10-3: Sally Reed uses a long-stemmed version of the Garrett Sea Hunter detector on a Padre Island seashore. She prefers this type of instrument because it is easy to use. The instrument is simply turned on — no ground canceling adjustments are necessary since this instrument automatically ignores iron earth minerals and salt water.

101

SEARCHCOILS

Searchcoils in a wide range of diameters from three to 12 inches and larger are provided for most Pulse Induction detectors. Preferred searchcoils are those from three to about eight inches in diameter. The small sizes permit quick and accurate pinpointing while giving good depth as well. In addition, these small searchcoils allow excellent maneuverability in tight places. This can be especially important when working under water where coins and other targets are imbedded in coral. When the individual coins can be more readily pinpointed and detected, they can be dug from the coral more easily and quickly. Small searchcoils also improve detection in areas with a great deal of trash or adjacent to metal structures. Searchcoils seven to eight inches in diameter are the preferred size for general purpose use. They provide excellent detection depth, sensitivity and pinpointing.

10-INCH TO 12-INCH SEARCHCOILS

Although these searchcoils should be used for maximum detection depth, they increase the complexity of pinpointing.

CAPABILITIES

Capabilities of Pulse Induction detectors are excellent with particular emphasis on detection depth. Availability of a wide range of searchcoils further enhances these capabilities. The Pulse Induction detector can perform as well as other types, especially in hostile under-

Figure 10-4: Robert Marx, during one of his many surf hunting expeditions, used a Sea Hunter attached to a Scubamate accesstory.

Figure 10-5: The author prepares to search for relics at a Spanish shipwreck site five miles off the coast of South America. You will note the Sea Hunter housing attached to the short-stemmed Scubamate accessory. The instrument is easy to carry and maneuver. The short stem model is preferred over long stem models for underwater hunting not only because it facilitates scanning, but because the operator need only extend his left hand forward to dig and retrieve any detected object.

water environments and over iron mineral/salt water elements. Operating with headphones improves performance even further.

APPLICATIONS

Pulse Induction detectors are preferred for coin, ring and jewelry hunting. They are not recommended for hunting caches and relics or for prospecting. Their performance is generally limited in these areas. A wide range of available searchcoils extends the applications for Pulse Induction detectors.

Pulse Induction detectors can be used with confidence in all areas of beach hunting, Figure 10-3, surf hunting, Figure 10-4, and underwater hunting. In fact, they are preferred over other types by many detector operators. These detectors can be operated at beach sites with dense concentrations of salt and black magnetic sand. The detector can be operated on dry beaches, then carried into the surf with no deterioration in performance.

Submersible Pulse Induction detectors, Figure 10-5, can be used under water to depths in excess of 200 feet as well as on the beach. Manufacturer's instructions must be followed, however, concerning submersibility. Some Pulse Induction detectors may be designed for only shallow submersion.

LIMITATIONS

Pulse Induction detectors generally require a larger supply of batteries than other detectors. Body-mounted units can minimize this weight problem, however. Increased expertise in pinpointing is required because of the slower audio response. Even though trash elimination is excellent, some small iron objects such as nails and hairpins may not be eliminated.

RECOMMENDATIONS OR CONCLUSIONS

Pulse Induction detectors gained in widespread popularity long after BFO, TR and VLF instruments. As models were improved, popularity increased almost overnight, especially hunting for coins, rings and jewelry on beaches, in surf and under water. The ability of these instruments is limited in cache and relic hunting and for electronic prospecting. They are recommended for hostile underwater environments because they are unaffected by adverse elements and because operation is simple. Do not hesitate to choose and use a quality Pulse Induction detector, especially if you find a configuration that you like.

The Computerized Microprocessor Metal Detector

The first detectors utilizing computerized, microprocessor-chip technology were introduced during 1987 and 1988. "Computerized" metal detectors with integrated circuits (ICs) were built in prior years, but they did not possess the ability to THINK. "Computerized," (IC) detectors simply took target data from the searchcoil receiver windings and conditioned it to control audible and visual indicators. On the other hand, true microprocessor instruments process target and ground mineral data by making millions of analytical computations per second. Let's look into this new breed of instrument and see how they benefit the user.

Computerized, microprocessor detectors must help the user by simplifying operating requirements and by automatically performing many adjustments formerly made manually. If not, design engineers have not done their job. Instead, they have returned the burden to the operator's shoulders and increased operation complexity. Microprocessor metal detectors should simplify the treasure hunter's life, not complicate it.

To explain the characteristics and abilities of microprocessor technology, let's discuss the new Garrett Grand Master Hunter, Figure 11-1. Even though its "inner" workings, Figure 11-2, are highly complex, the operational requirements are extremely simple. This detector is a "thinking" machine; it does most of the operator's thinking for him.

Both ground mineral and target data is "picked up" by the searchcoil receiver antenna. The data is fed into microprocessor circuitry via a receiver/converter circuit that changes the analog data to digital form. This data conversion is necessary because microprocessors can best use, in this application, digital data. The metal detector first checks its batteries and "reports" their condition to the operator. While the operator is scanning the searchcoil over the ground, the computer analyzes the earth's minerals and automatically adjusts the detector to "ignore" them. In less time than it takes the operator to read the detector's battery condition on the meter , the detector has adjusted itself. Ground minerals are balanced out; the operator can begin searching for treasure.

As the detector searchcoil is scanned over the ground, an unbelievable quantity of signals are being processed. In fact, as previously stated, millions of computations PER SECOND are being performed on the data being received. The data is algebraically and

Figure 11-1: The Garrett Grand Master not only was computer-designed from top to bottom but utilizes computerized microprocessor circuitry. It is the first "thinking" detector with a "brain" that performs all functions automatically. Millions of computations per second analyze the soil, detect targets and compare them with the detector's own pre-programmed "firmware." With extreme precision the detector maintains peak performance, rejects unwanted targets and detects treasure to depths greater than any other detector ever built.

trigonometrically manipulated and compared with the "mind" of the computer. Pre-stored at the factory in the microprocessor's memory, which is called FIRMWARE, is knowledge that operators used to have to store in THEIR memory.

Then, as you scan the searchcoil over the ground, detector circuits are analyzing the received data. It is actually ANTICIPATING data you'll receive. When target data comes through, you will be alerted to the presence of the target; that is, IF YOU WANT TO BE TOLD ABOUT IT. By adjusting two discriminating range selectors (ferrous metals and non-ferrous metals), you tell the detector what you want to dig and what you don't want to dig. Only if it's a "good" target will you get an audio alert. The meter, however, tells you the identity of all targets in case you want to know.

The Grand Master operates as follows: When the touchpad ON button is pressed, the microprocessor automatically analyzes all external conditions (ground minerals, etc.) and pre-set operator requirements, and sets all functions to GO. The operator simply begins scanning the searchcoil. The batteries are tested; ground minerals are balanced out; the operator's target discrimination requirements are brought from "storage;" audio threshold is set; outside interference including radio static and other electrical "noise" is analyzed; a maximum (optimum) detection depth is set into the detection circuits; and the detector self checks internal circuitry to make sure the detector is "Ready."

Dual range, panel discrimination controls are synchronized not only with the target I.D. meter but also with a unique audio system. Each range has its own signal with the coin range audio alert being a clear, unmistakable "bell" tone.

It is not necessary to look at the indicator to know in which range each detected target is categorized. Factory preprogrammed data is permanent and cannot be erased, even if the batteries are removed from the detector and left out for a year or longer.

As the detector is scanned, the detector is self-testing; that is, it self-adjusts to achieve optimum performance for all conditions including battery condition, temperature changes and even any aging of electronic components that cause their "values" to change. As target data comes in, the detector compares it with operator requirements and produces a proper audio alert and meter indication. False signals caused by conventional detector "back reading" are eliminated. Even large, surface and shallow objects are properly read on the meter, and the proper audio tone is given. This is achieved as the detector pre-reads the target. An analogy will help you understand this capability. When you look at the color of a wall, then turn the light off, you "remember" the color even though it is dark. This is not the old style "blanking" circuitry in use today in some conventional detectors.

There are two basic modes, ALL METALS DETECTION AND DISCRIMINATION. The operator selects the preferred mode by pressing the proper touch pad, Figure 11-3. When the detector is operating in the Discrimination mode, the detector automatically selects the optimum type of discrimination to "use."

Garrett engineers have known for years that different ground mineral conditions cause different discriminating performance. The Grand Master Hunter has various scanning methods stored in its memory "bank." As the detector is scanned and earth minerals change, the detector automatically readjusts itself to use the optimum type discrimination "method."

To precisely pinpoint and measure depth of detected targets, the PINPOINT/DEPTH touch pad is pressed and held. Audio signals are sharpened and an EXACT SEARCHCOIL CENTER beep indicates the precise location of the target in the ground. In addition, the meter pointer swings upscale and PEAKS when target center is reached. It does not peg the meter like conventional instrument meters. When the button is released, accurate depth below the searchcoil bottom is indicated on the meter. This reading is held until the detector detects the next target. The detection depth scale is calibrated from zero to 12 inches (30 cm).

The two discrimination range controls are "synchronized" with the I.D. meter. On a scale from zero to 100, targets are properly placed according to their conductivity levels. The left side of the meter is controlled by the FERROUS Range control. The right side of the meter

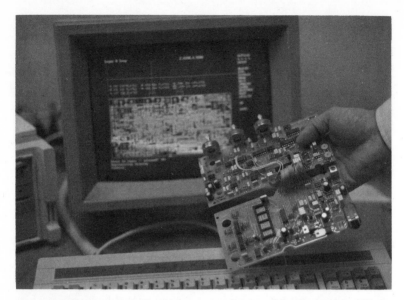

Figure 11-2: The computerized, microprocessor circuitry of the Garrett Grand Master Hunter performs millions of computations per second to free the operator from many of the adjustments and decisions formerly required. In addition, the "brain" continually analyzes its own circuitry and maintains itself in "peak" adjustment. It also selects the best preprogrammed electronic detection and discrimination functions.

Figure 11-3: Power and all modes on the Grand Master Hunter are controlled by this panel. To operate the detector, the operator simply presses the power ON touch pad and begins scanning. Microprocessors automatically adjust all functions. To change modes (All Metal, Discrimination, Pinpoint and Detection Depth) the operator presses the appropriate touch pad.

is controlled by the NON-FERROUS Range control. The operator knows exactly which targets will be accepted and which ones will be rejected.

This dual discrimination capability actually gives the operator FOUR RANGES: two reject and two accept. To properly set these ranges, the operator turns only two knobs to desired levels clearly marked on the panel. Objects to the left of the knob indicator are rejected. Objects to the right are accepted. Panel markings, as stated, correspond exactly with meter markings for all targets.

A unique feature is that aluminum pulltabs, which lie near the center of the non-ferrous range, can be dialed out. The detector accepts coins and rings above and below pulltab rejection. Between 75 and 100 % of all rings in a given area will be accepted while pulltabs are rejected.

No other detector has matched the depth performance of Garrett's earlier model Master Hunter instruments. This newest microprocessor instrument, the Grand Master Hunter, is capable of 50% or greater INCREASED detection depth. And, the discriminating circuits accurately identify detected targets at more than twice the depth of old style detectors.

Battery life has been extended with the use of six "C" cell batteries. Conventional batteries can be used or Nicad rechargeable packs are available. A unique feature of the Nicad packs is that individual "C" cell Nicads can be replaced. Other Nicad systems use factory-built "packs" that must be thrown away even though only one cell has malfunctioned.

What does the Grand Master Hunter mean to the metal detectorist? It simply means that the operator's performance is greatly improved in all phases of treasure hunting with this new "universal" detector. The operator can detect to greater depth, and considerably more discriminating accuracy is available. Additionally, the detector automatically reads all external and ground conditions and "sets" the detector's circuits for optimum performance. Much of this capability the operator cannot achieve with conventional detectors. "Mistakes" are virtually eliminated with this "thinking" detector.

The decade of the 1980s ushered in many detector innovations and improvements, but none can compare with microprocessor achievements. Treasures will be discovered that heretofore could never have been found. Professional performance and detection accuracy can be achieved, even by a child. We have truly entered the world of HI TECH metal detector performance. Treasure hunting and electronic prospecting will never be the same again.

CHAPTER 12

Where and How to Search the Beaches

While attending the First International Mining Conference and Exhibition in Sydney, Australia, I spent much of my off-duty evening weekend hours on hunting the beaches which were, apparently, untouched by metal detectors. My companions and I found coins, jewelry and other items as fast as we could dig, make a recovery and make the next searchcoil scan. Often, I recovered HANDFULS of coins from a single hole. We drew skeptical crowds. After seeing us recover about 10 coins from one hole, someone shouted, "I don't believe you are finding that many coins. You came here last night and buried them!"

Perhaps you are also skeptical? From the moment you discover your first "cache" of coins or piece of valuable jewelry, you will never again be a Doubting Thomas. The time will come when you find a single ring equal in value to your detector. And, quite likely, if you pursue this hobby forcefully, you'll occasionally make discoveries worth thousands of dollars.

Another rewarding aspect of beachcombing is the joy that comes from simply walking a beach experiencing the ocean breezes and the sand under your feet while listening to the tranquilizing sounds of surf and seabreeze, Figure 12-1.

A beachcomber is a person who searches along shorelines for valuable jetsam, flotsam, refuse and other lost treasure. "Keeper" finds can be anything valued by the finder or anyone else. The beachcomber's territory is often staked on two parallel sides by the shallow surf line and a macadam road. The other two dimensions often seem to disappear into infinity, Figure 12-2. Treasure digging is often as easy as kicking the sand with the toe of your shoe. The time is anytime...day or night...spring, summer, fall or winter.

Beach pickings are good almost anytime, but you'll learn that certain times are better than others. At first, you may be disappointed. Your finds may seem to provide small return for your efforts. But, remember, most new ventures begin awkwardly and without reward. Persist you must. Give yourself just a year; you'll be forever "hooked" and richer for your efforts.

"Beach pickings," Figures 12-3 through 12-6, include coins, rings, watches, necklaces, chains, bracelets and anklets, religious medallions and crucifixes, toys, knives, cigarette cases and lighters, sunshades, keys, relics, bottles, Asian glass and plastic fishnet balls, ships' cargo and other items that will soon fill barrels. And, for the very lucky and persistent hunter, the discovery of some lost pirate treasure or a cache of 17th century Spanish pieces of eight which were hidden ashore by early day explorers who never made it back to recover their wealth, Figure 12-7.

People shouldn't wear jewelry to the beach, but they do. Often, they forget about valuable heirlooms and diamond rings, Figures 12-8 and 12-9. Some just don't seem to care one way or the other. But, it's all the same for the beachcomber because all rings expand in the heat; fingers wrinkle and shrivel in the water and suntan oils merely hasten the inevitable loss. Beach lovers play ball, throw frisbees and engage in horseplay. These activities fling rings off of fingers and cause clasps on necklaces, bracelets and chains to break. Into the sand go these lost valuables. See Figures 12-10 through 12-13.

Coins, jewelry, keys and other beach "necessities" are placed on blankets. In a hurry to escape a sudden downpour or just through forgetfulness, the sunbather grabs and shakes the blanket. There go the valuables into the sand. Even though items are often immediately recovered, some are never found except by a metal detector, Figure 12-14.

Boys and girls play in the sand. Holes are dug and sand is piled up or made into sand castles. In this process toys, coins, digging tools, knives and other possessions are lost until the metal detector discovers them, Figures 12-15 and 12-16.

Perhaps, someday, you'll be as lucky as one beachcomber on Grand Cayman whose story was related by Robert Marx in *Argosy* magazine. The beachcomber spotted something shining on the sandy bottom in shallow water. To his astonishment it turned out to be a gold cross covered with diamonds. Without telling anyone, he

Figure 12-1: This lovely beach is one that many people would enjoy. A truly rewarding aspect of beachcombing is the joy that comes from simply walking the beach, experiencing the ocean breezes and sand under your feet while listening to the tranquil sounds of surf and sea breeze.

Figure 12-2: Ciro Plebe and Charles Garrett scan this beach near Ciro's home. In Italy. This beach, discussed in the text, loses its sand during the winter months as it is blown into a retaining wall. In early spring just prior to the beach season, bulldozers push the sand back out onto the beach. The perfect time to scan this beach is just prior to the bulldozer activity when metal detectors are the closest to the blanket of treasure.

returned later with scuba equipment and really struck it rich. Using only his hand to fan away thin layers of sand, he recovered a fantastic cache of treasure including a large bar of platinum dated 1521, various bars of silver bullion, a silver bracelet in the form of a serpent covered with emeralds and a large gold ring bearing the arms of the Ponce de Leon family. With no evidence of a shipwreck ever occurring in the area, he believes the treasure—which appears to be the booty of a conquistador—was probably buried ashore and eventually washed into the shallow water as the beach eroded.

Figure 12-3: Richard and Heather Ambrose of Montreal, Canada, are surf hunters and very successful ones. Here are a few of the gold rings and jewelry items they have found in the surf. Photo courtesy Richard and Heather Ambrose.

112

RESEARCH

Chapter 4 lists and describes many of the major and most common sources of leads. No list and discussion, however, can be complete. As you research the various sources, your techniques and abilities will improve. That's one reason why I encourage you to apply yourself aggressively to beach hunting for at least one year before you judge this aspect of treasure hunting. Don't be haphazard and sloppy in your efforts. Be diligent and you'll be amazed at your progress and success.

First, begin your research locally. Use every source of leads and information from old-timers to the chamber of commerce. Contact tourist bureaus as well as historical societies. Leave no source untouched in your investigation. To speed up your work, always be specific. Ask for information pertaining to both past and present swimming areas and resorts. Swimming was certainly one of the most popular activities of bygone days. Ghost towns, and there are always a few lying about in ruins, should not be overlooked.

When checking newspapers, pay particular attention to accident reports which usually give the location, or at least the name of a particular beach. Review the Sunday or weekend city news columns that announce the joys of swimming and sunbathing at local beaches. Advertisements of beachwear occasionally offer clues to areas of activity.

Don't overlook old postcards; antique shops can be a good source. If there is a postcard collector in your vicinity, pay him or her a visit. Old picture postcards, like those printed in this book, may be reliable X-marks-the-spot waybills to treasure.

Figure 12-4: Tom Edds spends a lot of time searching the Florida beaches and he is successful as shown by the finds in this display case and in other photographs in this book.

Figure 12-5: This nice collection of coins, tokens and religious medals was found by a Canadian treasure hunter, according to Keith and Mary Edwards who supplied this photo.

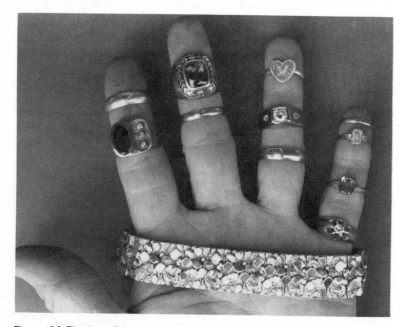

Figure 12-6: Thanks to Don Littlejohn of Fort Worth for letting us glimpse a few of the more valuable finds he has made in swimming areas in North Texas.

114

If you are not a member of your local treasure club, consider joining. The sharing of locations and success stories broadens everyone's knowledge, sharpens skills and increases success rates of members.

Don't be content to work only local beaches. Broaden your scope; it may pay rewards. For example, if you live in northern California, make a study of the history of the San Francisco Bay area. Many ships have gone down here, losing valuable cargos of silver and gold, much of which has not been found. Violent storms often churn up ocean bottoms and cast sunken treasure on the beach.

Never overlook the possibility of finding flotsam and jetsam washed ashore from offshore shipwrecks. Regardless of the age of a wreck, some cargo — especially gold, silver, copper and bronze items — will probably remain in fair to excellent condition. The principal cargo found in many old shipwrecks is silver and gold from the mines of Mexico and Peru, or gold from California and nearby states. Recent recoveries from old shipwrecks reveal that the typical ship's cargo consisted of cannon, gold and silver coins and bars, and personal relics. Often clumps of silver coins and discs are located. Other items such as English pewter and stoneware are often found. Be quick to take advantage of all opportunities to expand your treasure hunting horizons. You may also expand your pocketbook and require a larger safety deposit box.

When researching reports of shipwrecks, don't overlook Coast Guard and Life Saving Service records. Newspaper files and local and state histories are good sources of information. Insurance companies and Lloyd's Register may provide precisely the information you need.

Figure 12-8: This is a very unusual find made by Tom Edds on a Florida beach. It appears to be a Spanish real.

Figure 12-7: Thanks to Robert Marx for giving us a glimpse of this tremendous silver cache of 500 Spanish silver pieces of eight. Two treasure hunters were working a stretch of Florida beach immediately following a storm. In an area washed out by the storm, one of the treasure hunter's metal detectors sang out with a loud cry. Digging down, they found these coins. It is believed that Spaniards buried these coins at this site between 250 and 300 years ago and for whatever reason failed to return to recover their buried treasure.

Figure 12-10: Here are a few rings and religious items found by Alden Fogliadini, a successful beach and surf hunter who spends much of his time searching Northern California beaches. The author worked various beach sites on the Caribbean island of Guadeloupe with Alden and observed him as a very efficient operator.

Figure 12-11: Here are more of Alden Fogliadini's treasure finds. These gold rings are difficult to find, but it is obvious that Alden has mastered his detector and does not let excuses get in his way.

Assateague Island, off the coast of Maryland and Virginia, has proven to be the depository of much cargo from ancient shipwrecks. Treasure hunters, scanning the beaches with their metal detectors, have found valuable coins and relics, some of which have "marked" the location of larger treasures, Figure 12-17. Although much of the island is controlled by the National Seashore Service, portions are open to the public. Permission to search with your metal detector can sometimes be obtained on National Seashores; it doesn't hurt to request permission.

These examples of potentially productive areas offer ideas that may help you expand your territory. Treasure hunters often travel thousands of miles in their quest for treasure. You can do likewise, especially if there is a pot of gold at the end of your trail. But, I must stress the presence of considerable local treasure. Find it first; then hit the treasure trail.

As you search records, histories and old maps, be on the alert for clues to landmarks and locations. For instance, the name of a beach led me to the Spanish icon described later in this chapter. Wouldn't a name like "Massacre Beach" cause your ears to perk up? When I began uncovering what looked like human bones at the beach site, I knew the site was worth thoughtful investigation.

Stay alert to current weather conditions. You'll want to search at low tides—the lower the better. After storms come ashore, head for the beach. When oil spills deposit tar and oil on beaches, there's a good

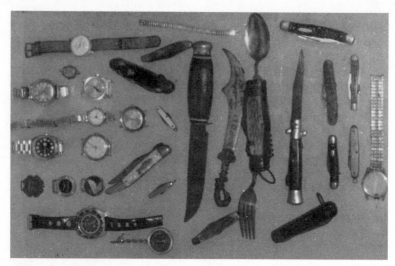

Figure 12-16: Here are a few more unusual finds made by Tom Edds on the beaches of Florida.

Figure 12-13: These finds made by Alden Fogliadini illustrate the author's contention that certain categories of jewelry items can be found at certain beach locations. The turquoise Indian jewelry indicates common items worn by lady sunworshippers and swimmers at certain beach sites.

Figure 12-17: Often treasure hunters scanning the beaches with their metal detector find coins and relics, some of which have marked the location of larger treasures lying just offshore in shallow water. These finds, plus the large ship's timber, indicate that an off-shore shipwreck is near by.

possibility bulldozer and other equipment used to remove it can get you much closer to treasure.

Watch for beach development work. When piplines are being laid and when seawalls, breakwaters and piers are being constructed, work these areas of excavation.

PERMITS

Be alert to regulatory laws and regulations. Quite possibly, most or all your beach areas are open to metal detectorists, but it is possible some areas are regulated. If a permit is required to search a given area, obtain one and operate within permit regulations. As an example, consider the regulations as set forth on treasure hunter Roy Sexton's Niagara Frontier State and Recreation Commission Permit. Its regulations permit hunting all year except during the period May 23 through September 7. No water hunting is allowed, only beach hunting. Hunting is allowed only on Beaver Island State Park and Evangola State Park. Certain digging and archaeological restrictions are enforced. But, there is no cost for the permit.

CLOTHING

Although you should always dress comfortably, protect yourself from the elements. Obviously keep warm in the winter and cool in the summer, but I caution you to shade exposed skin areas to prevent sun and wind burn. Skin specialists recommend the use of a high numbered sun screen. Use it often and freely. Regardless of the elements, you can protect yourself. This book instructs you in basics, but experience is the best teacher.

Figure 12-12: Here are many more lovely finds made by Alden Fogliadini in various swimming surf areas of Northern California. Note the four watches.

Figure 12-9: Here is another of Tom Edds' fabulous finds. He found this twin-diamond cluster ring on a Florida beach.

In the spring, summer and fall seasons I usually wear shorts or lightweight trousers, a shirt (usually with long sleeves), socks and comfortable shoes or sneakers, a wide brimmed cotton hat and a neck shield. During early morning and late evening hours I try to work open sunny areas. During the heat of the day, I work shady areas. Neither heat nor cold keeps me from working all day (8 to 12 hours) in my quest for treasure. I love hot weather, but yet I respect its fury. About one-half my water supply I use to keep my hat dampened. Keeping my head cool and protecting my skin from sunburn permits all-day searching to become a matter of course.

Treasure hunting, or any form of metal detecting must be considered play. But, I don't play when I hunt. The only rule I follow when in the field is to work from dawn to dusk and later, if necessary. Doing less is a gross misuse of time. Develop sound habits, be totally serious about your work and I am confident you'll find twice as much treasure. In fact, the difference between success and failure—separating men from boys, if you will—depends almost entirely on dedication to the job at hand.

Figure 12-18: Lisa Climer uses a Master Hunter detector to search the beach and very shallow water. She uses the automated mode which automatically ignores iron minerals and conductive salt water. She is using a scoop to retrieve her find. A scoop such as this can be used in loose, dry, sandy areas and near the surf where there is sufficient water to wash out the wet sand. Photo courtesy Mel Climer.

121

Figure 12-15: Boys and girls will play in the sand. In the process of making sand castles, countless toys, coins, digging tools, knives and other possessions are lost. This photograph shows numerous small toys discovered by a Canadian beach hunter. Thousand upon thousands of these tiny toy cars are found each year.

Figure 12-14: This rather odd assortment is typical of items found by beach hunters. Robin Botting of Wenona, Canada, made these finds, which include two groups of rings in the photograph. This photo clearly shows that valuable and sometimes not-so-valuable-but-interesting finds are made.

I never work barefooted, especially in sand dunes. I wear boots and I keep a sharp eye out for snakes. Rarely, do I dig with my hands, but use one or more types of diggers. I use knee pads, at least on one knee. In Chapter 27 I describe various other clothing items and gear.

The arrival of winter weather can signal the start of good beach hunting. Beaches become less crowded and the often violent weather increases its untiring efforts at erosion. As beaches erode, you should be first on the beach every day—the early hunter gets the treasure!

Cold weather hunting, particularly in the North and East and even on Gulf Coast beaches, requires more thought, more caution and more clothing than the same activity in warmer weather, You must keep yourself protected against lower temperatures, fierce winds and persistent drizzle or rain. Adequate protection, however, must not bind or restrict your movements, or else you will tire quickly.

My long thermals usually go on first, followed by loose-fitting outer wear. I've found that a lightweight windbreaker suit gives me considerable protection as an outer garment. The top piece has a zippered or button-up front, however, because as I begin to warm up, I first unzip the top piece. With my back to the wind, the unzipped top maintains body heat at the pre-sweat level. As the day warms, I may remove the top entirely.

I wear a Navy deck-watch type wool cap and either a separate rainproof bonnet or one that is attached to the top piece of my outer rain gear. Gloves are often a necessity; arm's length rubber gloves are a must for cold water work. While working on blustery days, I usually wear rubber boots. Sometimes I'll wear hip waders. You may ask why I wear rubber boots when I work dry beaches.

While they are not needed for dry beach work, I must be prepared when I discover a cut formed by wave and wind action. I never miss a chance to work a cut being formed as long as the water level and the elements permit. If land searching is producing only moderate success, I wade into the shallow water to seek troughs. Even though I enjoy hunting in the water during cold seasons, I prefer to keep my feet dry. If my feet stay warm, I usually stay warm all over.

I suggest goggles in high winds. If you wear glasses, wear goggles over your glasses, a type available from bicycle, motorcycle or skiing shops. Use goggles that are vented since the vents prevent moisture from forming. Those sold in motorcyle and skiing equipment shops are generally of better quality. Test them by pressing gently outward on the outside corner of one of the lens. If it slips easily out of its socket or rubber groove, don't buy this pair. In the field, the lens will never stay in place. Since lens are usually made of soft plastic, you must treat them with care to prevent scratches.

Always carry extra clothing, including dry socks and shoes. Include small waterproof canvases or paint drop-cloths to protect your car seats, floorboards and trunk from water and sand.

I encourage you to read and study Chapter 31. Take extra special care of your clothing and equipment or you'll wish you had!

EQUIPMENT

Wouldn't it be nice if treasure hunters could always dig holes only in the sand? Almost any type digger can be used in beach sand, except your hands. There is too much broken glass. I prefer two types of diggers: a heavy-duty garden trowel and a light-weight pick with a flat blade on one end. Just a quick whack with the pick, and I usually have my treasure. Of course, pinpointing is essential before you start hacking your way down to treasure. Begin by using a trowel or small shovel. As your pinpointing improves, you can graduate to a pick-type digger with a long handle. The long handle lets you uncover your target without kneeling on the ground. See Chapter 24 for more information on my recommendations.

Scoops are reasonably good in DRY, LOOSE SAND. A quick scoop, a few shakes and you have your find. In damp and wet sand, however, scoops are just a waste of time. It takes too long to work damp sand out of a scoop. If, however, you work the shoreline surf, a scoop can be effectively used. Onrushing surf and water will quickly clean the wet sand from the scoop. Figure 12-18.

Occasionally, you may need a strong, thin, digger-like screwdriver. A good percentage of my finds are buried in roots beneath trees and tree stumps. Digging becomes difficult amongst the roots, and a strong, thin, rod-type digger is required to loosen the soil. I left one "treasure" on the Caribbean beach of Guadeloupe because I did not have a strong digging tool or saw. A faint detector signal came as I scanned over the roots of a tree stump. As I dug deeper, the signal grew louder, but digging became more difficult. The root system was so tangled I could make only slow headway. My hunting companions were already loaded in the vehicle and were anxious to leave.

Still some distance from my target, I saw the need for a stronger tool and filled in the hole. As I walked sadly away, I promised myself a return trip with the correct tools.

And speaking of holes, some treasure hunters leave the holes they dig. DON'T YOU! Always, without exception, fill every hole you dig. Sure, it takes an extra moment, but you must do this for the sake of our hobby. And, you don't want someone to step into one of your holes and twist an ankle, do you? I have filled so many holes that I do it automatically. Even in mountainous regions and desert areas, I kick dirt into the holes I dig.

Other gear you need includes a general assortment of pouches, a secure pocket for especially good finds and a place for personal items. I often wear an Army-type web belt with a canteen and an extra pouch or two. If you hunt at night, you'll need a battery-powered headlamp.

METAL DETECTOR SELECTION

Much has been said about the selection of the proper metal detector. Still, a few more words of advice are in order. While the sand on most beaches looks innocent enough, the "wrong" type detector can spoil your day at the beach. Depending on ground mineral content, some detectors are practically worthless, others so-so, and yet others perfectly suited. A quality automated VLF with discrimination is your best choice.

On iron-mineral-free beaches such as those of Florida, a BFO, TR or most any of the later designs works well. If your BFO or TR has a discriminating mode, water-saturated sands can be worked easily. With discrimination control set near bottlecap rejection, salt minerals in the water are eliminated from detection.

Manual adjust VLFs give good depth in most beach sands, Figure 12-18. But, unless the circuits are "automated," heavy iron mineral black sand beaches may somewhat limit performance. If your VLF has a TR discriminating mode, you should set it at approximately the bottlecap setting. Of course, that setting imposes limitations, especially if you decide to advance the setting to pulltab rejection and dig mostly coins. I realize that most professional beach hunters will be aghast at that remark, since few professionals use any discrimination unless the beach is truly a "junk yard." Using discrimination, however, makes it more likely that you will miss valuable treasures. That's a fact of life. But, there are times when discrimination is needed.

The new automated VLFs have become popular with beach hunters. Many models ignore minerals, including salt water. Some instruments have an internal switch that cuts out salt minerals. Automated models can be operated from zero discrimination through pulltab rejection.

Pulse Induction instruments operate nearly flawlessly on all beaches, Figure 11-3. Giving good depth, they are a pleasure to use. Generally, they are heavier because of extra battery requirements and the heavier case needed by submersible/land models. One shortcoming of pulse detectors is that small iron pieces, especially nails and hairpins, may not be rejected. I have learned that Caribbean beaches can be a true hairpin junkyard, while U.S. beaches are generally free of them.

On beaches with black sand (iron magnetite) present, your choice of detectors is narrowed considerably. BFOs and TRs are out of the question because they cannot cancel the effects of the natural iron. Pulse Induction detectors ignore it as do manual and automated VLFs.

So, a choice must be made. A quality, automated VLF with discrimination is most desirable. These instruments ignore black sand and salt minerals, and you can adjust discrimination control to your desired setting.

If you own a BFO or TR, take it to the beach and use it for a while. Adjust the discrimination control near bottlecap rejection and try it over wet sand. You may have to make minor adjustments to find the correct setting. If the detector's audio cannot be "smoothed out," you are probably encountering black sand.

You should consider purchasing one of the late model automated (sometimes called motion) discriminating instruments. Give thought to buying one of the environmentally protected units, Figure 9-1. Then, neither rising water, rain, blowing sand, nor storms can send you home.

METAL DETECTOR NOTES

If your detector is not protected against the environment, carry along a plastic bag to slip over its control housing. When you set the detector down, sand will have less chance to work into its controls and circuitry.

Always use searchcoil skidplates to extend the life of your searchcoil.

Always, always (need I repeat, always?) use headphones for the greatest success. Wind, surf and "people" noise will mask your detector's signals causing you to miss many good targets. Any type of headphones are better than none, but the most desired are those with ear cushions and adjustable volume controls. Coiled cords are preferred along with right-angle plugs.

Figure 12-20: This low tide shot of a Galveston beach taken by Monty Moncrief shows a large sandy area exposed when the tide receded. Not only is there more dry land to work, but surf hunters can then walk greater distances out into the surf. Note the rocks in the foreground. These should always be scanned because during storm and other high water activity coins and jewelry can be cast into this area. The jumbled mass of rock prevents these items from washing back into the beach sand or back into the water.

Since large cushioned headphones can become quite hot, you might try the smaller versions even though their cushions may not mask as much noise interference.

Most searchcoils are submersible (check with your manufacturer, if in doubt), but not all detectors have a stem plug to prevent water from running back into the control housing. To be safe, immediately after using your detector in water, drain the lower stem. If you don't, the first time the searchcoil is raised above the control box, you may have a flooded instrument.

TIDES AND WEATHER

Wouldn't it be great if the ocean suddenly receded several feet leaving your favorite hunting beach high and dry? You could walk right out and recover lost treasure so much more easily. Well, the ocean does recede slightly every day during low tide. Nearly twice a day a full tide cycle occurs—two high and two low tides. Low tides are of greatest interest to you because the water level has dropped, leaving more beach area exposed. One-half foot drop in tide level can expose an extra ten or more feet of ground distance to the water's edge, allowing you to work not only more dry land but also a greater distance into the surf. See Figure 12-20. Low tides occur approximately every

Figure 12-21: This is a portion of a tide table which lists the month, the day, the high and low tide times and water heights. A fraction of a foot in ocean height change can result in many feet of beach being exposed. Also, many more outward feet of surfing is available to the surf hunter during low tides.

GALVESTON (Galveston Channel), TEXAS

Times and Heights of High and Low Waters

AUGUST

Day	Time h m	Height ft	m	Day	Time h m	Height ft	m
1	0125	0.7	0.2	16	0038	1.3	0.4
Sa	0724	1.1	0.3	Su	0409	1.2	0.4
	1449	0.2	0.1		0542	1.3	0.4
	2243	1.1	0.3		1607	0.0	0.0
2	0227	1.0	0.3	17	0218	1.5	0.5
Su	0718	1.2	0.4	M	1713	-0.1	0.0
	1545	0.0	0.0				

Figure 12-22: Study this photo carefully. It reveals many areas that nature has provided to increase your chance of finding treasure. The water-filled areas are low spots in the beach sand. These were filled with the tide that is now receding. The long body of water in left foreground marks the location of a trough. Troughs form along many beach stretches and they often run parallel to one another. Further along the beach are several pools of water that are also low spots that should be checked with your detector. Note that at the right end of the long trough, water is running back into the ocean. These should be checked as a depository of coins, rings and jewelry.

twelve and one-half hours. You should plan your work period to begin at least two or three hours before low tide and continue that long after designated low tide times. That's four to six hours of improved hunting. You can buy tide tables, Figure 12-21, or get the information from scuba shops, fishing tackle stores or the newspapers. If you plan to work inlet, cove and river areas, water current data may also be of interest. On some days, especially after a new or full moon, there will be lower-than-usual tides. Take advantage of these times. Also, listen to weather forecasts to learn of prevailing wind data. Strong offshore (outgoing) winds will aid in lowering the water level and tend to reduce breaker size and force. Offshore winds also spread out (thin) sand at the water's edge. This effect could result in decreasing sand that has built up over lost treasure. On the other hand, incoming waves and resulting larger breakers tend to pile sand up, causing it to thicken and increase in depth. Be alert to the lowest or ebb tides when you can work beach areas not normally exposed. You must get your timing right. Of course, you can work dry beaches during high tides and then be prepared to follow the tide out. That procedure offers maximum work time.

As you follow the tide out, work in a parallel path hugging the water's edge. Each return path should be nearly parallel to the preceding one. If your path length is long, each succeeding path will veer outward. Wide searchcoil sweeps can offset these veering paths, however. Be alert to the relationships between locations of your finds. It may be that you'll discover a trough, Figure 12-22, or other treasure deposit that needs additional scanning or work with a larger, deeper-seeking searchcoil.

Look for tidal pools and long, water-filled depressions, Figure 12-23. Any beach areas that hold water should be investigated since these low spots put you closer to treasure. As the tide recedes, watch for streams draining back into the ocean. These "mark" the location of low areas. If you will constantly keep in your mind the vision that only a few feet beneath the sand's surface a "blanket" of treasure awaits, your powers of observation will keep you alert to specific areas to search. After all, that blanket of treasure lying on the clay, gravel or bedrock BELONGS TO YOU, AND YOU ARE GOING TO GET IT. Continually watch for those low areas that put your searchcoil closer to it.

Weather is a major contributing factor to tide levels, and strong storms and winds can change tides drastically. A storm at sea moving

Figure 12-23: This photo shows a tidal pool, but it is an exceptionally interesting one since there are many rocks lying in the shallows. These rocks hold treasure that is washed in from the ocean. Note also the rocks in the foreground. Areas like this should be searched with your metal detector. Photo courtesy Monty Moncrief.

in your direction may raise the normal tide level several feet. When this occurs, wave action becomes so violent it is sometimes impossible (and dangerous) to hunt, even upon the beach. But, the stage is set, however, and you should hit the beach when calm returns.

Conversely, a winter storm reaching the coast with any strength at all can cause lower tides than those listed in the table and an accompanying compression of wave heights is noticeable. The water is often calm. These conditions and the changes they cause is a continuing process that controls sand deposits on the beach and in the shallow water. Storms often transfer treasure from deep water vaults to more shallow locations. For a change in your searching habits, plan a beach search immediately following a storm. If you are among the more hardy individuals, try working during a violent storm. It may be revealing. Indian John told me of working a Florida beach during a storm. Suddenly, at the water's edge, a gully began forming before his eyes. As it grew deeper, he suddenly saw the unmistakable color of treasure. I don't know how much he took from that glory hole, but he smiles when he relates the story. See Figure 12-24. Before working during a storm, however, read the safety precautions presented in Chapter 28.

Keep in mind that extremes in weather and surf conditions can make unproductive beaches suddenly become productive. Remember that storms play havoc with beach sands. Fast-running beach drainage currents can wash deep gullies in the sand. So, keep your eyes on the beach during violent weather. Study Figure 12-25.

Figure 12-24: Edward and Mary Perchaluk found numerous Spanish coins along this beach. Following a storm they used their metal detectors and discovered a large cache of Spanish coins at the cut shown in the center of the photograph. You will note that several people are looking at this low spot. The coins were there all the time, but a storm washed away the sands to place them within the range of metal detectors.

SAND FORMATIONS – NATURE'S TRAPS

Both wind and water move beach sand around in a continual process. Let me tell you of the time when I missed by only a few days what I believe would have been a "gold mine." On a stretch of beach along the eastern seaboard of Italy not far from Pisa, prevailing winter winds blow sand inland, uncovering harder packed soil. A retaining wall about 100 yards inland prevents the sand from being blown farther. Before each springtime bathing season, earth-moving equipment is deployed to return sand to the beach. Quite likely, considerable lost treasure captured within the harder-packed strata could be found during the winter months when the beach is stripped of sand blown inward. During a trip to Europe which included a visit to Italy, I came to this beach to test a prototype of a new beach/surf hunting detector. I arrived there immediately following the completion of the sand's redistribution along the shoreline. It was obvious the sand was from about two to four feet thick. My chance had been lost!

Another reason for working beaches immediately after a storm is that the beach continually reshapes and protects itself, Figure 12-25. Sands shift normally to straighten the beachfront and present the least possible shoreline to the sea's continuous onslaught. During storms, beach levels decrease as sand washes out to form underwater bars which blunt the destructive force of oncoming waves. Following the storm, the smaller waves return the sand to the beach.

To understand how sand, coins and jewelry continually move around, consider the action of waves upon sand. At the water's edge, particles of sand form the sand bank. When a wave comes in, the sudden immersion in water causes the grains of sand to "lighten" and become more or less suspended in the water. The constant churning keeps particles afloat until the next wave comes in. The floating particles are then carried some distance by the force of the water.

In the same manner, coins, jewelry, sea shells and debris are continually relocated, generally in the direction of prevailing wind and waves. As they move, waves and wind move material about until a spot is reached where the action of the water is lessened. Heavy objects fall out and become concentrated in "nature's traps." So, whenever you find areas with a concentration of sea shells, gravel, flotsam, driftwood and other debris, work them with your metal detector.

As your experience accumulates, you'll one day realize that treasure can be found outside the normal limits of the swimming area. How did this treasure get there? Possibly, at an earlier stage in time, the outlying stretches of beach were actually the swimming beach itself. For one or more reasons, (property disputes, beach erosion, etc.) the "old" beach was abandoned along with its buried treasure.

Another reason for this "mislocated" treasure is natural erosion that moved it. How does this happen? These redeposits do not "just happen" nor are they permanent. It may pay you to consider and understand those forces that create treasure vaults for you to find.

On your next visit to a beach where surf is especially violent, pay attention! When a wave comes in and breaks near the beach, notice that water has a brown appearance caused by suspended sand. When the crashing wave rushes up on the beach, it transports this sand and mixes it with other loosened beach sand. If the waves break parallel to the beach front, most of this deposited sand is washed back by the receding water and is deposited near where it came from.

Close observation, however, will reveal that waves do not come in parallel, but at an angle that sets up a current. The transported sand also comes in at the same angle. This angle of transport causes the sand to move further to the left or right of its origination point. Some of the displaced sand remains on the beach and some is washed back into the water at its new location. The result of this action is that sand is transported in the general direction that waves are moving. Study Figure 12-26.

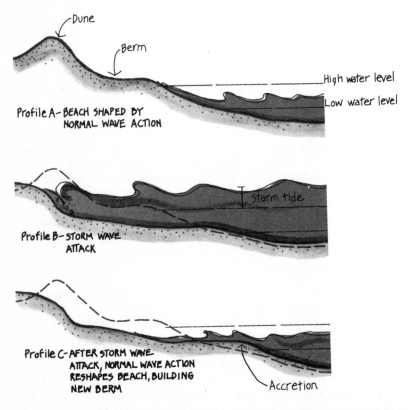

Figure 12-25: This is an illustration from the U.S. Army Corps of Engineers' Booklet, LOW COST SHORE PROTECTION, 1981. Notice how storm tides reshape beach sands.

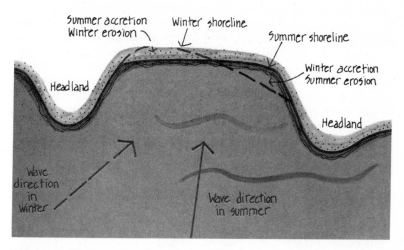

Figure 12-26: Beaches continually reshape and protect themselves. Sands shift normally to straighten the beach front and present the least possible shoreline to the sea's continuous onslaguht. Because wave direction is different in winter than it is in summer, beach contours change. This figure illustrates the shoreline variations that can take place as the seasons change. Illustration reproduced from the United States Army Corps of Engineers' Booklet, LOW COST SHORE PROTECTION, 1981.

Understanding this phenomenon is important because the same transport system (via storms and high wind) causes a redistribution of treasure from the point where it was originally lost. The ability of water to move heavier-than-sand material depends on its speed. Large waves and fast-moving currents can carry sand, coins and rings along a continuous path. When wave action slows down, movement slows down or stops. When wave action picks up, movement resumes. Growing shores (perhaps those severely eroded by prior storm action) are "nourished" by material that has been eroded from a nearby stretch of beach. Heavy treasure takes the path of least resistance, being pushed along the lowest points of cuts and other eroded areas.

As coins, rings and other jewelry are brought into these new beach areas, they become fill along with new sand. Being heavier, they gradually sink to lower levels and become covered. When that eroded beach has become fully "nourished," this buildup essentially stops, LEAVING YOUR TREASURE BURIED AND WAITING FOR YOU.

Perhaps you doubt that erosion and resulting treasure redistribution really take place. After all, during your many summer trips to the beach, everything looks serene and you have never seen coins and rings being washed around. Actually, it is usually during fall, winter and spring that weather patterns produce major face-lifting on beaches. Strong winds and high tides do most of the redistributing. Violent storms cause considerable damage. The classic northeasters that sweep

133

up the East Coast not only churn up beaches, but often cause millions of dollars of damage to property. Violent storms cause people to move inland as heavy snow, high wind and beach-grinding tides do their damage. High tides often flood beachfront communities with 10, 15 and sometimes 20 feet of water. Since normal high tides are only three to four feet, you can imagine the erosion forces that are set in motion. As much as 90% of the sand on a beach can be washed away during a violent storm. During the erosion process, considerable treasure redistribution takes place. Unfortunately, some treasure is washed out into the surf areas, where it may be found by surf hunters.

Since shorelines and beaches are continually being reshaped, you must be observant. One key to success is establishing permanent tide and sand markers. Your marker can be a piling or any structure you can readily observe at any time. Ideally, your water marker will be somewhat submerged during both high and low tides. By keeping your eyes on this water marker, you can determine water height at all times and know if the water is rising or falling.

Your sand marker is important because it is a gauge of sand height. The more of your sand marker that is exposed, the greater your chances of detecting treasure that lies out of reach during times of sand pileup.

There are high and low sand formations. High formations do you no good except to serve as height gauges when storm and wind activity erode cliffs. Imaginative beachcombers keep their eyes peeled for cliffs that begin to erode. You are interested in their lowest levels where you will find coins and rings as they become uncovered by the action of winds and waves. Eroding cliffs may reveal decades-old settlements and accumulations of treasure and debris. In your research, be alert for references to old settlements or ghost towns. What has been covered for many generations may be uncovered before your eyes today.

LOCATING THE BEST PLACES TO SEARCH

When you walk out onto the beach, where do you begin? How do you select the most productive areas? This is possibly the question I am asked most frequently by beginning beach hunters. Let experience be your teacher. You can pick up ideas from experienced beachcombers, but the final decisions must be based on your experience and your intuition. Experience will teach you of places that never produce and other places that are often rewarding. A knowledge of storm, wind and wave action will often come to your rescue as you study a new beach. I'll tell you of an experience where visual and mental study led me almost directly to an "x-marks-the-spot" location.

I was with a group of treasure hunters on a Caribbean island. Submerged at the entrance to a cove were numerous old and very large anchors protruding a few feet out of the water. We learned they had been placed there hundreds of years ago to prevent enemy ships from coming into the cove, then serving as harbor for a settlement. This historically active location interested me. One could just imagine enemy ships sailing in with cannons blasting and shore batteries returning the fire. Were ships ever sunk in the harbor?

A short distance away was an area called Massacre Beach. This name stirred my imagination with a scene of brutality so violent that this site should forever be remembered as a place of ruthless killing. What treasure hunter could resist standing on such a beach, visualizing the artifacts that must surely lie beneath its sands? As I studied the beach, I noticed an outcropping of coral protruding a few inches from the water and ending abruptly where sand met the sea. I thought that if there had been a slaughter there, relics might be found at the edge of the coral. Anything ever lost in the sand could still be trapped by coral that prevented high water from washing it back into the sea.

Also, I thought of sunken ships in the offshore water and of storms that hurled objects from their wrecks onto the beach. I walked over to the edge of the coral and turned on my detector. After only a few scans, my detector sang out with a "sound of money!"

At a depth of about one foot I dug into a shelf of solid coral that had become smooth from centuries of water and sand abrasion. When I moved my hand over the coral and failed to locate a target, I reasoned that it must lie below the coral. I scanned again and heard the detector frantically signaling the presence of something large and "valuable."

Again, I dug my finger around in the hole and my fingernails caught on something that moved. I grasped the object and lifted it out of the water. It appeared at first to be just a piece of coral. Looking again as I wiped away the sand, I saw that it was a man-made object either carved or cast of metal.

The "object" proved to be a Spanish icon made of pewter, Figure 12-27. The Virgin Mary was holding the Christ Child in her arms; halo rays adorned the heads. As companions surrounded me to examine my find, I forgot to recheck the hole in my excitement. The next day, another of the group was scanning the area and he found, in the same hole, a Spanish cob dated 1692. This date, plus features of the icon, date the religious relic to a few years prior to 1700.

My study of the area obviously worked in my favor. The name Massacre Beach prompted me to pay particular attention to the site. My knowledge of wind and wave action led me to the imaginary "X."

Beaches protected from winds that cause large waves are more popular than unprotected beaches. For instance, beaches on the west coast of the United States that face south are more protected from wind and heavy surf than beaches facing west and north. Popular beaches are usually wide with fine, clean sand and feature a gradual slope into the water. Many such identifiable sections of "lost" beaches should be hunted. Not all are connected to the mainland; some are separated by lagoons and marshland. Some have been converted into bird and wildlife sanctuaries.

Around populated areas many natural beaches have been changed or have eroded as a result of land development. Breakwaters, harbor extensions, jetties and damming or otherwise diverting streams and rivers have destroyed once-popular play areas. Search out these treasure vaults and reap a harvest.

Learn from my success at finding the icon. "Reading" a site requires recognition of key features and the forces that act upon them. Going pell-mell onto a beach and hunting here and there is for beginners. You've already begun this fascinating hobby, so slow down now and do it right.

There is a right and wrong way and I hope you'll choose the correct one. As I stated in my book, SUCCESSFUL COIN HUNTING, "Start right and be successful!"

You must begin by being at the right place at the right time. I have given explicit instructions directing you to research sources that will indicate productive sites. Discussions of tides, weather, and beach selection should put you there at the right time. Now, you must develop the skill needed to "read" the site. If you learn which features are important and why, much of the battle is won.

Sharpening your skills and powers of observation are a necessary part of your training. To obtain an idea of what can be accomplished, I suggest you read one or more of my friend Tom Brown's fascinating books relating his training and experiences under the tutorship of an Apache Indian. You'll be amazed at Brown's powers of observation.

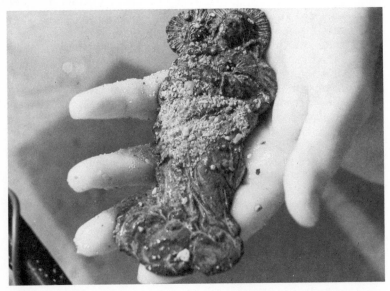

Figure 12-27: This Spanish religious icon found by the author on a beach in Guadeloupe depicts the Virgin Mary and Christ Child.

His ability to see things that others don't will astound you. While these are not treasure hunting books, per se, they will open your eyes and make you a better treasure hunter.

Some of the following is discussed elsewhere in this book. For convenience, however, let's draw upon the data one more time. The key to success is learning where treasure traps are located, then searching for them with your metal detector when covering sands are lowest. Certain features demand your attention, such as cuts, exposed shell, rock and gravel, exposed troughs, depressions, shallow pools, accumulations of jetsam, debris and driftwood, discontinuities, breaks and curves in the coastline, rock outcroppings, gulleys, sandbank cuts, exposed clay, bedrock and coral areas and other irregularities in the beach sands. Since nature is trying to help, you will do well to accept the help.

The obvious "other" places to search for beach treasure are man-made spots. Walk out on a beach and observe people at play. Watch children of all ages as they frolic. Then, when they tire of that activity, watch them scoot away. Coins fall from their pockets as they play games in the sand. Adults have their toys and games too, but they are sometimes more subtle — such as blankets and beach chairs. When people relax, Figure 12-28, down go coins and other items into the sand.

Search around trails, walkways, Figure 12-29, and boardwalks. Never pass up an opportunity to scan the base of seawalls and stone fences. People without lounge chairs often camp by these structures

Figure 12-28: Obviously, where people play, they lose things. Objects drop from pockets, from clothing, off chairs and tables and quickly sink into the loose sand. Be observant and increase the amount of treasure you find.

137

Figure 12-29: Don't overlook the possibilities of finding treasure along walkways. Scan the sandy and grassy areas to either side of paved walkways; where walkways are sandy, scan them also with your metal detector.

Figure 12-30: When you study beach areas, watch for treasure traps. In this photo there are many. Posts make excellent treasure traps as do the rocks along the sea wall. Note the trough that extends from left to right. Note, also, the waterway from the trough past the posts back into the ocean. Mark these areas for scanning to locate coins and rings that are being washed back and forth by the waves.

where they can lean back. Never fail to search around and under picnic tables and benches. Sure, you'll find lots of bottlecaps and pulltabs, but you will also discover lots of coins, toys and useful objects. Search around food stands, bath houses, shower stalls, dressing sheds, water fountains and under piers and stairs. Posts and other such obstacles are good "traps" where treasure can be found, Figure 12-30.

GRID SEARCHING

When searching a large section of beach, you should clearly define your area of search and systematically scan every square foot. There are many grid methods to use, some simple, some elaborate. The simplest, perhaps, is to guide on your previous tracks as you double back and forth. This method works if others don't destroy your tracks as fast as you make them.

Using a stick or other object you can draw squares in the sand. Work the first square completely and then draw an adjoining square and work it. Again, like the footstep method, this works if your lines and tracks don't disappear too quickly.

You can drive stakes into the ground, or just guide yourself on piers, water fountains, trees and other permanent objects.

Figure 12-31: This photo illustrates where troughs are formed. The first trough is partially filled with water. These are the low areas that place your metal detector searchcoil much closer to buried treasure. Other parallel troughs (not visible) also contain treasure. Often, lighter metals (trash) "fill" the close-in troughs while heavier metals (treasure) "fill" the troughs located farther out.

Some hunters prefer to walk a path parallel to the water. They then turn around, move about two feet away from the water and walk a return path. Others prefer to start at the high tide mark and scan down to the water. They then turn around and walk a return path about two feet to the side of the first path. This second method has more merit because you can more quickly spot a treasure belt (trough) if one exists.

You'll remember that troughs, Figure 12-31, sometimes form parallel to the waterline. There can be more than one trough a few feet wide or several hundred yards long. These troughs are "cut" areas that bring you closer to clay, gravel or bedrock where coins and jewelry accumulate.

What happens to these troughs when the tide goes out? They almost always fill with sand. You can sometimes find them if the treasure they contain is not too deep. Walk a scan pattern perpendicular to the waterline. Walk from the high tide mark to the water's edge. Each time you make a find, either remember where the find was made, or mark the location.

After you have scanned some distance down the beach and made several good finds, look back and study where you have worked. Observe the locations of your finds to determine if some pattern is developing. Most may have occurred in a narrow belt that runs parallel to the waterline. If so, you may have discovered the location of a covered trough where a storm or other wave action has created a treasure vault.

When selecting a stretch of beach on which to walk your grid pattern, try to choose one where you earlier observed a cut formed perpendicular to the waterline. Storms or high waves pouring back into the ocean form these cuts, usually at existing low points such as one formed during a previous storm. Cuts are important to you because they bring you closer to the treasure base and because coins and jewelry washing off the beach are pushed into them by the force of water drainage streams.

After reading about various searching patterns, can you see value in keeping precise logs of your treasure finds? Even with others working the same beach, it is likely that valuable patterns will emerge on the pages of your notebook. These patterns can actually show you where to look to find "hot spots." You may think that with others and yourself steadily working a particular beach, all its treasure will soon be recovered. What's the use in keeping track? You'll learn, if you continue working the same beaches year after year, that they are continually being replenished by "new" lost treasure and by "old" lost treasure that storms withdraw from deeply hidden moneybanks.

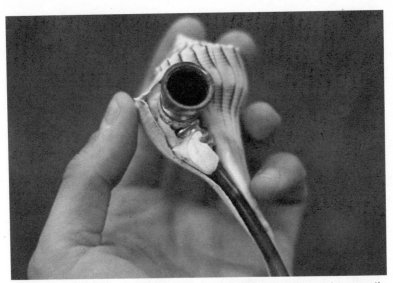

Figure 12-32: This unusual find is a pipe concealed in a shell. It was used, apparently, by a marijuana smoker who tried to conceal his smoking activity. Should someone walk near him when he was smoking, he simply turned the shell upside down and placed it on the sand, thus concealing his pipe.

Figure 12-33: These two members of the Western Australia Garrett Metal Detector Club, Vic Dimov and Rod Grayson, hold gold sovereigns and an 18-karat gold locket and chain they found while searching Western Australia's parks and beaches.

GENERAL SEARCHING SCANNING TIPS

The "eyes" of a metal detector probe deeply to spot treasure buried in the sand. Your detector scans beneath the ground untiringly and unerringly, ever alert to the presence of metal. Without a detector, your "take" would be considerably reduced. Even so, no metal detector can do it all. You must develop your powers of observation to be alert to what your detector cannot see.

Always watch for clues and for the unusual, Figure 12-32. Occasionally you'll visually find currency, marketable sea shells and other valuables. But the real value in developing keen powers of observation is that you never miss the signposts that point to detectable treasure. The rock outcropping, the gravel that is peeking through the sand, the slight depression or mound and the revealing accumulation of jetsam and debris might mark the location of a glory hole. Stay alert and be rewarded.

Do not race across the sands with your searchcoil swinging wildly in front of you. SLOW DOWN and work methodically in a pre-planned pattern. Unless you are in a hurry and want to locate only shallow, recently lost treasure, reduce your scan speed to about one foot per second. Let your searchcoil just skim the sands and keep it level

Figure 12-34: This is a closeup of a half sovereign gold coin found by Australian Vic Dimov. Photos courtesy Ted Sheehan.

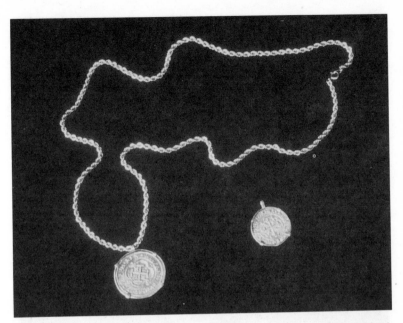

Figure 12-35: Two beautiful Spanish gold coins (escudos) are highly valued by coin collectors. Coins like the small one have sold for over $30,000, but larger ones have sold for over $60,000.

Figure 12-37: Can you believe it? But, believe it you can because it is true. This vast quantity of coins is proof that Tom Edds has mastered beach hunting techniques. He found these coins during a one-year period while searching Florida beaches.

143

throughout your entire sweep length. Overlap each sweep by advancing your searchcoil about one-half its diameter. Scan the searchcoil in a straight line. This method improves your ability to maintain correct and uniform searchcoil height, helps eliminate the "upswing" at the end of each sweep, and improves your ability to overlap in a uniform manner, thus minimizing skips. Practice this method; you'll soon come to love it.

A word is in order here about "hot rocks." If gravel is on your beach, some pieces may have the mineral content to be classified as a detectable "hot rock." A VLF detector may occasionally get a good reading on rocks and will sound off with a "metal" signal. When you detect the little pests, set your discriminating mode to "zero" rejection, switch into that mode and scan back over the spot. If it is a "hot rock," your detector will ignore it, or the sound level will decrease slightly. For further study of this phenomena, study MODERN METAL DETECTORS.

Figure 12-36: This 1882 United States gold coin and holder were located by a metal detectorist on a beach.

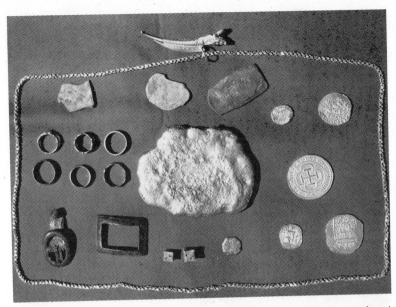

Figure 12-42: All of these items washed ashore from an offshore shipreck were found by a treasure hunter. Should you be fortunate enough to find a stretch of beach that contains gold and silver items like these, do not delay further investigation.

Don't ignore loud detector signals. Determine the cause. If it is a can or other large object, remove it and scan the spot with your detector. If you hear a VERY FAINT signal, don't ignore it. Scoop out some sand to get your searchcoil closer to the target and scan again. If you don't get a signal, check the material you scooped out—you may have detected a very small target. It might only be a BB, but at least you'll know what caused the signal. Remember, your metal detector won't lie to you; when it gives a signal, something is there, Figures 12-33 through 12-36.

If you search for 30 minutes in one location and do not locate "keepers," move to another spot. Don't become discouraged; go find treasure somewhere else, Figure 12-37.

During your search near the water's edge, when you begin detecting trash (pulltabs?) in a straight line parallel to the waterline, search for another nearby parallel trough. Remember there will sometimes be more than one trough created by the waves. The one closest to the beach may contain mostly light trash. Those farther out can contain heavier treasure items. To locate the second one, start from the trashy trough and walk out as far as you can safely go. Move over about two feet and walk back to the trash trough. Continue walking this grid and if there is a second trough within your grid, you'll find it. As explained earlier, you find it by keeping track of the location of "found" objects. A straight line pattern will develop.

When pinpointing, always be precise. Good pinpointing saves time and lessens the probability of damaging your finds when you dig.

TRASH AND THE TREASURE HUNTER

Marine debris has come of age. A committee for Texas Coastal Cleanup believes that plastic trash may be Texas' "Public Enemy No. 1." Fish and sea birds become entangled in plastic six-pack rings; sea turtles mistake floating plastic bags for jelly-fish and swallow them; sea birds peck at plastic pellets and feed them to their young. And, of course, hundreds of other items of trash are discarded on the nation's beaches every day. What can a beachcomber do about it?

Most detectorists carry out the metal trash they dig because all treasure hunters benefit from its removal. But, what about non-metallic trash? I know none of us carry trash containers around that are large enough to hold the plastic items and broken glass that can be found in only a few hours. But, let's join in by properly disposing of as much trash as possible. We not only do all beachcombers and sunworshippers a service, but we help safeguard our sea creatures and bird life as well. How about it...can't we join together and help one another?

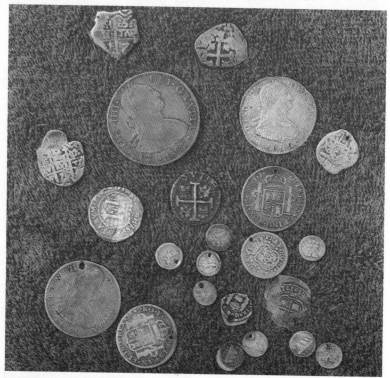

Figure 12-43: These Spanish coins dating to the mid-1700s were recovered on a beach in Key West, FL.

ADDITIONAL IDEAS ON TREASURE RETRIEVING

Various pinpointing and retrieving ideas and methods have been reviewed. Here are a couple of other suggestions that could increase your take. As part of your beach gear, consider adding a garden rake. When you encounter debris, seaweed and other materials spread over an area you want to scan, use this rake to clean it out down to the sand. Try to place raked materials where they can be picked up by beach cleaners and not washed back out to sea. Removal of any over-burden will let you scan your searchcoil closer to the ground, giving you extra depth for those deeply buried treasures.

Try exploratory trenching to locate out-of-reach troughs and glory holes. Choose a spot where you have found a concentration of good objects (not items flung from a blanket) and dig, if it's not illegal, a

Figure 12-38: You can often be of service to sunbathers by letting them borrow your instrument to look for newly lost items. This lass looks for a dropped necklace.

trench about a foot deep. This trench should be wide enough for you to insert your searchcoil in its normal scanning position. Be sure to scan the sand you dig out. The trench length can be as long as you like. If your are digging near a spot where you found several items together, determine whether you are in a natural drainage pattern. If so, dig toward the low side (in the direction water flows) because that is the direction coins and rings have been washed. If you are digging a trench to locate a trough, dig in a direction that takes you perpendicular to the "line" along which you were previously digging targets. You may have to dig several parallel trenches to locate the trough. Good luck! And...FILL YOUR TRENCHES!

MISCELLANEOUS PERSONAL TIPS

Plan your beachcombing expeditions around current (hourly) weather reports. Go prepared to withstand the worst.

Don't forget spare batteries. Make a list and review it THE DAY BEFORE you plan to make the trip. Check all gear before you leave.

Take along a friend, if possible. If you go alone, leave word where you'll be. Always carry identification that includes one or more telephone numbers of persons to call, including your personal physician.

Use caution and don't drive on unsure beaches. Carry along an extra tow rope and a shovel. You may have to dig your car some ramps if a tow vehicle isn't handy.

Search among crowds if there are no regulations to the contrary, but stay out of people's way. Angering the wrong person can result in a complaint filed against you. I'm sure you would not want to be the cause of having a beach put off lmits to metal detectorists.

As I have emphasized, pick up and properly discard all broken glass and bottles.

Return all valuable finds to their rightful owner. When someone asks you to help locate a lost item, try to oblige. Perhaps loan them your detector and teach them how to use it. You may bring another individual into the hunting fraternity, Figure 12-38. It is a good idea to have them stay right with you during the entire search. If they leave, the person might decide you found their lost item and accuse you of stealing it. That has happened. If you don't find the lost article, get the person's name and number — you might find it another day.

Use caution when you handle rings with stones. Often, mountings corrode during exposure. You wouldn't want to lose a two-carat diamond, would you? Examine jewelry with a pocket magnifier. If a stone is loose or the mounting has corroded, keep that ring in a container or at least wrap it to prevent the stone (or stones) from being lost.

We have mentioned your powers of observation. Occasionally scan or just walk along the waterline and observe the sands under the water. You may spot a coin shining in the water. Check the spot with your detector. It may only be a freshly dropped coin, or it could be the top layer of a glory hole.

148

Figure 12-41: Along a given stretch of a Florida beach, Robert Marx found these relics which indicate, in all probability, that a shipwreck lies just offshore.

Figure 12-44: This dry sand sifter built from plans printed in Warren Merkitch's THE BEACHCOMBER'S HAND BOOK is called the Amazing Money Machine. After many years of work he perfected this man-powered beach sifter and recovered many thousands of coins, rings and jewelry items and other miscellaneous lost things.

Learn what stinging jellyfish look like. During high water they often wash ashore and become stranded. Their tentacles can "sting" for many hours after the creature dies.

SPECIALIZED HUNTING

Be ever on the alert for "sea stories" and legends. Don't dismiss rumors of discoveries...some of them may be true. A major concern when you get active in such specialized areas as legend-tracking, Figures 12-39 and 12-40, is to locate the precise spot where rumors report that treasure was found. Beaches run for miles; they can can become severely eroded and they can become covered with mountains of sand brought in from the nearby surf. Spend time investigating these stories. Check with the newspapers, police records, historical societies and local coin

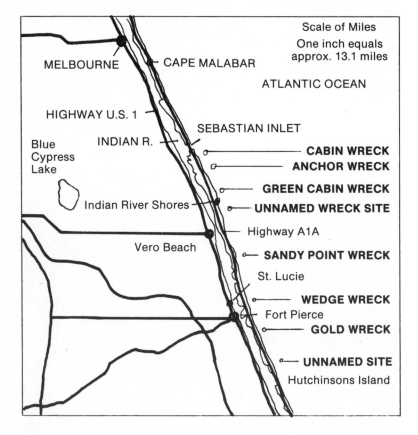

Figure 12-39: A 1715 hurricane drove a Spanish Armada into the Florida mainland. As a result shipwreck remains lie profusely along an area north and south of Fort Pierce. This map shows rough location of numerous of these and other shipwrecks. Fortunes have been found on the beach and in the water along this stretch. While the beach areas are mostly open to treasure hunters, some water areas have been claimed by Mel Fisher.

Figure 12-40: Robert Marx, while not diving, often strolls along the beach with his detector. Here he displays a few coins he found. You will note the coins have a varied amount of corrosion and tarnish. He is using a hip-mounted Garrett Sea Hunter detector.

shops. Uncover sufficient information to PROVE beyond doubt that the facts are correct. Then, you can pursue the tale knowing you are not searching for something that does not exist. And, when you locate unusual treasures such as those shown in Figures 12-41, through 12-43, don't put off investigating further. You may have just located a rich treasure ship!

THE AMAZING MONEY MACHINE

Warren Merkitch named his dry sifter the Amazing Money Machine, Figure 12-44. Many years ago he perfected a man-powered beach sands sifter and wrote a book describing the need for such a device, including detailed construction plans. Famed treasure hunter Karl Von Mueller, who owns Exanimo Press, Segundo, CO, 81070, prints and distributes Warren's book which is entitled the BEACHCOMBER'S HANDBOOK. The book, which you can obtain by sending $5 to Karl, is interesting and well-written, authored by a man who knows what he is talking about. One reading will reward you with many beach hunting tips, any one of which is well worth the low cost. The construction plans and operating instructions alone should sell for much more. The device is a sort of reverse lawnmower sifter that lets you "clean" a wide strip of sand and recover all metal and non-metal objects down to several inches depth. You pull the device through the sand. The rear section rolls on wheels while a front-mounted blade cuts through the sand. A built-in wire sifter lets sand and small objects pass on through, but traps larger objects.

The device can be used on dry sands and in water where the bottom is loose sand. It finds lost treasure and collects shells and even edibles. I saw one being used in an Italian surf to locate edible mollusks. I didn't ask the fellow if he also found treasure, but I am sure he did. In fact, I suspect mollusk hunting was only a sideline.

CHAPTER 13

Where and How to Search the Surf

There is a place...a treasure hunting place...an "all-weather vault"... where the treasure hunter can do his or her best any day...spring, summer, winter or fall. For the knowledgeable hunter, this place consistently produces the best treasures.

I am speaking, of course, of the surf...one of the "hottest" and newest treasure hunting locations. What exactly is surf hunting? Where does "beach hunting" end and surf hunting begin?

Visualize, if you will, the seashore divided into three sections or "zones," Figure 13-1. Zone One is the actual sandy beach — the picnic, sunbathing, and rollicking area between parking lot and water. Zone Three is the deep water expanse stretching out as far as the eye can see — strictly scuba diving territory.

Zone Two, our area of interest, our treasure vault — the area between Zones One and Three — is the shallow surf, from the foamy edge of the water to a depth of five feet or more. That's where treasure is kept — coins, jewelry, diamond rings, gold chains, gold and silver religious medallions and crucifixes. And, most amazing of all, access to this vault is free — free to you and free to me. Here's where you should stake your claim. I've staked mine there, Figure 13-2.

Other successful THers who have staked such a claim don't converse like ordinary coin hunters. When greeting a friend, they don't say, "Hey, I found ten silver coins today!" Instead, they say, "Hey, today's take was ten gold rings!" See Figure 13-3. They don't discuss their treasure in terms of silver ounces; they calculate it in pounds of gold. They keep their finds sorted in large containers.

Experienced treasure hunters know that surf hunting offers rich rewards. There are millions of coins and items of jewelry "stored" in the surf's treasure vault. Where people have been, that's where you'll find this treasure; it can't be any easier than that. Try this test. Visit a local park on any warm, pleasant spring or summer day. Count the people you see, Figure 13-4. How many did you count? Maybe 50? Now, drive to the local swimming beach. Count the people you see. How many did you count? Probably 50 plus several hundred more! Hundreds more who may lose valuable treasure.

Walk the beach and count the rings, necklaces, bracelets, ankle charms and other valuables you see the bathers wearing, Figure 13-5. How many are using tanning oil that makes fingers so slick that rings threaten to fall off momentarily? How many young people are horse playing or tossing a frisbee? Their rings and necklaces are likely to be jerked loose any moment, Figures 13-6 though 13-9. How many swim-

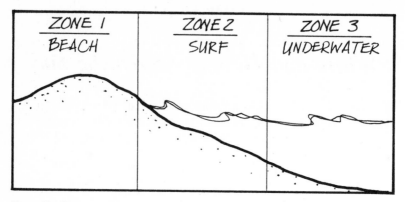

Figure 13-1: This is an illustration of the seashore divided into the three sections or "zones" where treasure can be found. Zone 1 is the sandy beach; Zone 2 is the shallow surf; Zone 3 is the deep water expanse — scuba diving territory.

Figure 13-3: If we could see Jack Lowry's face he would be smiling broadly. Here he gives us a glimpse of some of the rings that he has discovered while searching swimming areas and the ocean's surf. Photo courtesy Mel Climer.

Figure 13-2: What a delight it is to travel to faraway places and enjoy the rewards of searching white sandy beaches and the beautiful blue shallow surf.

mers carry their "hot dog" coins in their anything-but-safe bathing suit pockets?

You can be sure treasure will be lost at that beach every day. And, I don't mean "cheap" treasure either. People consistently wear expensive jewelry while swimming. They either forget they have it on, or they don't understand how they could lose it. But, lose it they will — by the buckets and barrels full.

That's one of the truly neat things about surfing: the supply of coins and jewelry is constantly being replenished. If you could somehow locate every lost item in any given surf (which, of course, you can't), next year the treasure vault would be "filled" again. Actually, you won't have to wait a year. Wait until the day following a storm and then try your luck. You'll be amazed how much you'll find that nature has brought up from the depths and deposited in your private treasure vault.

How much surf treasure can you find? In Chapter 3 you met several surf hunters who keep finding enough to come back for more. You met those who have given up all other forms of treasure hunting to devote their full time to surfing. How much you find is up to you. Learn to use your equipment; do your research and be persistent; you won't be disappointed.

Perhaps you have read the two WALK ACROSS AMERICA BOOKS by Peter and Barbara Jenkins. Their adventures were fascinating, weren't they? Well, I received a call from a detectorist who was setting forth on what I believe to be an equally fascinating but different sort of adventure. He was planning to walk across America and pay his way by surf and beach hunting at every location he came to. You know what? I believe he'll make it and he won't go hungry. He will find more treasure than he'll need.

In addition to the monetary aspects, other rewards come from this activity. You can't help but be healthier at the end of a long and vigorous surf-hunting season. I always feel terrific following even a single day in the surf. I have spent weeks searching several Caribbean swimming beach surfs. Following a day's hunting of six to eight hours, all I need to be refreshed and ready for the next day is a hot shower, a great meal and a good night's sleep.

You don't fatigue as much when you work surf as compared with working land sites. Especially is this true during hot, 100-degree summer days, provided you take care of yourself. In this and other chapters you'll learn my secrets of getting along in the elements.

The surf holds much less competition than you'll find on land. The ratio of water hunters to land hunters is easily 100 to 1. It's nice when there is little competition, Figure 13-14. Of course, water hunting requires a few more skills and there are dangers you won't find on land such as stinging jellyfish. But, about the only way you'll ever get tangled up with one of those fellows is to work with your eyes shut. There are other dangers and I have discussed them in Chapter 28.

You'll have to learn how to retrieve your finds in three feet of water using a long-handled scoop, Figure 13-15. At first, you'll feel foolish, especially when you make, perhaps, 10 tries before you final-

Figure 13-4: Can you count the people on this beach? There are easily more than a thousand and they are all potential losers of treasure. Such a crowd will easily lose hundreds of coins, rings, jewelry items and other treasures each day.

Figure 13-5: A treasure hunter sent this photo to the Garrett factory with a caption on the back reading, "Collection of coins, rings and jewelry found by one detector addict in one summer along the shorelines of Delaware."

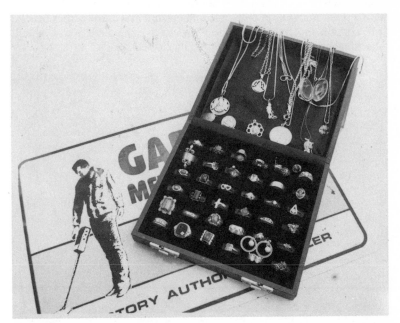

Figure 13-9: Our thanks to Mr. and Mrs. Bill Leclair of Massachusetts for permitting us to photograph a few of their valuable finds. These recoveries were made in swimming areas. They have developed efficient recovery methods, even their own scoop.

ly come up with your first water treasure. But, believe me, it soon becomes very easy.

You'll have good days, then bad days when you won't find enough to brag about. Maintain your enthusiasm anyway. Everyone has bad days, so don't sulk over your "poor luck," but, instead, turn your defeat into constructive planning.

Make up your mind that you'll do a better job of research the next time you are looking for that really special beach. Stop and review your situation: analyze your site, your timing, and your search methods. And, don't forget, bad days make the good days seem even better!

Well, are you ready to give water hunting a try? If you are tired of those dull everyday park finds, try going after gold in the surf!

RESEARCH

The most imprtant advice I can give you may very well be not to neglect your research! The one thing, the major thing, that separates successful treasure hunters from mediocre treasure hunters is research. Research is the key to locating the "hot" productive sites that really pay off in old and valuable coins and jewelry. Did you know that through research you can locate beaches most likely to yield high school and college class rings? Through research you can locate the beaches with mostly inexpensive jewelry and other beaches with the most expensive jewelry, Figure 13-16. Some beaches, you can learn, will contain a predominance of silver medallions and crucifixes. Other beaches will contain mostly gold religious pieces. All this data is available to the diligent researcher who takes time to learn.

Figure 13-6: This outstandingly beautiful man's diamond cluster ring was found in the ocean surf; the finder is unknown.

Figure 13-7: Jim and Ruby Ironside of Ayr, Canada, proudly display some of the beautiful rings they have found while working beaches and swimming areas. What a lovely collection it is! Jim and Ruby can be mightly proud of their efforts.

Figure 13-10: Surf hunters are continually amazed at the expensive jewelry that they find. Sunbathers consistently lose their treasure in the shallow surfs. Photo courtesy Don Cyr.

Figure 13-16: Through research you will be able to locate beaches with mostly expensive jewelry. Surprisingly, valuable jewelry items and lots of large denomination coins are found at this Caribbean nude beach site.

Did you know that some treasure hunters plan where they will be hunting one, two or even five years in the future? They know where they are going next, and they allow plenty of time while there. Should their present site prove unproductive, they have alternate sites nearby. They keep meticulous records concerning site location, time of year, water conditions and the quantity, quality and location of their valuable finds. They live with their log as though it were a Bible. They correlate one site's data with that of another and plan their trips accordingly. They return to some sites regularly and to some only once a year. The smart researchers make it their business to know which beaches high school and college students visit and when. They know when young people go there, not only during regular swimming and sunbathing times, but also during their special parties. They know that rich folks and the not-so-rich folks have their own preferred beaches. In areas predominantly Catholic, knowledgeable hunters know they will find religious jewelry. From ethnic studies, they know which beaches will produce mostly silver pieces and which sites the far more valuable gold pieces. From their studies, they know where the old, the really old, beaches are. That's where they go in search of valuable antique jewelry often worth the most when "sell" time comes.

I suggest you reread Chapter 4, especially the sections on Research Souces where I list and describe the "where" of hunting, such as newspapers, libraries, historical societies, the Department of Parks and Recreation and others. During your research of these sources you should specifically study the newspaper's recreational and lost and found advertisements. At historical societies you'll review area histories, photographs and postcards. At the Parks and Recreation Department, you'll ask for both new and old maps that locate long forgotten communities and public gathering places.

Figure 13-11: Here is another beautiful necklace found by Don Cyr. He mostly works in the water. He has found that it pays rich dividends.

Figure 13-15: Jack Lowry searches a Texas coastline. It was cold that day; you can tell from Jack's gear, a two-piece plastic suit, and waders.

Figure 13-12: Here are some beautiful items found by a Canadian surf hunter. Our thanks to Keith and Mary Edwards for supplying this photo.

Figure 13-13: It is obvious, that the Canadians who own this treasure spend a lot of time searching the water.

As for who to ask, start with fishermen, oldtimers and even "newtimers," the youngsters who may frequent the old out-of-the-way and often forbidden sites. And, speaking of newtimers, why not start with yourself? Ask yourself where you swam when you were young. I can remember five such places where my pals and I swam back during our growing-up days. One place is now an off-limits State Park; another is covered by asphalt; the third place is on restricted private property; the fourth I've worked, and the fifth, well...I am thinking about it. I've done some research. In fact, just today, I was told it is still being used. Not only that, but I learned from the same source where the site of a turn-of-the-century community is located with the exact spot pinpointed where the general store was standing. Maybe, just maybe, I can keep myself at this typewriter long enough to complete this book before I head south, down into Deep East Texas.

CLOTHING AND EQUIPMENT

Chapter 27 describes the kinds of clothing and gear you'll need for various weather and wading conditions you'll encounter. As your experience grows, you will accumulate your own preferred wardrobe. In cold weather, your clothing and gear should keep you warm, dry and comfortable. One exception is that while a neoprene wet suit won't keep you dry, it will keep you warm, very warm. If you don't care for the initial plunge into cold water, first pour warm water into the suit.

The type equipment you need depends upon whether you work shallow surf or deep-water surf. Shallow surf is defined as water depth that permits you to dig with your hands, a hand scoop, or a tool...in other words, at arm's length. Deep water surfing is hunting in depths of about five feet, or the maximum depth you can safely work.

The choice of retrieving tools depends upon soil conditions and your preferences. In sandy areas, a scoop is fast. If the soil is muddy or hardened clay, you will need some kind of digger. In deep water, a long-handled scoop is required to retrieve your finds. During moderately cold water searches, hip or chest-high waders and suitable underclothing will keep you warm and dry. When wearing waders be alert or else you may bend too far and, suddenly, you've got "convertible" gear: Your waders have been converted to a wet suit! The wearing of a waist or chest belt over waders might reduce the amount of water that comes in. Whatever type pouch (or pouches) you use, they must close and fasten tightly. Water-hunting treasure pouches must have a secure flap covering. Some surfers use a sturdy open-weave bag or pouch with zipper or drawstring. Whatever equipment your ingenuity comes up with, keep it in good shape. Don't lose valuables through holes! It's a good idea to have several pockets that let you separate treasure and trash. But, whatever you do, never discard trash without carefully examining every piece. You may have inadvertently placed a good find into the trash pocket. Also, that item that looked so corroded and unrecognizable may turn out to be a valuable object. When

Figure 13-8: And here is another photograph of another set of rings found by Jim and Ruby Ironside of Ayr, Canada. It is obvious that these folks have mastered their metal detector and the correct techniques of treasure hunting.

Figure 13-17: The tide is dropping and the beach sands are moving outward, providing the beach hunter and surf hunter more elbow room and space where treasure can be found.

in doubt about any find, examine it thoroughly, even placing it in an electrolytic bath for cleaning.

In warm weather your clothing should keep you decent yet protected from the sun's rays and other dangers such as sharp rocks, coral and stinging jellyfish. In shallow water you can stand and work or snorkel as you float. In deeper water you'll need a long-handled scoop unless you prefer scuba gear or a floating compressor hooka like Brownie's Third Lung. In strong breaker areas a floating hooka compressor is tricky to use. It's best used in a lake or other calm water areas.

You might try free diving. Others have, and prefer it. Surfers have learned to hold their breath for as long as three minutes. They swim along underwater, scanning with their detector and retrieving objects with their hand or a small tool. Then they pop up, take a breath and go back down to continue hunting. It sounds efficient, but requires experience to learn to fully conserve energy and get the most out of each breath. This method has some risk, however, and I do not recommend it.

Two amusing incidents were related to me by a fellow surfer who prefers to free dive when the conditions are right. Once, when he popped to the surface for air, he emerged in the midst of several youngsters. One frightened youth managed to stammer, "Wh..wh..what are you

Figure 13-14: This lone surf hunter has it all to himself. He probably enjoys it that way. Photos courtesy Monty Moncrief.

165

doing here?" My friend used his best and coarsest monster-of-the-deep voice to answer, "This is my home; what are you doing here?" Then he quickly submerged and swam away. Needless to say, he had the surf mostly to himself the remainder of that day.

Once when he was searching the bottom someone stepped on him and quickly jumped back, then cautiously touched the motionless body several times with his foot. Suddenly, there was a wild commotion; people began scrambling toward shore. He again had things to himself until a rescue squad came and began dragging for the "body."

Free diving is not for the fainthearted. It requires deep concentration, a will of iron and good swimming ability. Some say there is the likelihood of blacking out. Free divers do not venture beyond neck depth, but there is the possibility of unknowingly moving into deep water. A good swimmer would have no difficulty, but in case of an emergency, it could become a problem. Free divers wear goggles or a mask, swim fins, and a snorkel.

Some surfers use a flotation screen; others do not. If you use a converted land metal detector, you'll need a flotation device unless you mount the detector control housing on your body, or on the end of a very long searchcoil stem. The flotation device, of which there are several designs, is constructed with a one-half inch sturdy chicken wire screen. The screen opening should not allow a U.S. dime to pass through diagonally. If you are searching for smaller objects, the screen opening should be smaller. If your flotation device is large or contains your detector's control housing, the screen portion should hinge to permit rapid dumping of accumulated trash. The float can have recesses for the detector, a water bottle, your lunch and, perhaps, an extra tool or other necessity. Select a tube from the various automobile, motorcycle or bicycle sizes available. Since you are not supporting much weight, the tube does not have to be highway bus or truck size. You should position the screen so that its bottom surface is about one or two inches below the water line. This facilitates quick washing of debris, mud and sand. In fact, when you dump several scoops into a well-designed flotation device, surf action should quickly clean the material.

Some hunters have said they prefer to place several scoops of dug material into their screen before they examine its contents and retrieve their finds. This can be efficient if you use a zippered bag which takes extra time to open and close each time you store a find. If the bottom is heavy silt and mud, it might be quicker to dissolve and inspect a large amount of soil rather than stir through your smaller retrieving scoop each time you make a dig.

An innertube can be punctured accidentally. This is a problem only if your detector housing is mounted on the float. Even then, I think you would hear the air escaping and you could rescue the detector before it gets a bath. Also, the detector has no protection from rain or water splashed by swimmers.

When I work loose sandy bottom sites, I do not use a floating screen. As I start up with the scoop filled with sand and other bottom objects, I immediately begin shaking the scoop. By the time I have it up to the water's surface, most, if not all, the sand has already fallen through the holes.

I don't recommend a land detector for working deep water. In fact, I don't recommend using a land detector for any extended water hunting. It is too easy to become momentarily lax and forget that your detector needs constant supervision. It happened to me once when I was working the water's edge on a Cozumel beach. Because it was dry where I was working, I wasn't paying strict attention to the wave action. I stopped scanning to dig an object and without noticing, I placed the detector down too near the water. A high wave gave my control housing a good bath and ended all searching for the day with that detector.

You must tether a float to yourself or you'll lose it. According to Murphy's infallible Law, the first time you turn your back on an untethered float, it will head straight out to sea. I consider having to manipulate a detector and a long-handled scoop problem enough. Plus, it is not practical to use a float in surf areas when the waves are high. It will be constantly banging into you. And, it will never be where you want it when you need it.

In using a large open-basket screen, you invite thievery. Some individuals are naturally tempted when they see valuables laying in an open screen. A friend, Carl Ratigan, and I were working a Guadeloupe surf. Several boys gathered to watch. Carl brought up a scoop that contained what he described as "The most beautiful and valuable gold medallion of the week!" A boy reached into the scoop, grabbed the medallion and swam away.

Some have suggested constructing floats completely of non-metallic materials. They say that if you want to make sure no mud balls and other encrustation conceals treasure, you can scan the contents with your detector. While that has some merit, it is not the most efficient method. You should hand investigate and scan every strange item you discover. And, as I have said, take every "unknown" object home for closer scrutiny.

Your scoop and all other retrieving tools should be ruggedly constructed. You will be putting a lot of force on your scoop each time you make a dig. A plastic scoop may not stand up under the strain. The upper end of the handle should have a screw, lanyard, paint stripe or other marker to tell you at a glance where the scoop opening is located. A looped handle, which is the configuration I prefer, should be curved backward so that you don't have to lean too far forward to tilt the scoop into the required vertical position for proper digging. When you push the handle forward to position the scoop vertically, your hand will be about midway or lower down the handle. Then, you begin your backward pull while sliding your hand upward. You'll also rotate the handle to free the scoop from the muck. As you bring the handle backwards, you'll slide your hand over to the front section and grasp the handle as low down as possible. You then pull the scoop free of the bottom. The low position of your hand on the forward mounted handle section keeps the open end of the scoop in the upward position. Shake the scoop as you bring it up to remove sand and small debris.

Alden Fogliadini is a very successful water hunter. I have worked with him in the Caribbean and witnessed his phenomenal surf finds. A scoop which he manufactures and sells resulted from careful thought and much water retrieving experience. Stainless steel construction allows it to be disassembled for ease in packing and transportation. Also, it has three handle lengths. The mid-size handle lets you use it effectively without bending over when you work on the beach or in shallow water. The shortest handle converts it into a lightweight and sturdy hand scoop for shallow water and dry sand sifting. Next to your metal detector, the scoop is your most important tool. Select and use a well-designed, sturdy one for the highest efficiency. Alden's address and photos of his scoop can be found in Chapter 24.

SELECTION OF A SURFING METAL DETECTOR

Chapters 5 through 11 contain discussions about every aspect involved in the selection of the proper metal detector. As mentioned several times, a land detector can be used for surf hunting, but extra length searchcoil cables are necessary. Some manufacturers offer submersible searchcoils with nine-foot-long cables. Extension cables are available, but some means are needed to waterproof the connector, which is discussed in Chapter 24. The Beach Connection device will keep water out of cable connectors.

When you use a land detector in the surf, you must prevent the control housing from getting wet. Ingenious hunters have devised various effective waterproofing methods. One built a shoulder platform that keeps his detector not only high and dry, but also places the speaker near his ear should he not want to use headphones. Another hunter installed his electronics and controls in a construction worker's hat. I have seen photos of this device and it appears quite functional.

If you doubt whether your searchcoil is waterproof, ask your metal detector dealer or manufacturer. Not all searchcoils can be safely submerged. There are three designations you should become familiar with: splashproof, waterproof and submersible. Splashproof means the searchcoil can safely be used in wet grass and weeds. Waterproof means the searchcoil can safely be used in heavy rain. Submersible means the searchcoil can be safely submerged in water to the cable connector. In terms of depth, submersion is about 30 inches. To insure a searchcoil's water tightness, apply a bead of silicone rubber around the cable where it comes out of the searchcoil.

Figure 13-23: This beautiful 10-karat gold tiger-eye ring was found in the water by Canadian Don Cyr.

Most land searchcoils are buoyant. You must add weight to give the searchcoil either neutral or slightly negative buoyancy. A sand bag or a brick can be attached to the top of your searchcoil, and some hunters pour specially shaped weights using cement. Others attach lead weights to the stem. To keep from adding extra drag, lead can be poured into the lower stem. Keep lead or other metals at least eight inches above the searchcoil. A weight of from about one to three pounds is usually necessary. I perfer that my detector float somewhat vertically so that the searchcoil "bobbles" near the bottom. This keeps the handle near by. When I have recovered my find, I need only to reach over and take hold of the detector handle and continue my search. Some users recommend letting the stem and searchcoil float on the surface. This involves extra work and effort because you have to reach up to grab the handle and then force the searchcoil down to the bottom. To achieve the proper "float" and angle, it may be necessary to add buoyancy material such as cork or styrofoam to the upper end of the stem. Tape the cable to the stem at a point near the searchcoil to prevent it from snagging on objects.

No land detector can be as efficient as a submersible detector designed to be used in the water. There are submersible models such as the Garrett Beach Hunter AT3 and the Sea Hunter XL500 that were designed specifically for underwater work. Their design prevents water from seeping into the control housing and searchcoils. Both land (non-submersible) and underwater headphones are available for both models.

Your choice of a surfer model should be either an automated VLF model or a Pulse Induction type. The Garrett AT3 features automated VLF circuitry with a unique Dual Ferrous/Non-Ferrous Multi-Range Discrimination circuit. This circuit, described in Chapter 9, lets you select the metal objects you want to recover and rejects those you don't. You can accept most rings while rejecting pulltabs. Automated VLF circuitry needs no ground adjusting. The circuitry ignores black sand, iron earth minerals and salt water — automatically. This type detector and the Pulse Induction are the easiest to use. You simply turn on the power and adjust the audio for silent running or slight threshold.

True Pulse Induction instruments automatically ignore iron earth minerals and salt water. Some models feature the ability to reject such trash items as bottle caps and aluminum pulltabs. Elongated iron objects such as small nails and ladies' hairpins will be accepted, however, and some rings will be lost when the detector is adjusted to reject aluminum pulltabs.

Figure 13-19: These beautiful, and very valuable, late 17th century Spanish cobs were found by Carl Mathias in the surf at the site of a Spanish shipwreck.

DISCRIMINATION CHARACTERISTICS

Treasure hunting literature is filled with, perhaps, more "information and recommendations" about discrimination then any other subject. Some say discriminating metal detectors are practically worthless in the water; others swear by them. Actually, there are no "rules" when it comes to target discrimination. Let's review the merits of discrimination; you can make up your own mind.

Discrimination is fully discussed in Chapters 5 through 11; we are now looking at discrimination as it specifically relates to water hunting. As you probably know, discrimination is simply a term that detectorists use when discussing certain characteristics or capabilities of metal detectors. Metal detectors will detect the presence of all types of metal because that is the main purpose of metal detection. There are many metal objects present in ocean surf that are of no value to most hunters, namely bottlecaps, pulltabs and other man-made trash. Since the main purpose of most water hunting is the recovery of coins and jewelry, time is wasted when "junk" items are dug. Manufacturers have devised various detection methods (circuits) to measure and compare a target's conductivity with a predetermined value. Fortunately, most good targets have higher conductivities than trash targets. Trash, or low conductivity targets, read as "bad" or "reject." Gold, silver and copper have high conductivities.

The shape and mass of good targets sometimes cause difficulty. Rings are circular but, unfortunately, so are aluminum pulltabs. Since aluminum is a relatively high valued conductor, some rings and pulltabs LOOK THE SAME TO METAL DETECTORS. For decades treasure hunters dug many worthless targets to get rings. Detectors with discriminating circuitry such as the Garrett AT3 are designed to indicate with 75 to 85% accuracy, the difference between most rings and pulltabs. That accuracy level is *acceptable* to most hunters.

When a detector makes a decision about the conductivity of detected metal, it evaluates the combined conductivity of ALL metal objects within the field of detection. If, say, a high conductivity ring and a low conductivity bottlecap are lying in close proximity to each other, the detector reads their combined conductivity which will be lower than that of the ring. The detector may then read the detected "target" as "junk." That's why some hunters say discriminating metal detectors are no good for water hunting. They say they dig all targets, or they have developed a "system" for discriminating that lets them dig mostly good targets. They say that strong detector signals mean that the detected target is shallow and, therefore, it must be junk. They tell you to dig only weak target signals. Also, they tell you to ignore double "blip" signals which mean the detector has just detected a nail or a similarly shaped iron object.

The application of such theories may not improve your treasure/trash ratio any more than using a small amount of discrimination or one of the pulltab-reject detectors. All loud signals may not be junk targets. Often, water hunters dig shallow treasure that has just been lost or that a recent storm brought up from the deep. Also, a junk object standing on edge may produce a weak signal. Any experienced hunter will tell you that a ring or a coin standing on edge can produce a double "blip."

This is my recommendation: Purchase a surfing detector with discrimination; you can always turn the discrimination off. Then, when you want to use it, turn it back on. In some trashy areas with small iron targets, a slight amount of discrimination will avoid much of the trash and sacrifice little, if any, treasure. Since you will at least spend more time digging better targets, this may swing the balance in your favor. Also, pulltab rejection detectors let you spend more time digging for better targets. Yes, you probably will miss a ring or two. So, obviously the decision is yours. I urge you to experiment. Use various degrees of discrimination and keep a record of your finds. Also, thoroughly work an area using pulltab rejection. Then rework the same area using no discrimination. Compare the results. Keep in mind, however, that since an area can never be fully worked, your comparisons will never be 100% accurate.

When I discuss pulltab rejection, I refer to discriminating detectors that permit specifically selected objects to be rejected or accepted. The Garrett AT3 is one such model. Discriminating detectors that do not have this selection feature will reject a larger percentage of rings

Figure 13-26: Here are more of Don Cyr's valuable finds made in Canada's swimming areas. Don is primarily a water hunter.

when pulltab discrimination is dialed in. So, be knowledgeable in your decision-making. It is not complicated; study the earlier chapters and question your dealer or manufacturer until you fully understand how detectors work.

Additional thoughts on the use of discrimination: Some hunters, who use discriminating detectors, will find it very difficult and frustrating to work heavy trash areas. Some even refuse to work areas with a great deal of trash, preferring more productive sites. I recommend that you not avoid these locations with trash. Start by using only enough discrimination to reject small, rusty iron pieces. If you are still digging an overwhelming amount of trash, dial in more rejection. You may find an adjustment that lets you recover a fair share of good targets without digging too much junk. Also, use a smaller diameter searchcoil. Three to four-inch diameter searchcoils are known for their efficiency in junky areas.

Some hunters will tell you not to use discrimination because you will lose silver and gold chains. It's not just discrimination that causes these items to be lost; it is also that form factor. As you have already learned, eddy currents must be generated on the surface of metal for the object to be detected. Since chains have a tiny surface compared with their mass, these items present a poor target for detection. Consequently, you will locate about as many chains using a normal amount of discrimination as you will if you don't use any—especially if the gold or silver content is high. Start your training period using no discrimination. Pay attention to all signals. Especially learn the difference between bell-tone (if your detector has this capability) and regular sounds. Dig all targets and remember their signals. Gradually work with increasing discrimination until you are confident of the full capabilities of your instrument. Evaluate every new site; no two are alike. Your efficiency will improve in proportion to your expertise. The following discussion includes another method for successfully working high trash sites.

SEARCHCOILS

Metal detectors are normally equipped with an optimum size searchcoil for general purpose searching. For water hunting this size is between seven and nine inches in diameter. Smaller and larger searchcoils are available for some models. Smaller diameter searchcoils in the three to four-inch range are very efficient in heavy trash areas. Not only do they allow precise pinpointing but your discriminating capabilities will increase since fewer targets can be beneath the searchcoil at any given instant. Consequently, fewer good targets will be rejected. Larger searchcoils give greater depth, especially on larger objects, but pinpointing is more difficult. Also, in heavy trash areas signals will be more erratic and discrimination may be worsened.

If your searchcoil is not light colored, you may want to paint it with a non-metallic white or yellow paint. Its visibility will be enhanced. Purchase skidplates for all your searchcoils. Considerable sand abrasion can occur under the water. A skidplate prevents holes being worn in your searchcoil's plastic bottom and edges.

TIDES AND WEATHER

A section on "Tides and Weather" in Chapter 12 explains the cause and effect of tides and how they can aid the beach hunter. Low tides may be your most productive times since you can work farther out into the surf, Figure 13-17. Don't forget that swimmers also follow the tides out and take with them jewelry and coins to lose. When extra low tides occur, you may be able to work around platforms and other structures that you couldn't reach before, Figure 13-18. Around such play areas can be found an abundance of lost items.

Beach hunters know that stormy seasons aid in recovery of older and deeper finds. Winds and churning waves wash sand off the beach and deposit it in offshore bars. As sand is washed off, the beach hunter gets closer to the older treasure. Veteran hunters never pass an opportunity to work a cut or a pool of water. They know as they get closer to clay, gravel and bedrock, their chances improve. If you are only an occasional beach hunter, remember, remember and remember to

Figure 13-18: The water line along this stretch of Texas beach has receded quite a distance during low tide. As it receded it began to expose various rocks and obstacles where treasure can be trapped.

work all cuts and exposed areas immediately. Don't wait until tomorrow or a better time. Most likely, when you return, even if only an hour or two has passed, the cut or wash may be filled. Even embankments formed in the morning can disappear by evening.

Stormy seasons affect surf hunting because offshore sand deposits increase the distance to treasure. So, if your beach hunting buddy reports a heyday during stormy seasons, your day as a surf hunter is coming during the calm seasons when more gentle waves and winds return sand back to the beach. Be particularly on the lookout for troughs. Wave action, wind magnitude and direction and water depth combine to dig troughs that generally run parallel to the beach. These troughs are simply long low areas that range in width from a few inches to several feet and can run for hundreds of feet parallel to the beach. They can form near the water's edge as well as much farther out. Troughs are important because they are actually areas of reduced sand buildup.

Figure 13-20: Every chance you get, study the action of ocean waves and currents. Watch particularly for currents flowing outward as they are along the right side of this photograph. If you cannot discern water motion and there is no floating debris, pitch pieces of wood into the surf and watch their motion.

In other words, in troughs you can get closer to the treasure you are seeking. Some troughs extend down to clay. When you find these deep ones, you can sometimes spot treasure by eyesight.

Occasionally, you may find a glory hole that contains numerous coins, rings and other jewelry items as well as other heavy debris, Figure 13-19. At these spots and wherever you find treasure concentrations, work the entire area for several feet around. It may pay you to work your instrument here using a larger searchcoil. You'll get greater depth on a mass of metal. In fact, it may pay you occasionally to work the surf with these deeper seeking searchcoils. You may detect rich deposits that could not be reached with smaller diameter searchcoils. Watch continually for coral growth and bedrock areas. Treasure can become trapped in holes, cracks and low spots, as well as along the beachside edges of such material.

To study the effect of wind, waves and storms upon the beach and shallow surf, I encourage you to read WAVES AND BEACHES by Willard Bascom. He makes a complex subject very interesting. Bascom has also written another fascinating book, DEEPWATER, ANCIENT SHIPS. He tells how ancient, wooden ships that have sunk to great depths can be found in near-perfect states of preservation and how these ships can be raised.

LOCATING THE BEST PLACES

How do you know where to enter the surf to begin your search? Such ability generally comes with experience. Keep track of where you find the most treasure and always head there first. But, observe where swimmers spend their time. Where people play, that's where they lose things. Generally, you'll do better in areas that are enclosed. People generally do not play outside these enclosures. Of course, remember that where people are swimming today may not be where they swam decades ago. Also remember that treasure can "move" out of these areas. I always make finds near and around boundary chain or rope supports, floats, diving platforms and other permanent objects that protrude above the water level. Search protected areas, especially those enclosed by jetties and rock walls. These obstructions force people to stay generally within confined areas. Search in swimming areas of inlets and coves. They usually feature calm sea with reduced wave action. My experience has been that people don't like to swim in rough surf or where prevailing winds continually blow. Also, the violent action of the elements generally removes treasure from such places.

Watch where professionals work. Try to determine why they work where they do. If you ask, however, you may not get a straight answer.

Observe the surf during high wave and storm action. Watch where perpendicular currents are flowing outward, Figure 13-20. If there is no debris floating on the surface, pitch pieces of driftwood into the surf and watch their motion. Water, piled up on the beach due to wave, breaker and wind action, tends to flow outward in narrow perpendicular channels which are generally calmer then the wave areas. Treasure more likely will settle in these calmer areas then in areas of heavy wave action.

Work far out during low tide. Work along a path parallel to the shore in water as deep as you can. Then, move in with the tide. Keep alert for sudden, rapid, incoming tides.

BOTTOM CONDITIONS

When you find a clay bottom, shout for joy. Even very heavy objects have difficulty in sinking through clay and other hard packed soils. However, over a long period of time, the sandy bottom of an unused swimming area that has little agitation from waves or people, can become more compact. Even though there may be coins and rings within the layers of this sediment, it is very difficult to dig. I have found only one such place I believe to be loaded with treasure. Someday I may dig it out.

Heavier rings tend to sink deeper than lighter ones, primarily because of specific gravity. Chapter 19 contains a discussion about the settling properties of objects with differing specific gravities. Since glass and pottery made of clay have a specific gravity nearly the same as sand, bottles and similar objects that have been in the water hundreds of years may still be found just on or in the top layers of the ocean's bottom.

When you begin to work a new area, use a blunt probe to measure the depth to clay. If the overburden sand is a foot or more thick, you may not have much luck especially detecting deeply enough to locate heavier jewelry pieces. Gravel and shell-bottom surf areas may be productive because coins and lighter rings may have become trapped in the shell.

When you find areas where soft sand is piled above bedrock or clay, try to remove several inches of the sand over an area of several square feet. Then use your detector to locate coins or rings. When you find a good area such as this, you'll know what to do. Remember that in shallow water light wave action causes sand build up. But, light thin rings can build up with the sand. Heavy wave action results in sand removal near the beach, often exposing rock and gravel areas where you'll find the massive heavy rings. The larger the rock and gravel, the better your chances of finding the heavier jewelry. That's an old trick prospectors use when they are searching for placer gold deposits. Small rocks accumulated along the river's edge, forget it; large rocks, investigate.

Padre Island extends southward some 100 miles from Corpus Christi, TX. Several miles below Corpus Christi are two wash areas called Little Shell and Big Shell. Old-time treasure hunters know of these wide beach areas because failure to respect them often resulted in vehicles getting stuck. Another reason they know of them is because Spanish coins were often found there. But, far more coins were found at Big Shell area then at the Little Shell site.

177

Some hunters advise working at deeper surf depths; others advise working close to the shore. Actually, both can be good, depending upon the conditions. Treasure can be found in the more shallow water, but, generally, it is true that less trash is found farther out. Don't forget to keep all trash you find and discard it later. Just remember to be observant; watch the people and wave action; draw maps and plot your finds; think things through and continue to sharpen your skills. Always work smarter, not harder. Never confuse stubbornness with hard work. Be persistent and work smarter. Grid the areas where you work and develop searchcoil overlapping techniques. Use shore-based grid markers such as trees, posts, trash receptacles and other permanent objects. If no one is swimming or sunbathing, drive stakes into the ground on the beach or in the water. Another method to use is buoys. Any water-tight plastic container will suffice. Milk, bleach or detergent bottles and antifreeze containers make good buoys. Tie one end of a cord to the handle and a brick or other weight to the other end. The cord length should permit the buoy just to reach the surface. Otherwise, it will move around. If you can drive them into the bottom properly, long poles can be used.

Figure 13-24. Garrett dealer Gary Bischke regularly works beaches and surf in competition with his wife. This competitive sprit probably results in their finding more treasure than normal. Here Gary proudly displays the rings they found in one summer's hunting.

Sides of your grid square should be some 20 to 30 feet in length. When you complete a square, move the poles. You must, however, keep a record to the areas you have searched. When you finish for the day, mark the spot so you can start at the correct place tomorrow. Don't forget to record your finds and their location; it may become very revealing data.

SEARCHING TIPS

When you work a popular swimming beach and do not find pulltabs, someone may have just worked the site thoroughly. Since some hunters dig everything, or at least use minimum discrimination, they will remove everything, including pulltabs.

When working in surfs with violent wave action, always work sideways to the oncoming breakers. You need to present as little of yourself to the body-flattening waves as possible. and don't forget, some waves will be larger than others.

When scanning, keep the searchcoil near the bottom and lightly skim over the sand. If you hold the searchcoil very far above the bottom, you will lose detection depth. If you drag the searchcoil through the sand, you will be expending energy you need for a full day's scanning.

Dig all signals, regardless of magnitude! Some suggest not digging large signals. They reason that large detector signals merely indicate surface trash. But, treasure is sometimes found directly beneath such surface trash. Ed Morris tells of a friend who found a gold ring after he moved a "loud" tin can.

RETRIEVING YOUR TREASURE

When working in shallow water (arm's length-depth or less), use a scoop or digger, depending on bottom material and density. When the material is light, you can fan it away by hand or speed up the action with a ping pong paddle. Be observant when you are fanning since lighter junk items such as pulltabs can float away with the sand. No loss certainly, but you may just keep detecting them over and over again. When using pulltab rejection detection, however, you'll know that a pulltab can't be that "treasure" you just detected. Keep fanning and watch for a ring or coin to appear.

When working deep water, use one of the following scoop-retrieving methods that have been perfected. First, you must pinpoint the detected object. Then, bring the scoop forward and lightly touch the back edge of the searchcoil. Move the searchcoil out of the way and tilt the scoop forward and press on the butt end of the scoop with your foot. I don't like this method because I don't like the detector's loud squeal when the metal scoop comes near its searchcoil.

After detector pinpointing, some hunters place their foot lightly on top of the searchcoil, then move the coil away. They can place the scoop adjacent to their shoe to achieve correct scoop positioning.

Figure 13-27: Ken Schaffer made this unique find in the waters around Virginia Beach. When first discovered, it appeared to be just an ordinary ring, obviously, of an unusual design. Occasionally he would examine the ring, and one day he noticed that it appeared to be too light in weight to be of solid constructon. He began a close examination; lo and behold, it opened before his very eyes.

Figure 13-28: Here is the spy ring in its opened position. Ken Schaffer found this ring in a Virginia Beach surf. The United States Secret Service examined it and while they would not admit that it was a spy ring, they did say, "It is one of theirs, not one of ours."

Another method is to place your toe directly against the back edge of the searchcoil. Move the coil and lower your scoop until its forward edge touches your shoe's toe. This places the scoop digging rim (or edge) at the back edge of the searchcoil's detection pattern (see Chapter 5). Then, push outward on the top of the handle until the scoop is nearly vertical. With your foot press down on the scoop.

Still another method is to place your left foot beside the searchcoil and move the searchcoil outward to the right. Lower the scoop until it touches the heel of your shoe in the correct position for retrieval.

Regardless of the method you use, practice until you have achieved perfection, even digging several scoop depths, if necessary. Don't worry if you have to try several times at first to retrieve your object. It comes easier with practice. If you occasionally keep "losing" an item, the object may have been small enough to slip through your scoop holes. I had this problem once when I was digging everything at a beach site in Antigua. The "lost" objects turned out to be ladies' hairpins. Jack Lowry suggested I attach a magnet inside and near the bottom of the scoop to attract iron objects. That's a good idea to overcome that problem. If you get a signal but fail to scoop up a target on the first try, pinpoint it again with your detector. If the target moved, it could be a small object that sifted through the scoop. If you cannot locate it with your detector, it may be a deep coin or ring that was turned edgewise when the scoop contacted it. Try digging deeper to see if you can locate those mysteriously "lost" objects.

Here is a phenomenon you will observe: During a science class, you may have learned of diffraction, or the "bending" of light. This occurs when light passes through a water/air boundary. An underwater object such as your searchcoil will thus appear to be in a different place from where it actually sits. Until you get used to it, this sighting error may cause you to misjudge the location of your searchcoil and scoop.

Don't forget to recheck your holes. Do as I say; not as I did with the Spanish icon. As I was recovering it, several people came to see what I had found. In the ensuing excitement I forgot to recheck the hole. Later, one of the others in my group returned and found a nice Spanish coin there.

A FEW FINAL SURFING TIPS

On hot sunny days, wear a wide-brimmed cotton hat. Occasionally dunk it in the water and pull it back down over your head. It is surprising how cool you'll be even during temperatures well over 100 degrees. I have worked all day for days on end in very hot climates with absolutely no problems. I wear long-sleeved shirts with the collar turned up. I place a handkerchief under my hat and let the loose end shade my neck. In a surplus store I found a sun "shield" to protect my neck from the sun. Look at the accompanying photograph, Figure 13-21 and also Figure 13-22, and you'll see that it slips over the bill of a "baseball" style cap. The rear portion flows over the head and down to protect the neck and ears. The sun can't get to me when I wear it. It does have one drawback, however. I wore it one hot summer day in Idaho when Roy Lagal, Wally Eckard, Virgil Hutton and I were searching our own private "Treasure Mountain." While walking down a dusty trail, they suddenly jumped aside shouting, "rattlesnake!" I didn't hear the rattle, but fortunately I saw them jump aside. Cloth over my ears had kept me from hearing the snake rattle. No one had to tell me to carry the shield in my backpack or keep it pulled back away from my ears during the rest of our expedition.

It's best not to show your good finds to strangers. Let them think you are finding only junk and they will leave you alone. I like tots and you may also, but if you don't want to be pestered by them, don't give them your pennies or other coins you don't want. Every time I do so, I am soon covered with others wanting their share. Nothing is wrong with sharing or with charity in general, but these boys and girls will distract you. When you are hunting, you should concentrate only on your detector's signals. Don't be distracted. Consider the story of the Japanese karate expert. Using only his little finger, he defeated his opponent at arm wrestling. When asked how he did it, he replied that through concentration he directed his entire body power into his finger. Had he concentrated his power over a larger area (his arm and hand) he would have lost.

Occasionally, you'll find unusual items. One surfer found a small bundle of marijuana. Several Spanish coins were secured by string to

Figure 13-21: Here is one of the sun shields that the author often uses. Underneath the shield is a regular baseball cap with bill. The sun shield keeps the sun off the author's neck and face. Other shields are available that leave only the eyes exposed.

Figure 13-22: Another sun shield is worn in this photograph by Carl Ratigan, a very active treasure hunter who travels extensively into the Caribbean and to South America. In this photograph he is searching a Guadeloupe swimming surf.

the outside of the package. Since it was found off the coast of Florida, it is believed it may have belonged to an individual who was attempting to escape from Cuba. Ken Schaffer, H & S Detector Center, Virginia Beach, VA, found a very unusual item—a microfilm "spy" ring, Figures 13-27 and 13-28. The ring opened to reveal a slot into which could be placed miniature film negatives. He called in the Secret Service and asked them to examine it. Should you find unusual items, it may be to your best interest to contact the authorities.

One final bit of advice: Remember, you plan to search the surf not to find your own valuables, but other people's lost treasure, Figures 13-23, through 13-26. Leave all YOUR jewelry at home so some other treasure hunter won't be looking for it tomorrow!

CHAPTER 14

Where and How to Search Ocean Sites

Considering the vast amount of wealth lost in the ocean, it seems likely that a good percentage of all treasure hunters have dreamed of going after their share. Of those who think about it, probably no more than five percent get their feet wet. Searching for underwater treasure requires greater skills and a greater outlay of money than land searching. But think about the potential rewards. If a land searcher spends a thousand dollars for equipment and other necessities and finds $10,000 worth of treasure, the net profit is $9,000. If a water hunter spends $10,000 and finds $100,000 in treasure, net profit is $90,000. Even though the ratios are the same, the amount the water hunter banks is considerably more.

Let's assume (and probably correctly) that there is 100 times more sunken treasure than buried treasure. Let's assume, also, that there is one water hunter for every 100 land hunters. By doing a little multiplying, we come up with a "success potential" ratio of ten thousand to one, indicating that the water hunter is considerably more likely to find treasure. There are arguments against this kind of reasoning, but most arguments are based upon the assumption that it is easier and less time-consuming to find land treasure than underwater treasure. In some situations that is correct, such as coin hunting in a park, and relic hunting in a ghost town. But, in situations where large treasures are at stake, land hunting is not necessarily easier nor faster. I think what it condenses to is that thoughts (or fears) of water hunting and the required skills and equipment keep most people "safely" on land.

What are underwater treasure-recovery dreams made of? First, there is the discovery of a bronze cannon buried in the sand and refusing to surrender to the corroding effects of salt water. Next to it, a slow, careful hand fanning of the sand uncovers an ancient pirate's chest. A slight tug and the lid swings up to expose thousands of gleaming golden doubloons! While we all know it just doesn't happen that way, it's nice to dream.

Treasure is scattered everywhere on the ocean floors of the world, Figures 14-1 and 14-2. Largely unexplored regions hide many fortunes which can be claimed by those with determination to seek them out. In fact, man has been seeking sunken treasure for many thousands of years. Down through the centuries records explicitly record attempts by divers to recover sunken treasure.

Other than wartime, most ships meet disaster in shallow water. Reefs, or shoals, have ripped the bottom out of thousands of ships, spilling cargo into shallow water. Along the coastline of numerous Central and South American countries shallow reefs parallel the mainland. The remains of numerous vessels lie hidden in the ever-growing coral that relentlessly strives to conceal these sunken riches. We explored one such South American shipwreck site visibly marked by a stack of more than a dozen coral-encrusted cannon, Figure 14-3. It was strange to see these cannon stacked like cordwood, almost totally concealed by coral growth. How did the cannon become stacked like that? Perhaps the vessel was transporting cannon barrels and the seamen had stored them in one location on the ship. When the ship struck the razor-sharp coral reef, it broke up and quickly sank to the bottom. Over the ensuing decades the wooden ship succumbed to the teredo, leaving the ship's cannon cargo lying exposed on the bottom.

There were no other visible signs of the ship except for an occasional cannon ball. When we scanned the bottom with our metal detec-

Figure 14-1: Robert Marx locates a gold escudo. Where there is one, there could be many, many more.

Figure 14-2: A scuba diver inspects a cannon on the ocean floor near Bermuda in water 15 feet deep.

tors, it was a different story. The "eyes" of the detectors pierced through the coral to locate hundreds of metal objects that human eyes could not see. Using rock picks to hack our way through the coral, we discovered more cannon balls, various pieces of iron, and numerous pieces of eight. Sometimes the silver cobs came out in clumps of coral. When the detector indicated that the detected metal object was larger than a single coin, we would hack out large chunks of coral. Later examination of these pieces revealed numerous cobs bound together by coral.

Because of recent publicity given to numerous underwater treasure discoveries, I chose this as my next book. Metal detector manufacturers experienced surges in submersible detector sales immediately following televised reports of treasure hunters who had struck it rich under water. These increased sales proved that many treasure seekers are poised to strike—they need only the excitement, the proof that is generated by discovered treasure, Figures 14-4 through 14-7.

Even though many treasure laden shipwreck sites have been found, there are others...waiting. For every one found, a thousand others beckon us to the bottom.

SITE SELECTION

Not every vessel that sank carried recoverable wealth. Even the famed Spanish galleons carried little non-perishable treasure as they made their westward trek. On the other hand, eastbound galleons contained fortunes in hard money treasure. Records show that many of the ships that traveled from California around South America to the United States' eastern seaboard never reached port. These ships carried considerable wealth dug from the ground by California's gold-seeking 49ers. History reveals that many vessels went to the bottom carrying, not treasure, but relics well worth the cost of salvage. During World War II thousands of ships sank. Most were loaded with war equipment, but some carried great quantities of recoverable wealth.

HOW TO FIND YOUR SHARE

There are two ways you can find your ship—your sunken treasure: By accident, or through a systematic, organized search following clues tracked down in research. There is a joy in success either way, but your chances of accidentally finding wealth are almost zero. Certainly, there is the human desire to dash into the deep, make a few scans with your metal detector and hit the jackpot. There is something about human nature that causes us to think, "I will be the one. I will be successful without one bit of research."

The successful treasure diver is the one who follows a few simple rules that have been established by successful individuals. The first rule is selection of a ship worthy of your time. This ship must truly exist—strange as that statement may sound. It must not be the figment of

Figure 14-3: The author inspects a large stack of coral-encrusted cannon at a shipwreck site off the West Coast of South America. More than a dozen cannon were stacked up like cord wood.

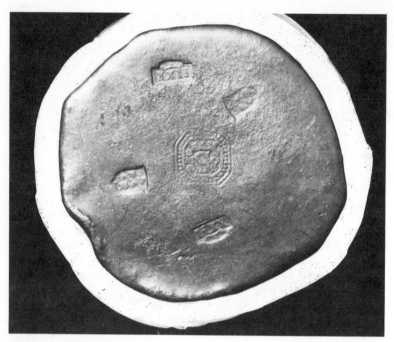

Figure 14-4: This is a 12-lb. gold disc found at a shipwreck site off the Florida Keys by Robert Marx.

Figure 14-5: These beautiful gold coins and the three unique toothpicks were taken from a shipwreck site off the Western Coast of South Africa.

someone's imagination. Its cargo must be valuable, and it must be recoverable. Never believe everything you read or hear about "your" ship. Some of the information contained in magazines, books and maps may be accurate — or none of it. You must get the facts yourself. You must do your own research. It's your money and time, and no one will search for the truth as you will.

Among the many shipwreck reference sources, you should consider Robert Marx's SHIPWRECKS OF THE WESTERN HEMISPHERE 1492-1825, Adrian L. Lonsdale and H. R. Kaplan's A GUIDE TO SUNKEN SHIPS IN AMERICAN WATERS and John S. Potter Jr.'s THE TREASURE DIVER'S GUIDE.

Before starting on any shipwreck recovery venture, you must clear one mental hurdle. You must believe, 100%, in yourself and your ability to succeed. Carrying shipwreck recovery all the way through to the end can be a costly, time-consuming, costly, energy-draining and — oh yes, costly — venture. Research, search and recovery efforts, expensive equipment, legal battles, hazards of diving, uncooperative weather, timetable maintenance, and energy-absorbing work must all be encountered and overcome. Long before your search ends, you'll want to throw in the towel and call it quits. If you begin by believing in your success and reinforce that belief daily, you'll keep progressing toward your goal. Consider Mel Fisher's success slogan which he uttered daily as he spurred his divers on to success against all odds and hardships... "Today's the Day!" That battle cry, and his belief in it, brought him success that'll live in the annals of treasure hunting.

Your selection of a ship can begin with tips from friends, divers, fishermen or oldtimers who may have gotten the information from other oldtimers. Then, you must gather source material about shipwrecks from books, logs, governmental records, histories, contemporary newspapers and other sources, including maritime archives, museums and libraries. If you can find confirming data (not material someone has copied from someone else) from two or three sources, you can be reasonably certain the story is worthy of further time and consideration.

The second rule is to establish absolute proof that precious, recoverable cargo was, indeed, on your ship. Ships' manifests and other data must record the existence of gold, silver, platinum or other non-perishable commodities. Next, is the cargo truly recoverable? What if, for instance, you could locate one of the sunken Spanish freighters bringing millions of dollars worth of mercury to Mexico's mine owners. When the ship sank, perhaps the hull broke up and the cargo was strewn over the ocean bottom. The quicksilver, likewise, would be strewn over a wide area where it quickly displaced all other lighter ocean bottom elements as it settled in thousands of cracks, crevices and other low areas. Such a cargo could not be recovered economically. Your only chance would lie in the good fortune that the mercury was transported in rugged, non-perishable containers.

Figure 14-7: Tony Ramirez takes aim with one of four Spanish guns shown in the photo. In the foregound is a unique Spanish iron cannon, and next to it is a sabre. The long slim item lying between the two guns is a small caliber Spanish cannon barrel. These items date to the 17th and 18th centuries.

Figure 14-6: A lovely sight, indeed, these Spanish coins include various Spanish pieces of eight, often called cobs. Included amongst these coins are those minted at Spanish Colonial mints in Mexico and Peru. Photo courtesy Robert Marx.

PINPOINTING THE SITE

Before attempting to search any unknown area, you should review hydrographic and oceanographic data. You should learn water depth, the location of reefs and other shallow and hazardous areas, and the directions of prevailing winds and currents. This, and other useful data, can be obtained from charts published by the U.S. Hydrographic Office and the U.S. Coast and Geodetic Survey. Sailing directions and coastal pilot books indicate areas restricted to military use, fishing grounds, shipping lanes, and other data indicating the feasibility of carrying out work such as you plan.

There are two methods for pinpointing a wrecksite. You can search a probable area after having narrowed it down as much as possible through research, or you can continue research until you have it pinpointed exactly. Both methods have been used successfully. The wisest course of action, as attested to by those who have searched successfully, is to exhaust all research methods and sources and do a little thinking and reasoning before scouring the bottom of an endless ocean.

It is estimated that up to 99% of all ships lost in the Western Hemisphere were lost in waters less than 30 feet deep. Most of these wrecks lie on sandy bottoms. Even though any lost ship will be difficult to locate, those in sand are easier to excavate. I know from personal experience that coral-encrusted shipwrecks are extremely difficult to excavate. So frustrating, in fact, that dynamiting the site often seems the perfect solution. Dynamiting is, of course, hardly a perfect, or even a logical, solution. But, after a very difficult day of hacking your way through coral encrustation, dynamiting just feels good to contemplate.

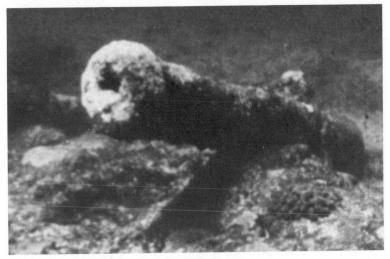

Figure 14-8: These cannon mark the site of a shipwreck that contained considerable treasure and artifacts. The remains of most old ships are scarcely recognizable as ships. Most wood succumbed long ago to the ocean's elements and creatures.

Figure 14-9: The author and companion let the eyes of Pulse Induction detectors scan through coral encrustation to locate Spanish coins and shipwreck artifacts. Retrieving óbjects embedded in coral is a very slow and painstaking process.

SITE NAME LOCATING

While I have not located underwater sites using site name locating, I have been directed to land-based treasure sites such as "Robber's Roost" in West Texas, "Outlaw Canyon" in Central Idaho, and Massacre Beach and Battery Street on Guadeloupe. John S. Potter, Jr., in his book, THE TREASURE DIVER'S GUIDE, tells of places discovered using place names. Chameau Rock put Alex Storm on the track of *Le Chameau,* and Thetis Cove was named after *H.M.S. Thetis.*

VISUAL LOCATING

If you are thinking about hopping into the ocean and discovering an ancient shipwreck by quickly spotting its hull, superstructure, and, perhaps, even its mast, forget it. You won't find these unless you discover a one-in-a-thousand vessel that was, by some quirk of nature, quickly preserved under protective sand and silt. Then, the day before you dove, it would be necessary for a record-setting hurricane to blast a path through the area, leaving your ship uncovered. Not likely!

The remains of most old ships are scarcely recognizable as ships. Most wood will have succumbed long ago to the ocean's elements and creatures. Some metal objects may remain, Figure 14-8, but they may be covered with sand, silt or marine growth. Nature seeks to return all man-made objects back to their natural state—wood and similar organic substances, back to the soil whence they came...metals, like iron, back to magnetite, or other ferrous material.

Marine growth begins to camouflage stubborn objects, even cannon, so that even the trained eye may not recognize it for what it is, Figure 14-9.

Wooden ships lost in sand, mud or silt may be the best preserved. The ship's structure and rigging may have become buried before the wood was completely devoured by shipworms. In either case—burial in sand, mud or silt or total encrustation by coral—ship locating will be difficult. More recent shipwrecks with iron hulls may be quickly found as the hulls generally remain intact and their size prevents them from being rapidly covered. Such ship's tall and massive superstructures, providing the ship came to rest in an upright position, can easily be spotted from a great distance.

Should you be so fortunate as to learn that the area of your search is clear water, an aerial survey should, perhaps, be your first step. Aerial surveying can be accomplished by using an airplane, helicopter, balloon or hang glider towed by the search craft. By hang gliding slightly off center, the boat's wake will not obstruct vertical viewing. Slow towing into the wind lets you glide much slower, and the use of polaroid glasses will improve your ability to see into the ocean depths. Scanning in the early to mid-morning, or from mid-afternoon to evening, may be the best time. While vertical sun's rays are needed to illuminate the bottom, reflections can be blinding. Also, angled sun's rays may cast shadows that enhance ship's components and other objects that protrude above the bottom. Be ready to document sighting with your camera (with polaroid lens filters) and to precisely mark or pinpoint the site on navigational charts.

During several successful attempts to locate underwater wreckage, we used the "shark line." Divers using scuba or snorkel gear were towed behind a boat. This method permits a large area to be covered thoroughly and quickly. There is, however, some danger in using this method, as the name implies. Also, fast towing causes rapid depletion of body heat and increases the likelihood of your face mask being pulled away.

Two simple methods to facilitate visual sighting, especially near shore, are snorkeling by fin-propelling yourself over the surface or by floating on a surf board with a built-in view window. During all visual sighting attempts, keep one or more small buoys with you. When a promising site is spotted, drop a buoy to mark the site. Make sure the line is long enough to reach the bottom. Another method is to drop off the board (or let go the tow line) when a site is located. A life vest, of course, should be worn to help you conserve energy as you await the towing boat's return. Using a self-propelled, underwater vehicle will give you greater freedom and can increase your coverage by as much as 10 times. Under some conditions, headlights will enable you to search at night or at times when visibility is bad.

You should develop an eye for spotting unusual features that mark the site of a shipwreck. Watch for anything unusual — especially, straight lines. Unlike nature's handiwork "topside" where trees grow vertically in straight lines, underwater growth is anything but straight. Straight and symmetrical man-made objects like cannon and anchors can be spotted even when encrusted with coral or half-buried in ocean bottom materials. Large marine growth or mounds, of sand and mud should be investigated. Mel Fisher's divers spotted a large mound lying in an otherwise flat bottom area. Curious, they scanned the mound with a metal detector and the instrument rang out with a multi-million-dollar "sound of money!"

Figure 14-10: The author makes preparations for a dive on a shipwreck site. The underwater camera and other gear was used by the Scuba World team who filmed these dives.

Ballast is often found lying in a heap and during the passage of time the heap gets larger as sand and silt and, in some areas, coral cover the stones or other ballast materials. Not all ballast piles, however, mark the location of ships. When large quantities of heavy goods such as gold and silver were loaded aboard, ballast was sometimes thrown overboard. Robert Marx has discovered ballast piles with no ship anywhere to be found nearby. Upon excavating the site, he found numerous man-made objects, but theorized that as unneeded ballast stones were pitched overboard, other useless objects were also discarded. Large anchors are often found lying on the seabed. In most cases, anchors mark the site where a ship was, at one time, in trouble. Ships' captains often rode out storms by casting out anchors in the hopes they would securely hold and prevent the ship from bring driven into shore. Reasoning follows that the anchor's direction may point to a shipwreck. In one of Bob Marx's books he tells of divers who found a large anchor. They swam in the direction it was pointing and found another anchor pointing further onward. A short distance along the same route they found yet another anchor, and then yet another — all pointing in the same direction. Near shore, the divers found the remains of a valuable cargo ship.

The application of "tools" is described in the following paragraphs. The function and use of these and other tools is described in Chapter 25.

In clear water the underwater sled has its advantages. You can skim along at any desired height above the bottom. Close skimming improves your ability to identify small objects and ship's components when they are covered by marine growth. Higher level skimming lets you see an area in greater perspective. Unusual straight line and other man-made geometrical objects can be better spotted when viewed in relation to a large area of natural bottom features and growth.

On sandy bottoms a blaster can remove tons of sand and debris quickly. Too much engine speed, however, can cause such a downrush of water that everything, including cannon balls, will be blasted away. Don't forget, too, when using the sandblaster, the entire perimeter around the spot being blasted will build up as materials settle back to the ocean floor. Such buildup will occur along the route of tidal flow.

Video documentation can be helpful, Figure 14-10. Underwater cameras can be attached to submersible arms on the underside of your vessel or controlled by underwater robots propelled and guided by an umbilical cord.

When sonar devices are used, large objects like ballast piles and ship's structures can be discerned. Liquid crystal and strip chart paper recording sonar devices provide quality, high resolution imagery, Figure 14-11. Expandable ranging allows you to "zero in" on suspect sites and get remarkable bottom detail. Recordings provide data for later study. It is important to indicate careful positioning information on the recordings.

Metal detector offer "x-ray" scanning to help locate submerged metal objects. Two surveying methods are available to you: submersible searchcoil scanning and submersible, self-contained metal detector surveying, Figure 14-12.

Complete metal detector short-courses are given in Chapters 5 through 11. Metal detectors will detect single objects as small as a coin to a distance of 12 inches or more outward from the searchcoil's bottom surface. A mass of coins and other metal objects can be detected to a distance of 4 to 6 feet. Larger objects like cannon and anchors can be detected to a distance of about 8 to 10 feet.

Submersible searchcoils allow you to remain topside while searching. These searchcoils are constructed with electrical cables and harnesses that allow underwater scanning to depths of 50 feet. The electronics are kept above water in your boat or other craft. The search-

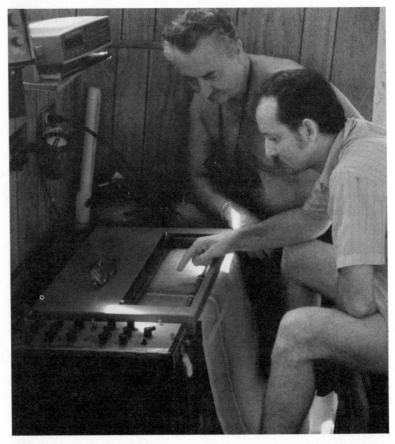

Figure 14-11: George Mroczkowski and Dave Graham operate a hydroscan recorder somewhere off the coast of Panama.

Figure 14-12: Two scuba divers using Sea Hunter underwater metal detectors search for clues off the coast of Panama.

coil is lowered to the bottom and then raised a few inches. As you guide your craft along a prescribed course, you metal-profile the bottom. Since the cord harness is made of white or yellow nylon rope, a diver can quickly follow it to the bottom to investigate the cause of a detector's signals. In shallow water, rigid poles can be attached to the searchcoil. This method provides better control over the searchcoil. Only one company, Garrett Electronics, manufactures submersible searchcoils with extended-length cable. These searchcoils have 50-foot cables and a nylon harness that is used to lower, raise, and maneuver the searchcoil under water. These searchcoils can be attached to several of Garrett's land detectors. The control housing with its electronic circuits is kept topside while the searchcoil is lowered into the water. Divers sometimes takes searchcoils under water and maneuver them over the bottom. A tug of the harness by the boat operator alerts the diver to the presence of detected metal. The diver can then investigate the metal source that caused the detector to respond.

SELF-CONTAINED SUBMERSIBLE METAL DETECTORS

Submersible self-contained metal detectors feature electronics, controls, indicators, batteries and the searchcoil mounted within a specially designed, submersible, water-tight housing. A suitable handle arrangement allows the searchcoil to be maneuvered over an area to be searched. Indicator lights, a visual indicator (moving pointer or liquid crystal) and an audible device (usually dynamic speaker-type head-

197

phones or a piezo electric crystal) are the detection devices that alert the diver to the presence of metal.

Self-contained batteries that power the detector for 10 or more hours are either rechargeable or standard non-rechargeable. There are several types of circuitry as explained in Chapters 5 through 11. Some models are stem-mounted, while others are convertible. The control housing is designed to be attached to the stem (stem-mounted) or belt-mounted to waist, arm or leg. When the housing is body-mounted, a short handle attached to the searchcoil allows the coil to be maneuvered over the search area.

Figure 14-13: This beautiful silver pocket watch discovered at a shipwreck site was made in London around 1680. The maker's name, Gibbs, is still visible. It is valued at nearly $5,000.

Figure 14-14: If ship's logs and other historical data are available, bronze cannon are often a positive means of identity. In addition to that, this cannon is worth a minimum of $25,000.

Metal detectors are valuable tools. They penetrate sand, mud, clay, marine growth, stone, rock and other non-metallic substances. Metal detectors can be used to locate wrecksites; to locate objects such as coins needed for wreck-dating; to locate non-corrosive metals containing inscriptions that identify vessels; Figures 14-13 and 14-14; to define parameters of a site by locating metal objects; to locate gold, silver, pewter, bronze, brass and other metallic treasures; and to check a "clean" area to make certain that all treasures, ship's rigging and other artifacts have been recovered.

The initial search for the site can be conducted by a diver (or divers) scanning an area according to a search-grid network. Since searchcoils will not "reach out" laterally, they must be scanned over as much of the target area as possible. Because most ships carried considerable metal, however, even a cursory scan of an area can often locate a wrecksite. Any grid-search method described in this chapter can be used, but the expanding circle method provides the most uniform searching pattern. A cord or rope is wound around a suitable spool, Figure 14-15. The spool is anchored and the diver slips his hand through a loop in the end of the cord. The diver then swims around the spool, scanning the detector searchcoil ahead. As the rope unwinds, it guides the diver in a controlled expanding circle. See Chapter 24 for construction details of this type guide-rope device.

Metal detectors with a built-in discrimination system are more versatile than non-discriminating types. For quickly surveying a site to locate only coins and other non-ferrous objects, the discriminating type should be used. This is a fast method to determine if the ship's cargo included treasure. Since non-corrosive metals survive longer than iron

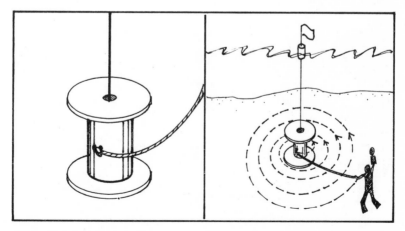

Figure 14-15: The expanding circle method of visual and metal detector site searching provides an extremely uniform means of bottom scanning. This illustration shows how a rope spool is deployed to achieve expanding circle searching.(See pages 306-7.)

Figure 14-16: When there is not time for a complete excavation of a site, a discriminating metal detector can locate only non-ferrous objects such as these which often give considerable information about the site. Makers' inscriptions are often clearly visible in non-corrosive metals even if buried beneath the waters for centuries.

Figure 14-17: When Robert Marx excavated Port Royal, he and his team located thousands of valuable artifacts. These silver and pewter objects were found at the site of one home.

Figure 14-18: Often ship's components and artifacts are better preserved when the ship-wreck occurred in sand and mud. Retrieving objects in sand is considerably easier than in mud and coral. Here a diver fans away sand overburden to reach a detected object.

objects, identifying stamps, insignias and other markings were usually affixed to these metals. Locating such pieces can hasten identification of the wreck.

A metal detector can speed up almost any shipwreck search for concealed treasure. When a sonar device locates a ballast pile, a quick scan with a metal detector will reveal whether metal objects are concealed within the ballast.

When a sunken ship is totally, or even partially, encrusted and there is not time for a complete excavation, a discriminating metal detector can locate only non-ferrous objects, such as coins, jewelry, navigation instruments and dinnerware, Figures 14-16 and 14-17. A metal detector with interchangeable searchcoils can be used another way. The small searchcoil can detect and precisely pinpoint individual and more shallow objects to speed up object retrieval. Not necessarily a problem in sand, retrieval efforts in concrete-like coral should minimize hacking and chiseling. When most non-ferrous, shallow objects have been recovered, a larger, more deepseeking searchcoil can locate bigger objects at greater depths.

Should you be fortunate enough to find your ship in sand, the first phase of recovery work will require only your hands. Slowly fan the sand away to create a cavity, Figure 14-18. As lighter materials flow away, heavier items such as coins, jewelry, china and other objects with a higher specific gravity will remain in place. In currents you may need to anchor yourself over the spot by holding an anchor rope, or grasping an underwater object. Don't try to hold on to coral unless you wear gloves; the glass-like substance can penetrate skin to cause pain and swelling. A ping pong paddle or a child's bounce-the-ball paddle makes fanning easier. A water jet can rapidly remove silt and light overburden, Figure 14-19.

SPECIALIZED INSTRUMENTS

If funds allow, specialized instruments can aid in your search for a shipwreck. Described in Chapter 25 are magnetometers and gradiometers, side-scan sonar, sub-bottom profilers and robot and manned submersibles. If it is known or suspected that your ship contained a considerable quantity of large iron objects such as cannon and anchors, a magnetometer will locate the magnetic mass by sensing the increase in the earth's magnetic field concentration. Of course, iron objects such as steel drums and other discarded iron trash will also create a detectable concentration of the earth's field, causing you to spend time investigating false leads.

Side scan sonar and sub-bottom profilers are capable of revealing remarkable detail of sunken objects. These instruments are not in-

Figure 14-19: This diver is using a water jet to remove light silt and overburden.

202

fallible, but they permit scanning a wide swath of ocean floor. Manned robots using video scanning were used to locate the *Titanic*. Their value remains unquestioned, not only during the original search, but also during all phases of surveying, mapping and excavation.

Whether visual or electronic scanning techniques are used, grid-search methods are essential. Haphazard searching wastes time, money and resources. Many grid-search methods, Figures 14-20 and 14-21, have been developed over the years. Use those that can be adapted best to your site and equipment.

SITE IDENTIFICATION

Now that you've found a wreck, is it really the one you have searched for? You must be certain because an extensive conglomerate of ballast, cannon balls, perhaps a few cannon, cargo, countless pieces of copper, lead, iron, bottles, pottery and tons of mud and silt (and perhaps tons of concrete-hard coral growth) will be found at most old shipwreck sites. You will be spending, perhaps, months and years excavating the site. What a pity it would be if the wreck contained not one ounce of treasure.

First, has any other salvage been carried out? Possibly, the salvage history with details of site, artifacts, treasure recovered and other data can establish the ship's identity. Coins and ingots provide conclusive evidence, but these may not be encountered until later in the excavation process. The ship's dimensions, number of decks, type of sheathing used, country of origin of cannon and hundreds of other clues are important in identification. Barry Clifford was able to identify his shipwreck immediately and without a doubt. He discovered what he believed to be the *Whidah*, a pirate ship that sank off the coast of Massachusetts

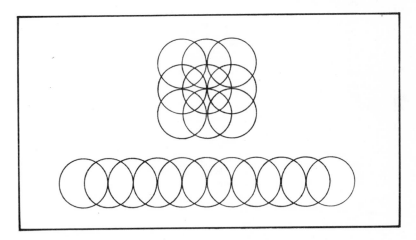

Figure 14-20: Illustrated are two circle grid-search methods to use when electronically scanning a site.

203

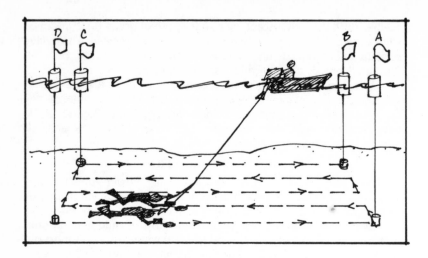

Figure 14-21: GRID AREA SEARCHING. A haphazard approach to shipwreck searching usually results in failure, or certainly reduces efficiency. A well planned, defined and coordinated search improves your efficiency and chances for success. The above illustrations can be applied to many search areas. Area size, weather and water conditions, water visibility and other factors should be considered in plans to implement a grid search. The buddy system is the safest and it speeds up the search and multiplies your chances of success. All illustrations by Mel Climer.

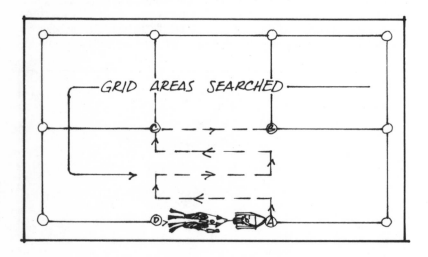

in 1717. From the site he pulled a large bell which had the ship's name clearly cast into its side.

SURVEYING AND MAPPING

Before proceeding to excavate, the site should be surveyed and mapped, Figure 14-22. Aside from archaeological considerations, much useful data can be obtained. Your task will be easier if the ship is not scattered over a wide area and if the ocean bottom is sandy. In heavy coral areas, your job will be much more difficult and require hand chisels, sledge hammers and, possibly, pneumatic tools.

Determining the area over which a ship is strewn will help you plan future excavation. More excavation time may be needed if the wreck is not contained in a small area. You'll need to know the type equipment needed. Your lease should clearly define the extent of your site. It is important to know the ship's orientation and determine bow and stern. You may want to excavate the stern first. The richest treasure, plus officers' and passengers' private wealth, Figures 14-23 through 14-25, can usually be found here. Silverware, china and other more valuable artifacts are also more likely to be found in the stern section.

SITE EXCAVATION

If you've made it this far, congratulations! Excavation has finally begun, and you're much closer to your bank's deposit window. Ex-

Figure 14-22: Before proceeding to excavate a site, it should be surveyed and mapped. Aside from archaeological considerations, much useful data can be obtained.

Figure 14-23: These eight coins were found clustered together. Apparently, they were the main components of some type of jewelry. Note the three holes in each piece. The author would appreciate hearing from individuals who have thoughts on how the pieces were originally fashioned together.

Figure 14-24: These nearly 500 Spanish dollars were part of a much larger cache located off the coast of South Africa. Note the small cannon.

cavation methods range from simply plucking a gold escudo out of the sand to deploying giant airlifts and blasters. Select and use those that best suit your salvage job.

A "center" of the wrecksite may contain most of the ship's cargo and other valuable artifacts. Try to establish an underwater grid system and keep it in place throughout your entire project for documenting the exact location of discoveries. The grid method is the most widely used on both land and underwater excavation sites. A grid pattern, of non-metallic pipe (if metal detectors are to be used), is generally built on a compass alignment basis with equal size squares of five to ten feet. As objects are excavated within each square, their location is indicated on a corresponding chart.

An azimuth circle system can be used that is much simpler and less time-consuming. An azimuth circle is mounted on a brass rod and driven into the bottom near the center of the wreck site. If the wreck is scattered over a large area, it may be necessary to place an azimuth circle at several points. The azimuth circle is aligned with magnetic north. A small chain (or non-metallic, non-stretchable rope) with distance calibration marks along the entire length of the chain is connected to the center of the brass rod with a collar to permit the chain to be rotated 360 degrees. When the chain is stretched to the object to be mapped, compass bearing on the azimuth circle and the distance to the object are recorded.

Figure 14-26: The hydro-lift utilizes a water jet stream to create a suction within the larger pipe. Sufficient suction is created to lift sand, rock, debris and artifacts from the bottom.

Figure 14-25: Spanish pieces of eight and artifacts recovered by Roy Volker from the 1715 Galleon, *Nuestra Senora de la Regla*.

Figure 14-27: Mel Fisher, Roy Volker and Robert Marx celebrate during a division of newly found Spanish treasure.

At sites where the bottom is uneven or with considerable marine growth and possibly large mounds of covered ballast, ship's cargo and various debris, standard grid techniques may not be feasible. In such cases, you can devise a "floating" grid network. Such a network should be securely anchored and be kept afloat by air-filled containers. The various small personal tools you may need include a flashlight, hammer or sledge, chisel, crowbar, geologist's pick, various floats, pouches, net bags and other containers. Lift baskets and containers will be needed. Lifting large artifacts requires lift bags and other buoyancy devices.

CHAPTER 15

Where and How to Search
Rivers and Streams

As early travelers moved across America, they encountered numerous streams that had to be crossed. There were few bridges across waterways of any size, much less the mighty rivers. At fords and ferry sites lives and goods were lost, especially during times of high water. Many travelers used water as a means of transportation, first in rafts and canoes. Eventually, barges and steamboats carried vast masses of people.

At countless places along waterways, people camped. They lost or abandoned personal goods or buried wealth for safekeeping. They sometimes died or fled without digging up their goods. Lewis and Clark, America's great explorers of the Louisiana Purchase, buried caches, several along rivers, some of which have never been recovered.

As volumes of water transportation increased, more goods were lost. Whole cargoes still lie beneath every waterway in the world. Some are of no value at all, but many lost cargoes are worth millions. Bridges collapse, safes loaded wtih gold fall into murky water to be tumbled downstream and, in most cases, lost forever.

Through research, planning and persistence, much of this lost wealth can be discovered. Fords, ferry crossings and bridge sites can be determined; Indian and settlers' communities can be located. I found the site of an old settlement in East Texas and discovered dozens of nice relics on the banks of the Trinity River until mosquitoes ran me away. Some winter day I'll go back and continue my search.

Sunken rafts, barges, steamboats and other craft can be located. There are numerous sources of information to point these places out to those who take time to search the records.

For over a century steamboats carried people and their goods down the rivers and the tributaries that empty into the Gulf of Mexico. Thousands of these vessels were sunk, scattering treasure the length and breadth of the Missouri, Ohio and Mississippi River valleys. Fortunes still lie along their bottoms.

The cargo vessel, *Berstrand,* sank in 1865 in the Missouri River near DeSoto Bend, north of Omaha, NE, carrying a rich load of mercury. When it was found in 1968 only a small quantity of mercury was found, but two million artifacts, 300,000 of museum quality, were found.

In 1820 a newspaper account reported the loss of a keelboat just above Owensboro, KY, at a point then called Haphazard. The cargo of silver and whiskey was being shipped south to pay Choctaw Indians for lands purchased by the Government. The vessel has not been found.

Historians and divers report discovery of wreckage from a 1778 flotilla of 10 ships sunk by the British in the Mullica River during the Revolutionary War. Two of the scuttled ships and possibly three more, were found about ten miles north of Atlantic City, NJ. The wrecks, containing historical artifacts, were found buried in mud and water less than 20 feet deep.

BOOKS

A library of books containing nothing but river wreck locations could be assembled. Thousands of sites of fords, ferry crossings, bridges and communities could be included to point out wealth for treasure hunters to find. And, diving is not always necessary since much of this wealth is either on dry land or in very shallow water.

FORDS

Hundreds of thousands of American settlers following the trails across our continent forded waterways. As they did, they left wealth behind. They lost treasure in the water, or they buried it for safekeeping during the night but failed to make a recovery the next day. You can locate ford sites by studying history to learn the routes of pioneers. When you search these water crossings, don't overlook the land around the ferry where buried caches and relics can be found. When you find coins, why not notify the local historical society and tell them? Dated coins are a practically irrefutable way to establish historical time periods of a site.

FERRY SITES

Bridges came much later at major water crossings. Enterprising individuals provided a solution by providing ferries to transport man and his goods. Not all crossings were successful. Goods lost in waters many years ago can still be found at that site or downstream where they became mired in muck or were stopped by an obstruction. On both sides of waterways, be on the lookout for lost relics, coins and personal items, as well as purposefully buried caches.

While reading one of J. Frank Dobie's books, I read about a cannon filled with gold that was dumped into the East Texas Neches River upstream a short distance from Boone's Ferry. The story revealed how a chest of gold was taken across the river and buried among the pines. This occurred in the early part of the 19th century when the Texans and Mexicans were at war. I found the site. I found no gold, but my brother, Don, found a flintlock rifle partially covered by a pile of rocks. At this site embankment "cuts" that guided traffic down to and out of the ferry docks were still visible even after nearly one and a third centuries. On the west bank a huge tree stump still anchored a rusty steel cable. About 100 yards west we found a brick road and building foundations. Later research revealed the site of a sugar mill.

There are many such sites along rivers, waiting to be found. In Chapter 17 you'll find numerous listings and descriptions of these sites and in other chapters you'll learn of treasures that have been found along various waterways.

SWIMMING HOLES

You'll find swimming "holes" in streams and at points along rivers, generally in the vicinity of cities and towns. They number in the thousands. Many of those places were far from attractive and in many cases bathers frequented them not from choice, but because there were no better places available to swim. Diversion, comfort and enjoyment during hot weather were precious and difficult to find.

LAND SITES

You'll often find shipwreck and other sites that were once under water now on (or under) dry land. Movement of water continually replenishes waterway sites and makes new ones. Islands can be formed almost overnight. Shifting riverbeds are caused by storms and high water. At points where water slows, sand, debris and other materials begin to pile up. As water flows around obstacles, areas are created when sand builds up in bars and islands.

Figure 15-1: Work rivers and streams at low water levels whenever possible. Visually search for remnants of civilization such as glass, china, pottery, arrow points and flint chips. The projective points and bone tools shown in the photograph were found in a Florida river.

Other dry land areas are created when rivers and streams change their course. Water continually seeks the easiest downhill path. Floods and erosion cause whole sections of rivers to move around. These locations can be found by talking to oldtimers and by studying old maps.

RIVER HUNTING

Shallow rivers with gently sloping sand banks are often used for swimming and water skiing. The river need not be wide or deep, but rather one that is slow running. The banks of such a river often have a series of sand bars used for recreational activities and camping. You should work beach areas (on the sand and in the water) and downstream from where activities occur. Deep pools and obstructions are potential collection points of coins and jewelry.

Don't expect submerged objects to be evenly distributed. Current, water flow, specific gravity of sunken objects and gravity are the determining influences that regulate distribution of debris. The outside of bends continually wash away while the insides build up with objects that settle out. Heavy objects come to rest in one area while lighter ones settle at a different location.

In clear water you may want to use snorkel equipment to locate good sites. They can then be sounded with probes and worked with a metal detector, air lift or hydrolift.

Remember to work rivers and streams at low water levels whenever possible. Visually search for remnants of habitation such as glass, china, pottery, arrow points and flint chips, Figure 15-1. Look also for building materials such as bricks, roofing tile, pier posts and other items. When you locate man-made objects, scout the site thoroughly, including any adjacent high bluffs. Usually man did not build in a flood plain, but on high, safe ground.

At a boat loading ramp I discovered a .22-caliber rifle at a depth of three feet. The bore was preserved almost perfectly. Preservation occurred because when the rifle was lost, it apparently plunged straight downward, forcing mud into the barrel to keep it dry.

In areas where you locate surface or shallow remnants of civilization, your search may be fruitful. Where there are no visible remains, valuables may be deep, requiring a good metal detector or dredge to reach through sand fill. A probe is a good tool to use for locating bottles, pottery and other large objects.

River searching can be the most tricky of all because there is no such thing as a safe, smooth-bottom waterway, Figure 15-2. Currents can be tricky and water speeds of up to 40 miles per hour have been measured. There are holes, depressions, logs, limbs, whirlpools and water so opaque you can't see your hand unless you press it against your facemask. River course and bottoms change dramatically in a single day's time. High water caused by upstream flash flooding can come crashing down on you. Barbed wire stretches across river and

213

creek bottoms to snag a diver. In deep rivers are rocks the size of automobiles that roll around on the bottom. Collapsing bluffs trap the unwary. Polluted water can be the source of typhoid and other diseases. Because of the treacherous nature of waterways, great caution and proper safety techniques are mandatory.

Diving, or even wading, can be hazardous. A partner is a must. A tethering rope with a quick-disconnect is a desirable safety accessory. A rope tied upstream lets you swing an arc, and you can let out rope as you work your way downstream.

An inflatable life jacket is good insurance. Tether your metal detector to your wrist to prevent its being lost. Work slowly and cautiously and take no unnecessary risks. Watch for boats, barges, floating logs and debris.

In this chapter and in Chapter 4, research sources are given to help you locate fords, ferry crossings, swimming "holes," dock areas and other promising sites. Riverboat shipwreck research sources are suggested. You should search through waterway histories. Check disaster and accident records and river transportation and historical books. Diaries and logbooks are an excellent source of data. And, don't forget the ever-rewarding source represented by historical society libraries. Old charts warned of low water and snags, which are treasure clues today. You may want to begin looking for old shipwrecks at these areas of potential disaster.

Figure 15-2: River searching can be very tricky. Certainly a metal detector can be used to speed up a search and improve efficiency. Richard Graham of the F.B.I. searches for material evidence that was thrown into this West Texas river from a bridge. He is using the Garrett Bloodhound Depth Multiplier attachment.

CHAPTER 16

Where and How to Search Lakes, Pools and Ponds

Lakes are defined as large, inland bodies of standing water. A pool is generally a small body of usually fresh water, often still and deep. It may not be entirely surrounded by land; a "pool" can also be a deep place in a river. Ponds are relatively small bodies of still water formed naturally or by hollowing or banking, the level being controlled by a dam. Throughout this chapter the term "lake" is used unless the use of "pool" or "pond" is required to be more specific or to clarify a point.

Lake searching can be an interesting type of treasure hunting around water; three distinct areas present themselves: recreational "beaches," swimming areas and deep water sites.

There are similarities between lake and ocean "beach" hunting and "surf" hunting. The types of lost treasure are generally the same. The types of deep water treasure found in lakes, however, often differs remarkably from ocean treasure. Boats and ships are both "lost" in each but the types of craft vary considerably. Also, in lakes there is more discarded and purposefully sunken "treasure" than in oceans because small bodies of inland water are generally more accessible than the ocean.

Experience has taught me that there is considerably more trash discarded in lakes than in the ocean. Also, there is usually more of nature's discards, such as leaves, sticks, tree limbs and even entire trees, to contend with. Ocean surfs can be, and usually are, self-cleaning. Both light and heavier "contamination" will soon be removed by the constant wind and wave action.

Not so with the still waters of lakes. Unless man does the cleaning, leaves, limbs and trash lie where they fall or are thrown. Trash accumulates to such an extent that cleaning it to search the bottom becomes a difficult, if not impossible, task. Also, the build up of sand, silt and mud can force abandonment of planned projects. My story of the lost slot machines, printed later in this chapter, illustrates the problem of lake contamination.

Difficult lake conditions can increase your chances of success. When a task is difficult, fewer individuals will spend time and energy to attempt it!

BEACH HUNTING

Lakes and ponds were often a focal point of early day communi-

215

ty life. They were the favored swimming hole, a source of water, a place for bathing and washing, and a location for picnics. On Sundays large crowds flocked to lakes to spend a pleasant afternoon. Since many lake sites, formerly on public property, are now privately owned, always check for ownership and regulations. Locate old maps and photos that pinpoint beach areas. Study Chapter 12 for a discussion of search techniques. Generally, the same activities that take place at ocean sites also occur at lake beaches. People lose things in the same manner. At lakes, however, picnics were the rule during early day periods. Time should be spent hunting the outlying regions. Since people generally wore street clothes to picnics, it is more likely that they (especially the men and boys who wore trousers) lost coins from their pockets. You may not find much jewelry, but older and more valuable coins will make up for the difference.

Children have always been provided playthings such as swing sets, slides and sand boxes. Early photos will show where play equipment was located. Try to find photos taken, say, every five years because when old equipment is torn down, it may not be replaced at the same spot.

Figure 16-1: Lake hunting is easier than ocean surf hunting if ocean breakers are large. In fact, the use of floats and dredges in ocean surfs is impractical. The individual in this photograph uses his float for sifting and carrying of tools.

Figure 16-2: Fran Peters (left) and Eleanor Hube search a Maryland lake. Note that Fran is wearing waders and warm upper clothing. Eleanor is wearing a dive suit. They are both using Pulse Induction underwater Sea Hunter detectors.

Be alert to maintenance schedules. Some lakes are drained yearly to lower water levels for cleaning swimming areas and replenishing beaches. Lakes are also drained to prepare for winter rains, to poison shoreline vegetation, repair dams and spillways and remove trees and stumps. When the water level of a lake drops only a few feet, beach areas can double in size. The newly exposed areas can be a real bonanza.

Occasionally, I travel to Arizona, specifically to the Quartzsite and Scottsdale areas, to test prototypes of new electronic prospecting metal detectors. While there, I often camp with friends including Roy Lagal and Virgil Hutton. The campfires burn brightly each night, sometimes until well past midnight. During one of our campfire "chats" I told the group about my progress in writing this book, and Virgil related this story:

When Virgil lived in Austin, TX, he normally searched for caches and relics at the various Texas fort sites. Deciding to try his hand at beach hunting, he located the site of an old lake swimming beach area and spent one entire winter weekend searching the sands. Apparently, this beach had never been worked with a metal detector. He found so many coins that two or three times each day he had to empty his

217

Figure 16-4: Don Littlejohn of Fort Worth located these silver coins in Texas lakes. Generally, fresh water lakes do not severely corrode silver coinage. Corrosion depends upon time in water and mineral content.

Figure 16-5: Bill Bosh is both a land and water hunter and from the looks of these finds, he has mastered water hunting quite well. Note the camera lens.

treasure pouch. The earliest coins dated in the late 1800s. There were Indian head pennies, buffalo nickels, seated Liberties, Barber dimes, Liberty quarters and Liberty walking half-dollars. He found one large Virgin Mary 18-kt. gold piece. He found 41 rings, 16 silver, 17 white gold and eight gold. There were two star sapphires and one diamond solitaire — a full carat mounted in a gold and platinum mounting, one diamond cluster ring, three ruby rings, three-stone emerald rings and four-stone pearl rings. Also, he found several silver and gold chains, crucifixes and Saint Christopher medallions. He said he often thinks about this lake and wonders if anyone has ever worked the water. We made plans to do just that on his next trip to Texas.

WATER HUNTING

Lakes have always been one of the quickest and easiest of places in which people could dispose of or conceal objects of almost any size. Stories of lake treasures abound in every community. Talk to the oldtimers and investigate what they tell you. When I was young, I remember hearing about outlaw loot that was thrown into the Fagley Lake in East Texas. When thieves had to get rid of stolen gold, they tied it in a deerskin and attached a section of barbed wire to the skin. The gold was thrown into the lake and the end of the barbed wire tied to a tree near the lake's edge. There's no record of that gold ever being recovered.

Over the centuries, outlaw bands, nervous thieves and even honest but untrusting folk have used lakes as their prime banking source. There are many gangster-era stories of bodies in cement jackets, weapons and stolen loot cast from a boat or bridge in the concealment of night. I always keep several treasure stories "going" at the same time. Here's one of them:

Figure 16-3: Club water hunts and contests are becoming more frequent. Here members of a Maryland club enjoy competing in a sponsored lake hunt.

219

In a small East Texas town, two men broke into a business, stole the safe and made their getaway. In pitch darkness they drove to a nearby lake and hauled the safe out on its earthen dam. Here, they tried to "crack" the safe. Alarmed by sounds of approaching cars, they rolled the safe down the steep embankment into the water. That was 20 years ago. The safe is probably still there. I've tried to locate it, but I have had no success. The lake bottom along the dam is filled with such a profusion of discarded metal that metal detectors cannot be used. By now, the safe has probably sunk several feet into the soft earthen dam. Someday I'll find it with probes or other means. It'll be a pleasure to split the contents with the insurance company.

Here's another story to whet your appetite: in 1887 near Great Falls, MT, outlaws robbed a train of $25,000 in gold coins and 25 small gold bars. With a posse on their trail the robbers hastily threw the bars and a portion of the coins into the lake. According to records, the men never recovered any of their stolen loot. One gold bar was found in 1971, but that is the last recorded recovery. This story, which was reported in a treasure magazine, states that those interested in this one should research the area around Haystack Butte and then check the area of the two nearby lakes.

Here's a true story that members of my family have been personally involved in since the year 1919. At that time my father, Wayne Garrett, was at an age when everything excited him, especially carnivals that occasionally traveled through. Most carnivals in those bygone days consisted of a few horse-drawn rides and side shows, just enough to excite a 14-year-old boy.

My father thought it odd one tent was not on the midway. There were no signs or side-show teasers to lure carnival-goers to it.

Their curiosity sufficiently aroused, he and his friends raised the tent flap and crept cautiously inside. What they saw amazed them — tables lined with slot machines stood on both sides of the tent.

Dad heard the whirring of slot machine wheels as people dropped in coins and "shook hands" with the one-armed bandits. Only occasionally did he hear the sound of money as coins fell into the winner's bowl.

Dad walked to the nearest slot machine, dropped in a nickel and pulled the lever. Wheels whirred as pictures of lemons, oranges and other fruit blurred past the windows. The wheels stopped, but no coins fell into the bowl. After a few unsuccessful tries, he stopped wasting his money.

Suddenly, a boy came into the tent and ran up to a young man standing near Dad, who heard the boy say, "The Sheriff's after you!"

The young man asked, "What do you mean?" The boy said, "He's looking to put you in jail for having these slot machines."

Dad remembers the young man turned sharply and fetched an older man from outside the tent. The two began loading the machines in the bed of a Ford Model T pickup. When they finished, the pair drove through a field, bounced across a gulley and onto a dirt road. Dad hopped on his bike and pedaled furiously to keep up with the pickup.

Because it was getting dark, the men could not see Dad who could still hear the truck even though he had fallen behind. He followed the truck down the dirt road until it turned into a recreational area called Jones Lake. Dad had been to the lake often—why, it was his favorite swimming hole. Pedaling closer, he heard the truck stop and doors slam. Leaving his bike, he crept closer. As he neared the lake he heard a loud splash, then another and another. When he could see the men, he watched as each carried a slot machine from the truck to the end of the pier and threw it into the lake. Dad remembers each man made about six trips, meaning at least 12 machines plunged to the bottom.

Often in the following years Dad came and swam in the lake. Each time he thought about the slot machines. One day when he was about 18, he decided to dive down and make a recovery. On his first attempt, he failed to reach the bottom at 10 feet. He hadn't realized the depth of the water in the area off the pier.

Determined to succeed, he dove again, groped around in murky water and grabbed one of the machines. On the next dive he dragged the machine a few feet along the bottom. After several dives, he had wrestled it into shallow water along the lake's edge.

He waited until night, then used a crowbar to break into the machine and empty the coin box. He then carried the machine back to the pier and returned it to its watery grave.

For more than 50 years Dad kept the secret of the remaining 11 slot machines. Because of his difficulty in getting just one machine and his fear of the Sheriff, he never tried again.

One day, however, as the two of us were driving in East Texas, he told me the story. Drawn like a magnet to the lake, we parked the car and looked the place over. I decided to make a recovery.

My father and my two brothers, George and Don, and Jim and John Cross met at the lake on a cold January day. Jim, President of Cross International, a Utah based underwater salvage company, was working under contract near Dallas to dredge a large lake channel. We decided to put his commercial equipment to good use at the East Texas lake site.

To begin the search, we scanned the lake with a Lowrance sonar, Figure 16-6, making grid surveys of the bottom. Fish were everywhere. At one point, the stylus on the chart mapped a long pencil-like shape on the paper about halfway between the lake bottom and surface. Someone said the mark represented the largest fish he had ever seen on a sonar printout. It may not have been a fish, however, as alligators have been in those waters for decades. None of us were particularly fond of encountering an alligator, but we were determined to find the lost slots.

The sonar showed the deepest part of the lake along the dam at about 18 feet. In many places the sonar drew objects protruding from the bottom. In fact, the whole bottom seemed to be covered with slot machines.

Selecting a likely area, Cross donned diving gear, Figure 16-7, to keep his body warm and used a two-way radio to communicate with those on shore. The lake was so dark his hand was visible to him only when pressed against his face mask.

Cross had only taken a dozen steps when he realized he was walking in heavy, knee-deep silt. He continued to walk into deeper mud, reaching six to eight feet as he neared the area of the present-day pier. Cross made his way through the mud by walking on the solid clay bottom. He discovered that the lake bottom under the pier was littered with junk of every size, shape and description.

Because visibility was zero, Cross walked slowly across the bottom until he bumped into something. Then he would reach down, feel the object and try to determine its identity. The first dive produced no slot machines.

A Garrett Sea Hunter Pulse Induction metal detector was used wherever it could be forced through the mud. In the "junkyard" beneath the pier, dozens of metal objects caused the detector to sound, but none of those resembled a slot machine.

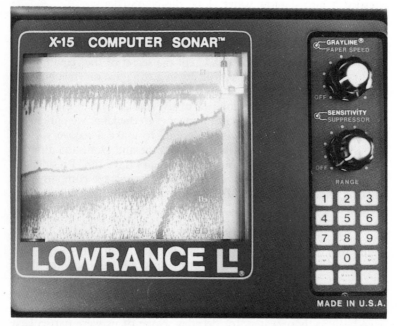

Figure 16-6: Here is a portion of a Lowrance sonar computer readout showing bottom contour and obstacles. Numerous fish can be seen as well as objects protruding from the bottom.

As Cross widened his search area from that of the first dive, he reported back, "I've found a motorcycle." Digging through the silt with his hands, he felt the frame and spokes of two wheels. As Cross resumed his search, he marveled at the huge quantity of bottles scattered across the bottom. His second search also produced nothing.

Later, Cross' brother John dove and began a circular grid search, using the detector and feeling his way as he went along. He found fishing poles, spears and more bottles.

"I've found something," he said suddenly. "I'm standing on top of it in mud that must be eight feet deep. The object is rounded and is roughly the size and shape of a slot machine."

In his excitement, he turned upside down, diving head first into the mud. Working with his hands, he began to uncover the object. We were certain he had found the first of the 11 slot machines.

But as the object emerged, it turned out to be a large piece of concrete. A park attendant later said park personnel had broken up an old concrete building and had thrown much of it into the lake.

Disappointed, but undaunted, he continued his search to find a wooden boat and what seemed to be the bed of a large wagon, about four feet wide and eight feet long. In the thick mud his energy was soon depleted and the lost slots were still as lost as ever.

While the divers were in the water, several of us worked the lake's edge with metal detectors. I knew the lake had been used for swimming for 60 or 70 years and I believed many coins, rings and jewelry might be there.

The mud along the banks, however, was at least two feet deep with tremendous quantities of tree limbs, broken wood, concrete and other junk strewn along the bottom. After about an hour we gave up our search for valuables. The only way to recover anything from this lake I thought, was to drain it and sift through tons of mud and debris.

The next day Cross and I, Figure 16-8, wore dry suits to work along the steep slope of the dam. He found numerous rotted posts sticking up out of the mud, confirming a theory we had about the location of early day piers. The most remote old pylon was 18 feet deep. Burrowing through the mud another 10 feet, he finally reached hard-packed clay.

Searching was difficult here too because of the vast amounts of junk. At one time Cross felt something bump into his backside from out of the muck, not once, but twice. Remembering the story of the alligators, he suppressed more than a twinge of fear.

I concentrated my search in the water along the dam. I made two passes along the embankment, searching with my hands as I pulled myself along on my stomach.

At one point well into a dive, I reached forward to pull myself along and grasped a rounded object. As I reached forward, I lost my balance and the object started moving.

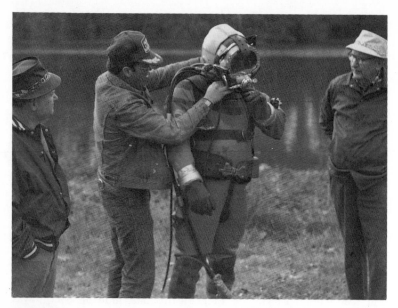

Figure 16-7: During a search for slot machines in an East Texas lake, Jim Cross suits up and prepares to dive. Gary Lee assists in fitting the helmet. The author's brother, George Garrett, (left) and Gordon Hall operated shore gear. A two-way diver-to-shore communications system is installed within the suit.

Figure 16-8: The author lowers himself, with the assistance of John Cross and Gary Lee, into the dam area of an East Texas lake near Lufkin. The men are searching for about a dozen slot machines that were discarded in this lake in the early 1900s as described in this chapter.

Reeling backwards to escape the "gator" I could imagine before me, I flipped over and began sliding uncontrollably down the steep embankment to the bottom of that 18-foot-deep hole.

When I finally stopped, I was tangled in a rat's nest of air hose, safety line, tree limbs and other junk. After a few anxious moments, I righted myself, untangled my line and climbed up the underwater incline. I knew there was nowhere to go but forward; so, I cautiously pulled myself along the bottom back into shallow water.

At one point, I again grabbed a rounded object. This time, however, I realized I had a tree root in my hand.

Continuing our underwater search throughout the morning, we found an endless amount of objects, but no lost slots. Near the end of the second day — cold, tired and alligator-jumpy — we decided to "call it quits." We packed our gear with visions of slot machines packed with buffalo nickels still haunting our thoughts.

As we talked later, we theorized that Dad's pier, circa 1919, could have been anywhere along two different shores of that lake. We believe that if the slot machines are still there, they most likely rest on the clay bottom beneath a combined depth of 20 feet of water and thick, suffocating silt.

And, the way we see it, they may be guarded by several hungry, but financially secure, East Texas alligators. I am continuing my search, however, developing new methods for locating the slots and swimmers' lost booty.

Recently, I received a letter and photographs from Pete Petrisky, owner of Deep Six, who had heard my "slot" story. Petrisky and local diver David Ferry, Figure 16-9, owner of Scubatec Dive Shop in Lufkin, did considerable research on the site and made numerous dives to locate the slot machines. He found hundreds of bottles and other of man's relics, but not the one-armed bandits.

Modern, efficient scuba equipment provides the underwater searcher with unparalleled opportunities for taking extended excursions into the aquatic world. Submersible metal detectors, surface suction dredges and other equipment provide the diver with tools for finding treasure. All that is needed are a few hardy, imaginative and determined individuals to venture into the underwater realm to locate sunken treasure where it is known to exist. Treasure that can be recovered consists of everything valuable from coins to jewelry, to outlaw loot, to sunken boats and ships. You can go after it, if you wish, and you'll mostly have it all to yourself.

Underwater lake hunting, however, is not a cake walk. The visibility, more often than not, is true "zero." Sand, silt, muck, clay and vegetation — tree limbs and even whole trees — cover the bottom. It's often a grope, probe and feel operation. But, of course, your metal detector can be the key to unlock the doorway to success.

You can expect difficulty in maintaining a grid search, but the

Figure 16-9: Following the unsuccessful attempt of the author and team members to locate slot machines divers Pete Petrisky and David Ferry take up the search. In the photo, David, who is owner of Scubatec in Lufkin, displayed some of the artifacts found. Note the sawed-off shotgun.

process can be improved by weighting PVC tubes in a grid pattern. The tubing can alert you to the limits of your search area as you feel your way along it.

Another grid search method is to anchor floats at strategic points Occasionally, during your search, you surface to take a bearing. Murky water lake searching is more diffiicult than night diving in clear water with lights because of the flaring, blinding effect of the light. You'll be tempted not to wear gloves since they restrict your sense of feel. Don't give in to this temptation because lake bottoms contain more broken glass, fish hooks and other dangerous objects than any other body of water. Searching river bottoms with bare hands is dangerous, but not nearly as much as working lake bottoms, especially near the shore or along piers.

Searching under piers and docks can be profitable but it is not without its dangers. Around piers you'll locate coins, knives, jewelry, tools, new and antique bottles, chairs, bicycles, sunglasses, fishing tackle, fishing poles, radios and cameras and pound after pound of lead and tin cans. You can expect to occasionally be snagged by some fisherman and run over by a boat if you aren't careful.

When diving, keep alert for overhead boats, as well as submerged fences, fish lines and nets and trees upon which you can become snagged. Poor visibility further adds to the complexities of lake diving. Strict adherence to buddy diving is necessary. Safety rules and procedures are discussed in scuba training manuals.

And, speaking of buddy diving, murky water, coins, jewelry and the like reminds me of a newspaper clipping I received from Ted Conard of Cache Inn Metal Detectors of Kent, WA. An article written by Peggy Ziebarth in the *News Journai*, tells of treasure diving in murky lake depths by a buddy team, Gary Robbins and Loraine Peterson. "Ever since I found a gold ring... I guess I've got gold fever," said Robbins. "I'm hooked too," Loraine quickly added. The pair had made 25 dives that summer in nearby Lake Wilderness. On Robbins' first dive he found four rings and several coins. On Loraine's first dive she found a coin purse that contained numerous coins including a "walking Liberty" silver dollar that she said must have been "mad money" that was lost nearly four decades ago.

They have found countless coins that date back to the 1920s and numerous tax and transit tokens from times "back when." They use a Garrett Sea Hunter with audible and visible light indicators. "When we make a find," Robbins said, "we get a light beep—sort of like a pinball machine racking up scores!"

For many years, William Houghton and fellow divers Brian Simpson and Richard Myers (state police troopers) have been bringing up treasures from one of Pennsylvania's recreational lakes, Figure 16-10. Houghton estimates that before their job is finished, they will have found 1,000 rings, plus many thousands of other jewelry items and miscellaneous lost items. Already, they have found nearly half the rings they estinated could be found, Firgures 16-11 and 16-12.

For 100 years, this lake has been used by persons seeking the fun and enjoyment that recreational waters have to offer. And, apparently, all during those 100 years, people have been losing their treasures. One day, Houghton, a scuba diver, decided to try his luck with his newly purchased Sea Hunter underwater metal detector. At a water depth of about six feet, he heard a faint detector signal. He dug 18 inches into the loose sand and retrieved a beautiful gold ring. "You're digging through the sand and all of a sudden it seems to spin right into your hand," Houghton said. "I could read the inscriptions and design. It was about as shiny as when it was new. There was just no tarnish." See Figure 16-13.

Since then, the Houghton team members have found a wealth of treasure. But, they don't claim one piece of it. They plan to return every item possible to the owner who lost it. Already many pieces have been returned. Working with Jeanie Craddock of the local school system, they catalog every item and then begin a search of school and other records. Ring initials sometimes indicate the original owners. The group contacts high schools and colleges to obtain yearbooks and arranges meetings with reunion committees.

The heaviest rings have been found in about 18 inches of mud. Other items found include Indian arrowheads, a Belgian-made shotgun dating to 1830, an antique ice-cutting tool, champagne glasses and 450 tear-shaped whiskey bottles. Many of the unusual and historical items are being placed in a museum. Congratulations to William and team members for the great work you are doing in recovering and returning prized possessions to their owners and for helping to establish a museum so that locals can enjoy viewing "treasures" from the past.

If you live near large lakes, watch for beach treasure cast ashore during storms. Violent storms with high winds can churn up the bottom and hurl things ashore. Watch for bottles, coins, shells, fossils, Indian relics and driftwood. When you see piles of driftwood and debris on the beach, search for valuable articles trapped within. Don't forget to beware of snakes. Stay alert in other ways as well. When you locate coins and other interesting things, consider the possibility that they came from an off-shore shipwreck or discarded cache. Always follow such "leads" through to completion.

I continually stress that hunters, even beach hunters, should fill all holes dug. This is especially important at lake sites because the ground is usually of a harder material that will not be self-healing like sandy ocean beach sites. Since some lake sites have considerable grass, good recovery techniques are a necessity. Leaving holes is the fastest way for you and all of us to be permanently barred from the sites that you abuse. FILL YOUR HOLES!

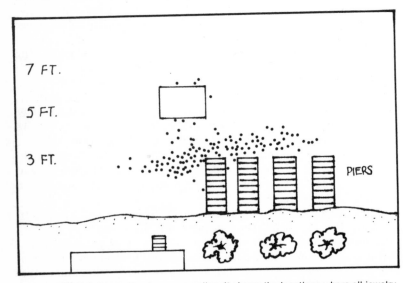

Figure 16-10: This illustration is very revealing. It shows the locations where all jewelry items were found in a very old swimming area. Note the large mass of objects found in the swimming area, per se, and then notice the trail of lost objects that leads out to a floating platform. Note, also, around the platform, numerous discoveries were made.

SEARCHING LAKE SWIMMING AREAS

Lake swimming areas can be as productive as the ocean surf. Some lake hunting will be much easier than ocean hunting, Figure 16-1. And, on the other side of the coin, some lake sites will be difficult. Beaches now being used are the easiest because they are usually kept clean of debris with the bottom loosened by swimmers. Old beaches that have not been used for years are generally more difficult to search. The bottom soil may become hard packed with the passage of time. If the park where the lake is located continues to be a recreational area (but with swimming areas closed), park users will quickly "fill" the lake with tons of discarded refuse.

If there are nearby trees, the area around the lake will gradually fill with leaves, twigs, limbs and even entire trees. Believe me, a swimming area that was once popular and could have been a perfect hunting site can become an almost impossible place to search after it has been closed to the public for only a few years. That's not to say that all abandoned places become impossible to search; it's just that some can be exceedingly difficult.

Before starting work at "your" lake site, make a thorough study to locate all possible swimming areas, past and present. Rely upon maps, photographs, postcards, histories and townspeople both young and old who know of prior activity. Study the shoreline carefully to identify areas that look promising. Gently sloping shore areas, especially with roads that lead to them, are promising sites that require further investigation. Use a "fish finder" sonar to locate shallow water sites. Concrete foundations and slabs may mark locations where public activities took place years ago.

Be alert to periods of low water. These occur during dry seasons, when the lake is drained and when nearby industry uses water faster than rain can replenish the supply.

Begin your search with a metal detector. Since fresh water does not contain salt, one detector "problem" is eliminated. Ground minerals will dictate the type, or types, of equipment you can use, Figures 16-2 through 16-4. If the ground contains no minerals, almost any type detector can be used. If ground minerals are present, either a manual or automated VLF or a Pulse Induction type will be required. As I have stressed, a water hunting detector is the preferred type, but since there are no breakers and high waves in lakes, a detector that can be used with its control housing mounted on a float will work satisfactorily.

If debris and an excessive amount of bottom fill prevent you from searching, you'll have to resort to other means. You can use heavy duty rakes to clean bottom debris, but raked material then creates a problem. You may not be allowed to rake it ashore. Certainly, you do not want to be raking it back and forth as you search the bottom. Select a site your detector says is "clean," or a site outside the normal swimming boundaries. Place the raked material and other trash there. Check with park officials prior to such extensive preparation.

After you have cleared the bottom debris, make a thorough scan of the site. If you find treasure, the effort will have been worth it, Figure 16-5. If you do not find treasure, you have some more work to do. Possibly silt has built up the bottom and placed the treasure out of reach of your metal detector. There are several steps you can take. With permission from the park officials or the lake owner, dig an exploratory trench starting at the shoreline and extending out as deep as you can dig. The trench must be wide enough for your searchcoil. Be certain to scan the material you remove from the trench. Place the material where it can be used to fill in the trench when you have finished your test project.

After digging and scanning several trenches, judge the site potential. If it was totally unproductive, you have selected a poor treasure hunting beach. Move to another site and continue your search.

If the bottom is loose and not hard-packed, a surface suction dredge can be used. Use a two-inch or four-inch size with a wire basket that catches all objects brought up from the bottom. The larger the dredge, the faster your work will proceed. Study Chapter 21 to learn techniques of dredge operating.

At some lake sites you'll find concrete ramps that were constructed for swimmers. One such ramp was provided for early-day swimmers in Dallas' White Rock Lake. Believing the area had never been search-

Figure 16-11: Here are some of the hundreds of rings and other objects located by William Houghton (left) and fellow divers, Dennis Riley (right), Brian Simpson and Richard Myers, from one of Pennsylvania's recreational lakes.

230

ed, I located the site and began my metal detector search. After several hours work, I was rewarded with only a few lead weights and fish hooks that were probably lost there only recently. Obviously, other treasure hunters had been there before me! I expected coins and rings in the mud at the end of the ramp. The ramp sloped downward and I knew that all lost articles would gradually slide down the ramp and fall into the mud. Not one did I find! It was disheartening, to say the least, but I was reminded again not to procrastinate. If you learn of a promising site, don't delay. Search the site as quickly as possible. Another truism was verified. There are other good hunters who are quite capable of locating hot spots and of using their equipment to locate lost treasure. Well...there is plenty to go around!

Figure 16-13: William Houghton dug about 18 inches to locate this lovely gold band. When found, it was without tarnish and about as shiny as when it was new. He could immediately read the inscriptions and designs. Photos courtesy William Houghton.

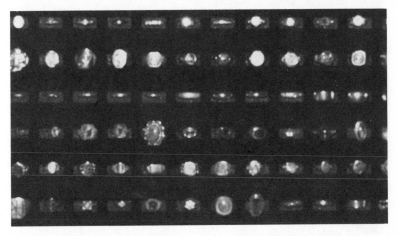

Figure 16-12: Here is a closeup of additional rings found by William Houghton and dive team members.

CHAPTER 17

Where and How to Search Miscellaneous Water Sites

There's a parallel between learning this business of treasure hunting and the way in which a tree grows. First, from the fertile earth pops a single bud that develops into a tree trunk. Then the trunk sprouts limbs. These limbs branch out and grow. Two branches bud into four; then four become eight...sixteen, thirty-two and more. Followed by the leaves. They pop out all over.

That's the way it is with treasure hunting. It keeps growing and growing—there's no end to it. Think about it. The earth, comparable to research, is a gigantic source of treasure leads. Out of research grows the trunk which is the foundation of treasure hunting. Each branch splits into two or more leads, then four, then eight and so on. Then, when you start finding treasure, it's like tree leaves popping out all over.

At first, 40-plus years ago, I knew nothing about treasure hunting. Then I began to learn. I studied material on the subject, which, although scant, represented WHAT WAS KNOWN AT THAT TIME. I'd go into the field to practice what I'd learned. I'd try to find treasure. I'd talk with other treasure hunters. There were times when I thought that surely, with so many people running about with metal detectors, there would soon be no more treasure to find. Well-meaning friends cautioned me against starting a company to design and manufacture metal detectors. They predicted that there would soon be so many people hunting that all the treasure would be found with no demand then for metal detectors.

The truth is, THERE IS LOST, BURIED AND SUNKEN TREASURE THAT WILL CONTINUE TO BE FOUND EVEN IF THE WORLD RUNS ANOTHER THOUSAND YEARS. Let me give you just three reasons. First, people are getting smarter. They are learning to do their research. They are finding where the more difficult treasures are buried and they are uncovering new leads that point to heretofore unknown treasure. Second, treasure locating equipment is getting better. Detectors are becoming more powerful; treasure can be detected deeper. Treasure that couldn't be found yesterday because of inadequate instruments, will be found tomorrow when new, improved detectors are made available. Thirdly, THERE IS A TEREMENDOUS AMOUNT OF TREASURE BEING LOST AND BURIED EVERY DAY. THE SUPPLY IS BEING REPLENISHED! But, that shouldn't surprise you. After all, the treasure you are finding now was lost or hidden in the past by people. Is there any reason to expect people to

232

stop losing or hiding treasure? Certainly not. Since man first walked the earth, he has dropped things and hidden and buried them for safekeeping. Lost treasure and treasure hunting is mentioned in the Bible. This business of treasure hunting will continue as long as man exists on the face of the earth.

At every turn, I learn of buried treasure. People who know I am a treasure seeker tell me stories. When I visit foreign countries, the story is the same. People want to tell me a story about buried treasure. In Mexico, for instance, I believe there's not one adult who doesn't know of a buried treasure. Throughout Mexico's turbulent history there have been so many revolutions, political upheavals and difficult, uncertain periods that it became automatic practice to bury what little you did have to prevent someone from taking it from you. Until just over a century ago, Comanche Indians made a yearly Harvest Moon trek from north of the Rio Grande River deep into Mexico, plundering, raping, killing and taking hostages as they went along. Mexicans soon learned to hide their valuables in anticipation of the onslaught that was sure to come. When the savages came, many people with buried wealth were killed or taken captive and the secret of their treasure lost forever...lost, that is until it is found by accident or until some enterprising treasure hunter comes along to discover it.

Now, after hearing all of that do you believe there are an unlimited number of places in your area to find treasure and an unlimited supply of treasure to be found? In this chapter I have listed and described many "uncommon" water locations where treasure can be found.

The remainder of this chapter is divided into four sections: BRIDGES AND BRIDGE SITES, WATERWAY SITES, OCEAN SITES and MISCELLANEOUS SITES. I expanded some listings to include additional data, with stories about site possibilities designed to put your mind to work.

BRIDGES AND BRIDGE SITES

There are many kinds of bridges, including vehicle, pedestrian and railway. And, there are many specific types of bridges, including earthen, covered, open and those built specifically for activities like sports (fishing and diving) and tourism. Bridges are permanent landmarks; they are interesting and there are plenty of them.

When an individual hides something, He plans to come back for it. Naturally he must have a way of remembering where it was hidden...a special object, tree, structure or landmark to mark the spot. The person on the run must quickly select a place with a landmark that will easily be remembered.

Bridges fit the requirements perfectly. And, if I might interject another thought, so do city limits, county lines and state boundaries. But, the very physical nature of a bridge makes it easy to remember and easy to find. An elderly gentleman kept his fortune in silver dollars buried in a field just off Highway 94 in East Texas at a point east of the Neches River bridge. Research indicates that Jesse James hid at least one cache near a railroad bridge just northeast of Garland, TX. During the Depression of the 1930s, workmen in Garland took up a collection of pennies. The fruit jar, in which they placed their coppers, was placed in wet cement as a bridge was being built on Saturn Road, midway between Miller Road and Kingsley Road.

An extortionist, fleeing from the F.B.I., stopped his car on a West Texas creek bridge and hurriedly disposed of incriminating evidence that the F.B.I. wanted. It was the typewriter on which he had written an extortion letter. See Figure 15-2.

You name it, and probably it has been hidden, discarded or lost either in the water beneath or near a bridge. Robbers have on many occasions dumped loot that was too heavy or "too hot to handle" by throwing it off bridges. Thousands or weapons have been so discarded.

Figure 17-1: When searching covered bridge sites, search beneath and downstream from the bridge. Also, search for weapons hidden within the covered portion and don't forget to check the approaches and surrounding ground for buried treasure. This is the 1869 Bell Ford covered bridge located on Indiana's East Fork White River.

Near Reno, NV, lies a large safe filled with gold and other valuables. It was being transported to higher ground just ahead of a raging river torrent. A weakened bridge collapsed under the weight of wagon and safe. Down it all came. Where the safe lies today under tons of sand and rock is anybody's guess. George Mroczkowski and I have searched for it and believe we have the safe's resting place narrowed considerably. Through research and interviews George was able to pin down the site, and continued investigation is underway.

According to researcher Michael Paul Henson, 40% of covered bridges in the eastern United States are connected in some way to a treasure. He also states that ghost sightings are often connected with them. Covered bridges, Figure 17-1, are safe shelters in times of inclement weather. They make perfect meeting places and locations for midnight gatherings. Many a traveler has spent the night under one. When searching these sites, look in the water both beneath and downstream from the bridge. Use your detector to search for caches and weapons hidden within the covered portion. And, don't forget to check the approaches for buried treasure.

WATERWAY SITES

INTRACOASTAL CANALS: Beginning in the 18th century and until the coming of the railroads, canals played an important part of the American way of life. In Europe canals and waterways have been used by man since he built the first floating apparatus. Searching is specifically suggested at those places where canals enter and leave communities, mills and taverns. Bridges and dredging sites should be investigated. As canals fell into disuse, they became the dump grounds for a community's trash. When you search these areas, expect to find coins, tokens, weapons, bottles and other interesting relics.

CHANNEL DREDGING OPERATIONS:

Don't miss these—much of the work has already been done for you. When giant scoops tear huge mounds of mud and muck from river and channel beds, you can count on the fact that there will also be many collectible goodies in them. Search the area where the material is placed. You'll find bottles, an occasional weapon and coins. Should you hit it lucky, you may also come up with some cache of outlaw loot or valuable relics. Try to keep track of the dredging operation. Should you locate coins, relics and, perhaps, some nice treasure, make a note of where in the waterway it came from. Search that spot under the waters of the canal as soon as possible.

While on the subject of dredging, let's discuss another type. In placer gold country some old recovery operations include the dredging of productive river sites. At locations where gold in paying quantities has been found, operators with dragline equipment dredge these productive sites and literally turn river and stream bottoms upside down. All recovered material is run through classifiers that permit dredged

Figure 17-3: Here is a closeup of Bob Bryan's 1879 $10 gold coin he found at a recreational site in Mississippi. Congratulations, Bob, as a member of the Gold Coin Club.

Figure 17-2: Gold coins are found more often then one imagines, and they bring much joy. Treasure hunters yearn for the day when they will make a gold coin strike. Bob Bryan of Missouri proudly displays a gold coin that he discovered with his metal detector. See Figure 17-3. Photos courtesy Smitty's Detector Sales, Desloge, MO.

gravel of a certain size or larger to be diverted from the ore processing equipment. The size of the classifier screens is determined by the large gold nuggets that are believed to be in the gravel.

As the oversize gravel is diverted, it travels on conveyor belts and is dumped in piles along the waterway. In case an extra large nugget is diverted, a spotter sits near the conveyor belt exit to stop the machinery. Not all such nuggets have been spotted. They slip off the end of the conveyor belt. Sometimes the spotter goes to sleep. Also, oversized mudballs can conceal gold and prevent it from being spotted.

To give you an idea how electronic prospecting pays off, consider this story of Roy Lagal, life-long prospector and treasure hunter. He has spent considerable time working old gold camps, bedrock areas and placer diggings. He has worked dredge piles along the highway near the Liberty Cafe in Liberty, WA. The area is a well-known gold producing site. While he probably won't tell you the total amount of gold he has found, he will tell you that the largest nugget he found weighed seven POUNDS!

Figure 17-4: Bob Sickler, well-known detector operator and equipment field test reporter for *Western and Eastern Treasures* magazine, specializes in searching recreational sites. "Searching through heavy snow is somewhat likened unto searching in water," explains Bob. "You can't see, but the detector can, as it readily penetrates the snow. And, too, when I search in winter, I usually have recreational sites all to myself."

Figure 17-5: Here is a closeup of some of the more unusual and valuable coins that Bob Sickler has found while working recreational sites.

Consider, also, that the dredge piles have been a favorite place for picnickers. There are several reports of the picnickers spying large gold nuggets laying on top of the dredge piles.

There are many other productive sites located along waterways. While I could expand upon each of them, I will simply list them in the following paragraph:

Steamboat landing sites; mouths of waterways; conjunctions of rivers; islands; Indian campsites; Indian trail crossings such as the two Comanche war trail crossings in the Texas Big Bend area; recreational boat docks; picnic areas; sites near settlements; fishing spots; water control operations and many, many others. See Figures 17-2 through 17-6.

OCEAN SITES

Chapter 14 discusses underwater ocean hunting and points out numerous places to search. In the following section I suggest several other possible locations along ocean coasts where treasure can be found.

ROCK AND CORAL OUTCROPPINGS:

These places are natural traps where treasure can be found. One of my most valuable treasures is a 17th century icon I found at a coral outcropping. Read the full story in Chapter 12.

PIRATE COVES:

Especially check inland for buried pirate treasure. Relic hunting should be excellent in these waters.

CHANNEL AND PORT DREDGE AREAS:

We've covered dredging in several sections in this book already. Refer to them for ideas.

DRY HARBOR SITES:

In some ports you've got lots of dry places to search. While touring southern Maine a few years ago, I visited some of the waterfront areas. I noticed the water had receded far out during low tides. There were dozens of potentially good sites exposed.

BEACHCOMBING SITES:

There are many places along the ocean's coasts that are known as treasure beaches. A peculiar quirk about winds and currents is that all kinds of debris floats ashore at certain beach locations. You'll find fish net floats, lots of rope, ship riggings, furniture, bottles, crates of cargo and goods, clothing, small boats and other vessels, plus an unlimited supply of other goods.

SHIPWRECK SITES:

These are the good ones—the ones that pay off. As we have discussed, when you start finding clues such as valuable coins and relics on the beach, you can suspect that a shipwreck may lie just offshore. It's up to you to do the rest. Two men found one such wrecksite. The Mother Lode was about fifty yards offshore. They used a dragline bucket which they carried out in a boat. A steel cable connected the bucket with a four-wheel drive vehicle. The retrieval method they used was to drop the bucket offshore and use the jeep to pull it in. Their recovered treasure filled a bank vault.

If you want to read a truly fascinating story, look for Lieutenant Harry E. Rieseberg's, THE SEA OF TREASURE. Read "The Search for the Golden Jacket's Treasure." This is the story of the *Golden Jacket,* that was driven by a hurricane in 1702 onto a shallow offshore rock outcropping. The ship disintegrated and its cargo, including over one million dollars in gold and silver, plus other coinage, was lost in the shallow waters. Occasionally, coins from the ship are still found on the beach.

Lieutenant Rieseberg describes the moments before the shipwreck: the hurricane's fury, monstrous waves, roaring waters, screaming winds, exploding whitetop breakers, the breaking up of the ship's oak timbers and the pitiful screams of the crew. It's the most vivid account of what takes place during a shipwreck I have ever read.

MISCELLANEOUS SITES

As you should believe by now, the list of places where treasure can be found has no end. Here are a few more for you to ponder:

NATURAL SPRINGS:

Don't overlook these treasure sites. They have been used by man since the beginning. You'll find treasure both in the springs and buried around them.

WELLS AND CISTERNS:

These are perfect places to discard junk or to dispose of something that best not be kept. You must use caution around these holes in the

Figure 17-6: Gary Burt of Edinburgh, Scotland, successfully searches recreational and other popular sites. Here he displays some of his coins, buttons and other items. Note the rings in the folder on the table. Thanks, Gary, for showing us your finds.

ground. Never work them alone. Watch for snakes and be on the alert for crumbling and falling bricks and stones. I should mention outhouses here. If you find one, it will probably pay you to dig it out. While we are on the subject of outhouses, consider this one. Research and tales indicate that Pancho Villa hastily threw a large treasure into a community outhouse built near one of the entrances to an old, deserted city in the southern area of the state of Chihuahua. The massive walls and buildings of this city still stand near the Batopillas River.

OLD SWIMMING HOLES:

Before concrete swimming pools, the storied "ol' swimmin' hole" was the place to go on a hot summer day. It might have been a natural sink hole fed by cold spring water, or just an oversized hole kept full by a running stream. I used to swim in one such creek, complete with rope attached to a high branch. You'll find these all over your area. Some that used to be free and wild have been taken over by park boards and a small fee is charged. Talk to oldtimers or write to the chambers of commerce in your area of interest. Request a list of old natural swimming hole site locations. Ask if metal detectors are permitted to be used.

WATERFALLS:

There aren't a lot of these around, but if you know of one, investigate it by all means. It's easy to visualize that heavy items flowing over a spillway may very well be accumulating at the base of the waterfall. Waterfalls attract people, so they would become natural places to discard something which was to be forever hidden from sight. Waterfalls are romantic places, so why not throw in a coin in exchange for luck or a down-payment on a wish? In gold country, waterfall sites could possibly be gigantic, fantastically wealthy placer concentrations free for the taking.

Other sites include natural sinkholes, watering holes, abandoned quarries, mineral-spring bath areas (spas), health resorts (search for caches of people who hid their wealth but didn't get well to recover it), baptismal areas, ceremonial pools, dredge boat dumpsites, beach cleaning dump sites, produce wharfs, fresh water cisterns and wells, and swimming pools.

SWIMMING POOLS:

If you are a good swimmer, you may want to dive to the bottom of every swimming pool you can find. Especially check motel and hotel pools, Figure 17-7. Carefully search by eyesight for dropped coins, lost rings and jewelery. You could get lucky and receive a reward — others have. All you'll need is your swimming trunks — unless you want to risk arrest — and a snorkel, mask and pair of flippers. Also, take a two-foot long set of tweezers or other device for retrieving items that have fallen through the strainer. These drain-plug strainers are often constructed with two-inch diameter round or square holes.

Figure 17-7: Whenever you have a chance and you are a good swimmer, don't fail to search the bottoms of swimming pools. Often coins and jewelry items are lost by swimmers. Since eyesight is generally all that is needed to locate these treasures, you should always carry with you a good set of flippers, mask and snorkel.

WATERING HOLES:

Ojo de Leon, nine miles west of Comanche Springs in West Texas is known for its great depth. In the 1800s a wagon master reached Ojo de Leon with a wagon wheel that had almost rattled to pieces. He cast it into the water for soaking, but the wheel disappeared from sight. He could not reach it even with a grappling hook. Since this depth may have prevented everything else from being recovered, it may pay an enterprising person to devise a means for cleaning out this or other watering holes.

HARBORS:

Harbors must surely qualify as the world's richest depository of sunken relics and wealth, Figures 17-8 and 17-9. I was in the Navy for four years and even though dumping was against the rules, I witnessed tons of debris, ship's gear and other objects being thrown over the side. When ships tie up alongside docks, refuse bins are provided. But, when ships anchor in the harbor, there are no refuse bins and all trash and garbage must be stowed until the vessel puts out to sea. You can imagine how much unwanted waste can accumulate in a month's time!

Surplus, obsolete and wornout gear must be disposed of. The order to "get rid of it" comes down to the seamen and get rid of it they do...right over the side...in port or out at sea. A group of divers made over 100 dives in an Argentina harbor. The United States Navy has

Figure 17-8: The author thanks Rune Fordal (left) for sending these photographs of himself and Arne Adolfsson. The men from Visby, Sweden, are presently excavating the *Lubecker* Warship which was lost in 1566 near Visby Harbor on island Gotland, at a depth of 15 feet.

Figure 17-9: This is a silver whistle dating to 1566 found by Rune Fordal and Arne Adolfsson (See Figure 17-8). Among the items found are more than 200 German Taler (silver coins), silver spoons, silver sword handles, hundreds of iron shot and many hundreds of lead objects. The men use Sea Hunter Pulse Induction equipment in their search.

243

a 100-year lease on the base. The divers found "treasure" during each dive. Among the boatloads of gear they found were hundreds of three-inch and five-inch brass gun casings. The divers stated that at certain sites, in every direction they turned there were brass casings. The sites were a veritable gold mine of brass. They found ship's rigging, brass portholes, porthole storm covers, a USN bell with clapper, hundreds of cups, bowls, plates and other dishes, and buckets full of kitchen utensils. One of their most prized finds was a brass 1944 Mark V deep diving helmet with breastplate.

Recently while talking with a friend, he told me about witnessing a remarkable find made in the harbor of Charlotte Amalie. He was walking along the beach when several men pulled ashore in a boat. He noticed the underwater detectors were of the Garrett brand. He asked the men if they had any luck, and told them he knew the man who manufactured the detectors they were using. The divers showed him several relics and then said, "Tell Mr. Garrett about this." They pulled a cloth bag from underneath the boat seat. The bag was filled with gold coins!

CHAPTER 18

Where and How to Find War Relics

My first exposure to hunting sunken Civil War relics occurred in Louisiana in 1968. Friends invited me to search for battlefield relics near Natchitoches. One member of the group was particularly interested in a small creek that trickled through the woods. At one point where it widened into a body of water about six feet across, a tree had fallen across the six-foot span. The relic hunter walked slowly across it, skimming his searchcoil over the water.

"I just got a faint signal!" he shouted. After a few seconds digging with his shovel he reached into the water and raised a mud-caked cannon ball aloft. He pitched the cannonball onto the embankment and made another detector scan at the same spot. He grinned and dug into the mud again. With a whoop he brought up an identical cannon ball. To this day, I distinctly remember the water depth to be arm's length. The right sleeve of his short-sleeved shirt was wet.

Why were there two cannon balls in the same hole? Why were they in the water? There is a good probability that they were purposely dumped. And, there is a good chance there are many more in that hole waiting for someone to come along with one of today's superdeep detectors that can reach greater depths than the old-styled detector my friend was using.

The search for sunken relics may not be an activity all treasure hunters enjoy. But, for those who don't mind extra adventure in their search for the big one, such pursuit can be exciting and profitable. The discovery of a sunken Civil War "time-capsule" containing a wagon load of rare historical treasures is a relic hunter's dream come true — one that is never forgotten.

Following is the story of one individual's successful recovery. In Louisiana's deep woods several miles from the nearest road, a relic hunter located a wagon-load of sunken 10-pound Civil War Parrott shells. In a shallow creek, his detector indicated metal. Digging down about a foot he recovered one of the shells, complete with wooden sabot. Excited, he laid the shell on the bank and scanned again. Another loud signal told him to dig. Excitement mounted as a second shell was discovered. For over an hour the relic hunter dug Parrott shells from the creekbed. Satisfied he had recovered the entire cache, he sat on the bank thinking about his success. He had spent hundreds of hours searching Louisiana Civil War sites, but nothing had been as rewarding as this effort. He had carefully done his research and had located the site where a retreating army had crossed a bridge, spanning what was then a much larger stream. A private diary revealed that a wagon load of munitions caused the bridge to collapse. The munitions spilled into the water and there was no time for the soldiers to recover the cargo.

Before the relic hunter could load his finds in a vehicle, he suddenly felt a sharp chest pain and became nauseated. His strenuous work in the water, and the excitement of his success had been too much. He suffered a heart attack! Not being a person to surrender easily, he placed a shell under each arm and walked toward the road, leaving the other shells, his metal detector and other equipment behind.

This story has a happy ending. The man reached his car and was able to drive to a hospital. Friends brought out his cache of shells. Today the relic hunter continues his pursuit, becoming as excited as ever when he discovers another historical treasure.

Such success is not achieved without effort, patience — or a minimum of discomfort. This advice may not be welcome or encouraging in a book written to stimulate water hunting. But it is written not

Figure 18-1: The author thanks Larry McCoy of Mobile, AL, for sharing this photo of war relics found in the Blakely River near Spanish Fort. It's easy to see why Larry is excited as the objects he found are very rare and desired by most relic hunters.

to be discouraging. As a person who has been involved in this activity for 40 years, I am continually impressed with people's capacity to do whatever is necessary to achieve success. Certainly, I am not encouraging anyone who has just suffered a heart attack to hoist 20 or 30 pounds and hike out of the woods. Moreover, what I am saying is that effort, coupled with determination, will produce rewards.

Determination, such as that described above, is perhaps more of a trait amongst relic hunters than any other group of treasure seekers. Successful battlefield and war relic site locating and recovery often require a special rigor not required, say, in coin hunting. Coin hunters go to just about any park or school campus and find coins. Not so with the relic hunter. Lengthy library research, coupled with considerable field reconnaissance, is necessary for success.

One especially good reward for the water hunter is that he is usually the first one to the sites he has researched. You see, only a small percentage of relic hunters are water hunters. The relic water hunter has much in his favor because specialized underwater metal detectors and water gear are required. Underwater searching and recovery are much more difficult and time consuming, but the rewards are rarely matched.

War relics can be found in lakes, streams, rivers, Figure 18-1, and in the oceans on a much larger scale than two cannon balls. Retreating armies hastily discarded war materials in water to prevent their being used by the enemy. Ferries, steamboats and lake and ocean-going vessels were shelled or set ablaze and much of their cargo is still resting where it sank to the bottom. Vessels set ablaze often floated miles downstream before sinking, which makes their discovery more difficult.

All relic hunters are familiar with General William T. Sherman's March to the Sea. He left terrible destruction in his path but failed to discover many hidden fortunes in treasure and buried caches. Well in advance of General Sherman's march, people were alerted to the pending destruction. They fled, with as much wealth as they could carry. What they could not carry — gold, silver, jewelry, priceless heirlooms and much more — they quickly dumped in wells, cisterns, ponds, lakes, streams and rivers.

Most of this wealth was recovered when the surviors returned to their homes. But much was not recovered. Occasional finds made by persistent hunters prove that Ante-Bellum treasure still awaits discovery.

As General Sherman encircled Savannah, the Union Navy shelled one of Savannah's lifelines, a Coosawhatchie River bridge. Relic hunters made a thorough search of the site and found hundreds of pounds of Civil War shell fragments, plus dozens of whole projectiles including the three-inch Hotchkiss, 10-pound and 12-pound Parrott, 12-pound Bormann and several rare Navy 3.4-inch Schenkl shells.

In the closing months of the great struggle, as Northern troops began overrunning Southern cities and towns, Confederate soldiers dumped tons of munitions in watery graves. Munitions recovered by

Figure 18-2: This photo shows examples of relics found by Civil War relic hunters.

today's treasure hunters include 2.2-inch baby Mullane shells, 6-pound and 24-pound explosive balls, 4.5-inch Dyer shells with lead sabots, Rains hand grenades, 3-inch high base reed shells with Girardi fuses, 3.67-inch detachable nose Hotckiss projectiles and many other type munitions.

Other weaponry to be found at river crossings and bridge sites include Sharps carbines, Enfield rifles, bayonets, Colt revolvers, swords (some with scabbards), bugles, pocket knives, mini-balls by the thousand, Figure 18-2, religious medals and other personal items, tools, wagon parts and even Civil War-era bottles.

Searching "black water" is seldom a cup of tea. Even in depths of only three to four feet, swift currents compound search and recovery problems. Proper equipment and techniques facilitate successful search and recovery at most locations.

At some sites, bridge timbers can still be located. Artillery fragments and relics along shorelines mark locations of sunken relics. Low water is the best time to locate and search potential treasure sites.

Before attempting underwater recovery, an understanding of metal preservation is necessary. Even solid cannon balls, if left unpreserved, will slowly crumble after 100 years under water. Chapter 29 describes processes you can use to preserve most relics you'll discover.

Some relic hunters donate discovered prizes to local museums. This not only increases the historian's knowledge of an area, but provides tangible proof to future generations that no country is free from war.

Locating a sunken Civil War vessel can be very rewarding because such a site is, in reality, a "museum" containing war materials, goods and those personal items necessary for survival 125 years ago. Excavation and recovery using archaeological methods is the only way to achieve full knowledge of the historical site, to recover and preserve its artifacts. On Dec. 12, 1862, the ironclad *U.S.S. Cairo* was sunk in Mississippi's Yazoo River. A Confederate torpedo exploded and tore open the *Cairo's* bow. The Union gunboat sank in 12 minutes as the first armored warship ever sunk by an electrically detonated mine. Approximately 100 years after she sank, the *Cairo* was located in 25 feet of water by metal detector searchcoils lowered from a boat. A few feet of mud covered the ship. A tremendous quantity of relics were found on the craft. So important was the find, the *U.S.S. Cairo* Museum was constructed at the National Military Park in Vicksburg. The *Cairo* is being reconstructed and will be rebuilt exactly as she looked in 1862.

A ship from the long-lost Texas Navy, the battleship *Zavala,* was found by Clive Cussler in Galveston, under an unpaved parking lot near Pier 29. The uppermost of the 201-foot ship's three decks was about 10 feet below the lot's surface. Cussler and his team, who used core drilling equipment to locate and verify the ship, have located 52 other shipwrecks around the world.

One hundred five years after the *CSS Georgiana* sank, she was discovered and identified by Lee Spence of Charleston, SC. The *Georgiana* was attempting to run a Federal blockade off Charleston harbor. Crippled by shell fire, the *Georgiana* signaled its surrender. Using the lull in the firing, the captain ran his sinking ship aground to permit its crew to escape. The furious Union seamen tried to torch the ship, but only the upper part burned. The *Georgiana* was soon forgotten. Spence found the wreck approximately one mile offshore near Isle of Palms. Needless to say, locating, exploring and salvage of a wreck with such historical significance is an experience of a lifetime.

CHAPTER 19

Where and How to Find
Bottles and Relics

There's something about searching for bottles...a certain fascination and charm that exists no where else in treasure hunting. They have been prized for centuries and even though popularity of bottle-collecting is highly cyclical, today's treasure hunters are finding them to be a stable aspect of the hobby. During times of great popularity, bottles — including junkers — commanded decent prices. Even during lulls in bottle collecting, higher valued bottles retain their value or increase as the years pass.

Slowly, but surely, bottle, or glass collecting as it is often called, is increasing in activity and gaining new recognition. Frequently, various treasure, collectible and diver magazines print stories about bottle collecting. As writers divulge the location of good hunting locations, more and more people are become curious and try their luck.

Not only is there value in bottles, there is a certain pride in ownership. "Look at this beautiful bitters I found!" Bottles make handsome yet charming displays as the limitless variety of shapes, colors and types permit collectors to fill shelf after shelf with striking arrays, Figures 19-1 through 19-3.

The beginner soon finds himself advancing from "curiosity seeker" to becoming a died-in-the-wool addict as more valuable bottles are discovered. Bitters, medicine, poison, sure-fire quick cures, embossed beers, pop bottles, snuff and inkwells are only a few of the many types to be found, Figure 19-3.

Everyone agrees there are limitless numbers of bottles waiting to be found. The key, however, to successful bottle hunting is research. Good, productive locations must be found. You can find more locations than you could ever search.

Obviously, bottles will be found where people once lived or congregated. The more people, the better. To locate these productive sites, a study of history is necessary. Where were towns, military posts and forts, waterfronts, bridges, fords and mill ponds located? Where are other historical sites of decades and centuries gone by? A study of newspapers, maps, historical accounts and other sources will reveal many of them.

Your success will be directly related to research. Don't forget, glass collecting is like "getting a bug." Once you've contracted the bottle bug, there is no escaping its clutches. The continuing thrill of finds keeps you hooked. So, do your research, keep your tools busy, let patience

250

Figure 19-1: Here are just a few valuable glass wine bottle finds attributable to Robert Marx's extensive underwater salvage efforts. These bottles date from 1645 to 1800 with the older bottles on the lower shelf.

and perseverance keep you motivated and keep on hunting...and finding. The rewards are yours to enjoy.

PRODUCTIVE BOTTLE-HUNTING SITES

Bottles are found in some of the strangest places. The following list is by no means complete. But, these locations will get you started in the right direction; as you gain experience, you'll find your own productive locations.

Old homesites, towns, forts, military installations and industrial plants that were once located along rivers and near lakes and ponds;

Large trash dumps, many of which were located near these water sources;

Fords and ferry crossings;

Bridges;

Wells and cisterns;

Along rivers, streams, ponds and lakes;

Outhouses (dry land searching, but nevertheless productive);

Shifted river sites (dry land searching);

Popular beaches and picnic sites;

Old waterfronts in present day cities and towns;

Channel dredging sites;

Sunken river vessels;

Sunken boats and ships in lakes and oceans.

251

RECOVERY METHODS, TIPS AND PROCEDURES

When bottles are lost in water they become covered with sand, entrapped in sediment or, in the case of the ocean, become encrusted by reef organisms. Bottles falling into and becoming entrapped in holes or near rocks, boulders and in other productive spots, are generally in better condition because they are protected from the elements. Depending upon the type of bottle, pollutants and organisms that attract it as well as its underwater environment, some bottles survive better than others. You'll find bottles that are badly corroded while others show only mild film residue. Some will become pitted while others develop a heavy encrustation.

Beginning bottle hunters are often surprised to discover by sight alone a 100-year-old bottle lying on top of bottom sands. Perhaps someone, while standing on a bridge, tossed the bottle into the river. Then 100 years later someone discovers the bottle simply by eyesight. Why was the bottle not buried deeply, perhaps under 10 feet of sand?

Figure 19-2: This is a Spanish olive jar in the author's collection found at a 1733 Spanish shipwreck site near the Florida Keys. The glazed glass jar is 12.5 inches tall and 9.5 inches in diameter. Olive jars date from the 1700s and are very significant finds. Ceramic containers were used to keep a variety of consumables aboard Spanish ships.

Specific gravity and size and shape have a lot to do with the depth at which objects will be found. The specific gravity or weight of an object compared with that of surrounding materials, say river sand, governs the pull of the earth's gravitational field on that object. Water, sand and rock motion tend to keep the river bottom materials loosened allowing heavier objects to sink. Small rounded objects like musket balls can more readily sink down through sand and silt than can a rifle which can become snagged on boulders, logs and other objects to prevent further settling.

Since glass, pottery, china and other similar objects are made of various earth materials such as clay, their specific gravity can be the same as riverbottom sand and mud. The gravitational pull upon man-made objects is the same as upon surrounding materials. Thus, the objects don't sink but can be tossed about by water and sand movements.

WORKING LAKE SITES

Find pier and dock locations by watching for piling stubs. Study old maps and early photos for long-gone piers, docks and amusement areas. During drought seasons, receding water lines allow construction pilings, bottles and shards to be spotted. Mill ponds are usually shallow or have shallow portions so that bottles can be spotted by wading.

Don't be fooled. Just because you cannot see bottles, that doesn't mean they aren't there. Every lake and pond has its share. Especially will bottles be found in abundance around locations such as amusement and recreational centers, near fishing piers and along dams. To give you an example, when I worked an East Texas lake searching for slot machines, we encountered a staggering number of bottles. Everywhere, at every turn, we found bottles. The mud and silt was eight feet deep in places and at every level we found bottles. The deeper we went, the more valuable the bottles became. The bottles were there. We couldn't see them from the bank, but we found them when we worked the bottom!

WORKING RIVERS AND STREAMS

Near the ocean rivers rise and fall with ocean tides. For best results in finding good locations, work during low tide. Watch for bottles, shards, broken china and other debris. In shallow waterways work around exposed boulders and sunken logs where bottles collect. Work fords, ferryboat areas and old swimming holes and under and around bridge sites. Also, work downstream from these places. At bends of rivers the water slows down and can become shallow. Bottles can more readily fill with water and sink at these locations. Look for areas where embankments have washed away. Especially in cultural areas, you are likely to find bottles and relics that have washed into the water from eroding embankments.

WORKING CHANNEL AND WATERFRONT DREDGING SITES

These sites can be very productive. As draglines do their work, decades of history are scooped up and deposited ashore. If you are fortunate to be present during such operations you can expect to reap rich rewards. You'll find many bottles by eyesight, but as you dig through the reclaimed dredge material your chance of uncovering many other valuables is increased. You'll need standard digging and recovery tools. It can be hard and dirty work, but the rewards can be great.

WORKING FOSSIL SITES

As you work bottle sites, you'll occasionally discover fossils. Shark's teeth and the bones of prehistoric creatures are being found in many locations. For instance, off Maryland's Calvert Cliffs some of North America's finest Miocene marine fossils are found. The teeth, some nine inches long, indicate that ancient sharks may have been larger than today's whales. The best times to search areas like this are in the winter after storms and strong winds have churned up the bottom. And, in many areas, diving is not necessary since finds are made in water two to five feet deep.

THE TOOLS AND CLOTHING YOU'LL NEED

Everyone, sooner or later, will develop personal tools. That's because certain specialized tools such as scoops, sifters and probes are not currently manufactured. You can start with traditional purchased items such as shovels, pitch forks and pronged garden trowels. A good set of waders and rubber gloves may be a necessity. Refer to Chapter 24 for tips on various types of specialized recovery tools.

Figure 19-3: This photograph shows a portion of the bottles and other items found by Bill Houghton and fellow divers in a Pennsylvania lake. Millions of bottles, many quite rare, lie in lakes, ponds and the waterways of the world.

CHAPTER 20

Where and How to Find Nature's Gold

Prospecting for gold has been a favorite pursuit of man since he found and picked up his first gleaming nugget. Every imaginable technique and method for recovering gold has been tried. This chapter describes popular methods available for successfully recovering gold from mountain streams.

Keep in mind that methods presently being used, except the use of metal detectors, are successful because gold is relatively heavy. Its specific gravity is higher than other elements you'll encounter. That means that gold has the greatest pull exerted on it by the force of gravity. Gravitational pull is the reason why gold can be found in water streams and rivers. Gold settles to the bottom of streams and collects in "traps" while rock and sand tumble on downstream. That's where you come in. With the right kind of knowledge on how to locate the gold and the right kind of gear needed to recover it, you can find your share, Figure 20-1.

Other heavy elements such as black sand, platinum, copper, mercury (used by early-day miners) and gemstones such as garnets can also be found. They are deposited in streams by the same forces of gravity that act upon gold. The recovery techniques described in this chapter will permit you to find these elements.

It takes training and experience, but you'll soon learn to recognize gold when you see it. There's nothing else like it. It looks like, feels like and acts just like...well, like gold. It's heavy. It comes in many different sizes from the consistency of fine powder to chunks weighing a hundred pounds or more.

To understand how gold collects in natural "traps" you must think of a river or steam as being one big sluice box (described later) with natural bedrock cracks and crevices and other traps functioning as riffles. The forces of gravity, water, sand and rock cause gold to act the same way in a waterway as it does in a sluice.

Let's start at the beginning...at the mother lode source high up on a mountain. A vein of gold becomes exposed as rain, wind and earth movement slowly causes surrounding earth to loosen and erode. The vein eventually begins to break up, and pieces of gold tumble, slide and otherwise work their way down the mountain slope. Eventually, over a few million years, give or take an eon, the gold finds its way into a waterway. Forces of gravity and moving water, sand and gravel gradually force the gold downstream. The gold movement

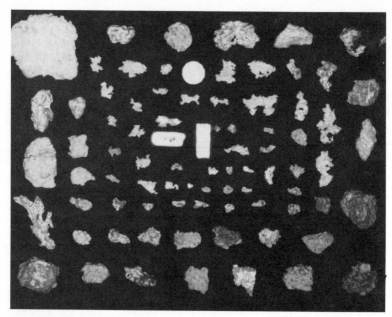

Figure 20-1: With the right kind of Knowledge about how to locate gold and the right kind of gear needed to recover it, you can find your share.

continues in two directions, downstream and down in the waterway toward bedrock, the rock-hard bottom of the steam. When gold reaches this level, it can go no farther vertically. It then continues its downstream trek until it reaches a bedrock crack, crevice or low spot. As gold settles into these "traps," it displaces less-heavy material. Here, the gold accumulates. Over a period of many years these concentrations, known as placer (pronounced as plaster with the "t" removed) grow larger. Other heavy objects and sediments such as black sand (magnetite...iron mineral) and even gemstones also find their way into the "traps."

Now, not all gold is found in cracks and crevices. Some gold, and lots of it, is still in the process of looking for a crevice to fall into. Where is it? Still in its downstream trek. Smart prospectors, however, are like bloodhounds. They know, from experience, the routes gold can take. The following discussions will help you become a gold bloodhound too. As gold tumbles along, it follows the shortest route. When it reaches a bend in the river it doesn't go way 'round the bend. No, it takes the shortest route and hugs the inside of the bend. Because water moves more slowly there, gold is more likely to settle. Gold that doesn't get temporarily trapped at river bends gets stopped at other places such as when it washes up behind (downstream from) boulders and rocks. The water is much quieter and slower there, giving gold a good chance to settle. If you'll watch water flow, you can see that

256

as it slows down behind obstructions, light, floating debris such as leaves and twigs come to rest there on the surface of the water and beneath.

Tree roots and similar obstacles make good traps that will stop gold in its downstream trek. During floods, the extra forces of water can cause gold to become dislodged from these resting places to be thrown around until it again becomes trapped. As a result, gold has been found trapped in roots, moss growing on rocks and in other unlikely places.

Today's gold sleuths use every known clue and possible technique to locate placer gold deposits. They know that gold is heavy and will sink to bedrock. They know it follows the path of least resistance. And they learn to look for natural obstructions such as boulders where gold can become trapped. Then, when promising locations are found, man uses a various and sundry assortment of tools to retrieve the trapped gold.

Following seasons of heavy storms and rains, there may be less overburden in the stream beds making it easier to reach bedrock where gold is trapped. Also, high water often dislodges gold from inaccessible spots, adding to the available supply you can recover.

When you begin prospecting waterways, look for bends in the river and other slow-water stretches. Pay particular attention where a tributary or another stream joins your river. Where larger (and heavier) rocks are found along the banks, it is likely that heavy gold has also settled there. Check also behind boulders and gravel bars. If you find gold, even a few colors, you should suspect that there might be more...lots more. Now, it's time to go to work!

Before you begin your study of equipment recovery methods, this review of how gold is trapped in nature's sluice boxes should help you understand man-made gold pans, sluices and other devices. Knowing how the "process" works helps you to understand how to use available equipment. Right? Certainly!

I'll admit, man-made tools do it on a much smaller scale than nature, but the process is exactly the same. When you shovel an alluvial mix from bedrock and put it into your gold pan, sluice or dredge, you have just taken gold, sand, rock and water and started it downstream in your own private waterway. As you agitate your device and the mix starts down the sluice, you are simulating nature's process. Water keeps the mix moving down the sluice until the heavier elements (namely gold and black sand) become lodged in your man-made traps. Can the process be more simple? No. As long as you have sufficient water and suitable agitation that causes the gold to settle to the bottom into traps (riffles) that are correctly designed, then you will come up with gold, Figure 20-2.

THE GOLD PAN

Gold pans, see Chapter 24, have been employed for thousands

of years. They have been made of wood, ceramic, metal and plastic. In fact, every conceivable container, including automobile hubcaps, has been used at one time or another. My favorite is the "Gravity Trap" gold pan with its patented 90-degree riffles. A gold pan is simply a container into which alluvial mix is placed, along with water. Built-in riffles are the traps that stop the gold and keep it in the pan while your swirling and tilting motion causes the lighter sand and rocks to flow off the pan's edge, Figure 20-3.

Figure 20-2: Roy Lagal, father of modern electronic prospecting methods and author of numerous books, demonstrates gold panning techniques in an Idaho river. The pan is the patented 90-degree riffle Gravity Trap pan, designed and patented by Lagal and distributed worldwide by Garrett Electronics. This pan is the world's most popular.

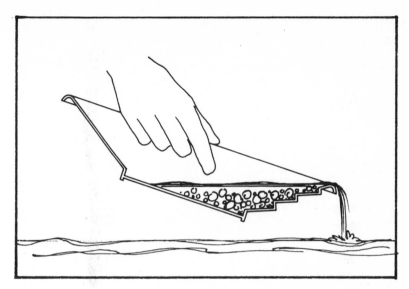

Figure 20-3: This illustration shows how the 90-degree Gravity Trap riffles do their job. The sharp, right angle, riffle traps trap the gold while letting lighter materials flow off.

The all-important point to remember, and I have already mentioned it several times, is to make sure your panning procedure completely dissolves the mix, Figure 20-4, freeing the gold to settle to the bottom. Then, the uppermost layers of the material can be washed off the sides of the pan.

You should take your gold pan wherever you go. You never know when you might stumble onto a likely looking spot, Figure 20-5. Just remember (and how could you forget?) that gold is where you find it and you can find it by sniping. Sniping is a quick, easy technique of examining a likely looking spot to determine if gold is present. You dig down to bedrock behind a boulder, for instance, and pan your recovered mix to determine if gold is present. In fact, you can check out hundreds of likely places in a day's time as you try to determine which areas are worth further investigation.

The gold pan is an indispensable tool for cleaning up sluices and dredges. Resulting concentrates are washed from the riffles into the pan where you can quickly recover your trapped gold. Pan the contents until you have mostly gold and sand left in the pan. The gold can be placed in a container for safe keeping with remaining black sand placed in a larger container for later recovery of the finds, Figure 20-6.

THE SLUICE

The simplest, full-scale device for placer mining is the sluice box. Like the gold pan and dredge, the sluice is a man-made stream bed on a very small scale. A sluice is a trough with a series of built-in riffles to serve as gold traps. Sluices are of varying lengths, the shortest

Figure 20-5: The author (right) and Roy Lagal listen as a Mexican miner tells tales of fabulous gold and silver strikes made along the Batopilas River which runs along the southern part of the state of Chihuahua. The men are shown in this photograph using the Gravity Trap pans to snipe for pockets of black sand and silver.

Figure 20-4: The author snipes along a small stream bed to locate pockets of black magnetic sand and gold. He is holding the Classifier above the 14-inch Gravity Trap pan. After placing rock, sand and other materials into the Classifier, he twists and shakes the Classifier to let the smaller materials flow through into the pan.

Figure 20-6: Carl Ratigan, center in dive suit, inspects the material being processed in a four-wheel separator. These devices do an excellent job of separating gold from lighter materials. Photo taken in Costa Rica on one of Carl's gold claims.

of which is about two feet. Lengths of 15 to 20 feet are occasionally seen, Figure 20-7.

A section of the stream is selected where the sluice is placed so that water flows freely through it. Boulders can hold it in place but it must be possible to adjust the slant of the sluice. Water volume and speed must also be controlled.

You can easily shovel several tons of mix through a small sluice in a single day. Periodically, when the traps are filled with concentrates, the sluice must be cleaned. Understanding the correct use of your sluice and gold pan, plus an understanding of how and where placers are formed enable you to operate a sluice successfuly.

SNIPING

Now, you've read this chapter, perhaps studied a few other books. So, you are ready to go. You have gathered your gear and scouted an area. But, how do you find gold?

Since you have studied this chapter, you know it can be found at bedrock level. So, you investigate the river banks until you find bedrock and follow it into the water. Then, to find cracks and fissures, you must remove all sand, gravel, clay and boulder overburden. Use shovels, brooms and any other tools to loosen and remove the material. The currents will help you.

After you find cracks, use your crevicing tools to clean them out. Use your pry bar to break open the cracks if you need more space to remove the material. When gold is flipped out, it will sink, not wash

261

Figure 20-7: Large scale mining operations such as this one in Costa Rica can process many tons of material a day. These twin sluices can process 50 cubic yards of material per hour. Photo courtesy of Carl Ratigan.

Figure 20-8: The author uses his personal 2-inch backpacker dredge for sniping along this shallow creek. Even though he is using a power jet, the suction nozzle would prevent losing prime whenever the nozzle is removed from the water. The power jet, however, gives more suction.

downstream. Place all material you remove from the crack into your gold pan for panning. Use your tweezer and sniffer to retrieve flakes and nuggets. If you cannot do a complete job, make plans to use a surface dredge.

Continue sniping by locating all stream obstructions and protruding boulders. These can be worked by digging to bedrock and running a sample of the mix through your gold pan. Scout for tree roots, moss-covered rocks and other traps where gold might be waiting. After you find promising amounts of gold, make your plans for a larger scale operation.

SURFACE SUCTION DREDGES

Surface suction dredges, Figure 20-8, derive their name from the fact that they are mounted on appropriate flotation devices that float the engine, pump, sluice boxes and classifiers on the surface of the water. The engine, usually gasoline powered, drives a water pump. The pump creates a vacuum which pulls water in through a strainer and intake hose. This water is pump-forced through another hose to a nozzle where it is discharged at high velocity into a larger intake nozzle. This jet of water creates a vacuum that pulls in a much larger quantity of water through the nozzle intake. This nozzle is the business end of the dredge. Thus, it is obvious that a suction dredge is nothing more than a vacuum cleaner that pulls in water, sand, rock, gold, silver and various other materials.

Dredges come in many sizes, ranging from approximately one-and-one-half inch up to eight, ten and twelve-inch sizes, Figures 20-8 and 20-10. The size of a dredge is measured by the inside diameter of the main intake hose. The nozzle, however, is reduced in size slightly, with the suction end always smaller than the inside diameter of the hose. This is a design feature that keeps large rocks and other objects from becoming lodged inside the hose.

Small two-cycle engines, larger four-cycle gasoline and even diesel engines are used to power the pumps. The size of the engine depends upon the size of the dredge.

There are two basic types of intake nozzles: the power jet and the suction nozzle. The power jet configuration gives the greatest amount of suction and lift. This nozzle, however, is not suitable for surface or shallow work because when the nozzle is lifted above the water, it loses prime. The suction nozzle, on the other hand, does not lose prime, even when held out of the water, but it does not have as much suction as the power jet.

Water, sand, rock and other debris are pulled through and deposited in the riffle tray. Lighter materials — water, sand, rock — flow back into the stream while heavier materials such as gold, silver and black sand are retained in the riffles. The size dredge you select depends upon several factors. If your site is remote, perhaps you should consider a two-inch backpacker model. They are light and easy to set

Figure 20-9: The author, on the left, observes Roy Lagal, center, and George Mroczkowski clean the Mexican silver contents of a 2-inch dredge riffle tray into 14-Inch Gravity Trap gold pan. The gold pan will be removed to separate rocks and larger materials from the gold. Curly Jones, in the background, operates the dredge.

Figure 20-10: These twin 5-inch American surface suction dredges are designed and manufactured by Allan Trees, American Gold Dredge Manufacturing Company.

up and operate. Larger dredges are heavier, but they will process considerably more material than a two-inch size. In some areas, governmental agencies allow only the smaller dredges to be used.

The best angle to set your riffle box permits them to run about three-quarters full. If the tray is too flat, riffles will not work. If the angle slope is steep enough to show more than 50% of the riffles, the angle is too steep and the riffles can't do their job.

Another factor to consider in selecting a dredge is whether it will be used for other jobs such as coin recovery from a swimming pool or recovery of objects from a shallow sunken shipwreck. Study the manufacturers' literature and ask questions. Get answers before you decide which model to buy.

When you have located a hot spot through your sniping procedures, it is time to set up the dredge. Select a spot where there is sufficient water for operation. The dredge must float freely to insure the riffle tray remains at the proper slant. The pump intake nozzle must have sufficient water for proper operation. Tie the dredge to keep discharge of the mix downstream and away from your nozzle operation. Set a bucket on the river bottom and weight it to keep it in position. The level of the stream must be higher than the bucket so that the bucket stays full of water. Place the pump intake strainer in the bucket. This reduces the amount of sand being pulled in through the intake, thus reducing pump impeller wear.

If the water is shallow, you should use a suction nozzle. If the intake nozzle gets out of the water, you won't lose prime. When you have sufficient water depth, however, more suction is available with a power jet intake nozzle.

One mistake beginners make is to jam the nozzle into the sand in an effort to make it work harder. This is called "hogging." If you overload the intake, you'll probably have to shut down the pump soon and clean out the hose. Take your time and learn to work the nozzle properly. Work slowly, especially at bedrock level and in other areas where gold is present.

There is much that can be learned about dredge operation, far beyond the scope of this book. I suggest you read, THE GOLD DREDGE, by Allen Trees. Study your equipment instruction manual before operating any new equipment. Failure to do so may result in burning out your pump. But, a far more expensive loss may be that of considerable gold because of improper operation.

Another interesting and efficient method of gold recovery is deploying the GOLD CONCENTRATOR, Figure 20-11. It is essentially a dry land operation. Material is shoveled into a hopper. Water, pumped in from a nearby source, washes the material, separating the heavier elements from the lighter.

ELECTRONIC PROSPECTING FOR GOLD

My books, MODERN METAL DETECTORS and ELEC-

TRONIC PROSPECTING, the latter co-authored with Roy Lagal, discuss how metal detectors can locate gold and other conductive metals. I recommend you study these books (see Appendix I) to equip you better for beginning your work with electronic equipment. The proper use of metal detectors in prospecting is the most difficult of all applications to master, but rewards will surely be in proportion to your effort.

There are several types of metal detectors; namely, the BFO, TR, Pulse Induction, VLF and Automated VLF. Forget the first three when you go prospecting. In this chapter we'll discuss the use of the VLF and Automated VLF instruments.

Figure 20-11: This is the unique Gold Concentrator manufactured by American Gold Dredge Manufacturing Company. Dry materials are shoveled into the hopper. Water pumped in from the stream separates the materials.

The VLF designation means that the detector operates in the very low frequency radio spectrum of 3 kHz to 30 kHz. It means nothing more, nothing less. However, since this type detector is a very capable instrument, some models are lovingly and appropriately called all-purpose by users and manufacturers alike. The main feature of the VLF detector is that the disturbing influence of earth iron minerals can be cancelled. That is, the detector can be adjusted so that iron minerals are not detected.

Elsewhere in this book are discussions of metal detectors. Here, we will briefly outline their capabilities for, and cover the basics of, underwater gold recovery.

There are two kinds of VLF metal detectors, the MANUAL-ADJUST VLF GROUND CANCELING and the AUTOMATED VLF GROUND CANCELING. Certain models of the Manual-Adjust VLF are designed to be all-purpose detectors, Figure 20-12. That is, they will perform almost all treasure hunting and electronic prospecting functions. They can be adjusted to cancel iron earth minerals and they have, basically, two modes of operation, all-metal detection and discrimination. The all-metal mode does just that—it detects all metal. The second, or discrimination mode, allows the operator to adjust the detector to eliminate certain undersirable metal items such as nails, foil, bottlecaps, certain small pieces or iron and aluminum pulltabs.

In almost all electronic prospecting applications, the all metal mode is used. Only in high junk areas is it "permissible" to use discrimination and then only the smallest amount needed to reject troublesome pests such as nails or other tiny pieces of iron. Even then, some nuggets will be lost.

VLF manual-adjust models generally offer a wide range of searchcoils to use. The most important sizes to you, the electronic prospector, are the Super Sniper three to four-inch and the general purpose seven to eight-inch diameter searchcoils. The Super Sniper searchcoils are necessary when sniping near and under boulders and when searching in tight places for nuggets and placer. They are also good for ore sampling (high-grading), testing of ore samples to determine content.

General purpose searchcoils are the most widely used. They are good for nugget hunting, ore sampling, sniping and other work. Larger searchcoils such as the 10 and 12-inch sizes should be used only after you have gained detector experience. In some areas, the larger coils are indispensable when nuggets are quite deep. Since larger searchcoils cover more area, scanning efficiency is improved.

To sum up, Manual-Adjust VLF Ground Canceling detectors are the preferred types to use for electronic prospecting because they are the deepest seeking; they have the ability to cancel the earth's iron minerals; they are all-purpose with the ability to perform just about any task, plus some manufacturers offer a full range of available search-coil sizes.

Figure 20-12: Virgil Hutton recovers materials for panning after getting a signal with his detector. He is searching for nuggets and concentrations of black sand. Certain detector models like this Garrett Master Hunter are designed to be all purpose detectors. They will perform almost all treasure hunting and electronic functions.

Automated VLF Ground Canceling types, while designed primarily for coin hunting and general purpose work, are not as capable as Manual-Adjust VLFs. Nevertheless, the newest versions of the automated types are acceptable for nugget hunting and placer sniping. Keep in mind they won't detect as deeply nor detect nuggets as small as the Manual-Adjust VLFs. Also, the automated types do not have as wide a range of available searchcoils. Some models, however, can use the Super Sniper and slightly larger than general purpose sizes.

Prospectors who are content to locate only larger nuggets can use the automated types. Also, these types can be used to scan a location and define its productive areas. If a quick scan of a site produces a few large nuggets, it can usually be assumed worthy of closer examination. A manual-adjust detector can then be used for the deepest and most thorough detection.

NUGGET HUNTING

To search for nuggets, use the all-metal mode. If you are using an automated detector with discrimination mode, rotate the trash rejector control (discrimination knob) to zero. This is basically all-metal capability. Since manufacturers do not set their detector's "zero" at the same reference point, capabilities of different brands may vary.

Adjust the detector to cancel iron minerals (please refer to your metal detector instruction manual). Automated types ignore earth minerals automatically. Lower the searchcoil to within a few inches above the ground, Figure 20-13. At a rate of about one foot per second, scan over the ground.

In this mode you'll dig lots of junk pieces of metal. You may tire of digging junk, but at least you'll know that if you pass the searchcoil over a nugget, you've got it. If there is a large quantity of iron junk, switch to the discrimination mode and dial in just enough discrimination to reject the most troublesome nails or small iron pieces. Always remember, however, that with discrimination, no matter how little, you run the risk of losing gold.

Figure 20-13: The author uses his Master Hunter to scan for nuggets along this small, shallow stream bed. The VLF all-metal mode is utilized and all targets are dug. Even though trash items are detected in this mode, the all-metal capability lessens the possibility of missing good nuggets.

Figure 20-14: California prospector Roy Roush searches for nuggets and black sand concentrations in this Southern California river. Roy has been active in the field of treasure hunting and electronic prospecting for many years.

Occasionally, you may detect what we call "hot rocks." These pests are nothing more than worthless chunks of ore that cause the detector to detect them as metal. There are methods explained in our literature that enable you to ignore hot rocks. Some practice is necessary, but you can quickly learn to identify them.

PLACER SNIPING

Searching for placer on dry land or in the water, Figure 20-12 and 20-14, is, in reality, identical to nugget hunting. You may be looking for lesser gold densities since placer is often an accumulation of fine gold particles. Black sand will be present that may look like a detectable hot rock to the detector. This only serves to enhance the ability of the detector to locate placer concentrations. When sniping, you may have better results by using the Super Sniper searchcoil. It is smaller and will more readily detect smaller gold densities. Also, the little searchcoil can be more effectively maneuvered around boulders and into tight places in your quest for gold.

The keys to successful metal detector operation are: First, Learn about the capabilities of your detector by studying your manual. Second, Learn how to adjust your detector by studying your operator's manual and the books I have recommended. Finally, Practice, practice, practice! You can't short-circuit any of these three steps and be successful. Believe in your detector, have patience and persevere; success will be yours.

TOOLS YOU'LL NEED

In addition to your gold pan, classifier, sluice, dredge and metal detector, there are certain small tools you will need in order to operate in an efficient manner.

Snipping tools are available from many Garrett dealers. The short-handled Estwing pick is tough and it is recommended. For heavier work, you may want to invest in a 27-inch Estwing pick. It can save you lots of back-breaking effort. A crevicing tool is pointed on one end for digging and cleaning crevices with the other end flattened for scraping. Two sizes of tweezers are recommended. The longer version is good for extracting nuggets from deeper crevices and rocky niches, with the shorter size for the smaller stuff. A suction bottle is a must for retrieving gold from crevices and your gold pan and sluice.

I recommend the Gravity Trap Gold Pan Kit which contains the world's most popular pan, a 14-inch professional model, a 10½-inch pan for quick sniping and finishing (removing black sand, gold), a classifier for removal of large gravel and a gold-guzzler suction bottle.

Personal items include a snorkel and mask to use for work in shallow water. You may also need a weight belt to hold you in place.

STAKING A CLAIM

There are areas available for public use. But, before working a site, determine if it has been claimed. This should be indicated by a pile of rocks, a sign or post. To determine which areas you can work and to stake a claim, check with the offices of the state's Division of Mines and Geology, the Bureau of Land Management, the State Forest Service and the County Recorder's office. You can write to these various agencies to obtain the information you are seeking.

VIDEO SERIES AVAILABLE

A new series of video tapes, produced by Garrett Electronics, covers all aspects of metal detecting, dredging and panning. These tapes are available at your nearby Garrett equipment dealer or they may be ordered directly from the Garrett factory. To obtain the name of your nearby dealer, call TOLL FREE, 1-800-527-4011 or in Texas, 1-800-442-4889.

CHAPTER 21

Where and How to Dredge
For Coins and Jewelry

While no studies could obviously be made, it is probably safe to assume that at least half of all coins, rings and other jewelry lost at the beach or pool are lost in the water. Beach hunting, especially the surf, presents treasure hunting's newest frontier. There are numerous other sites where coins and jewelry can be found. Underneath and downstream from bridges, at tourists' stops and along major pedestrian thoroughfares a multitude of treasure can be found. People cannot resist the temptation to pitch in a coin and say a wish. This practice started thousands of years ago in Europe and continues to this day. Whenever a traveler came to a bridge, he or she would throw a coin in the water and make a wish or mutter a plea to some multitude of gods.

I visited several such sites in Europe. In Rome there is one bridge still carrying pedestrian traffic after two thousand years. I was anxious to get in the water here and try my luck but being pressed for time, I only worked a short while along an embankment downstream where I found various items of modern jewelry. Upon inquiring about the lost items I learned that flood waters occasionally wash over the bridge where jewelry and souvenirs are sold to tourists. Floods sometimes take these souvenir merchants unaware and wash their canopies, tables and merchandise into the river. My guess is that in a space of one mile downstream from this bridge there must be millions of coins and items of jewelry.

You may scoff at my beliefs, but let me tell you another story. While visiting Berne, Switzerland, I stopped while crossing a major bridge in the heart of the city. Upon looking into the water I was amazed to find it perfectly clear with visibility to the bottom. In the water was a veritable montage of copper and silver colors. I was amazed to discover that I was looking at thousands upon thousands of coins! To this day I can scarcely believe what I witnessed with my own eyes. That river has been a public waterway for two thousand years. Can you imagine how much treasure lies along its bottom? Obviously, I wanted very badly to work there with my dredge, but when I learned it was against the law, reluctantly, and sadly, I went on my way.

When you consider the thousands upon thousands of pedestrian bridges in the world, you begin to realize just how much wealth awaits the dredge operator. Beneath the bridge at Royal Gorge, CO, thousands of pennies and five-cent pieces have been recovered, as well as numerous rings and wrist watches. Coins found there are thrown by tourists as good luck pieces. The jewelry found is attributed to rings and watches coming off arms and fingers as a coin is flung. Thousands of coins have been recovered with dredges from the Russian River near the town of Monte Rio, CA.

Other lucrative river sites are located beneath and downstream from bridge crossings in Reno, NV, where countless rings have been found. Apparently, many women who have come here over the years for a divorce are so fed up with marriage that they fling their rings into the water in a final show of defiance. Some actually purchase cheap rings to throw away during this ritual of claiming their freedom.

Often, in the various treasure publications, stories are printed about successes of dredge operators in recovering coins, rings, watches and other jewelry from swimming areas.

LET A DREDGE DO THE WORK

As mentioned, probably half the valuables lost at swimming areas are lost in the water. This has been proven many times, not only by users of detectors with submersible searchcoils, but more recently by persons using surface suction dredges. There are submersible dredges, but for various reasons they are not popular. We will discuss only surface dredges in this chapter.

Figure 21-1: This versatile 2-inch backpacker dredge can be used not only with the standard riffle tray for prospecting, but when dredging for coins and jewelry. The perforated basket shown here nestled into the end of the tray catches all materials. The smaller material flows out while larger materials, coins and jewelry, are trapped in the basket.

273

Figure 21-2: This is a closeup showing how the coin basket fits into the riffle tray of this 2-inch Garrett backpacker dredge.

Suction dredges, when used at swimming beaches, will bring lost coins, rings, watches and similar valuables up through the hose to be deposited either on the standard riffle tray or into a basket, Figures 21-1 and 21-2. The standard riffle tray is not suitable, generally, for salvage because coins cannot be trapped as easily as gold. The force of water acting upon the broad face of coins will sometimes propel them right off the tray. My own dredge is equipped with a wire mesh basket where all objects pulled from the bottom are dumped. Water, sand and small objects fall through the mesh back into the water. Two people are needed to operate a dredge most efficiently, one person using the nozzle with the other keeping the accumulated rocks, other debris and, of course, the good finds—coins and rings—clear of the wire mesh to allow sand and water to pass through. Broken glass and fish hooks, among other things, will be dumped into the basket. You are forwarned! Be prepared, especially for an occasional snake which will be pulled up alive through the dredge. If you are successful in locating and dredging some of the earlier swimming areas, of which there are thousands throughout the United States, you could easily pay for your dredge equipment each day of your operation.

Be very careful to keep the rubber tube or float balanced. The float must sit level in the water. If you mount the engine too far to the edge, the float will tip over or not float level. Also, be extra careful when operating an inflated tube float because if the tube becomes punctured you can guess what happens.

274

WHAT SIZE DREDGE TO BUY?

Determine what is the largest sized object you want to retrieve from the bottom and buy a dredge with as a diameter rating at least one-half inch greater. Of course, the larger the dredge, the greater the speed at which you can work. Larger dredges, however, are more difficult to manage. The four-inch size is considered the upper limit for one person to operate.

Some dredges are designed for multi-purpose use; they are suitable for both gold prospecting and for underwater treasure recovery. The two dredge illustrations depict various ways which dredges can be put to good use by an underwater treasure hunter.

At some swimming sites you may have to go deep into the sand, perhaps two feet or more, before the site will become productive. But, when you start pulling out silver dollars, halves, Barber quarters, Buffalo and Liberty nickels and Indian Head pennies, your efforts will be rewarded. Some coins will come out heavily encrusted, but others will look like new. Some will be black, some pitted, while others will be worn smooth. The condition depends upon time in the water and upon the soil mineralization and composition of decaying matter. A dredge, especially when used for recovering coins and jewelry in deep water, is a two-person operation. The main problem is the difficulty of containing large items or those with a broad surface in a standard riffle tray.

When a wire basket, constructed of one-quarter-inch mesh, is used, only sand and small rocks and debris will pass back into the water. Larger rocks, pieces of metal, bottlecaps, pulltabs and all other items pulled in by the dredge will remain in the basket along with coins and jewelry. Junk items and valuables alike can't get out. Consequently, the basket must be cleaned regularly, depending upon the volume of junk encountered. Here is where the second person is necessary to keep the basket clean while the nozzle operator works.

An extension arm allows you to use the dredge in water as deep as you can wade. You hold the handle end of the extension while you maneuver the intake nozzle along the bottom. You must not "hog" the nozzle by jamming it in the bottom, or you'll quickly fill your hose with sand or mud. One of the best ways to use a dredge, especially in warmer weather, is to snorkel. You float along on the surface while you look down into the water and operate the intake nozzle.

Obtaining permission at private swimming holes is a wise course of action. Unless a property owner understands what you are doing, they may become irate as they see you make what they think to be 40-foot-deep holes and destroy their property. In sandy areas your holes will fill in quickly. There is some danger to swimmers who might step into holes, but proper operating procedures will fill holes as fast as you make them. Work in straight lines with the dredge discharge end trailing along behind you. As sand and other dredged materials flow

Figure 21-3: This diver is shown using a surface dredge suction nozzle to siphon out sand and coins and rings lost in this swimming area.

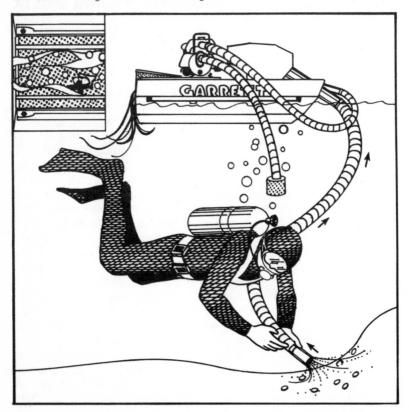

back into the water, the holes are automatically filled.

Dredging causes absolutely no ecological damage in swimming areas. In fact, how could just a little air pressure cause more damage than hundreds of swimmers who spend their day kicking up tons of sand? A dredge operation.however,brings up lots of edible items from the bottom and supplies them to the hungry fish free of charge.

CHAPTER 22

Making Money
In Underwater Salvage

Who can forget John Wayne's great undersea adventures in the movie classic, WAKE OF THE RED WITCH? He battles a huge man-eating octopus for possession of a chest of pearls. He dons a deep-sea diver's suit and descends to the ocean bottom to recover five million in gold from the hold of an 1860s three-masted schooner. The ship, precariously perched half over the ledge of a deep chasm, adds frightening suspense as it threatens to fall into the abyss. Thunder, lightning, wind and roaring waves plus other Hollywood excesses forever plant a concept in the movie-goer's mind of the dangers always confronting the diver seeking treasure. It appears that the underwater treasure hunter must surely lead the most exciting, adventure-filled life it's possible to experience...or, so the movies would have you believe.

This fine old movie and the other so-called true-life adventure stories have attractd as many men to the underwater world as have the treasures found by real-life salvors like Mel Fisher, Bob Marx, Burt Webber, Barry Clifford and others.

Of course, the real world of today's commerical/treasure salvor bears little resemblance to that of his counterpart on the silver screen or the color TV tube. Fighting the real world of salvage laws, months of separation from loved ones at home, rusted equipment, storms at sea and even modern-day pirates are the adventure stories these men tell. But, treasures found, or, at least, the promise of treasures to be found are the real incentives that keep them returning to the ocean depths. And, believe me, there is adventure to be found there!

While a chest of golden escudos may be the sought-for treasure, a bronze cannon worth $25,000, a large ship's propeller worth $5,000, an anchor and chain worth $1,000, or just a collection of rare 1800s bottles are treasures sufficient to keep men coming back for more.

There's little glamour in underwater salvage—it's mostly hard work. True, treasure salvors dive for "instant wealth," and, while they might not admit it, for adventure or for the simple reason, "I just had to do it!"

The sport of underwater salvage may not make you rich, but you can add to your income and to your showroom of conversation pieces. Certainly, there is nothing wrong with setting your sights on your very own Spanish galleon. You should also be prepared for such mundane items as sunken boats and motors, lost anchors and chains, bronze relics and other ships' antiques—and even plain old scrap metal. After

278

all, there's enough sunken wealth to keep you in salvage equipment, compressed air and the necessary square meals that let you continue, perhaps forever, in your dreamer's quest for the truly big one.

The kinds of lost and discarded goods you can locate under water include boats, Figure 22-1, motors, anchors and chains, propellers, boating gear, fishing gear and fishnets, rifles, shotguns, pistols, knives, tools and tool boxes, rings, watches and other jewelry, eyeglasses and other personal items, relics and ships' artifacts, golf balls, scrap bottles, stolen loot, contraband, weapons, material (law enforcement) evidence, Figure 22-2, ships' cargo, aircraft, Figures 22-3 and 22-4, automobiles and diving gear.

To locate potentially good sites, keep your eyes and ears open. Read everything you can find on the history of disasters in your area. Make it a habit to talk with divers, boat captains and crew, marina operators, insurance agents, local law enforcement agencies and others who may possess knowledge of lost articles, shipwrecks, boating accidents and disasters, downed aircraft and other water-related events. Study Chapter 4 for tips on research.

The following is a list of contacts you should develop. Make known to them your activities and your willingness and desire to search for and recover sunken objects and vessels: The reclamation departments of the Army, Air Force, Coast Guard, Navy, National Guard, state and local police, sheriffs' departments, Civil Defense, Flood Control and river and port authorities.

EQUIPMENT

The type equipment you need depends upon the type recoveries you plan to make, Figure 22-5. In addition to your regular, personal dive equipment you'll need marker buoys, lift bags (don't use your BC), numerous lengths of nylon line and rope for scanning, towing and air lift attachments and a various assortment of tools including pry bars, metal saws, drag hooks and other items. Depending upon the location, you may need a boat, an inflatable, Figure 22-6, a raft or a floating platform, Figure 22-7. In many search and recovery activities a metal detector is an indispensable tool.

Other tools and equipment you may need include wrenches, chisels, hammers, wire cutters, tin snips, nails, canvas, come-alongs, block and tackles and flashlights.

SEARCH METHODS AND PROCEDURES

Review Chapters 14 and 15 for a discussion of various search and recovery methods. In deploying search guide ropes you'll need to know basic knots such as the square knot, half and full hitches and the bowline.

All operations should be carefully planned with every member of your team knowing first aid and safety procedures. Teamwork is the key to successful, accident-free searching, with every member not on-

Figure 22-1-A-B-C-D: In these four photographs is shown the racing boat, the LIBERTY II, which was recovered from Pennsylvania's Conneaut Lake by William Houghton and Brian Simpson. They located the boat on July 13, 1985. The boat sank on a timed trial run shortly before speed boat races on Labor Day 1922. A foundation was formed to restore, maintain and operate the boat again on Conneaut Lake. She belongs to the people of the area and is managed in their interest by the Foundation's Board. Photos show the remarkable perfection achieved during restoration.

ly dedicated to his or her job but willing to share the work. Make a thorough study of the water, currents, tides, bottom conditions, weather forecasts and history and likely boating and shipping activities. Keep safety equipment such as lines and flags ready for instant use. Every team member should know how to use every piece of equipment. This is best accomplished by classroom study and actual practice under the water.

Underwater metal detectors are designed to detect ferrous and non-ferrous metals. These metals can be located even though concealed below and within aquatic growth, bottom soil and rocks, wood and other non-metallic materials. Objects as small as a single coin can be detected to distances beneath the searchcoil of 12 inches or more. Large metal masses such as boats, motors and safes can be located several feet below the searchcoil. The metal detector's capability of "reaching out" into the unknown can make a big difference in the recovery of objects hidden by murky water or buried beneath silt and mud.

Knowing what you are looking for will help you select and use the proper equipment. Magnetometers can sense the change in the earth's magnetic field density caused by iron objects. These instruments are of no value, however, as an aid in locating non-ferrous materials. The metal detector can locate both ferrous and non-ferrous objects. Size, shape and depth can be determined to a degree. Experience is needed, however, to comprehend these parameters.

Figure 22-2: The author assists Garland Police in recovering a safe which was stolen and thrown into a North Texas rock quarry.

Figure 22-3: Members of the Shoreham Aircraft Preservation Society, 1940/45, of London, located a downed World War II aircraft and recovered as much of the airplane's components as possible. Photos courtesy Alan B. Biddlecombe.

Before beginning your metal detector search for, say, an anchor chain, try to determine in which direction the chain lies. Then swim at right angles to the chain's orientation. Unless the chain is buried deeply in mud and silt, this method is fast. Locating small, isolated objects is more difficult and requires a grid search deployment of a detector.

Figure 22-4; This is the Mercedes Benz engine which the Shoreham Aircraft Preservation Society, 1940/45, of London, recovered from a crash site following clues given in World War II records.

Should you be called upon to locate a pipeline, a magnetometer can be used, provided the pipe is iron. A metal detector can be deployed using the right-angle scan technique. Should you be required to determine pipeline depth, the best method is to use a probe. Depth, however, can be reasonably well determined by the use of a metal detector. If you know the size of the pipe and can test it above water, or if there is an exposed section underwater, you can calibrate the meter reading for various detection distances. Then take underwater site measurements and correlate your findings with your calibrated readings.

If you understand trigonometry, you can devise other methods for determining pipeline depth.

Figure 22-5: This member of Cross International, a commercial diving company, based in Orem, UT, with gear allowing deep dives in cold water. Its two-way communication system improves efficiency and, of course, gives the diver a greater sense of security.

Figure 22-6: Members of the Cross International Commercial Diving Company prepare a diver for underwater search and recovery. Note the underwater detector the man is holding. Beneath the waters lies a modern-day town flooded when a river was dammed by a mud slide. Cross International was contracted to locate the exact position and condition of railroad tracks, highways and other structures.

Figure 22-7: Jim Cross (left) and other members of Cross International utilize this floating platform to conduct operations. Note the diver in the elevator on the right. Many aspects of commercial diving are extremely hazardous and all possible safety precautions and the best possible equipment must be utilized.

The use of sonar should not be overlooked. A sonar signal travels through the water and when it strikes an object, a signal rebound occurs. The rebound signals are recorded on a visual screen or recording paper. There are numerous kinds of sonar devices including hand-held proximity locators, "fish" finders, sub-bottom profilers and side scan. These devices are discussed in Chapter 25.

Because the treasure salvor often works in black water and in other dangerous environments, direct communication with the surface is important. Should an accident occur such as diver entanglement, then help could be summoned immediately. Chapter 28 contains a discourse on night (black water) diving.

Direct communication permits a continuous exchange of information which should include discussions of problems and solutions. Guidance is achieved as topside team members continually monitor the position of divers by observing the location of air bubbles.

DISPOSITION OF RECOVERED VALUABLES

How do you dispose of recovered treasure that you don't intend to keep in your collection? There's a ready market for everything; Chapter 29 suggests some sources where you can sell your recovered items. The Bibliography includes more references that list individuals who collect and buy just about everything.

CHAPTER 23

The Metal Detector in Marine Archaeology

The metal detector can be eyes that "see" into the ground to locate metal objects of interest to archaeologists. All types of conductive metal, without exception, can be detected. Objects as small as a pinhead can be found. Large objects can be detected to depths of about 20 feet. Metal detectors are so sophisticated they can classify various types of metal into categories and accurately indicate depth. Ground minerals and the ocean's salt water pose no problems. Automatic detectors are simple to use. Just turn them on. Most other functions are accomplished automatically.

Some archaeologists use metal detectors, while others, apparently, refuse to consider their use. Metal detectors are simply tools, not unlike electrical resistance surveying equipment used widely by archaeologists. So, why don't more archaeologists use this tool that can help them in their work?

Metal detectors have found archaeological treasures that probably would never have been discovered otherwise. A metal detectorist found a bronze head of Emperor Hadrian. A few years later another hunter found a complete, larger-than-life-size bronze statue of the same man. In England, metal detectorist Ted Seaton found a religious pendant believed to have belonged to England's King Richard III. The pendant was found at a depth of about 14 inches. It was found alongside a well-worn footpath—probably a site that would never have been excavated archaeologically. A most valuable find, it sold at auction for an amount in excess of two million U.S. dollars, Figure 23-1. Books can be filled with stories of treasures and artifacts found with metal detectors that probably otherwise never would have been discovered. If the use of a metal detector can contribute to historical research, why not use it?

Two scuba divers conducting a routine search beneath the emerald-green waters of the Gulf of Mexico about 40 miles west of Key West, FL, scanned their metal detector over what appeared to be a large mound of coral. The detector screamed loudly. The pile turned out to be a mix of ship's weights, pieces-of-eight and ingots of silver as big as loaves of bread. The "mother lode" discovered that afternoon turned out to be one of the biggest caches of sunken treasure ever found—a fortune in silver, gold and emeralds carried by the Spanish galleon, *Nuestra Senora de Atocha,* that sank in a hurricane in 1622. The estimated value of the treasure she carried is 400 million dollars.

Figure 23-1: Metal detectorist Ted Seaton of England found this religious pendant believed to have belonged to England's King Richard III. This precious 15th century relic sold at auction for two million American dollars.

In addition to its riches of silver and gold that had lain buried on the ocean floor for more than three centuries, the *Atocha* is also proving to be a scientific bonanza. Duncan Mathewson, chief archaeologist for Treasure Salvors, Inc., the Florida-based group of divers and investors that sought the *Atocha,* calls the vessel, "an enormous time capsule, as important as Pompeii, or even King Tut's Tomb."

Mathewson has been diving on historic shipwrecks off Florida and in the Caribbean for more than a decade. He is recognized as one of the world's foremost authorities on shipwreck archaeology. He is a co-founder and chairman of the Atlantic Alliance for Maritime Heritage Conservation, a coalition of sports divers, shipwreck salvors, maritime historians and marine archaeologists. The organization is dedicated to the conservation of historic shipwrecks and other maritime resources.

Mathewson calls the hand-held metal detector a "very important and effective tool" in underwater archaeological research. "Archaeologists are only beginning to get an idea that they can do serious archaeology with a metal detector," says Mathewson. "I'm trying to get them to understand the detector is not simply an instrument to be used to find the 'goodies,' but it also can be used to help map sites when they really can't do it any other way. If you find a distribution of metal objects on a site and you map that, then you've learned a good deal about the archaeology of the site."

Using a metal detector can also lead to artifacts that otherwise might never be recovered. At the *Atocha* site salvage diver John Brandon found gold links that formed a chain several feet in length. The links had fallen into cracks in the underwater hardpan and were recovered from an area that had been described as "clean" by other salvage divers.

The search method used by the Treasure Salvors team involves the use of large L-shaped tubes called "mailboxes." Two are mounted at the stern of each search boat. Once the mailboxes have been pivoted into place over the boat's spinning propellers, they direct the prop wash downward toward the search site. They not only push clear water down to the site to be excavated, but they dig a deep crater in the sand. Then, the divers equipped with metal detectors go down. They scan the entire area, including the sand berm formed around the hole.

Detectors used by these divers are of the pulse induction type. Each diver merely sets the audio control to his, or her, preferred threshold level and starts scanning. Pulse induction detectors are not affected by ocean salt or black magnetic sand.

Even though some underwater detectors can be submerged to depths of 200 feet, divers at the *Atocha* site used detectors at a depth of about 55 feet. But, they have also used them successfully in much shallower waters, such as off the coast of Ft. Pierce, FL, where Spanish galleons dating to 1715 have been found. "The water's depth doesn't affect the metal detector," says Mathewson.

Before recovering any artifacts, divers under Mathewson's supervision lay down grids of non-metallic orange tubes over major finds and exposed portions of the vessel. The grid sections are marked with numbered floats.

Recovered artifacts — from coins to cannon balls, iron locks and sword blades — are sealed in plastic bags and marked with a number for computer coding.

Treasure Salvors maintains an archaeological laboratory at the company's Key West headquarters. A description of each find is entered into a computer. Later, the finds can be studied in relation to one another. Mathewson also supervises photographing, drawing and weighing of each artifact.

Mathewson believes that scientific examination of the *Atocha* and its cargo will provide enlightenment on a wide variety of topics. He notes, for example, that the ship was built in Havana in 1618, a generation after the defeat of the Spanish Armada off the English coast. The *Atocha* could thus shed light on what innovations had been incorporated into galleon design by Spanish shipbuilders. At least five years of investigation and recovery work are necessary to complete examination of the *Atocha* site.

Metal detectors are also being used successfully by archaeologists excavating dry-land sites. A noted professor who teaches historical-site archaeology says that the detector enables him and his students to do a better job of excavating and writing reports.

Archaeological excavation normally begins with the construction of one or more control grids, which are used as an aid in mapping and as a method of recording the artifacts found within the site. It is after grids are laid out that archaeologists call upon the metal detector, sweeping the searchcoil over the square to be excavated. Whenever the detector signals the presence of a metal object, a small flag is planted. No excavation begins until the electronic survey has been completed and the square flagged.

"Using a detector gives us pre-knowledge of exactly where every metal artifact is located," the professor says. "We don't miss a thing once we start to dig. The detector increases our expertise."

Not only does the detector enable the archaeologist to find a greater percentage of buried artifacts, it also helps prevent damage to them. "Suppose you're digging a site and you come upon a buried piece of thin metal, perhaps a tin can that's been down there for 70 or 80 years. A carelessly used trowel could penetrate the metal. But when you know the metal is there, you proceed with caution," the archaeologist observes.

"A metal detector can help make for safe digging, too," he states. "If there are buried electric power cables or other objects that are potentially dangerous, you can seek them out and establish where they are before you begin digging."

Figure 23-2: Four members of this group plan a two-month expedition following the route Moses and the Israelites took during their departure from Egypt about 1400 B.C. From left to right team members are Astronaut Jim Irwin, Dr. Roy Knuteson, Dick Ewing (team leader) and Charles Garrett. Jim Irwin has made several searches for Noah's Ark. On the right in the white shirt is Ron Wyatt, an explorer who also has made several searches for Noah's Ark. The men will utilize their equipment knowledge and expertise in their search for proof needed to establish the true route that the Israelites took in their exodus from Egypt, across the Sinai Peninsula and into Saudi Arabia.

This archaeologist has been using detectors in his scientific investigations for more than a decade. He tested several different types before settling on the Garrett Deepseeker, a sensitive and stable instrument.

Rick Sammon, President of CEDAM International (Conservation, Education, Diving, Archaeology and Museums), and members utilize land and underwater metal detectors on their expeditions. CEDAM is a very active professional group of people dedicated to the discovery and preservation of both land and underwater historic sites and shipwrecks.

Metal detectors on many occasions have proven themselves. In Ireland a metal detector survey was made around the ballast stones of the wreck of the Armada ship, the *Santa Maria de la Rosa.* The survey was made to locate the precise position of the ship's cannon. Numerous targets were located but no detector signals indicated the presence of objects the shape and mass of cannon. Excavation proved the cannon lay elsewhere. On a wreck, called the *Kyrenia,* a large concentration of lead objects that might have been overlooked outside the excavation area were located with metal detectors.

Several individuals and I plan to spend from one to two months following the route Moses and the Jews took following their departure from Egypt about 1400 B.C., Figure 23-2. Team leader Dick Ewing has spent years planning this expedition. Team members Astronaut Jim Irwin, Dr. Roy Knuteson and I will participate by bringing our equipment knowledge and/or expertise into play during the various searches. Irwin will man various aircraft deploying photography, infrared and other specialized airborn equipment into play. My responsibility will be to handle land and underwater metal detection equipment at the various sites.

OTHER SUGGESTIONS FOR METAL DETECTOR USE

An initial survey of a given land or underwater site will locate all metal items down several feet deep. This pinpointing of metal objects helps the archaeologist to determine scope, layout and other characteristics of the site.

A site can be scanned for metal artifacts of all types or just non-ferrous, high conductivity metal items such as those made of copper, brass, bronze, silver, pewter and gold. Since these non-ferrous metals do not corrode rapidly, they may bear visible data permitting dating, country of origin, type of cargo or other valuable research information. A complete detector scan of a site, with markers placed at each target location, helps in determining the areas most likely to be productive. When coins are found, quick dating of a site can be made. A metal detector survey of a "suspect" area can "prove" the site is one the researcher wishes to investigate. The same investigation can also prove the site is NOT the one to investigate. To some extent, metal detectors can determine when ground-zero has been reached. A complete scan will reveal whether other metal objects (and possibly whether other non-metallic objects) are present below existing levels.

DETECTOR SURVEY OF KNOWN WRECKS

Whenever a wreck is to be studied and excavated archaeologically, it may be desirable to conduct a metal detector survey of the site to enable the excavation to proceed in a more orderly and planned fashion. Information can be obtained on the extent of the wreck, the direction in which it is lying, the location of cannon, anchor and other ship's rigging. To accomplish this survey, a non-metallic grid is placed in position. Detectors are used to locate every detectable object which can then be dug or simply size-determined. It is easy to distinguish between a cannon and a coin or other smaller item. Of course, several metal objects closely associated may appear as one large piece of metal. To some extent, iron can be distinguished from non-metallic objects. By using these methods, a metal-object profile of the wreck can be developed.

At an underwater site such as the resting place of the *Titanic,* personal artifacts and ship's components are strewn over a vast area. One convenient, simple way to locate most of the buried strewn metal debris is to use metal detectors. Approximate locations of each found item could be made or a vast grid network could be deployed. A non-metallic grid network could be set up for metal detectors to locate every piece of buried metal. Certainly, this would be of great value when there is not sufficient time to completely excavate a site or when murky conditions prevent a photo mosaic.

RESCUE ARCHAEOLOGY

Rescue Archaeology, sometimes called "Salvage Archaeology," is a techique archaeologists use during emergency situations when a site is soon to be covered by rising waters of a new lake or by the construction of buildings, highways and railroads. This technique is also used at canal excavation sites.

In such situations archaeologists realize that only a small fraction of the historical relics can be saved; but, even a small part is better than nothing. Thus, compromises are made, as quickly as possible, to recover relics from the site. The metal detector can be the perfect tool to help the archaeologist in this plight. The metal detector will quickly locate all buried metal objects. A marker is placed at each location with a team of people following the detector operators to recover the detected items. One metal detector can keep numerous "recovery" teams busy.

Using Rescue Archaeology, much knowledge of the history of a site can be obtained that might otherwise be lost forever. A community can be rewarded with the knowledge of a portion of the history of

292

Figure 23-3: Metal detectorist Gary Weicks found the flintlock mechanism shown in this photo of a Hudson Bay gun. Realizing the gun's importance, he contacted the National Forest Service and is now working with Forest Service archaeologists to prove that the area was a rendezvous site of early-day fur trappers.

their ancestors. Educational museums can be established for the townspeople. The foregoing discussion about Rescue Archaeology was taken from my book, MODERN METAL DETECTORS, which contained a chapter with case histories and suggestions for use of metal detectors.

THE ARCHAEOLOGIST AND THE TREASURE HUNTER

The subject of metal detectors has long been hotly debated. Some archaeologists steadfastly refuse to acknowledge the detector as a viable tool and even brand users as mere artifact collectors. But through the efforts of many archaeologists, the value of the metal detector in research is being realized.

I am on the side of both the archaeologist and the treasure hunter. In both my writing and work in the field I would never encourage or instruct any "treasure hunter" to remove even a single artifact from a valuable historical site. I place historical knowledge far above any monetary value to be gained from artifacts. The treasure hunter should never encroach upon an established or defined historical site. Neither should an archaeologist, as an archaeologist, encroach upon treasure sites by imposing general restrictions on sites that represent no value to archaeology.

Tens of thousands of sites contain relics and treasure from the past. But, never in ten thousand years can the archaeologist locate and excavate them all. For the archaeologist and historian to attempt to keep the treasure hunter from all such sites is wrong. Not only will all the "historical" sites never be discovered, the passage of time will continue to destroy them along with their artifacts and treasure. Why not let the treasure hunter search for and recover treasure from sites that archaeologists know realistically they will never work?

On the other hand, historically important sites should not be touched by the treasure hunter. To remove even a single item is the loss of great knowledge about that site and the customs of the people who lived there. Archaeologists are the Sherlock Holmes of science and history. They relentlessly investigate our heritage to provide valuable knowledge about our past. It's remarkable how their investigation and analysis reveals the finest details of life as it took place thousands of years ago. Work is very demanding and thorough. Consequently, they don't need anyone to come along and destroy even a single shred of evidence. They need all the help they can get.

Why can't the archaeologist and treasure hunter work together? It's been proposed and discussed many times. Some critics of treasure hunters strongly oppose any such coalition. To do so, they believe, would confer an unwarranted respectability on the treasure hunter. Instead of recognition, the treasure hunter is often detested and likened unto looters and thieves. Granted, there are some treasure hunters who, without regard to the law or the value of ancient sites, willfully destroy sites as they remove artifacts and treasure. But, are all archaeologists really "clean?" Are there no misplaced artifacts or treasure concealed in home closets and cellars? Never are all members of a profession or calling perfect. Has there never been some minister, banker, law officer, archaeologist or treasure hunter who hasn't "gone astray?"

And what about the thousands of sunken vessels and cultural areas destroyed by erosion? What about bulldozers and earth-moving equipment of developers and and builders? Don't they destroy countless sites every day?

Well, neither side can win 'em all, nor should either expect to. Each should try, however, to see the other's point of view and realize that we should work together, or at least, not hinder the other. Certainly, working together makes the most sense. It has worked before as proven at numerous locations including the Custer battle site at the Little Big Horn.

A start would be for each side to learn the true nature of the other's complaints. What are the real objection of archaeologists? And, what is the treasure hunter's gripe? WHY WON'T THE TWO GROUPS WORK TOGETHER? Certainly, each can learn a lot from the other. I believe that if most treasure hunters knew how to recognize a valuable historical site when they found one, they would stay away from them and would direct the archaeologist to their locations. It has happened many times. Also, if the treasure hunters knew what was historically important, they would be careful in their recovery work and would supply important site and artifact data to the proper people. Many metal detectorists would gladly, without charge, work with archaeological groups. The archaeologists could achieve many objectives simply by educating treasure hunters on the basics of archaeology and the importance of certain objects. Since the metal detector IS an important tool of discovery, archaeologists could benefit from knowing how to use it. Few are the metal detector users who wouldn't welcome the opportunity to instruct others in the use of their equipment. Metal detector manufacturers would offer free training for archaeologists. I would. I have written three times to a Texas state archaeologist and offered such training at no expense to the scientists. Furthermore, I have offered the use of my skills with a metal detector at historical sites anywhere in Texas at no charge. I am still waiting, after several years, for an answer, yes or no.

What can you, the treasure hunter, do to protect historically important sites and help close the gap between the treasure hunter and the archaeologist? You can start by trying to understand the archaeologist's point of view. You can become an amateur archaeologist and learn something about archaeological methods and techniques. You can acquaint yourself with the background and aims of archaeology. There are several reference books listed in the Bibliography. Try to form a partnership with your local archaeological community, with historical societies, museums and universities. Reach out to them. Offer to work as a site volunteer using your metal detector when and where it would be useful.

Stay alert to the possibility that you may someday discover an important archaeological site. For instance, should you be working a beach or surf area and locate a bronze axe, contact your local or state archaeologist. You may have discovered the site of a ten-thousand-year-old settlement.

Learn the nature of the responsibilities of your state's archaeologist. Ask your State Senator or Representative for such information. Obtain a copy of your state's antiquities law and learn what it says. Read it carefully to determine your rights, provisions for licenses or permits and which agency or individual has the authority to issue such documents.

Encourage local archaeological groups, museums and historical societies to establish a central clearing house where you and other amateur archaeologists and historians can turn for information on identifying and preserving important locations and finds. When you make such discoveries, contact this group and report them. Ask if they are interested in the site and joining you in your work. Make your contacts first by telephone or a personal visit, and then by letter. Certainly, you would want proof that you disclosed the location of an important site. Be businesslike, serious and ready to propose a plan. Offer to continue working the site using archaeological knowledge and methods you have learned, and to report data about finds. Welcome the opportunity of having an archaeologist monitor your work. Each time there is a successful encounter between professional archaeologists and treasure hunters, a closer bond is cemented. I know of many persons who have shared their finds with historical groups and federal, state and local authorities. In almost every case, they were made welcome and encouraged to continue working. Also, such contacts resulted in their being granted permits to work in areas otherwise restricted to the metal detector operator.

A metal detectorist discovered several bronze axes in Northern Michigan. He reported the find to authorities. The site has become very important archaeologically. Another treasure hunter, Gary Weicks, found the flintlock mechanism of a Hudson Bay gun, Figure 23-3. He made contact with DeWitt Bailey of London to obtain data about manufacture and distribution of the weapon. The treasure hunter, realizing the gun's importance, contacted the National Forest Service. He is now working with two Forest Service archaeologists. A complete metal detector survey, similar to the one performed at the Custer battle site, is being planned. The area may prove to be a rendezvous site of early-day fur trappers.

To sum up, do not trespass in restricated areas and on known archaeological sites. Joan Allen in her book, GLITTERING PRO-SPECTS, points out that doing so is stupid, inconsiderate and, of paramount importance, is against the law. She further compels us, "To remember that each time we go out with a metal detector, we are an ambassador for an activity that is rewarding in very many ways. We must face up to our responsibilities as both treasure hunters and citizens. The reputation and future of ourselves and others who enjoy treasure hunting will be secure."

Let us develop a rapport with archaeologists and learn from them. Learn applicable laws and take an active part in writing and passing good legislation. Be ready to teach others about treasure hunting and metal detecting. Be ever responsible to insure conservation and proper management of our archaeological resources.

CHAPTER 24

Treasure Pouches, Hand Tools and Various Other Devices

Selecting and properly using correct tools is essential to maximum success in treasure hunting as in any other field of endeavor. If you are wise in your choice of tools and proficient in using them, your rewards should be great.

This chapter describes equipment and tools needed for beach hunting, surfing and underwater recovery. Chapter 25 describes specialized equipment such as depth recorders, sub-bottom profilers and submersible craft. Metal detectors and accessories are described in Chapters 5 through 11. Various "how-to-use" metal detector instructions can be found in other chapters.

BEACH HUNTING EQUIPMENT AND TOOLS

Treasure pouches are available in one, two and even three-pocket designs, Figure 24-1. In the one-pocket style, everything you find — treasure and trash alike — goes into that single pocket. At the end of the day, you must sort through the entire contents to recover "keepers." Even with a two-pocket pouch that holds treasure in one pocket and trash in the other, you should carefully inspect your trash visually before discarding anything.

I recommend that all detected items be placed in a recovery pouch. At intervals you can inspect your trash and discard it properly. I emphasize that last word because all of us treasure hunters can help keep beaches cleaner by properly discarding trash. The next hunter (possible even you) will not have to contend with trash. And, even if your detector is a discriminator, remember that reject targets resulting from trash that you have cast aside can diminish good target detector signals.

Some hunters prefer their "treasure" pocket to have a snap, zipper or velcro fastener. For beach hunting a secure pocket is not particularly necessary unless you often lay down to rest or you have the habit of tossing your pouch on the ground or in the trunk of your car.

Some beachcombers use three-pocket pouches. One pocket is used for trash, one for most finds and the third for more valuable finds. To me, all treasure finds are "keepers" and I don't want to lose anything I find. When I find an especially attractive item, I stop searching and take it to my vehicle or camp. When I am searching long hours, I sometimes set up a tent where I can occasionally return to eat or rest in the shade. On these trips I place all finds in my stowed gear.

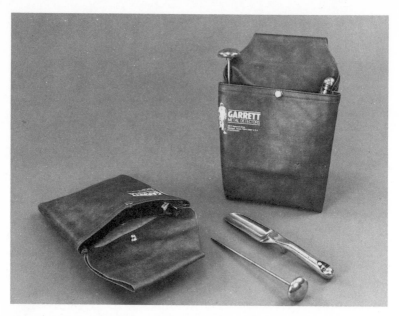

Figure 24-1: There are many styles of treasure pouches available. The text describes construction and desired features.

Figure 24-2: Our thanks to Gary for permitting Bill Welsch to photograph his treasure "harness." Everything Gary needs for a day's treasure hunting can be carried in the back pack. The various belt-mounted pouches hold coins, rings and other found treasures.

Pouches should be waterproof to prevent soiling of your clothes. The fabric should also be rugged and able to withstand lots of weight and rigorous use. A non-fraying cord or other suitable means of securing the pouch to yourself is required. Many pouch styles can be mounted on a belt. I often wear a web belt that holds a canteen, a tool kit and two or more extra pouches for miscellaneous items such as sunscreen, a small camera and first aid kit. Sometimes, I wear my treasure/trash pouch on this belt. A web belt is versatile and allows you to carry any number of things securely, Figrure 24-2.

The digger or retriever to be used depends upon the beach sands, whether coarse or fine, wet or dry and upon the individual's preference. I prefer a long-handled, lightweight, flat-bladed pick, which with one blow usually dislodges the object. If I still can't find it, one pass with the detector searchcoil tells me where the object is — still in the ground or on the surface. Occasionally, I'll use a wide-bladed trowel with which I can quickly cut a hole and remove the sand and detected object with one circular motion. Another recovery method for loose sand is to use a cup-size plastic container. Sweep the cup through the sand, then under the searchcoil. If your metal object is in the container, the detector will tell you so. See Figure 24-3.

Some beach hunters use a garden trowel. When you need to dig deeply through packed ground and tree roots, you'll appreciate a heavy duty digger.

Figure 24-3: Here are various digging devices available to treasure hunters.

Figure 24-4: This long-handled scoop, manufactured by Alden Fogliadini (see scoop description, Chapter 13) is the author's favorite. Figure 24-5 shows the available handles which increase the scoop's versatility.

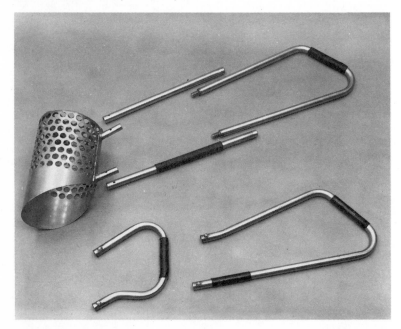

Figure 24-5: Alden Fogliadini's water scoop is made even more versatile by the short and medium length handles as shown. The selection of a field-proven, rugged scoop is very important to the surfer. For information write to Aldo's Scoop, 6180 Via Real #1, Carpentena, CA 93013.

Sand scoops and sifters can be useful at times. When sand is very fine and completely dry, you can use a sifter to scoop up your target along with sand, then shake it and your treasure will be on the sifter. When sand is coarse or damp, however, you'll probably have to shake the sifter for a minute or so to remove all the sand from your sifter. In damp sand you may never get the sand out unless you submerge it in water. In situations like these, a sifter is a waste of time.

You may also be interested in the Estwing long-handled recovery tool. Because the device has a long handle with a digger/scoop, you do not have to bend down each time you make a find. You can drag it through the sand, scoop up your find and pocket it, while you remain standing.

SURFING EQUIPMENT AND TOOLS

Open-pocket pouches are very risky. I encourage you to use a pouch with a secure closing device such as a zipper, snap or velcro. The trash pocket can and should be the open type because you will quickly become weary of unfastening its pocket every time you recover junk. Opening and closing a treasure pouch each time you find money or jewelry is trouble enough. But, you are glad to do it because you are preventing loss of found treasures.

Belt pouches with a single, large pocket for trash and a smaller pocket with a fastener are available. Any pouch used in the water must have drain holes. Some surfers prefer to use a zipper bag or a screwtop plastic bottle attached to a string. The bag or bottle is worn around the neck.

When you work in shallow water, you can use a hand sifter to recover detected objects. When you work in water deeper than about 18 inches, you must use a sifter with an extension handle. There are many designs. I prefer the type that has a handle loop, Figures 24-4 and 24-5.

There are several reasons why I prefer the loop-handle design. When you are not retrieving a find, you may slip the upper end of the handle loop over your arm for easy carrying. The most important reason, however, is because the loop handle is very efficient to use. To dig, place the scoop blade at the correct place on the bottom. Grasp the rear section of the handle loop and push it forward. This action places the scoop in a near vertical position for digging. After you have pushed the scoop into the sand with your foot, pull backwards on the handle. Slide your hand down the forward section of the handle loop until you reach the scoop. If the water is too deep for you to reach the scoop, you can make a succession of "jumps" along the handle, each time pulling the scoop further from the soil. This is difficult to do with some plain handle scoops because of their center of gravity. When you pull upward, plain-handle scoops tend to rotate. When loop-handle scoops are pulled free of the bottom, they don't rotate like scoops with a single straight handle.

Figure 24-6: The Beach Connector is a sealing tube that protects searchcoil extension cable connectors. Standard-length land searchcoils, if guaranteed submersible by the manufacturer, can be used to depths of about three to four feet. An extension cable (and some means of waterproofing the connector) allows the electronics housing to be body mounted where it is kept dry above the water.

There are several methods you can use to recover detected finds. You must practice to learn exactly where to place the scoop. In the beginning you may have to make a dozen or more tries before you are successful. Even with experience, more than one "dig" is sometimes necessary.

Because light-colored shoes can be more easily seen when you are working in murky water, you'll have an easier time of positioning a scoop at the point of your toe when your shoes are light colored. When shaking sand from the scoop, shake it away from the path you are walking to minimize visibility reduction. Also, when you let water currents clean your scoop, make sure sand washes away from the direction you are walking.

When surfing with a submersible metal detector, a correctly designed long-handled sifter is the only recovery tool you need.

THE BEACH CONNECTION

Some hunters use their land detectors in shallow water by attaching the housing to the upper portion of their chest or mounting it on a flotation device. This procedure, however, requires an extension cable inserted between the searchcoil cable connector and housing connector. You must waterproof the connector. A waterproofing device I have tested is the BEACH CONNECTION, Figure 24-6, manufactured by The Beach Connection Company, P.O. Box 175, Ashland, KY 41105. The device will remain watertight to a depth of about six feet. Number

75-1875 protects connectors with a maximum diameter of ¾ inches. Number 100-1875 protects connectors with a maximum diameter of one inch. Use the smaller size, if you can, for less bulk.

DETECTOR AND SCREENING FLOTATION DEVICES

Most metal detectors can be used in fresh water if the electronics housing remains dry and the searchcoil is submersible-rated to the depth you will be working. Non-discriminating BFOs and TRs cannot be used in salt water. To cancel the effects of salt water, a detector must have a discrimination circuit adjustable to bottlecap rejection. At this setting, salt water will be ignored. Most automated detectors can be used in salt water.

To keep the housing high and dry, it can be mounted on your body, perhaps with a backpack. You must, of course, be able to reach the controls.

There are about as many flotation devices as there are people designing them. An automobile innertube or styrofoam device can be easily constructed, Figure 24-7. PVC tubing makes an excellent float/screen. Monty Moncrief built such a device especially for the benefit of readers of this book. It's best to mount the metal detector one foot or more above the water by suspending it from an inverted "L" bracket attached to the float. Remember, however, the housing must not be too high for you to reach the controls. Of course, the cable length of your searchcoil must be adequate.

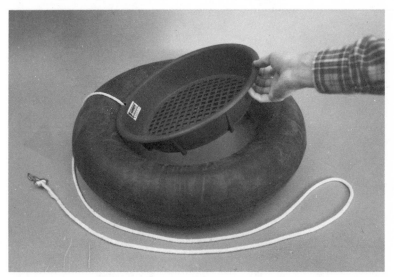

Figure 24-7: This sifting device works quite well. Its center part is the Garrett Gravity Trap gold pan classifier. A motorcycle tube or large bicycle tube make satisfactory flotation supports. Smaller tubes permit the classifier bottom (screen) to lay partly submerged which facilitates cleaning of sand and small debris.

Figure 24-8: When searching for gold, the gold pan is an indispensable tool. This is the Garrett Gravity Trap Gold Panning Kit that contains the two main gold pans, a classifier, suction bottle, the GOLD PANNING IS EASY book, and a companion "How to" video with the same title.

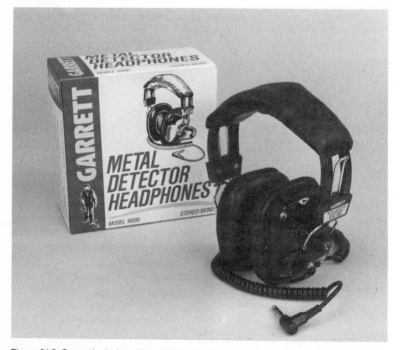

Figure 24-9: Correctly designed headphones will enhance metal detector signals and block "outside" interference noises. Headphones can easily improve a metal detectorist's performance by 25 to 50%.

Your sifting screen should float slightly below water level. Submersion in water helps keep it clean. Depending upon the amount of rock, shell and other debris on the bottom, you'll occasionally have to dump the unwanted material. Some means can be devised to hinge the screen for quick dumping. Also, keep it tied securely so that it will remain nearby and not float off to China. Be sure to build in one or more "pockets" for treasure, trash and other items.

UNDERWATER RECOVERY EQUIPMENT AND TOOLS

This section covers hand-held recovery tools, lift bags and other devices. Major equipment such as hooka rigs, inflatables, boats, site gridding devices and the like are discussed in Chapters 14 and 26.

At some sites, you can just fan your hand and the sand will blow away. At others you'll need a pick to break coins and other detected items from coral growth. A strong diver's knife should be on your check list. A good sheath mounting location is on the lower leg just above the ankle. A secure locking strap is a must.

Suitable bags or containers should be part of your equipment for keeping the things you find. Nylon netting bags are good. In sandy or heavily silted areas, a probe can be used to pinpoint solid objects.

The Estwing prospector's pick is a good tool You can fasten it to your wrist with a lanyard. Larger picks may be needed such as the 27-inch Estwing model.

LIFT BAGS

Lift bags are available in a variety of sizes and shapes. These include pillow bags, buoyancy balls and open-mouth lift bags. Open-mouth bags are not popular, however, because they cannot be laid on their sides without losing air. Lift capacity of bags ranges from 50 pounds to 12,000 pounds. Bags are very strong, durable and lightweight. They can be rolled into a compact roll for storage and easy handling under water. A bag with a 100-pound lift capacity weighs approximately 10 pounds.

Bags are usually constructed of a neoprene bladder bonded to an outer shell of nylon coated with a layer of polyurethane rubber. This coating is tough and flexible yet highly resistant to abrasion and to most chemicals, particularly gasoline and diesel fuel which are commonly encountered during salvage operations.

Other features of lift bags include inflation and dump valves to maintain buoyancy, as required, and straps or lift points for attaching objects to be lifted. Attaching objects securely permits you to tow them after they have been raised. Air bladders are available without straps for placing inside cars, boats and barges.

MISCELLANEOUS RECOVERY TOOLS

Grappling hooks can be used to recover objects from cisterns and wells. Three or four-pronged hooks come in all sizes. Their main disad-

Figure 24-10. To protect your metal detection equipment select a suitable carrying and storage case. They are of two types, hard case and the softer zippered bag.

vantage is the ability to "stay hooked" to almost anything. If the object proves too heavy or large to retrieve, you've lost a hook and some rope.

USING MAGNETS TO RECOVER IRON OBJECTS

A magnet will attract iron objects, but not non-ferrous metals such as gold, silver and copper. Most magnets have an eye hook or means for attaching a rope. They are rated according to the pull they will exert on an iron object. A magnet will attract iron rust just as it will attract solid iron. Whenever the magnet is not in use, an iron bar should be placed across its open end. Always use care when placing the bar on the magnet. To remove the bar it may be necessary to slide it off.

PROBES

In loose sand and lightly compacted soils, probes can be easily inserted two feet or more. With practice, you will be able to determine if you have contacted metal, glass, wood or rock. Construct your own probes with any type of rod material. Small sizes are preferred but the rod must not bend easily. A small "bullet" welded on the tip will reduce the amount of drag when you pull the probe from the soil. Only slightly larger in diameter then the probe rod itself, the bullet should be pointed or rounded to facilitate insertion. A suitable, yet solidly attached, handle should be mounted on the upper end.

SPIRALING CIRCLE SPOOL

Various grid methods will insure 100% coverage of an area you are scanning. The "spiraling circle" search is a popular method. Use a spool with rope or line wound upon its core. Anchor the spool at the center point of your search area. The spool must not rotate. The preferred method is to spiral outward. Place one of your hands through a loose-fitting loop formed by the end of the rope. Hold the rope and begin swimming around the spool as you scan visually or with a metal detector. Swimming in this controlled circle will permit you to search an area without skipping. The amount of "feed out" per revolution around the spool depends upon the width of the path you can effectively scan. (See page 199.)

If you wish to "feed out" at the rate of 36 inches for each revolution, the spool core diameter should be approximately 12 inches. Use the following equation for determining your desired spool core diameter:

CORE DIAMETER = "FEED OUT" DISTANCE ÷ 3

BUOY MARKERS

You may need several small buoys. These can be constructed using bleach or other plastic containers with sufficient line attached. A brick can anchor your buoy except in high wind or rough weather.

Buoys can serve as site markers or markers for your recovery baskets. When you fill a basket, follow the line topside and haul in your finds.

DIVER'S FLAGS

Areas with boat traffic require you to position dive flags to warn boaters. But, don't rely entirely on the flag to do the job. Some boaters haven't the slightest idea what a dive flag means. Others may ignore them. So, always approach the surface cautiously.

UNDERWATER BEACON TRANSPONDERS

In traffic lanes and locations where total secrecy is essential, you can plant underwater beacon transponders. These battery-powered devices transmit a low frequency signal at a given interval. The receiver, mounted in your boat, precisely locates underwater sites. Depending on power, life of your batteries can be several months.

There are many other miscellaneous tools and equipment pieces including the ones shown in Figures 24-8 through 24-10 that searchers need. Study manufacturers' literature and acquire the items that will improve your efficiency and protect your equipment.

CHAPTER 25

Specialized Locating—
Equipment and Methods

Thousands of potentially rich underwater treasure sites have attracted both the professional and the amateur. While not everyone seeking sunken treasure strikes it rich, those who do fuel a fire that grows ever brighter. The desire to find sunken wealth leads men to search farther and deeper, pushing not only their limits but also those of the equipment and methods they use. Consequently, diving for treasure demands development of improved equipment required by the needs of man's aggressive pursuits.

This chapter introduces you to some of man's inventions. From the simple view-sled to the Side Scan Sonar/Sub Bottom profiler to Robot and Manned Submersibles, man's technology has responded to develop new equipment as needed. Even as I write this chapter, men continually expand the limits of underwater exploration by perfecting equipment that stretches today's imagination.

Equipment described on these pages is being used every day. Select from it to the extent that your requirements and budget allow. Professional equipment should be used to the fullest extent possible so that nothing can hinder progress toward achieving your goals.

SURFACE VIEW-SCOPE

A glass-bottom bucket or view-scope is a simple yet excellent device to permit a visual search in a body of clear water—river, lake or ocean. To construct a view-scope, bond a round, clear glass plate into the end of a PVC pipe or other suitable tube. Glass shops can readily cut a 1/4-inch thick piece of glass to any diameter you require. Waterproof silicone will securely bond the glass in the proper size tube. For good visibility, the diameter of the tube should be large enough for viewing with both eyes. A safety sling will prevent loss.

UNDERWATER PHOTOGRAPHY

Photography can be a useful tool for the dedicated treasure hunting enthusiast. Every good photograph is valuable as a permanent record of data and information that might be lost forever. Before-and-after site documentation can be invaluable and time-saving. By leisurely studying photos you can discover features overlooked at the scene. When a study of reconstruction of a shipwreck is required, grid/photography documentation can help accomplish it. A complete photographic record of finds has many advantages, including its use as a record in case of losses through fire or theft.

Don't feel intimidated by all the technical information you've read or heard about. The selection of an adequate camera, a study of its operating manual, an initial training exercise and a basic knowledge of photographic fundamentals are the starting basics. Mastery begins by learning to concentrate on technique.

Begin with specific subject selection rather than randomly shooting everything in sight. If you have a plan, a goal to be achieved, you've won most of the battle already. A critical study of your photographs taken as you progress is the fastest means of developing photographic expertise.

Don't be afraid to ask for help. Check out books from your library and study them. Soon you'll be asking yourself what the fuss was all about. There are many good cameras on the market including professional Nikonos models and the Hanimex 110/35mm amphibians. Depending upon water depth and required print quality, you may be able to use one of the waterproof "swimmer's" cameras that do everything except select the subject to be photographed. Various waterproof camera housings are available. The Helix Company, 325 West Huron Street, Chicago, IL 60610, (312) 944-400, stocks a complete range of underwater cameras and equipment. The Ikelite Company, 50 W. 33rd Street, Indianapolis, IN 46208 (317) 923-4523, manufactures a wide assortment of underwater camera and equipment housings.

AERIAL PHOTOGRAPHY

Since 1969 various types of infrared and water-penetrating film have been produced which, when used with polarizing filters, locate from the air those images of sunken objects not visible with the naked eye. These special films have been used to record ocean-bottom detail and to find underwater archaeological sites. Precise location of sites is difficult with aerial photography unless it is near a coastline, or specially placed buoys are used.

Film manufacturers, including GAF Corporation and Eastman Kodak, can provide additional information to those who wish to investigate the use of aerial photography.

Pre-flight groundwork for aerial photography is very important. A marine navigation chart provides a graphic planning tool for laying out the area(s) to be photographed. Water depths are shown and flight lines will enable a pilot to fly your search area. When over the area you plan to photograph, make at least one dry run to familiarize yourself with its features for any possible changes prior to actual "picture taking." An excellent source book is INTERPRETATION OF AERIAL PHOTOGRAPHS.

A few helpful hints will assist you in the successful use of this type of research activity.

A. The camera "sees" what the eye sees. If water is dirty, deep

Figure 25-2: This is the Hydrofin developed and manufactured by Hope Diving Developments Limited. This underwater sled when towed by a boat allows the diver to skim along effortlessly under the water at any desired depth. It can be towed at speeds up to 5 knots and is highly maneuverable and easy to use.

(50 ft. or deeper) or turbulent, effective aerial photography will probably not be possible.

B. Because glare and reflection reduce photo coverage, mid-morning (9-11 a.m.) and mid-afternoon (1:30-4 p.m.) time periods are best for aerial photography. The afternoon period may be extended during the summer months. A clear day with less than 20% cloud cover is necessary if detail is required in your photography. This is not only because of clouds blocking the view but also because of cloud shadows.

C. Vertical or near vertical photography will produce the best results. A helicopter is preferable as it can remain in an almost stationary position. A fixed-wing aircraft should be banked in a slow turn when photographs are being taken.

D. A fast shutter speed (1/500 sec. or faster) will reduce image motion caused by aircraft flight and vibration.

E. Slide film (color) usually produces the best photography. Use a haze filter and SLIGHTLY overexpose for water penetration.

F. Check ALL camera equipment and film, and clean aircraft windows prior to take-off.

SURF BOARDS AND PLANING SLEDS

An easy way to visually inspect large bottom areas quickly is to be towed along the surface. In addition to mask, snorkel and fins it is a good idea to wear a slim-line or inflatable life vest. Towing speed must be slow or the water pressures may become too great. Extended towing can also rapidly deplete your heat and energy.

A surf board with a glass viewing port can be an efficient device when the water is sufficiently calm. Rough weather will cause the view port to bound out of the water, creating visibility problems.

Various underwater sled designs are available. One such model is the Hydrofin, manufactured by Hope Diving Developments Limited, 10 Farndale Avenue, Palmers Green London N1 3 TAQ, London, England. This device allows a diver to survey areas precisely in a minimum of time. Use of such a device also eliminates the need for massive diver effort. The Hydrofin, Figure 25-2, has a detachable instrument console that will accept a dive watch, depth gauge and compass. It has a camera-mounting bracket and all necessary handles, arm rests and a towing eye. At a speed of approximately five knots a diver can maneuver at will over and around obstacles from surface level down to any practical depth. While its advantages greatly outweigh its disadvantages, the Hydrofin's main restriction is that you must go where the towing vessel takes you. Even then, a simple direct-coupled sound system can be devised to permit the diver to instruct the boat pilot.

A towing sled can be built of PVC tubing and aluminum sheet metal. The device should have a rudder, bow planes and watershield. Bow planes permit lateral motion, and a waterscreen lessens water pressure on the face and body.

UNDERWATER METAL DETECTOR SEARCHCOILS

An inexpensive method to locate metal objects under water is to use a metal detector searchcoil. The Garrett Master Hunter includes a 12-inch diameter searchcoil, Chapter 8, Figure 8-3, which is constructed with 50 feet of waterproof cable. The searchcoil can be lowered and maneuvered over the bottom while the electronic housing is kept above water. Objects as small as a coin can be detected. Larger objects such as motors and metal boats can be detected six to eight feet below the bottom of the searchcoil. Maneuverability and coverage is good except in swiftly flowing water. Even then, the searchcoil can be weighted to improve stability.

With the searchcoil attached to the end of a 10 to 15-foot pole the operator can control and maneuver it from a boat or pier. Various other searchcoils with standard cable length are available. These, also, can be attached to a pole for shallow water searching.

The Garrett Bloodhound Depth Multiplier attachment which can triple the Garrett Master Hunter's depth capability on large objects is shown in Figures 25-3 and 25-4.

For further information on submersible searchcoils and metal detectors, contact Garrett Electronics, 2814 National Drive, Garland, TX 75041, (214) 278-6151. Telex 4630163.

Figure 25-3: This is the Garrett Bloodhound Depth Multiplier that multiplies the depth capability of the Master Hunter series of detectors. It is a land unit, but when properly protected can be utilized underwater. See Figure 25-4.

Figure 25-4: Garrett Electronics assisted General Electric engineers in the development and construction of a plexiglass underwater container to house the Bloodhound Depth Multiplier. The Bloodhound was used to search underwater for an engine flywheel which broke loose from an airplane engine and rolled into a bay at Honolulu.

Figure 25-5: This is the Tekna DV-3X self-propelled underwater vehicle. It permits the scuba diver to travel four times faster and ten times farther on a tank of air while reducing air consumption by 50%. The rechargeable batteries offer a range of up to 3 miles.

SUBMERSIBLE SELF-PROPELLED VEHICLES

Self-propelled vehicles permit a scuba diver to travel four times faster and ten times farther on a tank of air while reducing air consumption by 50%. These small, self-contained, battery-powered vehicles give you an exhilarating feeling as you glide almost effortlessly along the bottom, maneuvering over and around obstacles. Rechargeable batteries offer a range of up to three miles on a single charge. The units are constructed of high-impact, non-corrosive materials. A headlight improves visibility during cave and night dives. For information on Tekna Diver Vehicles, Figure 25-5, contact TEKNA, P.O. Box 849, Belmont, CA 94002 (415) 592-4070.

THE BLASTER

The Blaster, also affectionately known as the "Mailbox," was first used as an excavation tool by Mel Fisher. Hampered by murky water, he diverted his ship's prop wash downward to force clear water to the bottom. To Mel's surprise and delight, water velocity also blew sediment away exposing heavier materials such as ballast, relics and treasure.

There are many factors governing the design and operation of a Blaster: diameter and length, its attachment to the boat, protection for divers, proper boat anchorage, speed of props and length of time operated. An improperly operated Blaster can damage sites and cause treasure to be lost. Excessive Blaster force has cut through coral, propelling cannonballs 50 feet and blasting emeralds as though they were fired from a gun.

VIDEO DOCUMENTATION

The relatively low cost and simplicity of operating video equipment places it within the realm of everyday use by both topside and underwater explorers. Home entertainment cameras and recorders produce superb "viewing" quality.

While the days of film are not over, the arrival of videotape eliminated headaches associated with shooting and processing film. Video cassette recorders utilize magnetic tape, instead of the emulsion film of photography that requires extreme care in handling, developing and processing. Tape is inexpensive and reusable and has near-perfect storage qualities. Editing and assembling your own movies is not difficult, especially if during filming you plan ahead by allowing

Figure 25-6: AquaVideo manufactures a line of high quality submersible video equipment housings. The various housings shown here can contain various of the present-day video recording systems. More than 30 standard design housings are available and custom-fitted housings can be made.

314

ample "on scene" leading and trailing footage. Also, make sure exposures are correct (most cameras feature automatic exposure) and capture sufficient event footage and extra action and closeup takes to enhance the finished product. Home video comes in two formats: VHS and BETA with VHS being the overwhelming favorite. Remember that VHS and BETA tapes and recording equipment are not interchangeable. You can, however, have your footage transferred from one to the other, but image quality will suffer.

Before selecting any equipment, a thorough study is advised. Renting and testing several models is not a bad idea. The more you know about video recording, plus the best possible understanding of your filming and later usage requirements, the better you will be able to select what's best for you.

Panasonic and Sony offer complete underwater systems. Video cameras, recorders, light and batteries are built into especially designed, highly functional and maneuverable underwater housing.

Companies such as AquaVido manufacture high quality submersible video equipment housings, Figure 25-6. They offer free advice and literature. Contact AquaVideo, Inc., 5056 N.W. 159th St., Miami, FL 33169.

Exotic deep sea equipment such as remote-control cameras play key roles in underwater surveys to locate and explore sunken ships and shipwreck sites. Video cameras provided instant initial viewing of the *Titanic* and its wreckage. A remote-control camera explored the *Titanic* and sent up vivid color footage of the ship and its wreckage to help its discoverers plan later manned-vehicle exploration.

DEPTH FINDERS

There are numerous models of depth finders—sometimes called fish finders. These instruments can provide information on depths and bottoms. A piezo-electric crystal transducer encased in a suitable plastic module is mounted on the underside of a boat or on a pole under water. When an electrical current excites the crystal, it expands, sending a shock wave downward into the depths. Any object it strikes, such as fish, logs and the bottom, cause a reflective wave which, when it reaches the transducer, excites the crystal. The resulting current signal is amplified and conditioned to activate lights or recorders and in some cases, audible alarms.

Even the simplest models accurately indicate bottom depth and proximity to large submerged objects. Devices like various of the Lowrance models produce paper recordings of bottom contours and submerged objects such as fish, stumps, piers, boat motors and objects as small as a few inches. Remarkable and exacting data is immediately available for immediate or later analysis. These models are programmable to depths in excess of 1,000 feet. Any portion of the vertical range can be selected to fill full paper height thereby giving great detail of the bottom or of objects protruding from it. Many ob-

315

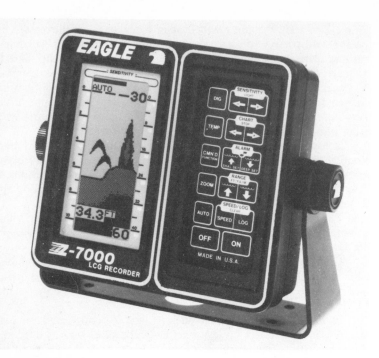

Figure 25-7: This is one of the new Lowrance Eagle sonar instruments. The readout of this new Z-7000 log recorder is a liquid crystal graph (LCG). This new Eagle provides versatile high-tech non-paper graph recording that provides precise definition of fish, lake and stream bottoms, structures and other underwater objects. It has 17 scales ranging from 0 to 10 feet to 1000 feet and features bottom zoom capability in each range.

Figure 25-8: This is a diver-held cesium magnetometer manufactured by Varian of Canada. This is the same type as used by Burt Webber in 1978 to locate the Spanish Galleon *Conception* off the coast of the Dominican Republic.

jects, such as boats and motors, are often outlined with remarkable detail providing instant object recognition, Figure 25-7. Contact Lowrance Electronics, 12000 E. Skelly Drive, Tulsa, OK 74128 (918) 437-6881 for information.

MAGNETOMETERS AND GRADIOMETERS

On November 26, 1978, underwater explorer Burt Webber and his *Sea Quest* crew used a cesium magnetometer to discover the wreck

Figure 25-9: This illustration is an artist's conception of the Klein Hydroscan sidescan sonar/sub-bottom profiler technique. Note the remarkable three dimensional detail of the following hydroscan recording images.

Figure 25-11: This is a Klein 500 kHz sidescan sonar record of *Vineyard Sound Lightship* which was sunk Sept. 14, 1944, off the coast of Massachusetts in water 75 feet deep.

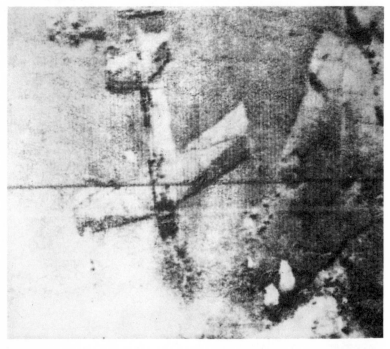

Figure 25-13: This sonograph of a small airplane located in the harbor at Gloucester, MA, was recorded by a Klein 500 kHz, very high resolution, sidescan sonar system.

of the Spanish galleon *Concepcion* off the coast of the Dominican Republic. An estimated $40 million in silver and gold on board the *Concepcion* highlighted capabilities of the model used, as shown in the accompanying photograph, Figure 25-8, which was produced by Varian Associates of Canada.

Magnetic iron and steel objects such as anchors, cannon, cookstoves and parts of ship's rigging cause a local change in the earth's magnetic field. This change, or "anomaly," can be detected by a magnetometer some distance from the magnetic body. The detectable distance and signal strength depend upon object size. The greater the mass, the greater will be the anomaly.

Magnetometers consist of a sensor mounted on a staff. The electronics and display unit are mounted in a waterproof housing. Magnetic field strength is converted to a tone which is fed into the diver's headphones. Changes in the audio tone are caused by anomaly detection. Even in poor visibility, the diver will know of nearby iron and steel objects.

The gradiometer is essentially two magnetometers, mounted in one instrument that measures the difference in field strength or gradient between two sensor points. The gradiometer is a simpler instrument, in principle, since it is only necessary to measure the difference in field intensity, the absolute value of field strength being irrelevant.

There are four type of magnetometers: cesium, proton precession, fluxgate and optically pumped. The complexity of optically pumped magnetometers restricts their general use. Of the remaining three, only fluxgate magnetometers are directional in that they measure the field component through the axis of a mu-metal core.

Magnetometers and gradiometers are available in hand-held, portable and towable configurations which may be towed under water, across ice and through the air. Their development long ago reached the stage where highly reliable systems are commonplace.

SIDE SCAN SONAR

For more than 40 years, Nessie, the legendary Loch Ness monster, shared the dark waters of its Scottish lake with something equally big and fierce and almost as famous. During World War II, a Royal Air Force pilot ditched a 14-ton Wellington bomber in the long, narrow lake in the highlands of northern Scotland. Records indicated the plane was in the lake, but no one knew its exact whereabouts.

In the late 1970s, several teams began systematic sonar studies of the lake using side scan sonar and the newly developed sonar subbottom profiler. They made numerous important discoveries, one of which was the Wellington bomber. Other "finds" included various other planes, sunken vessels, strange rows of what appeared to be rocks and several "unknowns" that, for all the world, looked just like Nessie, or at least how the creature is "supposed" to look.

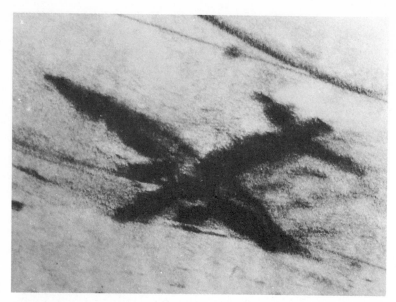

Figure 25-12: This is a photo of the Klein sidescan sonar record of a Wellington Aircraft which was downed in Scotland's Loch Ness during World War II.

Figure 25-10: This is a Klein Hydroscan sidescan sonar record of the *USS Hamilton* sunk in the War of 1812. Photo courtesy Canada Centre of Inland Waters and Royal Ontario Museum.

Figure 25-14: This is a photograph of the Wellington aircraft (Figure 25-12), being raised from Scotland's Loch Ness.

Side scan sonar is a widely accepted tool for mapping topography of sea and lake beds. Scanning hundreds of meters on both sides of a moving ship, it provides an excellent means to rapidly survey any area of interest.

Sub-bottom profiling is the deployment of high resolution sonar to profile shallow bottom sediment layers. This is a vertical scanning system as compared with the side-angular scanning of side scan sonar.

Both systems are built into rugged, portable and self-contained housings called "tow fish." Side scan sonar beams project outward from the "tow fish" along the sea bed on both sides of a moving vessel. Objects or topographic features produce echoes which are received by transducers. The sub-bottom system transducer projects a conical beam straight down toward the sea floor. Echoes from the bottom matrix excite the transducer which produces signals that are processed by graphic recorders.

The accompanying illustration, Figure 25-9, show an artist's conception of the Klein HYDROSCAN Side Sonar/Sub-Bottom profiler technique. Figures 25-10, through 25-13 show numerous craft located with Klein systems . Note the remarkable, three-dimensional detail of the Hydroscan recording images. Figure 25-14 is a photograph of the plane recorded in Figure 25-12.

My friend, Martin Klein, president of Klein Assciates, has just sent me information of their new sonar system with a high resolution thermal recorder, the System 590 Klein Digital Sonar. The heart of this system is the new Model 595 Graphic Recorder. Some of the features include image correction, record expansion, sophisticated annotation and ease of operation through menu-driven controls. The 595 has a new, fixed head, high speed, high resolution, dry thermal printer in which each dot is individually addressed to produce 16 distinct gray shades. The recorder uses the latest dry thermal paper which is plastic-based, tear-resistant, scratchproof, odorless, archival and dimensionally stable.

The system includes the unique Klein Simultaneous Dual Frequency 100 kHz/500 Side Scan Sonar Towfish, which allows a new level of versatility in detection, classification and signal analysis. The 595 will also work with all existing Klein Side Scan Sonars, Sub-Bottom profilers and Microprofilers. For additional data contact Klein Associates, Inc., Klein Drive, Salem, NH 03097 (603) 893-6131

SEA FLOOR MAPPING

The sea floor-mapping system of Environmental Equipment Company produces a "plan view" map of the seafloor's topographical features, all appearing in the correct size and shape. Analogous to aerial photographs of land areas, the seafloor images are accurate maps depicting the size, shape and location of various natural and man-made objects such as shipwrecks, downed aircraft and lost objects. For further information contact: EG&G Environmental Equipment, 151 Bear Hill Road, Waltham, MA 02154 (617) 890-3710.

Figure 25-15: Because man's quest takes him deeper and deeper into the oceans, robots and manned submersibles are being constructed to fill those needs. This is IUC Canada's Beaver Mark IV 2000-foot submersible which was built to U.S. Navy specifications. It offers life support of 360 man hours minimum with emergency battery and lighting systems. Its cruising speed is 2.5 knots with top speed 5.7 knots. It can lift 1500 lbs.

ROBOT AND MANNED SUBMERSIBLES

Whether it be Spanish galleon, a downed aircraft or a luxury liner, it doesn't stand much of a chance of staying lost any more. The *Titanic* was pinpointed when a robot submarine captured it on film and videotape. A submarine then carried researchers below to make extensive surveys of the sunken liner.

Robots and manned submersibles, Figure 25-15, are becoming more important in man's exploration and conquest of the depths. The Alvin, a research submarine operated by the Woods Hole Oceanographic Institution in Massachusetts,can take a two-man crew to depths of about three miles. Never has man gone so deep and done so much while there. It's intriguing to think about using today's high-tech equipment...exciting to the mind to think about what tomorrow may bring in equipment designed by men determined to get there regardless of where and how deep "there" really is.

For further information on the Beaver Mark IV 2000-foot submersible, as shown in Figure 25-15, contact IVC Canada, 900 Palliser Square, 125 Ninth Avenue, S.E., Calgary, Alberta T2G OP6, (403) 263-1680.

CHAPTER 26

Scuba, Snorkel and Personal Accessory Equipment

The selection of skin and scuba equipment is based on the function and use of each component in relation to your need for it. A thorough knowledge of each piece of gear as it relates to equipment technology will help you select the most suitable and best equipment for you. Your selections can determine the level of enjoyment and success you will experience in the water.

Visit your local dive stores. Talk with divers and instructors. Visit dive clubs, read and review *Skin Diver* and other diving magazines. There are numerous styles of each piece of equipment; new innovative gear is announced in almost every issue of dive magazines. You'll want to purchase the latest equipment that meets your dive requirements and adapts to your present gear.

Personal diving equipment can be categorized in three groups: Fundamental, SCUBA (Self Contained Underwater Breathing Apparatus) and Accessories.

FUNDAMENTAL EQUIPMENT

Fundamental equipment is required for shallow dives such as beginner diver familiarization, exploratory surface/shallow water dives and recreational diving. All pieces should be selected based upon need; that is, will you be shallow diving or will you also venture into the depths with scuba gear? Fundamental equipment includes face mask, snorkel and swim fins.

FACE MASK: The mask is your window to the underwater world. The space between your eyes and the glass allows you to see clearly underwater. Goggles are not acceptable for diving because they cannot be equalized. They can be used for snorkeling unless you feel more comfortable with your nose within the mask. Fit and comfort are the two most important features to consider. A mask should be snug but comfortable, have tempered glass and finger-wells or a nose pocket to allow access to the nose for ear clearing. The two problems I am personally confronted with are leakage and fogging. I think my moustache causes most of my leaks. Everyone experiences fogging. There are liquids you can use that help prevent fogging, and you can also spit—yes, spit—into the inside of the lens, rub it around and rinse with water. Consider also prescription lens masks.

SNORKEL: A snorkel allows you to breathe without lifting your head out of the water while floating on the surface. With proper buoyancy adjustment you can swim along on the surface and breathe through the snorkel while viewing the underwater world. Then, by holding your breath you can dive beneath the surface for a closer examination of some object of interest. The snorkel is also used when scuba diving to conserve tank air when on the surface. There are several types of snorkel, including contour and flexible hose. Get one that fits comfortably when attached to your mask strap. Do not get one with a ball or other leakage prevention device mounted on the upper end.

SWIM FINS: These are for propulsion and they free your hands for other activities. Various sizes and configurations are available in full-foot and open-heel designs. The type that best suits my purposes are the open strap type with medium length and flexibility. I always wear wet suit boots with a walking sole. Here are my reasons: With a strap I can adjust the holding tension. Boots eliminate pressure of the foot pocket on my toes. When not diving or snorkeling, I remove the fins and don't have to worry about stepping on glass or other sharp objects. I have learned that boots with walking soles are perfect when metal detecting in the surf. Also, boots keep my feet warm. The only problem I have encountered wearing boots is the odor that sometimes appears after several days of steady use. This doesn't hurt anything but the boots should be thoroughly dried after use or they will rot.

SNORKELING VEST: According to Scubapro, their snorkeling vest facilitates snorkeling in several ways and adds a measure of safety. You float slightly higher, thus reducing pressure on your lungs and making it easier to breathe. Your swimming profile can be adjusted to minimize water resistance. When resting, additional air provides more buoyant resting support.

When diving, the vest allows slight positive buoyancy at the surface, then buoyancy decreases as you descend, thus aiding descent. Then, as you start up, increasing buoyancy (due to less water pressure) helps the ascent. Also, as you load your pouches with treasure, added vest air offsets treasure weight.

Then in emergency situations, a vest with a CO_2 cartridge will supply 15 pounds of positive buoyancy at the surface.

The complexities of diving multiply when you advance from snorkeling to scuba diving. You are ready for scuba when you have become thoroughly at home with your basic gear. When you are perfectly at ease with your face under water while breathing through a snorkel and when you learn to stop swimming with your arms and learn to use your legs for propulsion, you are ready for scuba.

You should not proceed further and definitely you should not purchase scuba gear until you have taken and passed one of the recognized courses such as PADI and NAUI. Inquire at your local dive shop, police or fire department or perhaps check your yellow pages for the location of a nearby instructor. I took the PADI course but I cannot tell you if it is better than NAUI. You'll hear pros and cons. The value you receive from a course depends upon the instructor and your efforts rather than the name of the course or its curriculum.

Select an instructor who is certified. This will enable you to apply to one of the recognized schools for your dive card upon your successful completion of the course. You must have this dive card to get air at dive shops. Select an instructor who teaches classes regularly. Also, I suggest you select one who has a swimming pool available for course training and tests. An instructor who supplies you with all equipment except a mask, snorkel and fins has more plusses.

SCUBA EQUIPMENT: There are several items you'll need when you begin scuba diving. The minimum scuba assembly consists of the following: air tank, tank valve, back pack, regulator and weight belt. Other desirable accessories are recommended.

Scuba equipment allows you to remain under water for an extended period of time. Here is where the treasure is waiting! Select your equipment carefully and you'll be rewarded with successful underwater excursions.

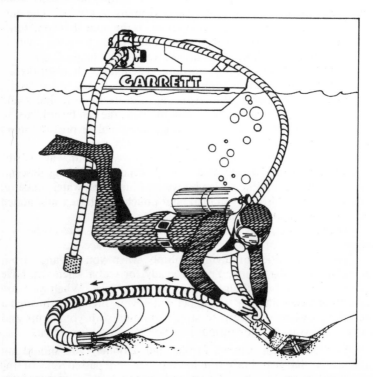

Figure 26-5: Diver uses scuba gear as he clears an underwater site. See Figure 14-26.

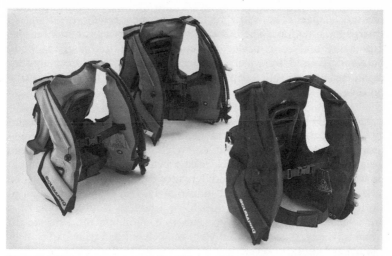

Figure 26-1: The buoyancy compensator (BC), one of the most important accessory pieces of equipment for a diver, is described fully in the text. Scubapro of Rancho Dominguez, CA, manufactures a high quality line of scuba equipment and accessories which the author has used for years.

AIR TANK: The air tank is a cylindrical metal container that safely stores fresh air under high pressure. Common sizes are 38, 50, and 80 cubic feet. Typical air pressure is 2300 psi. Attached to the tank is the tank valve to which a two-stage regulator is attached. Boots are available to slip over the tank and form a shock-absorbing flat bottom for handling stability.

TANK VALVE: This mechanism screws into the tank and acts as a shut-off valve. The two types of valves are the K-valve which is a simple on-off device and the J-valve which has a safety alert mechanism. A spring shuts off air flow from the tank when pressure drops to 300 pounds. This is designed only to alert divers. A pressure gauge should be used to monitor the amount of air remaining.

BACK PACK: A backpack holds the tank securely and comfortably on the diver's back. Most back packs are designed with two shoulder straps, a waist belt and, usually, a metal strap to hold the tank to the frame. If you use a buoyancy compensator (BC), you may not need a backpack since most BCs have their own tank support assembly.

REGULATOR: The regulator hose routes tank air into a double stage air pressure reduction and regulation device. The regulator reduces tank air pressure and supplies air to the diver at a pressure equal to the surrounding pressure. So, regardless of water pressures, which increase as a diver descends, the regulator furnishes air at a pressure exactly equal to outside body pressures. A very functional and desirable rig is one that offers multi-port connections to attach a regulator, BC with an extra octopus attachment regulator and an air pressure gauge. The extra regulator permits buddy breathing in emergency situations. The BC with its tank supply acts as an inflatable life jacket and as a device for compensating for changing body buoyancy caused by water pressures. Some air pressure gauge attachments also feature a depth gauge. See Chapter 31 for a discussion on dive gear care.

WEIGHT BELT: A weight belt is used to offset positive buoyancy allowing the diver to achieve neutral buoyancy. The slimmer and more muscular a person is, the less weight that person requires. Lead weights are attached to a quick-release belt. No straps or gear should be worn over this belt. In an underwater emergency, a diver must be able to jettison the weight belt immediately. If it snags on an item of clothing or equipment, a diver might be in serious trouble. Some belts are available with zippered pouches that eliminate the lead weight while traveling. Just prior to diving, the belt is filled with lead shot or sand. Lead shot, however, is sometimes hard to find; because sand is much lighter, heavier people may require a great deal of it.

Figure 26-2: Brownie's Third Lung is a floating gasoline engine-powered compressor that supplies air for one or more divers. Hooka gear such as this frees the diver from wearing compressed air tanks. See Figure 26-3.

ACCESSORIES AND EQUIPMENT

BUOYANCY COMPENSATOR: This apparatus, Figure 26-1, could be considered an integral part of scuba gear. It is one of the most important accessory pieces of equipment for a diver. Other than functions explained in the Regulator Section, it features a CO_2 cartridge for emergency life jacket inflation; a mouthpiece allowing the BC to be filled with lung air; overpressure and dump valves; and pockets for various items. Finally, a diver who wears a BC and knows how to use it properly has a feeling of extra security. Some professionals even believe that a BC can be used in a severe deep dive emergency to permit a diver to rebreathe air for a couple or so lifesaving breaths.

Figure 26-3: These hooka divers are enjoying the freedom of diving without wearing compressed air tanks. Their air is supplied by the floating Brownie's Third Lung as described in Figure 26-2. Photos courtesy Steve Lucas & Associates.

329

DIVING WATCH: This is one that is watertight and has a rotating bezel with calibrated marks allowing the diver to time his dives. Luminous hands are a desirable feature.

UNDERWATER LIGHT: Many types are available. If dark water is expected, you'll need one.

DIVING KNIFE: Numerous sizes, styles and models are available; it is a must for the treasure hunter. The knife is usually worn on the leg but I caution you not to rely upon the manufacturer's securing straps. On a dive in Texas Squaw Springs, I surfaced to find my knife missing. The sheath was still attached to my leg but the knife was

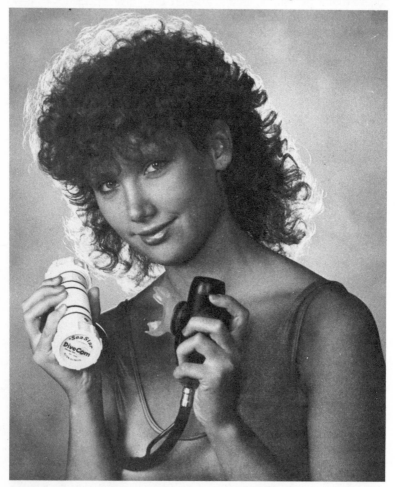

Figure 26-4: This young lady is displaying the Divecom underwater communications device manufactured by Sea Star Electronics, Alton, IL. The device turns on automatically when you enter the water. A microphone installed in the regulator mouthpiece picks up the voice. Electronic circuits amplify the voice and transmit it to other divers up to 20 feet.

gone. The handle strap had slipped over the end of the knife. Devise a method of securing your knife that will let you retrieve it quickly when needed. I suggest that you attach your own velcro strap.

ALTERNATIVE AIR SUPPLY: There are several to consider. Some gold prospecting dredges have an extra air compressor that provides the underwater goldseeker with air. Other surface air compressors are available that float on an inflatable tube such as Brownie's Third Lung, Figures 26-2 and 26-3. Air supplies other than your back-mounted tank are referred to as HOOKA RIGS. Read your instruction manual when you use one. You must prevent gasoline engine exhaust air from entering the air compressor air intake.

The PONY bottle is a small accessory air tank with built-in regulator. The PONY is used as a reserve system if a diver's regular scuba system fails or the main air supply is depleted.

OTHER MISCELLANEOUS GEAR

A gear bag is a must to keep a diver from dropping gear as he or she moves about. A gear bag protects equipment and provides a neat place to store it. Pack gear in the reverse order in which the equipment will be needed. Wet suit should be on top with weight belts and fins on the bottom.

Communications equipment, Figure 26-4, compasses, small gear, various bags, repair tools, dive tables and many other accessories are available. Chapters 24 and 25 include other gear.

CHAPTER 27

Personal Preparation: Clothing and Gear

Comfort is essential to the enjoyment of treasure hunting. In warm weather, perhaps the only clothes needed are shorts, a T-shirt and sneakers. In cold seasons protective insulation is crucial. Clothing must offer protection from both air and water while permitting considerable freedom of movement.

You've been exposed to hot, warm and cold weather all your life. You have learned to survive comfortably. This chapter will concern primarily those conditions you'll encounter in the water and the type of clothing demanded. Some people are hot natured; some, cold natured. Let these suggestions be guidelines for selecting gear for your greatest comfort and utility.

BEACH HUNTING

During warm seasons, you can wear just about what pleases you. Certainly, foot, head and skin protection are the key considerations. I wear a scarf and sometimes a neck shield that attaches to my hat. Often, I wear soft, cotton gloves. My coin and treasure pouches are water resistant and very sturdy. Sometimes I take a poncho or water repellent beach suit along in case of rain. But, more often than not, I enjoy the rain, whether I'm treasure hunting or jogging. During my four years in the Navy aboard a ship that was continually traveling from one climate to another, I learned that weather is a friend, not an enemy. I despise TV weather forecasters who say, "Well, folks, we've got some pretty drab, nasty and terrible weather in store for you." Frankly, ALL types of weather are a wonder and enjoyment to me.

Dress for comfort in hot weather. Personal articles should include a canteen (I use the military type on a web belt), snacks, digging tools, sunscreen, knee pads and toilet paper.

During cold weather, out come long pants and shirt—even thermals, if necessary. Insulated boots are good, especially if you have cold feet. A seaman's type wool cap and gloves can be lifesavers. During wet seasons a poncho is good, except it often gets in the way, especially when you stoop to dig. The two-piece lightweight rain suits are better, but hotter.

Thermals, jogging suits, multi-layered clothing are all good. Primary considerations are warmth, mobility and dryness. Non-porous clothing that makes you perspire yet does not provide the ability to get rid of moisture can make you uncomfortable. You may have to do some experimenting, but give cold weather hunting a try; you'll like it.

For digging on your knees you might try ready-made or home-built knee pads. Optimal Enterprises manufactures two styles of knee pads called Kneel-Eze. They are made of tough neoprene with a velcro elastic strap. You can write to this company at 245 Fischer Ave., D-6, Costa Mesa, CA 92626 (712) 549-5211.

Thick, tough rubber pads prevent skin abrasion and sore knees. There are two disadvantages to wearing knee pads. If the bands become too tight, they will restrict blood circulation and/or cause discomfort. The second disadvantage is that dirt and sand may work its way inside the pads, soiling your trousers. You might try making your own as Duane Caldwell wrote about in *Lost Treasure* magazine. He described an efficient, simple method of constructing knee protectors by cutting two lengths of rubber from an automobile innertube. The sections, each a foot or more in length, are worn over the pants' legs at the knees and can be held in place by rope or strapping that comes up and attaches to the belt or clothing. Large safety pins can also be used to attach the protectors.

SURFING

During warm seasons, just about anything goes in the water. I rarely wear anything more than shorts, a T-shirt, protective footwear, a wide-brimmed hat, neck protection and soft cotton gloves. I use lots of sunscreen, number 12 or higher. In areas where you may encounter

Figure 27-1: This is another of the author's headgear which he occasionally wears during cold weather. It completely covers his face and neck with the exception of the eye port. See also Figure 13-21.

333

coral, submerged logs or jellyfish, you should protect arms and legs. Sometimes I wear polarized glasses that reduce surface reflection of the sun.

One trick that works for me is wearing a soft, water-absorbent hat. Occasionally, I dip it in the water, then pull it back down over my head. The slowly evaporating water keeps my head cool and comfortable. My friend Roy Lagal jokingly suggested that my brains might "cook" when the water turns to steam. Actually, water slowly evaporates to remove heat which results in cooling of the skin. Often, I wear World War II military headgear. I wear different styles, as shown in Figures 27-1 and 13-21, which I purchase at Army/Navy stores.

Cold weather presents several options. You can stay dry by wearing hip or chest rubber boots. Internal clothing or thermals and socks will keep you warm. Arm-length neoprene gloves, with another cotton pair inside, keep your arms and hands dry and warm. This gear is available from sporting goods stores, mail order cataloges and Army/Navy stores. Jogging suits and insulated underwear such as that worn by cross-country skiers should be considered. Select insulated articles only after some experimenting. If your inner clothing soon becomes saturated with body sweat, you've dressed too warmly. Several thin layers that let moisture escape while trapping air are the best combination. Remember, when clothing becomes wet, it loses most of its insulating properties. Outer, water-protective gear must be ventilated to let the moisture escape.

Should you fall or be struck by a sudden ocean wave, your boots could fill with water. You'll quickly become cold and uncomfortable; you may even find it difficult to reach shore. For such occurrences keep one or more extra sets of clothing along with you. If you have a long drive home, a pair of warm, dry socks and shoes will feel mighty good. Carry along a covering to protect your auto seats and floorboards because surfing gear will become wet and sandy—if not downright muddy.

In the next section you'll read about wet and dry suits. They have their pros and cons, but they get the job done.

DIVING

In warm water a bathing suit alone will be sufficient for dives of short duration. Remember, however, that water will take 25 times more heat from your skin than air of the same temperature. Just wearing an upper sweat shirt will provide some comfort. A 1/8-inch or 3/16-inch wet suit, especially the upper section, will give you all the heat-loss protection you'll need. If there are coral, logs and other objects on which you can snag yourself, wear the entire suit.

Gloves are a must when working around coral. I dove in the waters off Colombia without adequate hand protection and suffered the consequences. The currents were very strong and I maneuvered myself around by grasping various coral growths. A few days later my finger tips began to swell. My doctor, who had treated many such problems, said glass-like bits of coral had penetrated my fingers. The material caused a swelling and burning sensation which lasted about two months. Several layers of skin peeled off.

In colder water you'll definitely need a cold weather suit. Wet suits, Figure 27-2, which are the most popular, are reasonably priced and provide considerable freedom of movement. Various thicknesses from 1/8-inch to 1/4-inch are available with thicker suits needed for coldest conditions. I prefer the long-john bottoms. Those that come just to the waist (like trousers) are available, but long-johns resemble old-fashioned farmer's overalls, complete with shoulder straps. You'll need boots for warmth. See Chapter 26 for my recommendations. During extremes, a hood should be considered, which will also mask detector headphone sound somewhat. Be certain you have sufficient neck space when you buy a hood because you don't want the hood so tight it cuts off blood supply to your brain. You'll also need gloves. When wearing a wet suit in the surf, you may need to wear a quick-release weight belt for stability. Make certain it is the very last item you attach to your waist. You might also consider weights that you wear around your ankles.

Figure 27-2: Treasure hunter Jim McGarr is both a land and water hunter and cold water doesn't keep him at home. During cold water seasons he wear a scuba diver's wet suit as shown in the photograph. Wet suits, which are very popular with surfers, are reasonably priced and provide considerable freedom of movement.

Some divers prefer a dry suit. Manufacturers, when touting their "better" dry suits, point out that wet suits compress as you dive. Diminishing wall thickness results in reduced insulation properties in proportion to depth. Personally, I've never noticed much loss but most of my diving has been only to about 30 to 40-foot depths which is double atmospheric pressure.

Dry suits are just that; they keep your body dry, whereas wet suits must trap water between your skin and the suits. The water warms up to skin temperature, and you stay warm. Dry suits cost more than wet suits and they don't give you the freedom of movement of thin wet suits. You can wear thin insulating pieces which give you added warmth. You can control the volume of air in some dry suits, but you should never inflate one in order to get more buoyancy to bring up treasure. Dry suits can also be used for dry land and beach hunting.

This HEAT EXPOSURE SUIT CHART includes suit thickness approximations for various water temperature ranges.

TEMPERATURE ZONE (Fahrenheit)	REQUIRED WET SUIT PROTECTION	UNPROTECTED DIVER TOLERANCE TIME
WARM		
85 degrees and above	Partial	Working diver may overheat
75 degrees to 85 degrees	1/8"-3/16"	Diver at rest chills in 1-2 hours
COOL		
65 degrees to 75 degrees	3/16"	2-1/2 hours
60 degrees to 65 degrees	3/16" to 1/4"	1-1/2 hours
COLD		
55 degrees to 60 degrees	1/4" (or dry suit)	1 hour
50 degrees to 55 degrees	1/4" (or dry suit)	1/2 hour
45 degrees to 50 degrees	3/8" (or dry suit)	Protection is critical
EXTREME COLD		
Below 45 degrees	(Special thermal suit)	Death in less than one hour

CHAPTER 28

Safety First

Accurate knowledge will not only help you dispel many unreasonable fears, but can materially reduce the chances of encountering problems. It is the UNKNOWN that we fear most. Always Remember the motto of the Boy Scouts: Be Prepared.

This chapter contains three sections: Safety on the Beach, Safety in the Surf and Safety while Diving. Study the entire chapter even though you do not intend to become involved in all three phases of treasure hunting. If you are a beachcomber...who knows? Someday, you may decide to take the plunge to find underwater treasures that others are finding. And, someday you may need to instruct or help a friend in water safety.

It pays to learn and be prepared before plunging into potentially dangerous situations. Certainly, this chapter is not meant to frighten. Rather, it seeks to alert you to possible dangers. Beachcombing, surfing and diving are treasure hunting's newest frontiers, and much lost wealth is waiting to be recovered. Thousands of dedicated detectorists regularly spend time on our beaches, in the surf and under water searching for treasure.

First of all, it'll pay you to stay in good physical condition. Diving is an especially rigorous activity, even diving in a stream in search of gold. Don't be afraid of the water. Working hard all day on the beach or in the surf can be relaxing, enjoyable and rewarding. I wouldn't say that unless I had experienced the rewards myself. Don't forget, while you are learning safety rules, teach them to all family members. When I was a Boy Scout, we were taught that the best way to avoid trouble was to be prepared for it.

STAY AWARE OF THE WEATHER

Keep track of weather conditions and forecasts. Stay tuned to the NOAA weather radio station in your area. You'll need a shortwave receiver tuned to one of these mHz frequencies, 162.40, 162.475 or 162.55. Here, you can listen to continuous weather reporting that includes updates on humidity, atmospheric pressure, wind strength and direction, temperature and tides. You'll be told of expected hail, strong winds and severe storms of all types. You'll also hear radar reports, advisories, tornado alerts, boat warnings, forecasts, extended outlooks and cold front information.

FIRST AID KIT

Regardless of your activity, you will always do well to keep a first aid kit handy. There are many kits on the market; whether you purchase one or make up your own, there are certain items it should contain.

The container should be easy to open and of non-crushable, waterproof construction. If necessary, it can be taped to keep out moisture. It should contain an American Red Cross First Aid textbook. Suggested items include soap (antibacterial), aspirin, scissors, tweezers, safety pins, flashlight (disposable), waterproof matches, antihistamine tablets and ointments for marine life injuries and stings (also good are alcohol, vinegar and meat tenderizer), antibiotic ointments (apply after cleansing to minimize infection), lip balm, skin lotion, cleansing swabs, burn ointment, triangular bandages, adhesive compress bandages and assorted dressings, tourniquets, baking soda and a non-prescription ointment for relief of local pain. Also, two quarters taped to a card with emergency numbers and your name, address and telephone number typed or clearly printed. Other items can be added.

SAFETY ON THE BEACH

Probably the worst things that will befall the beachcomber are sun and wind burns. Even they can be avoided by wearing sunshades, proper clothing and using the proper sunscreen. Among other mishaps are the following:

Cutting your hands, knees and feet on broken glass.

Suffering cuts caused by fish hooks, electrical cables and other sharp objects.

Getting caught in a sudden storm. Even though your chances are remote of being struck by lightning, Take Cover! Don't stay on the beach during a storm. Listen to the NOAA or other weather radio stations for continuous weather broadcasts.

Being physically attacked by hoodlums, drunks or others. If you lack confidence about an area, work in pairs—out of the water, as well as in. Some beachcombers carry a can of "mace" or similar deterrent, not stored away in a bag but where it is readily accessible to them.

Being attacked by animals. Often when I jog or work in unfamiliar areas, I wear a four-foot length of chain around my waist. A quick-release clip attached to one end makes a neat fastener. Only a mighty strong-willed animal will stay around after one blow from my weapon. I'm glad, though, that I've never had to use it.

Being robbed or molested. I suggest you never tell anyone, even children, the amount of treasure you are finding. The quickest way to discourage people is to show them a few pulltabs and bottlecaps. They'll suddenly lose interest and even the children won't be so anxious to help you dig. Never tell inquisitive people how much your detector is worth. Just say, "Oh, they don't cost very much; besides, this detector was a gift." It probably was a gift, either to yourself or from your spouse.

Digging up explosives. In the years of World War II and since some beaches have been used from time to time as bombing and artillery ranges. Now, these areas are certainly few and far between. Nevertheless, if you dig up a strange-looking device that you suspect might be a bomb or artillery shell, notify the police immediately. Let them take care of it. Then exercise caution when digging in that area, or just stay away entirely.

Stepping in holes. You won't fall in the holes you dig, certainly, but joggers and others might, if you fail to cover them. Fill your HOLES!

Burns from live coals. When campfires are covered and not doused with water, coals remain very hot even till the next day and can cause severe skin burns. Watch out for coals, even when they appear cold.

Toxic waste. Toxic waste is an increasingly serious problem that should keep you away from any area or any piece of flotsam or jetsam that looks or smells bad or that you suspect of being contaminated in any way.

SAFETY IN THE SURF (SHALLOW WATER)

Surf hunting is just as safe as beachcombing when safety guidelines are followed and attention is paid to the environment. Don't take chances such as working in water up to your neck. If you insist on working in heavy breakers, you'd better plan on being knocked flat.

Use common sense and stay aware of potentially dangerous situations.

Among possible mishaps that could befall you are:

Getting seasick. Don't laugh, especially if you are prone to seasickness when you ride in a boat or on a ship. Some ocean surfs are rough; if you are unaccustomed to the rocking motion caused by breakers, you could get seasick. If that happens, just get out of the water.

Becoming fatigued. Be constantly aware of how you feel. When you grow even slightly tired or weary, pay attention to yourself. You may want to leave the water rather than wait until you are exhausted.

Sun and wind exposure. Appropriate attire and sunscreen are a must — even though some medical experts are now suggesting that sunscreen may be hazardous to our health! Apply sunscreen with a Sun Protection Factor (SPF) of 12 or above to all exposed areas 45 minutes before exposure. Most sunscreens require time to penetrate and adhere to skin cells before their ingredients can become active. Don't wear sheer clothes but preferably dark cottons which offer greater protection than synthetics.

Suffer from hypothermia. Subnormal body temperature can occur following long exposure in water. And, it doesn't have to be wintertime for hypothermia to occur. Anytime you become drowsy, feel overly fatigued, start shivering, become dizzy, or become disoriented or nauseated, get out of the water and into warm clothing; drink hot liquids. You might need medical aid. Do not underestimate the problems associated with hypothermia and long exposure under water. The human body is a marvelous machine and has an excellent heat regulation system in its normal environment of air. When the body is submerged in water, the situation changes dramatically. You can remain perfectly comfortable in air at 70 degrees. In water at this same temperature you will quickly become chilled and very uncomfortable.

Water absorbs body heat 25 times faster than air. In cold water, skin surface capillaries constrict to prevent excessive heat loss. As skin temperature drops, the body begins to shiver, resulting in muscular effort and energy outflow. Continued immersion can result in extreme discomfort and hypothermia.

The following Heat Exposure Chart compiled by the United States Naval Institute provides guidelines to help judge "safe" times when surfing and diving. See Chapter 25 for discussions of protective clothing and dive suits.

HEAT EXPOSURE CHART
Physiological Effects of Temperature

Water Temperature (Fahrenheit)	Approximate Time to Exhaustion or Unconsciousness	Death
32	15 min.	15 min.-1-1/2 hr.
50	30 min.-1 hr.	1-2 hrs.
60	2-4 hrs.	4-8 hrs
70	3-7 hrs.	6-24 hrs.
80	12 hrs.	relatively safe

Making contact with dangerous sea creatures. Contact with sea urchins, jellyfish (especially the Portugese variety), horseshoe crabs and seals and sea lions can cause misery. Avoid them. Jellyfish are easily seen. They look similar to small, blue or pink balloons floating on the surface. Long, stinging tentacles float underwater, sometimes to great depths. To prevent stings wear gloves and use large rubber bands or velcro to secure your trousers securely to your ankles. Do not touch dead jellyfish lying on the beach.

Water motions and currents. There are several kinds of ocean surf and river water motions and currents. Let's consider them:

Orbital currents are caused by wave and breaker motion. Water is propelled toward the shore. The resulting water that piles up on the shore rushes back into the ocean, generally in water "troughs." When you stand in these troughs you can feel the outward pull. When the next wave breaks, it tries to propel you toward the shore. These are generally harmless water motions. Swimmers over the world regularly play in them in surf areas.

Undertows are water currents that flow back out into the ocean. When water is cast ashore it piles up before beginning its outward flow as incoming waves break. Although these currents usually present no cause for concern, on beaches that slope steeply toward the ocean, water surges can become violent. Such areas should be avoided. Generally, undertows are not considered dangerous although you can get tossed about by incoming breakers. If you get caught in an undertow, swim parallel to the beach a few feet until you reach calm water.

Rip currents, sometimes called riptides, can be the most dangerous. As large waves break on the beach in quick succession, water is piled up faster than it can recede back to the ocean. This larger-than-normal water volume seeks channels in which to escape. As water rushes out to sea in the rip channels, persons may be caught and pulled into deeper water. The best way to escape from a rip current is to swim parallel to the shore. After a few feet, you will reach calm water where you can proceed normally back to shallow water.

Some riptides cannot be seen from the shore. Watch for floating debris to indicate water movement. Ask the lifeguard to point out the locations of possible riptide areas.

Watch for floating dangers. Don't expect boaters and surfers to watch for you, watch for them yourself. I narrowly missed being struck by a large windpropelled surf board as a fellow came zooming into the swimming area where I was working. Be ever on the alert for motorboats, sailboats, surfboards and floating logs. During times of rough surf and high winds, large logs can be propelled rapidly on and through the water.

River currents are often deceptive and can carry you out from shore. These currents rarely follow the contour of the riverbed even in comparatively straight stretches. Projecting land areas, islands, backwaters and windings of the river course cause currents to wander back and forth from bank to bank. In working along river banks, pay attention to these currents and when they begin to feel strong or to change direction, move to a safer area. Unusual and sometimes strong currents can be found at the junction of rivers and at their mouths where they empty into the ocean. Opposing forces of currents and tides create these unexpected water movements.

Weeds and grasses are sometimes encountered by water hunters, and they often serve as a trap for coins and jewelry. These areas are not a serious menace. Quick thrashing movements of the feet and searchcoil tend to wrap the growth around the legs, searchcoil and stem. Slow movements will let the growth untangle itself.

Hazardous bottom areas. Holes, steep slopes, vegetation, dropoffs, rocks and coral can cause problems for the water hunter. Generally, if you walk forward and scan the searchcoil in front of you,

you will be able to detect most, if not all, of the above hazards. You must always be prepared for the unexpected.

Hazardous "dry" areas. In dry seasons or when, say, the level of a lake has been dropped, be on the alert for muddy sink holes. The surface may appear dry while underneath the soil can be very wet and soft.

Panic situations. Probably the greatest danger facing those who enter the water is panic. Sudden overwhelming fear, accompanied by loss of reasoning, contributes to almost all water accidents. Condition yourself to resist panic; try to think calmly about each problem you face. Acting quickly and without thinking carefully can gain you nothing. Fear can be overcome; let your reasoning take control to allow you to THINK your way out of difficult situations.

Polluted water. The best solution is to know about and stay out of unsafe water areas. Polluted water, such as a poisoned mill pond, can do worse than hurt your health; it can kill you. Even if you do not swallow the water, it can cause you problems—sometimes, even if you do not touch it. Polluted water presents the danger of infections even modern medicine cannot cure. To locate hazardous areas, contact public health officials.

Unexpected river waves. When detecting in rivers, be aware of ship movement. Barges or ships moving by can create strong and fast-moving waves powerful enough to knock a person off his feet.

Hip boot dangers. Even though hip boots seem the ideal solution for keeping dry and warm, they can present problems. You must be on guard lest you bend over and let water spill into them. In the surf, unexpected large waves can crash over you to fill your boots. Either case can certainly spoil an otherwise pleasant afternoon of surf hunting. But, more than that, your life can be threatened. Struggling to reach shore while wearing a set of waders filled with water can be a very difficult and dangerous task. Tie a belt or rope around the upper section of chest-high boots.

Physical problems. Long exposure to water can cause leg cramps. If cramps occur, move toward shore immediately while massaging the cramping muscles. Cold water has been known to cause severe stomach cramps, especially just after eating. Apparently the water interferes with digestive processes causing the disturbance. When hunting in the surf, develop an easy, relaxed method of scanning, digging and retrieving. A slipped back disk could suddenly place you in a very dangerous situation, especially if you are alone.

Wear a life vest. Buy and use a good one such as the model that inflates whenever a CO_2 pressure cartridge is punctured. The vest stays flat until you need it. I hope you never do.

Safety under water. If you plan to scuba dive for treasure, it's imperative that you take one of the scuba courses such as that of the Professional Association of Diving Instructors (PADI). I once did a fair amount of scuba diving, and even taught a scuba course at Southern Methodist University in Dallas. I later lost interest in scuba diving and was inactive for about 15 years. In the early 1980s when we began to develop underwater metal detectors at Garrett Electronics, I became active again to test our new detector prototypes. Realizing that I needed to refresh my knowledge of scuba diving, I took the PADI course. I was shocked at how little I knew about the latest in diving procedures and the advances that had been made in the manufacture of diving equipment. It was obvious—I needed that course!

When you take the course and during your dive time following graduation, you'll learn a lot about safety. This is not a diving book, however, and I do not inted to expand upon the subject. I simply urge you to take an up-to-date course and learn as much about safe diving practices as possible before venturing into the deep. A few cautions, however:

Even though snake bites and shark, alligator and crocodile attacks are rare occurrences, use the utmost caution when entering waters where these denizens are known to live.

Hypothermia is more likely to be a problem when diving than when surfing.

Even though you use a diver's flag, never swim rapidly to the surface. Ascend to 10-foot depth, stop, rotate completely around while scanning the surface. Then, proceed cautiously upward. As soon as you break surface, immediately rotate and scan the entire horizon to detect approaching boats.

Always dive with a buddy. Know the capabilities and limitations of your equipment and your buddy's equipment. Know the area you intend to dive, including hazards, weather conditions, local emergency numbers and weather-alert radio frequencies. Know dive limits and the location of the nearest decompression chamber. Maintain your equipment flawlessly. Never use unsafe or marginal equipment.

Never "lose your cool" during the excitement of recovering sunken treasure. Never compromise on a dive. Pre-plan and stick to it. Never try to get "one-more-dive" out of a dangerously low tank. Always use common sense. Don't panic! Know your buddy and watch out for each other.

WRECK DIVING

Wreck diving can be dangerous. Never go alone. Take extra tanks and a pony tank. Be aware of your time limits. You'll need a light for seeing and signaling and keeping close to your buddy. You'll need a dive knife and maybe a smaller backup knife. Carry a spool of line to mark your exit route and, perhaps, a kit with the tools you'll need to remove a souvenir or yourself if you become entangled in the ship's gear.

343

NIGHT DIVING

It's best to dive during a full moon. If you dive from a boat, exposed lights above and below the waterline are necessary. These exposed lights will serve as beacons to guide you home. So will a shore light if you enter from land. Try to avoid swift currents, caves, wrecks and other obstacles. Carry a knife, a battery and chemical light, a compass and a whistle. A six to eight-foot buddy line with loops at each end is good but can be hazardous.

If possible, explore the area first during daylight hours. Check your buddy's equipment and have him check yours. Plan your dive. Know your light signals. Keep calm.

The above is, at best, a very short course on the perils of night diving. I suggest that you read some of the diving books that treat this subject in depth. Then, STUDY THE MATERIAL.

A FINAL WORD OF CAUTION

Always observe warnings regarding trespassing, danger areas and underwater obstacles. Test all diving areas for depth each time before you dive; waterways can change and present dramatic differences in depth. Never dive alone, and do not allow children in or near the water without constant supervision. Many streams, lakes and ponds that appear peaceful and calm can be deep and cold or have swift currents.

And one sincere request: Leave each place in better condition than you found it.

Many natural sites represent a fragile environment that can be easily damaged or destroyed. Please leave only footprints—not pop-tops, cans or other symbols of our "disposable" civilization. Remember, a fellow treasure hunter may want to work the area someday and you may even want to come back yourself.

CHAPTER 29

How to Clean, Preserve, Display and Sell Your Finds

Do you remember those movie scenes where the sunken Spanish galleon lies on its side in 35 feet of water with its masts in place and fish—even a few sharks—gliding silently over its decks? I'm sure you also remember the cannons still standing guard to protect the Spanish treasure spilling from a gash in the ship's hull. All of this after 300 or more years in the salt water! Scenes like that are best forgotten.

Why should you forget it? Because, at shallow depths the action of wind and waves, the electrolytic effects of warm salt water and the destructive effects of teredo worms would have long ago reduced the ship, its rigging and its treasure to an unrecognizable heap that would now be covered by sand or encrusted with coral. It's possible you might discover by eyesight a ballast pile, a stack of coral-encrusted cannon balls or perhaps a badly corroded cannon or anchor resting on the bottom.

The teredos, better known as shipworms, will have devoured every trace of wood by attaching themselves to it and eating it completely in just a few years. Gold, platinum and pewter will remain unharmed, but other metals will be in various stages of chemical decomposition. Iron will either have been converted or be in the process of conversion into crystalline magnetite. Copper and brass change chemically into chlorides that produce the familiar green color. Bronze remains in excellent condition. Non-electrical materials such as pottery and glass will remain in their original condition except for surface film or coral growth.

Common sense must certainly be considered an important factor in the successful recovery of artifacts. These items are hundreds of years old; they have been existing all that time in a relatively hostile environment. Certainly, all artifacts must be handled with utmost care if they are to survive at all, much less in a presentable condition. Objects like coins can be picked up and placed in a bag or other secure container. Fragile items should be placed in a rigid container or better yet, hand-carried to the surface. Large objects must be lifted in a basket or with lift bags.

A complete study of retrieval, cleaning and preservation should be made before attempting shipwreck salvage. The water action of wind and waves, the natural forces of marine life and the chemical action caused by sea water are the main destructive forces. Of course, some preservation will have occurred. Objects buried in soil often will

345

Figure 29-1: Few metal detectorists can match or exceed Tom Edd's treasure displays. Here are just a few, a very few of his many found treasure items.

Figure 29-2: Here are three displays of Canadian found treasures, as shown by Keith and Mary Edwards.

be surprisingly well preserved, and coral growth can protect objects.

Retrieval of artifacts other than gold, platinum, silver, copper, bronze and pewter invites disaster unless the objects are kept in water. Drying of organic materials such as leather, paper, bone and rope can result in total destruction within a few minutes. Shrinkage occurs as water evaporates from wood; rot and decay will speed up; cracking and warpage will soon follow. Iron, when exposed to air, will deteriorate rapidly.

Although salt water is a more harsh environment than fresh water, protection of objects recovered from both is essential. Buckets and plastic bags filled with water are used most often to recover objects from the bottom. Once artifacts are aboard your vessel, the task of preservation can begin immediately. Unless you have containers large enough for complete submersion of all objects, it is best to leave the larger items on the bottom until preservation can be done properly. Glassware and porcelain objects do not need water submersion but demand utmost care in handling.

Since this chapter presents only basic guidelines in the retrieval, storage, cleaning and preservation of artifacts, you should undertake a serious study of the conservation of objects you recover from underwater sites. The Bibliography contains reference sources.

Artifacts recovered from the sea are commonly encrusted with layers of calcium carbonate, magnesium hydroxide, metal corrosion products, sand, clay and various forms of marine life such as shells, coral, barnacles and plant life. Conglomerations may contain a single item or hundreds of items. Since damage to artifacts can occur when encrustation is removed, x-rays are indispensable for determining the context of an encrustation and for serving as a guide in artifact extraction. If you do not have access to a conservation laboratory, you can have conglomerates x-rayed at medical clinics and x-ray laboratories.

ENCRUSTATION REMOVAL

Attempt to remove encrustation only when a substantial amount of the original metal is left. Deposits can be removed from large objects by gentle tapping with a rubber mallet or sand blasting under low pressure. Smaller objects can be cleaned chemically or in an ultrasonic bath. The chemical process consists of a bath in a solution of 10% nitric acid and 90% fresh water, followed by several washes in fresh water to remove all alkaline traces. There is a time element in this process as the acid will attack silver, copper and pewter.

Chiseling along cleavage lines can loosen encrustation from cannon and other very large objects. Electrolysis can loosen encrustation and hasten its removal. When using mechanical means, extreme care should be used to prevent surface damage. Encrustations from objects can also be removed with pneumatic air scribes or electric scribes and vibrotools. A combination of tools can be deployed to free movable parts such as cannon swivels, loaded breech chambers and various components. Encrusted breechblocks and bores of cannon can be cleaned with tube drills or by the slower process of hammer and chisel and sandblasting. Since sandblasting can cause surface pitting, care must be used.

After encrustation has been removed, the objects must be cleansed, examined and evaluated to determine correct conservation treatment. Gold needs no treatment, nor does silver; but, copper can continue to deteriorate unless treated. Ferrous metal objects present preservation difficulties as do wood and other materials. Some objects may be badly corroded but retain their original shape. They may require a wax or other synthetic consolidant. Other specimens may be so badly oxidized and fragile that they can only be saved through casting and making of replicas.

A CONSERVATION DISCUSSION
GOLD AND GOLD ALLOYS

High purity gold and high gold alloys do not require any treatment. Even after thousands of years, the noble metal looks the same. Occasionally coral encrustation is present and a slight discoloration may occur if other corrosive metals were in contact with the gold. Consider carefully before you remove coral encrustation because Mother Nature's work can often enhance the value of such items. Copper compounds can be removed with citric acid. Corrosion of silver in low grade gold alloys can be removed with ammonia. Ammonic hydroxide (NH_4OH) is a strong, basic solution irritating to skin, eyes and respiratory system. Use a solution below 25%.

Figure 29-3: Edward and the late Mary Perchaluk of Stratford, CT, display some of their finds at the Black Diamond Hunt in Moonlake Park in Pennsylvania.

348

SILVER AND SILVER ALLOYS

Corrosion most commonly encountered with silver will produce silver sulfide and silver chloride. Both compounds are stable and will not corrode the remaining silver any further. In copper alloys corrosion forms cuprous chloride which can continue to corrode the copper component. Prior to conservation, marine encrustation should be removed. In some cases it can be removed by immersion in 10 to 30% formic acid solution. Concentrated formic acid (HCoOH) causes painful wounds when it comes in contact with skin.

Further conservation alternatives for cleaning silver and silver alloys are: 1) galvanic cleaning, 2) electrolytic reduction, 3) chemical and 4) stabilization and consolidation.

GALVANIC CLEANING

This treatment utilizes mossy zinc or aluminum in caustic soda followed by an intensive rinsing and dehydration in a water-miscible solvent before a covering of clear acrylic lacquer. The following treatment is preferred.

ELECTROLYTIC REDUCTION CLEANING

Electrolysis causes direct current to pass through the artifact, removing chloride and sulfide ions from silver chloride and silver sulfide. Silver remains in a metal state. There are two electrolytic reduction cleaning methods: normal reduction and consolidative reduction. Normal electrolytic reduction uses a fully rectified direct current power supply. Consolidative reduction employs a partially rectified asymmetrical alternating current power supply. Both techniques require that a metal core be present in the object. Use a stainless steel

Figure 29-4: Thanks to Jim and Ruby Ironside of Ary, Canada, for supplying this photograph of a display of some of their finds made at recreational sites.

anode (+) surface area. Stainless steel beakers can be used for ferrous and non-ferrous materials. Two electrolytes, formic acid (5 to 30% HCoOH) and sodium hydroxide (2 to 15% NaOH-without aluminum crystals) are used to clean silver. Current density is .01 amp per square centimeter. Since a current with inadequate voltage can cause copper (from the crust, cathode screen or copper components) to be deposited on the artifacts, and excessive voltage (or too long an electrolysis action) can cause silver to be reduced, experiments should be conducted to determine the most efficient current density and whether an alkaline or acid electrolyte is best.

Suggested electrolytic reduction cleaning solutions:
For cleaning iron and steel:
8 oz. lye
2 oz. laundry soap
1 gal. water

For cleaning copper and brass:
1 oz. lye
5 oz. washing soda
2 oz. trisodium phosphate
1 oz. laundry soap
1 gal. water

For cleaning tin and zinc:
4 oz. sodium bicarbonate
4 oz. washing soda
1 gal. water

WARNINGS

When cleaning encrustation from large objects, wear gloves and safety glasses. Since removing crustations and working with various electrolytic cleaning processes is messy, old clothes should be worn. A rubberized apron and rubber gloves should be worn when working with acids.

Caustic soda (sodium hydroxide) is strong, basic and highly active with aluminum and H_2O. That's why manufacturers add aluminum crystals to "plumber's helpers."

Various anode materials such as platinized titanium, stainless steel and carbon are used, depending upon the desired solution. If stainless steel is used in sodium hydroxide, it will oxidize after prolonged electrolysis, resulting in the destruction of the anode and depositing iron of the anode on the silver. A mild steel anode should not be used in formic acid as it will quickly break down and invariably result in iron deposited on the silver.

No chemicals of any kind should be flushed into home or industrial sewage. Not only is it illegal, but plumbing may be damaged. An individual I know set up a copper portrait business in her home.

She discarded waste and diluted copper solutions into the bathtub and sink drains. After about two years of using this convenient disposal method, her copper plumbing was eaten away. What made matters worse was that she lived in a home built on a slab foundation

The above "don'ts" reinforce the need for you to study electrolysis techniques throughly before attempting to use them. The Bibliography lists several excellent conservation publications.

CLEANING COINS AND SMALL OBJECTS

A simple, safe method to remove corrosion and encrustation uses a solution of citric acid and salt. This electrolyte solution contains one teaspoon of citric acid (a harmless substance primarily used as flavoring in soft drinks) and half a teaspoon of table salt dissolved in a cup of water. A stainless steel electrode plate connected to the positive wire of a low voltage (3 to 6 volts) power supply is placed in the solution on one side of a glass container. An alligator clip or other connector is attached to the coin or artifact to be cleaned and positioned on the other side of the container. A current of about 20 milliamperes flowing through the solution will cause corrosion and minor coral encrustation to loosen. The artifact can then be cleansed with a toothbrush or other soft bristle brush and a soda paste. The accompanying illustration and caption suggests one design of the above cleaning apparatus and method. Test various objects before attempting to clean valuable specimens.

Figure 29-5: These double-sided coin displays, made by Robin Botting of Winona, Ontario, Canada, are a unique way to exhibit coins and other finds. Most displays do not permit viewing of both sides of coins. Another interesting display is to use a large, wide mouth jar fashioned with vertical slide trays for mounting found treasure.

TUMBLING

Tumbling is a common method for cleaning coins and small objects. Tumblers are not expensive, and they are available in various sizes. Instructions and recommended cleaning agents and solutions come with each tumbler, but be sure to consider recommendations of the manufacturer. Be specific as to the type of material you have to clean. For additional information on tumblers and associated products, write to Finch Products, P. O. Box 213, Birch Run, MI 48415.

CHEMICAL CLEANING

A great many silver objects recovered from the seabed require only limited treatment. Tarnish caused by sulfur compounds can be eliminated with commercial silver cleaning solutions.

STABILIZATION AND CONSOLIDATION

Silver coins are sometimes found that have completely converted to silver sulfide. About all that can be done is to record data from the coin's impression in the surrounding encrustation.

CONSERVATION OF FERROUS METALS

Several methods are available for cleaning ferrous metals. Electrolytic cleaning is probably the best when measured by simplicity, maintenance and versatility. An electrolytic cell consists of a vat with an anode and cathode (the artifact) and a suitable conductive solution, the electrons of which are collected by the anode. Chlorides are drawn from the specimen and migrate toward the anode and walls of the vat. Positively charged ions in the artifact's surface compounds are changed to metal and remain bonded to the object's surface. Many factors must be understood and controlled in this process, such as electrolytic solution, amperage, clip construction, anode material, water purity and duration of electrolysis. At the completion of this process, the objects should be submerged in running water for seven to ten days and brush-cleaned often, followed by another bath in distilled water for a week. Artifacts are then heated to remove all moisture. A sealant such as paraffin is used to prevent air and further moisture from making contact with the object's surface. Clear flat lacquers, epoxy or polyurethane resins or plastic sprays can also be used.

GLASS AND BOTTLE CLEANING

The weathering, corrosion and encrustation of bottles and objects made of glass depends upon the soil, nearby objects, the composition of the glass, temperature and age.

Depending upon the type of body and glaze, ceramics are affected in varying degrees. Porcelain is least damaged, although its painted exterior may be eroded away. Glazed pottery, covered with a waterproof vitreous layer, fares better than porous, unglazed pottery.

Marine growth on ceramics can be removed in a 10% solution of nitric acid. Iron and lead oxide stains can be removed in a bath of 5% solution of sulfuric acid.

Figure 29-6: The author's friend, Walter Stark, of Merrit Island, FL, made this belt buckle and gave it to the author. Walter used two Spanish reales found on Florida's beaches.

If the glazed layer on pottery is imperfect, do not use acids. The pieces should be bathed in fresh water to remove salts and then dried and coated with several layers of clear plastic or lacquer spray.

Most bottles require no treatment other than soaking in a soda solution. First, remove all sediment with a high pressure hose. Tough contamination can be removed by carefully probing with a wire or small wooden dowel. Fill with a soap solution and let soak for several days. Cleaning with a bottle brush or a gentle shaking with unpopped popcorn kernels will clean most bottles. Bottles encrusted with dried algae, calcium or lime deposits can be cleaned by soaking in a water and vinegar solution. Sulfuric acid can also be used. Baby oil or lemon oil can be used to add shine and luster to badly corroded bottles.

COIN AND JEWELRY CLEANING

Gold is almost always recovered as bright and shiny as the day it was minted into coins or made into jewelry; it requires no preservation treatment. Soaking in a bath of 10% nitric acid will remove any tarnish caused by association with other metals.

Depending upon conditions, silver is affected in varying degrees. Some objects will be found completely converted to silver sulfide and nothing can be done to preserve such an object except to encase it in plastic. Such specimens must be handled carefully to prevent them from crumbling into powder.

Electrolysis can be used to clean heavily encrusted objects. Following this treatment, the objects should be further cleaned to include brushing in running water or rubbing with a paste of water and baking soda. An important step in the preservation of any object is deciding what you will do with each coin and jewelry item. The patina that many silver coins and medallions and other pieces will have is im-

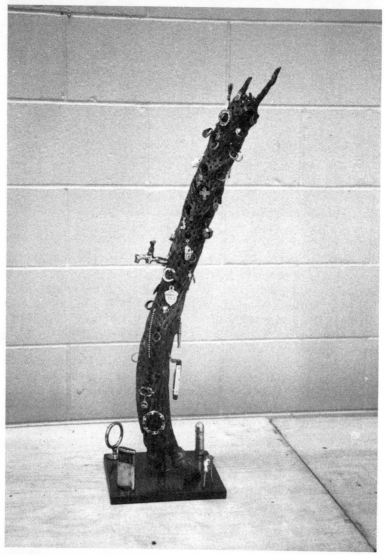

Figure 29-10: Ralph Harriott of St. Williams, Ontario, developed this method of mounting his treasure finds. Thanks, Ralph, for a a neat idea! Photos courtesy Keith and Mary Edwards.

possible to duplicate in the laboratory. Consequently, some buyers and collectors prefer to obtain pieces with patina intact. Also, when you locate items encrusted with coral, you should consider leaving the encrustation; it sometimes enhances the desirability of the artifact.

Copper, brass and bronze objects usually suffer little from salt water immersion. Calcareous deposits can be removed by immersion in a bath of 10% nitric acid, followed by immersion in fresh running water. The same acid bath can also be used to remove the green patina, but consideration should be given to leaving the patina. When the patina is left, corrosion continues but at a miniscule rate.

There are many commercial cleaners which are more or less satisfactory for cleaning silver and copper objects. Perhaps the most important consideration is that you must not use harsh chemicals or excessive scrubbing techniques. Scratching and marring a coin's surface will decrease its value.

DISPLAYING YOUR TREASURES

Imagination plays a key role in your display of artfacts. A ship's wheel, bell or porthole looks great mounted in a panelled den. An unusual artifact such as a corroded clock or other instrument becomes a conversation piece when mounted on a wooden base. A brass porthole or door viewport can make an unusual picture frame or mirror. Objects such as a large, globe-shaped potato blender are stunning when utilized as lamp bases.

Coins and other flat items can be placed in plastic-front display cases, Figures 29-1 and 29-2, which can be purchased at most coin shops. Larger objects can be placed in shadow-box frames, Figures 29-3 and 29-4, the depth of which is determined by the heights of the

Figure 29-8: Here is another display showing an assortment of treasures found by a member of Canada's Golden Triangle Detecting Club.

355

Figure 29-11: Art and Marlette Steinke of Mid-West Metal Detectors in Bloomington, MN, found this coral-encrusted pistol on a Texas beach. See Figure 29-12.

Figure 29-12: The x-ray of the pistol as described in the previous photograph clearly reveals the details of a coral-encased revolver.

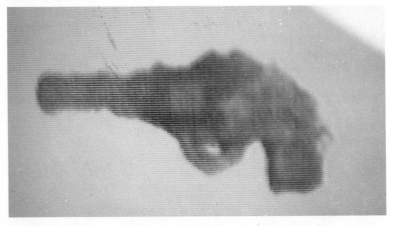

largest objects to be displayed. One enterprising individual purchased an old motorized revolving watch display case. He placed various jewelry items he had found on the "buckets." When friends wanted to see all the items he had found, they pushed a button and watched as the display rotated. See Figure 29-5 for a novel way of displaying both sides of coins and tokens. Attractive displays on a neckchain can be made of unique or more valuable coins. Holders can be purchased for most coins. For shaped coins such as pieces of eight, handmade holders can be made by forming flat silver strips around the coin's edge. An eye can then be soldered to serve as the eyelet for hanging the coin on a neckchain or bracelet. If you can encase items in plastic, attractive belt buckles, Figure 29-6, and other jewelry can be made. For more ideas see Figures 29-7 though 29-10.

Art and Marlette Steinke, owners of Mid-West Metal Detectors, Bloomington, MN, found the coral encrusted gun shown in Figure 29-11. An X-ray, Figure 29-12, indeed reveals the object is a pistol.

SELLING AND EVALUATING YOUR FOUND TREASURES

There are buyers for all types of found treasures. The key is to learn the value of coins, jewelry, relics and other collectables. Learning to evaluate your finds and determining their "going rate" comes with practice and a current knowledge of gold and silver prices. Comparison shopping in jewelry stores and coin shops helps keep you abreast of values. It is important to learn coin grading so that you can correctly evaluate your coins. You'll need to learn how to determine gold content and know the meaning of various markings stamped on the silver and gold jewelry pieces.

Pure gold is 24K (karat) or 1000 fine. A gold alloy of 50% is considered 12K or 500 fine; three-quarter gold is considered 18K or 750 fine. Most gold items are made of 10K to 18K gold. There are 20 penny-weights to the troy ounce. Each troy ounce contains 480 grains. Government regulations require that gold items be marked for purity. If you cannot locate a karat or fine stamp, then the item is not gold but made of plated-over base metal. You can test jewelry with nitric acid. With a ring, make a drag mark on a piece of soapstone. With three other rings clearly marked 10K, 14K and 18K, make a mark parallel and close to the first mark. Using an applicator, spread a line of nitric acid across the four lines on the soapstone. The lowest karat line will begin to disappear more quickly than the higher karat lines. Observe which of the three ring lines disappears at the same rate as the line made by your test ring. The gold content of your ring will be the same as the content of the ring that made the comparable line.

To determine whether your ring or jewelry item is truly gold or silver and not just plated, scratch it in an inconspicuous place. The cut must penetrate the surface of the object to be tested. Drop a tiny amount of nitric acid on the cut. Most cheap alloys will fizzle and bubble under the acid. Copper and brass fizzes bubbly green. Silver turns to a creamy or slight brownish haze. Lead will haze a deep gray or black. Gold will not be affected. Thoroughly wash items in running water after testing them to remove all traces of the acid.

If you plan to sell your gold jewelry, you'll need to purchase a scale that weighs several troy ounces. Knowing the gold content of your finds will help you avoid being cheated. You'll know exactly how much to ask. Dealers usually offer 50 to 75% of the true worth of the gold. You may be able to develop a continuing relationship with a particular dealer who will pay you up to 90% or more. Any dealer who

357

purchases your gold has a right to make a profit. Remember that there will always be charges for smelting and refining. Consider for a moment that a smelter charge of 10% and only a 10% profit for the dealer reduces the value of your gold by 20%. Such mathematics show why it is difficult to sell gold jewelry for a price approaching the value of gold.

One way to get more for your jewelry is to sell the items directly to your friends or at flea markets. People will often pay far more than gold value for a nice crucifix, ring or other jewelry item. Antique jewelry commands high prices.

You will need at least a "talking knowledge" of semi-precious stones, pearls and diamonds, And, don't forget all the new and mostly worthless "fake" stones flooding the market. Just because that ring you found looks too old to have a synthetic stone, you could be wrong. Synthetic stones have been around for decades.

With a scale you know how to use, it'll be easy to determine the value of your finds. Let's use the following equation to work through one example:

$$\text{SPOT (\$/ounce)} \times \frac{\text{dwt (object)}}{20 \text{ (dwt/ounce)}} \times \frac{\text{object K}}{24K} = \text{GOLD VALUE}_{(\$)}$$

SPOT is the value of gold for that day. Check the newspaper or call a coin shop for SPOT value. Dwt (object) is the pennyweight of the object in question. Object K is the karat weight of the object which will be stamped somewhere on the object.

Let's say you have a ring that weighs 10 pennyweight (one-half ounce) and is made of 12K (one-half purity) gold. Spot for the day is $300 per ounce.

$$\$300 \times \frac{10\text{dwt}}{20} \times \frac{12K}{24} = \$75$$

The value of your ring calcuates to be $75 (gold content). If your dealer offers to buy it for 60% of gold value, you'll receive $45.

THE PRACTICAL BOOK OF COBS, by Frank Sedwick is an excellent reference book. The author gives information on the history, identification, values and the buying and selling of Spanish coins.

ADDITIONAL TIPS FOR TREASURE DISPOSITION

You can seriously damage coins by cleaning and scrubbing them improperly. It's best you make no attempt to clean your more rare and valuable coins. Let the buyer do his own cleaning. Don't forget that silver coins are worth more than face value. To get top value for your coins consider using shop bid boards. Chances are, you'll realize considerably more than the dealer will offer. Heavily encrusted coins can be x-rayed, Figures 29-11 and 29-12, to reveal the true nature of the encased item(s). Some x-ray labs charge $20 or more for single x-rays, so

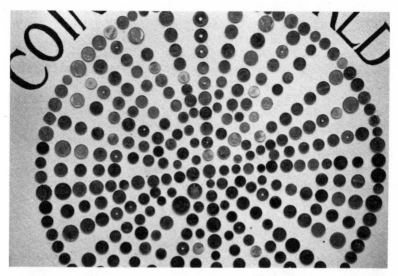

Figure 29-7: This unique way to display coins and tokens found by treasure hunters is shown by Keith and Mary Edwards.

x-ray more than one item at a time and call around for best x-ray prices.

Take the watches you find, regardless of condition, to a watch repairman. Because some parts are difficult to find, watch repairmen will purchase old watches for parts. You can donate your finds to a charitable organization. Local museums and historical societies love to display relics that were lost during pioneer days of the community. The Smithsonian Institution will accept your valuable artifacts but they have 100 million (at least) items in storage. Chances are, your relic will never be viewed by the public unless it is extremely rare or valuable. Perhaps the Smithsonian Institution should auction off some of its treasure to help pay the national debt? Just a suggestion!

Antique shops will purchase your artifacts, but you might consider leaving items on consignment. You'll probably realize more from an outright sale.

Auction houses will dispose of your finds to the highest bidder. There are several to consider. One often heard about is Christies, Manson & Woods, Ltd., Rokin 91, 1012-KL, Amsterdam, The Netherlands. These auctioneers do a remarkable job of disposing of recovered sunken treasure. There are numerous auction houses in the United States. Contact your local coin shop or consult antique buyer's guide for their names.

One handler of treasure is the Joel L. Malter & Co., Inc., 16661 Ventura Blvd., Suite 518, Encino, CA 91316 (818) 784-7772. Malter specializes in ancient coins, including those found with metal detectors, and other treasures from the ancient worlds of Egypt, Mesopotamia,

Greece, Italy and the Orient. They publish an auction catalogue and a magazine called the *Collector's Journal of Ancient Art*.

A quarterly newsletter which reviews any and everything regarding Florida area treasure salvage, auctions, coin shows and treasure exhibits, is *Plus Ultra*. Recent issues included data regarding the history and markings of the escudos of Lima and Mexico. Book reviews and discussions of famous shipwreck recoveries such as the *Atocha* are regular features. For subscription information contact *Plus Ultra*, Quarterly Newsletter of Florida Treasure Brokers, P.O. Box 1697, W. Palm Beach, FL 33402.

Anchors, chains and other salvage items can be left on consignment at yards that handle used marine goods. You take a percentage when the goods are sold. Since anchors are always in good demand,

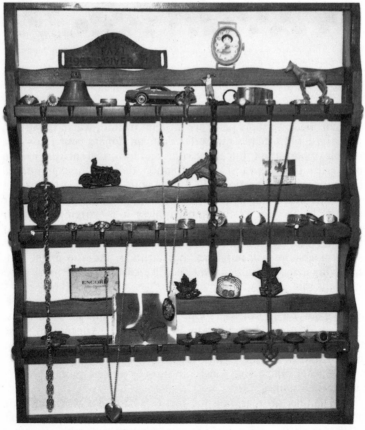

Figure 29-9: This wall rack makes an excellent display support for unusual treasures and finds.

you can sell them directly to your friends or other boating enthusiasts. Metal items can be sold for scrap. Keep metal items sorted by type—one barrel for brass, another for copper and still another for aluminum. Give lead sinkers to fishermen friends. Who knows, they may someday snag a valuable wreck and give you its location. Lead, however, can be sold or used to make weights for your belt.

You can make your own jewelry creations and transform scrap gold and silver into handsome and saleable items. Design your own rings, pendants and other jewelry items! Becoming a silversmith is not difficult and can make your leisure hours profitable.

DISPOSING OF GOLD NUGGETS

If you have been successful prospecting, you can sell your gold to a jeweler or gold buyer, but, remember, gold nuggets are almost always worth more than gold content, if you can find the right buyer. Both ladies and men are ready-made buyers for nugget pendants. Learn how to mount your nuggets and you can double or triple the amount you'll get for attractive nuggets. Nuggets can also be designed into jewelry creations.

SELLING YOUR BOTTLES

I am continualy amazed at the quantity of bottles I locate during my underwater salvage. In East Texas where we searched for lost slot machines, I estimate there are five thousand bottles in that small lake.

Modern beer and soft drink bottles are worthless but bottles just a few years old begin having value. Flea markets are good outlets for bottles. Since they make excellent conversation pieces and decorative items, you may be able to establish markets among friends.

TREASURE: BUYING AND SELLING

If you are interested in buying or selling treasure, relics and antiques, there is a publication you should obtain: the WHO'S BUYING AND SELLING GUIDE. Its publisher, Charles Culbertson, a treasure hunter, developed this alphabetized guide to help sellers find those who want to buy and vice versa. If you are interested in selling or buying coins, jewelry, toys, antiques, bottles, books, knives, cookie cutters or just about anything in between, contact The Good Folks, Shiloh Publishing Company, 302 N. New St., Staunton, VA 24401.

CHAPTER 30

Laws, Taxes and Agreements

FIRST ADMONITION: Learn the applicable laws in the area of your search. Seek counsel. With regard to a significant treasure, take reasonable steps to avoid losing it through ignorance of the law.

In the realm of rules, regulations and laws, absolutes such as black and white are rare. There are, instead, many intermediate shades of complexity and interpretation. Governing the citizen treasure hunter there are federal and state laws and city ordinances. And many are the local differences.

"Ignorance of the law is no excuse." This often repeated, but true, statement is one that you should keep in mind at all times. There is no excuse for not knowing laws that regulate activities you pursue. You should be familiar with every aspect of applicable regulations. For instance, if a law states that you can metal detect on a given beach, does it also say WHEN you can detect? It might stipulate that metal detectors are allowed during minimal periods of swimming and recreational activity. What does "minimal" mean? It may mean that you can hunt during any season other than a stated swimming season, say from May 1 through Labor Day weekend. Or, it might mean detecting is permitted during nighttime and winter months only.

If you find a coin on the beach, can you keep it? If you find a coin in the shallow water of an ocean beach surf, can you keep it? If you locate a boat in an inland lake, can you raise and keep it? Maybe you can retain those items; it may be you'll need to abide by certain laws before you become the rightful owner.

You must heed "No Trespassing" laws. In certain areas, trespassers are not the rightful owners of any treasure they find. Without a permit or rightful claim of ownership you may not be able to keep what you find. You may not only have to give up your treasure but pay a fine for trespassing and destroying property.

It is possible for you to be jailed if you break the law. There have been those who have served jail or prison sentences when they were found guilty of either failing to pay federal and state income taxes on found treasure, or of searching historical sites. Remember that all land and water areas are owned by someone. Also, most property and goods are owned by someone. The law decides whether you can keep what you find. Generally, you are required by law to make an attempt to locate the owner of property you find or turn all found items to lawful authorities who will attempt to locate the owner. When they cannot, within a specified time, the property becomes yours.

Obviously, this chapter cannot contain all you need to know concerning the laws that pertain to your treasure recovery work.There are thousands of laws concerning treasure-trove, salvage, permits, trespassing, property owner/treasure hunter search agreements, division of found treasure and a myriad of other things. This chapter, then, is intended only as a basic guide to start you in the right direction to protect yourself and to help you keep all, or as much as possible, of the treasure you find. Further study on your part is necessary.

FINDERS KEEPERS?

There may be some accepted truth to that statement, but Finders/Keepers does not apply in all situations. Many states have laws prohibiting the tampering with or removal of historic artifacts from on or under lands owned by the state. If "artifact" is not clearly defined, it could be anything made and lost by man, recent or otherwise. Generally, for an item to be classified as an artifact, its age, monetary value and appeal to an archaeologist or historian must be considered. We can safely believe that officials are not interested in relatively recent objects. And, too, their concern with shipwrecks and their cargo may be limited because such treasure is generally covered by Admiralty laws, although other federal laws may also apply and, as in Texas, state laws may play a very singnificant role even well out into the offshore waters. A toy found on a beach, a recent coin found in a surf or an old bottle (of which there may have already been catalogued one thousand of them) found in a river, may not be of interest to anyone except you, the finder. Any object out of context (a mile from a wrecksite) is little value to an archaeologist or historian. But, when that single object is present within a wrecksite, its value increases sharply.

Finders/Keepers may not apply to an object you find on private or posted property if the landowner decides to dispute your claim to the object. On the other hand, Finders/Keepers generally applies to any "owner-not-identified" item you find alongside a roadway, at a deserted ghost town or at a swimming hole no longer in use. Although we must remember that all land is owned by someone and the owner can always dispute your title to found objects (and probably will dispute title if the find has significant value), it is much safer to make prior arrangements for division of the booty with the landowner and to do so in carefully drawn instruments if you anticipate the treasure is of considerable financial worth.

In fact, Finders/Keepers seems to apply to just about any found object when you are not trespassing, when you are hunting legally on any public land and when the rightful owner cannot be identified. Of course, anyone can claim ownership of anything you find; it may then be left to the courts to decide who really is the rightful owner.

TREASURE TROVE

In the United States, Treasure Trove is broadly defined as any gold or silver in coin, plate or bullion and paper currency that has been found concealed in the earth or in a house belonging to another person, even when found hidden in movable property belonging to others such as a book, bureau, safe or a piece of machinery. To be classed as Treasure Trove, the treasure must have been buried long enough to indicate that the original owner is dead or unknown. There are five categories of found property: abandoned, concealed, lost, misplaced and property embedded in the soil.

Abandoned property, as a general rule, is a tangible asset that has willfully and intentionally been discarded or abandoned by its original owner and thus becomes the property of the first person who discovers it. An example would be a household item such as an old television set discarded into a trash receptacle. If the trash collector or anyone else decides to take the set, he can do so legally.

Concealed property is defined as being tangible property hidden by its owner to prevent its observation, inventory, acquisition or possession by other parties. In most cases, when property has been found and fits into this category, the courts order its return to the original owner. Sometimes the finder is given a small reward, more for his honesty in reporting the find than for his efforts in making the discovery.

Lost property is defined as property which the owner has inadvertently and unintentionally lost, yet to which he legally retains title. There is, however, a presumption of abandonment until the owner appears and claims such property, providing that the finder has taken steps to notify the owner of its discovery. Such a case might arise when someone finds a lost wallet that contains documents identifying the owner. It is the general rule that all property must be returned to its owner; he may, or may not, at his discretion, give the finder a reward. In fact, in almost every jurisdiction, there is a criminal statute that makes it a crime to withold "lost" property.

Misplaced (or mislaid) property is defined as property intentionally hidden or laid away by its owner who planned to retrieve it at a later date but then forgot where the item was hidden. When found, such property must be treated the same as concealed property with attempts made to find its owner. If this cannot be done, the property generally is ruled to belong to the owner, or occupant on whose premises it is found, and the courts generally award the finder some amount of the object's value.

Things embedded in the soil constitute property other than that described as Treasure Trove, such as antique bottles or artifacts of historical value. The finder acquires no rights to the object, and possession of such objects belongs to the landowner unless declared otherwise by a court of law. Generally, the courts split the value of the find fifty-fifty between the finder and owner of the land on which the object was discovered even if the finder did not break any laws. Remember, a person entering private property and removing objects without permission can be prosecuted for trespass and larceny, whether or not "No Treaspassing" signs are visible.

Some states recognize the doctrine of Treasure Trove; others do not. Some have laws that state that all found property is treated as either lost, misplaced or abandoned. In some states, each case to reach the court is treated individually at the discretion of a judge. Court cases generally occur when treasure or artifacts are found by someone on private property, or when a find is publicized and someone claims rightful ownership of the find.

You may have heard the story of the Connecticut treasure hunter who found in a Fairfield County swamp a 20-pound chunk of lead which turned out to be a fragment of the statue of King George III that was toppled from its Manhattan pedestal by jubilant patriots upon the signing of the Declaration of Independence. Research revealed that after the statue was destroyed, many of its pieces were melted down into musket balls by patriots, while other pieces were spirited away by a Tory Loyalist who wanted to spare the king any further indignity. Thus, the court ruled that the piece of metal found by the treasure hunter was not intentionally "abandoned" but merely "mislaid" by persons who had every intention of retrieving it, meaning that it belonged to the owners of the land unless the Tories show up to reclaim it!

MISCELLANEOUS REGULATIONS AND LAWS

If you wish to search an old well or cistern, you'll need permission of the landowner. If your search leads you into a river, you'll need to contact your state's authority. You can obtain permission to search a privately owned lake by securing permission from the landowner; but, the owner has proprietary rights to whatever is found. If a lake has a connecting navigable waterway, search rights may come under the jurisdiction of the U.S. Corps of Engineers and ownership of sunken treasure may be regulated by Admiralty antiquities laws, even though some states may claim ownership.

To recover coins and jewelry from a swimming hole in a city park, you'll need to obtain permission from the city, generally through its park commission or board. You may be required to locate the owner or turn found items in to police who will attempt to locate the rightful owner. In some states, if you find "lost" property, you must turn it in to the authorities or you risk losing it entirely. If no one claims property you turn in, it could become "finders/keepers," but the courts may decide that part of it belongs to the landowner or even the present tenant. Some states require you to obtain a permit before searching state property. Other states do not have permits, but all have rules. If you enter the Padre Island National Seashore Park on the

Texas Coast, a federally controlled park, you risk loss of any metal detectors in your vehicle, whether or not you are found using them in the Park. In the state of Maine, there are regulations for the use of metal detectors. They do not permit metal detectors at their historic sites or memorials, and they do not allow digging in state parks, except on the beaches. Detectors are permitted on beaches only during periods of light recreational use. Upon entering a Maine State Park, you should check at the gate. They will furnish you with a permit at no cost. The reason for the permit is to know who is searching with metal detectors when someone loses a valuable piece of property such as a watch or ring.

If you will study the last sentence, you'll realize that there are laws concerning the ownership of found items. Not everything found is considered Treasure Trove; for instance, a detectorist found an individual's ring. Through research of the person's initials, the finder located the owner. The finder called the owner and reported the find. The finder stated that he expected the owner to pay a reward. The owner said, "No, I won't pay you anything. I own the ring and I want it back." The finder then stated that he wouldn't return the ring. The owner then changed his attitude and said, "O.K., what is it worth to you? I'll pay. Where can I meet you?" When the finder met the owner at the designated place, the police arrested the finder. I haven't learned the outcome of that one yet, but I'll bet it wasn't to the finder's liking.

The moral to that story is that when you return an object, it's best not to demand a reward. If a person publishes an offer for return of a lost object, its owner must pay the stated reward. If the term, "Generous offer" is published, perhaps you should ask what is meant by that. What may seem generous to the owner may be peanuts to the finder.

There are laws that prohibit destroying private property. Digging a hole, even under water, is considered destroying private property. Whenever you obtain permission to search an area, make sure the person giving the permit understands you will be digging holes. But, be quick to inform him that you will also be filling your holes...and do so!

In some areas, federally owned lands under the jurisdiction of the Bureau of Land Management or the U.S. Forest Service permit treasure hunting. Treasure hunters are welcome, provided they do not destroy property or deface national monuments. The managers want to know you are there, however. To obtain permission, write to the park ranger in charge of the particular area you wish to search.

BEACH HUNTING

State laws very considerably with regard to treasure found on beaches. In some states, beach areas between low and high water marks (usually defined as being the sand dunes above the beach area) can be searched without a permit. Neither the state nor adjacent landowner can claim a share of what you find unless they can prove ownership of your found objects.

You should not enter "Posted" or "No Trespassing" beaches without obtaining permission. Even in states where all beaches are declared public, do not search fenced or posted areas without permission.

On city beaches, there may be ordinances regulating metal detecting. You may be able to hunt anytime or only during certain hours. In all likelihood, the beach you want to search will be open to you; just the same, it is well to investigate, even if there are no "No Metal Detecting" signs posted. It would certainly be a discomfort if you broke a law and had your vehicle and equipment confiscated and were forced to wait for some time to appear before a magistrate. It's your option whether you obtain a written permit or just accept an oral one. If you get an oral "O.K.," at least get the name of the person and a copy of rules and regulations for metal detector users. Then, make certain you read it often to be aware of what you can and can't do.

For instance, Connecticut beach hunters should be aware of these rules stated in a Jan. 1, 1984, directive issued by the Department of Environmental Protection:

"The use of metal detection devices is permitted on land under the jurisdiction of the Departmental Protection under the following conditions:

1. The activities shall be limited to surface collection except where digging is permited in sand areas devoid of vegetation. However, no collecting or digging will be allowed in areas of sand dunes adjoining the beach area proper. Digging must be done by hand with all motorized devices prohibited. All holes dug must be refilled immediately before the collector leaves the site.

2. Use at a swimming beach shall be limited to times of 'no swimmer' use or at staff discretion.

3. Persons using a metal detector are required to use a trash apron to store all materials found. The collector may retain articles found, except items of a personal nature such as jewelry and watches which must be turned in to the manager in charge. Any material the collector does not wish to retain shall be placed in a waste receptacle.

4. No specific permit is required at this time.

5. Staff may close any area to this activity for purposes of maintaining visitor safety and preserving significant artifactual remains."

SURF HUNTING

Most surf areas are open to treasure hunters but some are not. You may have to get a permit from the state or from the person to whom the state has already awarded a search permit. In areas where a person owns the beach to the water, you may be able to search in the water.

The searching of National Seashores such as Texas' Padre Island and North Carolina's Hatteras is prohibited. In some national park areas, you may get permission but you may be required to turn in historically valued items.

The use of motor-powered devices such as dredges is prohibited in some surf areas. And, in some surf areas where you must get a permit, you are required to fill your holes.

Unless otherwise regulated, most beach areas from the high tide mark out to beyond depths in which you can't very well hunt, are open to the public. Some land beach owners have been known to take it upon themselves to declare adjacent water as their property and force off "trespassers," sometimes by gunpoint. Territories of all navigable waterways come under the jurisdiction of the Army Corps of Engineers. They control it, they regulate it and most beach water areas are open to the public for boating, swimming and/or other activities...unless the Corps of Engineers forbids! It's best, however, never to argue with a "loaded shotgun." Leave such property owners to themselves.

UNDERWATER HUNTING

If you wish to recover a sunken yacht, you have two basic courses of action. You can offer to raise it for the owner and/or insuror and charge a fee for your services. You could also purchase the sunken vessel "as is" and raise and restore it yourself. In either case, you stand to profit. You cannot, however, simply recover the yacht and claim it as your own.

Let's take another case, the location and salvage of cargo from a Spanish galleon. Oceanside states and states with navigable waters may require a permit or license that gives you the right to search for the vessel you are seeking. You may have to pay a fee and obtain a security bond before you can begin your search.

After finding the wreck, it has to be identified, usually with old ship drawings or coins and relics found aboard.

Then, to protect your discovery against claim-jumpers and to avoid legal problems, you'll have to go into Federal District Court to "arrest" the wreck. You, or a diver, acting on orders from a Federal Judge, will swim to the bottom and "serve notice" on the shipwreck. The notice, encased in plastic and tethered into the wreck by a short length of rope, informs anyone who might happen along, that "a warrant shall issue for the arrest of the (name of ship), her appurtenances, her furniture, her cargo and her apparel." The notice is part of the maze of legalities, technicalities and technology into which modern adventurers must venture in order to hunt shipwreck treasure. The court seeks possession of the wreck until rights of possible claimants to it can be determined. In effect, you, or your company, are merely the custodian of whatever you bring up. The courts then determine ownership. In the case of centuries-old Spanish shipwrecks, many could step forward, including Spain itself as original owner of the vessel; a descendant of the ship's captain; and even the country, perhaps Mexico or Peru, from which the gold'originally came.

If the courts decide in your favor, then the ship is yours subject to any treasure you may give to the state and, of course, all applicable income tax levies. Of course, special situations exist, as on the Texas Coast where, contrary to other states, Texas owns the Continental Shelf extending out into the Gulf of Mexico and the State lays claim to all treasure found "on its land," even under hundreds of feet of coastal waters.

YOU SHOULD KNOW...

When you become "custodian" of a shipwreck, you may also become responsible for all problems concerning it. If fishermen snag their nets on "your" ship or gear, you may have to pay for the loss. If "your" ship becomes a menace you may have to have it hauled into deep water or demolished. Dismantlement costs of a WWII cargo ship might be expensive. If someone claims injury from "your" wreck, you may be responsible. You may, also, NOT have 100% rights to keep others off "your" wreck. Others could recover treasure and demand and collect a fee from you under Admiralty laws. You may have another problem, if, during your salvage you discover that another ship's cargo and contents somehow became "mixed" with yours. In other words, you are suddenly excavating two ships, including one in which you may have no legal right. What happens then? Well, I guess that's what laws and lawyers are for, to untangle problems...and ship's rigging.

MARITIME LAWS

Maritime laws are sometimes referred to as Admiralty laws because they were once administered under the jurisdiction of admirals. Maritime law regulates navigation and commerce on the world's ocean and navigable inland lakes and rivers. It regulates all vessels from small boats to giant ships, and its laws pertain to insurance, property damage, contracts and personal injuries.

Maritime salvage laws are designed to reward those who rescue ships and property from the perils of the sea. These laws guarantee a monetary reward to those who salvage property and return it to its owner. The property in question must be lost or abandoned, its owner unknown or not available and the property in peril of the sea. If the owner is not interested in such property, it can be yours. If the owner cannot be found, you may have to make your claim in Admiralty Court where the judge can declare you rightful owner. That is what happened when Mel Fisher won the right to salvage the Spanish galleon, *Atocha,* in Florida waters. Mel's lawyers used Admiralty Salvage law to win their case; Florida's own state Antiquities Law became null and void, as far as their claim on the *Atocha* was concerned.

INCOME TAX LAWS

All treasure hunters must pay income tax on profits derived from the sale of treasure, artifacts or any objects found. The profits received are treated as normal income. Expenses incurred in the salvage of the goods are deductible according to and regulated by income tax laws. Taxes are due during the year you sell or receive value for your found goods. If you donate artifacts and treasure to qualified recipients, you may earn a tax deduction for a charitable contribution. It will probably be necessary for such goods to be appraised by a qualified appraiser and you should have a statement from the charitable institution stating that such goods were, indeed, accepted. There are certain Internal Revenue Service rules that govern amounts that can be claimed as a deduction.

You should keep complete, accurate records of all money you spend in your activities related to treasure recovery. Expenses include equipment cost, transportation, lodging, meals, rental fees, license and legal fees. Obviously, if you don't know all your expenses, they cannot be charged against the profit you receive from selling treasure. Remember, however, the IRS may question your expense items. These expenses are not fully deductible from other "ordinary income" if it is determined that your treasure hunting is a hobby rather than your principal business.

GETTING PERMISSION

You may be astonished at what you can do simply by writing a letter and requesting permission to search a given area. Don't overlook this method to obtain permission to search an otherwise "unsearchable" area; many treasure hunters testify that it works.

Don't assume that an area such as a state park is off limits. Within many park systems metal detectors can be used in non-archaeological areas such as sandy beaches. Some areas can be searched if you'll first obtain a permit from the park's chief ranger or manager. Park managers may grant you permission to search for a specific lost item, such as a ring or valuable piece of jewelry. If you get permission, you must abide by all the rules of the permit. Hunt only during stated times and in stated areas. Don't destroy buildings, vegetation, or even the ground by digging a hole larger than necessary to retrieve the article. Then fill your holes! Leave every area in as good a shape as you found it. One bad move on your part, and you and everyone else may be banned, perhaps forever, from that park and possibly even others. Park managers change jobs often and if you make one enemy, you may be barred everywhere he goes.

You may possibly secure treasure hunting rights to certain areas by agreeing to turn over to the officials all found artifacts of historical value. In return, you can request to keep modern items such as coins, rings and other jewelry. Plus, you should also take out all trash.

You and your entire club may be able to "break the ice" with reluctant city and other officials by offering to "adopt" the area you wish to search. You promise to remove all trash, both dug and found, cover all holes, possibly specify that only digging tools like screwdrivers be used and agree to assume the responsibility for all club members who don't abide by the rules. You can offer to repair their damage or pay a penalty. Also, you could agree to look after the park and when you find other hunters who, say, do not fill their holes, you will instruct them in proper digging and recovery procedure. Those who do not obey the rules or who attempt to damage property are to be reported to park officials.

RULES AMONGST OURSELVES

Clubs can invite local lawyers, archaeologists and historians to attend meetings and to serve as guest speakers. Ask them to talk on treasure trove, salvage laws, trespassing, permits and landowner/treasure hunter search agreements, archaeology, excavation methods and archaeological and historical site information. Getting to know these professionals could lead to the "discovery" openings of many sites.

All metal detectorists should consider joining and actively supporting local treasure hunting clubs. Participation in club activities is one of the best ways to learn about laws and regulations that treasure hunters should know about. If your club is not a member of the FMDAC (Federation of Metal Detector and Archaeological Clubs, Inc.), suggest to the members that the club contact FMDAC at, RD2, Box 263, Frenchtown, NJ 08825. The Federation actively monitors laws, restrictions and proposed legislation that affects us all. Through their efforts, our voice is being heard as never before. Restrictive laws have been abolished or modified, resulting in many new and formerly restricted areas being opened to responsible metal detectorists.

It should be understood amongst ourselves that the code of ethics of the treasure hunter is in force at all times and that every team member must abide by the rules. Be quick to remind a fellow treasure hunter to discard all trash in the proper receptacle and to fill all dug holes. Police your own group; you may prevent good areas from being closed.

Learn the following rules or at least keep a copy tacked in a convenient place where you can review them occasionally.

METAL DETECTORIST'S CODE OF ETHICS

I will respect private and public property, all historical and archaeological sites and will do no metal detecting on these lands without proper permission. I will keep informed on and obey all laws, regulations and rules governing federal, state and local public lands. I

371

will aid law enforcement officials whenever possible. I will cause no willful damage to property of any kind, including fences, signs and buildings, and will always fill the holes I dig. I will not destroy property, buildings or the remains of ghost towns and other deserted structures. I will not leave litter or uncovered items lying around. I will carry all trash and dug targets with me when I leave each search area. I will observe the Golden Rule, using good outdoor manners and conducting myself at all times in a manner which will add to the stature and public image of all people engaged in the field of metal detection.

DIVIDING FINDS

When you and a friend go treasure hunting, you may agree that each person keeps what he finds, or you may agree to split everything found. What happens when you make a single, valuable find? You both write down what you believe the item is worth. The one who makes the highest bid takes the item—and pays to the other the value of his higher bid. The "winner" has the item he wanted and he pays what he thought it was worth. The friend gets more than what he believed it to be worth. Another solution is for the low bidder to take the item and pay the friend the higher bid but not to exceed an amount twice the low bid. This second method tends to keep the bidding low but, in the event the "friend" purposefully inflates his bid, the winner is protected by the ceiling value.

SEARCH AND SALVAGE AGREEMENTS

Avoid heartbreak...insist upon an agreement between yourself and property owners. And please notice I said, "property owners." Even though the husband owner of a beachfront gives you permission, his wife may take all you find if she hasn't signed the agreement.

When you are dealing with governmental agencies and the stakes are high, you should consider employing an attorney well versed in all laws peraining to such matters. The following is an example of a simple agreement between land owners and a treasure hunter. Depending upon the property laws applicable to the site you wish to search and the anticipated dollar value of your finds, you may want to consider a more detailed, custom-drawn agreement.

SEARCH AND SALVAGE AGREEMENT

This agreement, dated this   day of 19,   , between
                    ,hereinafter known as the Property
Owner(s), and   , hereinafter known as the
Salvagor. In consideration of the Salvagor's undertaking to devote his
time and equipment in a search of the premises described as:

the Property Owners hereby agree that the Salvagor shall receive as
compensation for his services (one half or other fraction) of all money,
jewelry, artifacts, and
discovered by the Salvagor, subject to the laws of this community. The
Salvagor is given full authority to work in, on, or about the said
premises at any reasonable time, subject only to such notice as the
Property Owners may require in advance of such work. Each party
waives any possible claim against the other for liability for any careless
or negligent act or omission of the other arising out of or in the conse-
quence of the search herein provided for. This agreement shall be effective for   months from the date thereof.
Executed at

Salvagor   Property Owner

                                                Property Owner

Note: Property may be described generally as a house and lot, or
a farm or tract of a particular street or road address, owned by the
Property Owners, or by use of the legal description, if available.

This agreement is a copy of an agreement used by a treasure
hunter during one particular treasure search. It should be modified to
satisfy all applicable laws and requirements of all parties when and
wherever it is used. Be certain the "owners" are not just renters.

DEALING WITH FOREIGN GOVERNMENTS

I'm not going very far into this one...just far enough to tell you that you can fully believe that in some situations, a courtroom filled with Philadelphia lawyers, all on your side, may not be able to help you acquire what you know is yours based on a contract signed by both you and a legal representative of a foreign government. It seems to be the new order of the day that many governments have decided they aren't giving anything away. If you find foreign landbased or off-shore treasure, whether you have a search permit or not, you will pro-bably need the best legal assistance available...and even that may not help you one bit. You may wind up not only without treasure but with a prison sentence.

ANOTHER PROBLEM YOU MAY ENCOUNTER

Granted, most foreign countries seek tourists with money to spend, but when you come through Customs loaded down with strange-looking equipment cases and businesslike luggage, you can ex-pect delays and possibly confiscation of your goods, at least until you leave the country. All of your documents and letters of permission from tourist departments may be totally ignored by Customs Officials. Believe me; I speak from experience. On one trip to a South American country with the Scuba World team we had been "invited" to make a film for televising in the United States designed to attract American tourist dollars to that country. When we arrived with numerous suit-cases, bags and television "equipment-looking" cases, we were stop-ped cold at Customs. Finally, we were allowed to come into the coun-try minus all strange-looking equipment cases, which meant that camera equipment needed to make this "tourist-dollar" film, was held by Customs until the day we departed one week later.

All this took place—and is probably being repeated this very minute at a Customs post somewhere in the world—because some developing countries, some that know nothing about scientific in-vestigations, and some that have had their "antiques and relics" plundered, are suspicious of any kind of high technology investigation and explorations. They simply say No; then they are safe.

CHAPTER 31

Equipment Maintenance and Field Repair

Salt water with its corrosive effects will damage practically everything. After equipment is used in the field, especially in salt water environments, cleaning and maintenance are critical factors to prolong its serviceable life.

EQUIPMENT MAINTENANCE

CLOTHING

Regular and thorough washing of clothing you wear when beachcombing, surfing and diving is all the care needed. Sneakers, boots and waders should have sand rinsed out after each outing. Never dry these items using heat but let them dry in open air. You can use paint thinner to remove tar and oil from personal items. Baby oil works but it does take longer.

SNORKEL AND SCUBA GEAR

All snorkel and scuba gear should be rinsed in fresh water as soon as possible after each use, especially when you have been working in salt water. I always at least hose down my gear, but whenever possible I fill the bathtub with water and give the equipment a thorough soaking. Boots, waders, dive suits and hoods should be turned inside out. After washing away all mud and sand the articles should be left to dry in the open air. A towel can be used to absorb much of the water to hasten drying. Never use heat to dry these articles. Let them dry thoroughly before storing. Whenever dive boots are worn for long periods, they will develop a disagreeable odor. Wash them in a solution of soda and water and let them dry thoroughly.

Your dive mask and snorkel should be cleaned and all water and foreign matter blown out. Your scuba regulator is the most critical. It should be thoroughly rinsed in water, using successive clean baths. Blowing through the regulator while depressing the various valves will clear out sand and other contaminants. Follow the manufacturer's recommendations concerning periodic cleaning and inspection, no matter how little the equipment may have been used. Cost is minimal; but whatever the price, it's worth it. Air tanks should be inspected according to manufacturer's recommendations. Unless dive shops find an updated inspection date, they will refuse to fill air tanks.

TOOLS

Tools you use that are made of iron or steel, and even stainless steel, will eventually rust. You can prevent rust to some extent by washing all items in fresh water immediately after they are used. Let them dry before storing. You'll notice I said stainless steel will rust. You must care for these items the same as you would any other metal-fabricated tools.

USE A CARRY/STORAGE BAG

You'll save yourself a lot of grief if you keep and carry your gear in a protective bag. A bag will help prevent damage to equipment, and you are less likely to accidentally drop or lose items.

DREDGES AND OTHER POWER EQUIPEMNT

Use fresh water to clean out accumulated sand and debris as soon as possible after the equipment has been operating. This is especially important if the equipment has been used in salt water. Always follow manufacturer's recommendations for cleaning and storing. CAUTION: Never run your dredge pump dry. To do so will damage the pump. Lubricate all items as specified by the manufacturer. Always run combustion engines until the carburetor is empty of gasoline. If you don't, the next time you need the equipment, its carburetor and jets may require cleaning.

METAL DETECTION EQUIPMENT

When you use your detector on the beach, sand will somehow find its way into the stem and control housing. In fact, it'll find its way into everything! Many years ago, after an extended stay on Texas' Padre Island, one member of a search group found sand in a factory-sealed cigarette package! The following maintenance procedures will keep your equipment in top-notch working condition. The detector stem should be completely disassembled and flushed with fresh water. A soapy solution can be used to aid removal of stubborn materials. A lubricant is not recommended nor desirable unless the lubricant is positively non-sticky and will not attract any particles such as sand or grit. Wipe the detector with a damp cloth. The searchcoil can be cleaned with a garden hose. Do not let water get into the cable connector. Protect the cable from sharp blows and avoid kinking it. Open any portals and battery doors and check the interior. Clean out foreign material such as sand or leaves. Never use forced air to clean a detector. Air that is blown in a detector control housing can force dust and debris to become lodged in the electrical controls and cause them to fail.

You can tell visually when water gets in the housing of underwater detectors that are constructed with transparent control housing. If this occurs, immediately remove the access door, drain the water and let the detector thoroughly dry for at least a day while sitting in an open area. Never place a metal detector or a searchcoil in an oven or other heated area for drying. Normal temperature is sufficient. Dessicant packs can be dried by placing in a 400-degree oven for one hour. the indicator card will be blue when wet, but turn pink when dry.

Properly designed underwater detectors utilize dual o-ring seals that prevent water from entering into the control housing. Nevertheless, detectors will eventually require maintenance. When control shafts are rotated, microscopic particles of matter gradually work their way into the o-ring seals to cause leaks or sticking controls. If this occurs, it is advisable to return the detector to the factory for proper repair and replacement of o-ring seals. When underwater instruments are received at the Garrett factory for cleaning, inspection and new seals, the detectors are given a six-atmosphere pressure test to insure the equipment is ready for underwater work.

When using your detector, inspect all exposed connectors daily. Each time you charge the batteries, inspect the battery and clip connection. All contamination and corrosion should be removed using a pencil eraser. Be careful not to short the terminals of the battery with the metal casing on the eraser. Any spring clips that appear to have opened should be closed with a slight pressure of your thumb and forefinger. Visually inspect all detector components during maintenance and cleaning operations.

Give your detector reasonable care and regular maintenance checks; clean it when needed, and your detector will give you many years of trouble-free performance.

FIELD REPAIR

Check the batteries first if your detector stops working. Some people just forget to replace batteries. Now, new batteries certainly won't correct all your detector problems, but they are usually the source of the problem when a detector stops working. Always carry a fresh set of batteries on every hunt. Even though the battery check meter or indicator says the batteries are good, test the detector with fresh batteries any time it fails.

NOTE: The following sections were reproduced from the author's book, MODERN METAL DETECTORS and various Garrett instrument instruction manuals.

Make sure you insert new batteries correctly and they test satisfactorily. Regularly give your detector a thorough visual inspection. Check battery terminals for tightness. Carefully examine the detector by looking through any doors and portals and observe every component for damage. Look for wires that may have been pinched when you last changed batteries. When panels are replaced, detector wires can be pinched, setting up a potential problem that can result in failure in the field. If your detector is factory-sealed, never open it. At best you risk having your warranty voided.

BATTERY CHARACTERISTICS

There are four types of batteries for use in a metal detector: carbon zinc, heavy duty, alkaline and nickel cadmium (Ni-Cad).

CARBON ZINC cost the least and deliver current for the shortest length of service. They operate most efficiently at temperatures from 32 to just over 100 degrees Fahrenheit. They are more prone to leak corrosive acid than alkaline and Ni-Cads.

HEAVY DUTY (zinc chloride) are generally more expensive than carbon zinc but will give additional service. They are more prone to leak corrosive acid than alkaline and Ni-Cads.

ALKALINE (alkaline managanese) cost more than carbon zinc and heavy duty types and give more current for a longer period of time. They last longer in storage and are less susceptible to leakage. Their performance is better in extreme temperatures. Their use is probably cheaper in the long run than carbon zinc and heavy duty types.

NI-CAD RECHARGEABLES (nickel cadmium) feature a manufacturer's claim that they can be recharged one thousand times. They are more expensive than other types. Longer life and best performance can be obtained if they are used often and recharged immediately at room temperature. They will take a "set" if repeatedly used the same length of time. For example, if repeatedly used one hour per day and then recharged, the Ni-Cads will take a "set" and one hour is the maximum length they will deliver current. It is often good to let the batteries run down completely before recharging. At least once every three months completely discharge and restore a full charge to extend battery life. Ni-Cads will power a given circuit 40 to 50% as long as carbon zinc. For example: If carbon zinc batteries power your detector 20 hours, Ni-Cads will power it for eight to ten hours. Since Ni-Cad operating voltage is less than the other types, Ni-Cads will register at a lower level on meters and lights designed to check batteries on detectors.

SEARCHCOIL AND SPEAKER CONTAMINATION

Contamination such as dirt, black magnetic sand, small metal shavings or other matter works into a searchcoil cover or speaker to cause erratic sounds that are annoying and appear to indicate a faulty detector. It is easy to clean out a searchcoil cover. If black magnetic sand particles are sticking to the speaker cone, turn the detector upside down to let the material escape. Test the detector by activating it. Sometimes, the vibration of the speaker cone will loose particles that have become magnetically attached to it. A small magnet can also be used to pull the particles out.

CABLE CONNECTOR INSPECTION

Erratic sounds can be produced when the cable is slightly twisted at the point where it enters the removable cable connector. To check this problem remove the connector cable clamp screws. With the cable clamp removed, visually inspect the wiring. Rotate the wire slightly to test for broken connections. These broken connections can be repaired with a small soldering iron. Making repairs of this type, however, requires some knowledge of both electronics and soldering. As soon as possible, have a reputable technician check your emergency repairs. NOTE: Some detector connectors are factory-molded, which virtually eliminates broken connections.

TESTING SEARCHCOILS AND CABLE

Erratic operations and no audio can be the fault of the searchcoil and/or cable. Pick up the detector, turn it on, grasp the searchcoil and gently twist it back and forth. Gently pull on the cable where it goes into the searchcoil to determine if the wiring is broken. If wires break in the field, you can sometimes press the searchcoil cable or tape it in such a way to permit you to finish the day's searching. Permanent repairs will be necessary, and it is in your best interest to make them as soon as possible. Don't expect a "field expedient" to solve a problem permanently. If erratic operation persists, the searchcoil my be faulty, and you should replace it.

INTERMITTENT SOUNDS

Check the battery connections. In fact, these connections should be checked occasionally to make certain they are tight. Check carefully for corroded batteries. Sometimes batteries will leak a small amount of battery acid, creating corrosion on the contacts.

NON-DETECTION

If a coin lying on top of the ground produces no detection, make sure you have your detector correctly adjusted in the ground elimination mode. If you are using TR discrimination, make sure you press the retune button or tune the detector searchcoil at the correct operating height. If you retune the detector while the searchcoil is held in the air and then lower it toward the ground, heavy ground minerals can detune the detector to such an extent that coins on top of the ground will not be detected. Also make sure that you have not turned your trash elimination control too high.

AUDIO THRESHOLD DRIFT

If your detector audio threshold won't set, but instead, slowly drifts up or down, check your batteries. Some detectors require warmup time. Make sure you have allowed adequate warmup (five to ten minutes). Removing your detector from an air-conditioned car, then operating it in direct sun can cause components to heat too rapidly, necessitating a few minutes warmup time.

DETECTOR STOPS WORKING AFTER
YOU SUBMERGE THE SEARCHCOIL

If a manufacturer states that searchcoils are submersible, you should be able to submerge them up to the cable connector. Submersible searchcoils have been known to leak, however. Sometimes the cable covering has been punctured either by careless handling or by thorns when the detector was brushed up against bushes, a barbed wire fence or other sharp object. Searchcoils can be punctured under water by sharp coral. Water can seep into punctures and run through the cable into the searchcoil. Also, searchcoils have been known to leak when taken from the hot trunk of a car and plunged into cold water. The hot, expanded air inside the searchcoil cooled, causing a vacuum to form which pulled water in through a punctured cable or at a juncture. If you suspect water seepage is causing your searchcoil to fail, let it dry for several days in a warm place. Do not place it in a hot oven; this may permanently damage the searchcoil. If you can locate where the water seeped into the coil, repairs can be made with silicone material which can be purchased in tubes at most hardware stores. Apply this generously to the location where you suspect the leak occurred and let it dry thoroughly before using.

After water searching, do not elevate the searchcoil above the level of the control housing. Any water that is trapped in the stem may flow back into the housing. It may be necessary to remove the lower stem to drain accumulated water. Searchcoil skid plates are recommended because they provide excellent protection for your searchcoil.

INTERMITTENT AUDIO, UNSTEADY THRESHOLD SOUNDS

This, in all probability, is caused by operating the detector near high voltage power lines, televisions, TV transmission lines, airports or another metal detector. Citizen-band radios operating nearby have also caused this problem. Your solution is to move away from these electromagnetic interference sources. Co-axial searchcoils eliminate a great amount of electromagnetic interference.

If your detector appears to fail, unplug your headphones! A broken headphone wire will cause erratic operation, or you may lose audio. If this happens, you can continue your search using the speaker alone if you do not have a spare set of the headphones.

SHORT BATTERY LIFE

If this occurs and you use Ni-Cad rechargeable batteries, read the battery section in this chapter. If it occurs with regular batteries, place a fresh set into the detector and keep a record of the amount of hours the new batteries give you. You may find your batteries were actually not fresh to begin with. Use headphones instead of the speaker to extend battery life; your detection efficiency will improve as well.

NO DETECTION DEPTH

If your batteries are strong, if your detector correctly tunes and if you can achieve threshold sound, in all probability, the problem lies with you and not the detector. Of course, searchcoils can fail. If you have a spare searchcoil, place it on your detector and check for depth. If the detector is still giving poor depth detection, re-read manufacturer's instructions and carefully follow operating procedures.

CHECK POINT LIST

Many of the previous problems and a few more have been compiled into this check list. If your detector fails to operate properly, perform these checks:

1. NO OPERATION
Battery checks zero:
Check battery holder and battery cable connector.

2. NO OPERATION
Battery checks normal, power on:
Check for disconnected connectors.

3. OPERATION NORMAL
Battery checks zero:
Check joints at battery check switch and other wiring points.

4. SOUND NORMAL
No meter operation nor battery check:
Check for disconnected wire to meter.
Check for defective meter.
Check for joints at battery check switch.

5. NO SOUND
Meter operation normal:
Check for disconnected speaker connector.
Check for loose wires at speaker.
Check for damaged headphone jack or plug.
Jack springs can "spring" open.

6. CONSTANT SOUND
Substitute a good coil.
Check pushbutton or Master Control switch and associated cables.

7. METER OPERATION LOW OR COMPLETE FAILURE
Check for pinched wire.

8. WILL NOT TUNE (Cannot achieve threshold)
Substitute a good coil.
Check pushbutton or retune switch and associated cables.
Clean connector pins. (Use pencil eraser.)

9. INTERMITTENT OPERATION
Check for loose terminals on battery holder or batteries.
Check for tarnish on coil connector pins.

10. BATTERY HOLDER DIFFICULT TO INSTALL
Look for restriciting wiring.
Use flat file (six or eight-inch) on battery holder or tray to smooth out nicks in runners, etc.
Check for bent or misaligned battery tray and mating connector pins.

11. MODES REVERSED
Control switch connected backwards.
Wires reversed in control switch cable connector.

12. ERRATIC OPERATION
Substitute a good coil.
Check for excessive stem movement.
Clean coil cable connector pins.
Check for loose connector and housing screws.

ADDITIONAL TIPS

Your detector is a sensitive electronic instrument. Although it is built to withstand rugged use, care in transporting and handling will extend its life.

Do not subject detector to high temperatures by storing in hot sunlight or in heated automobile trunk.

Keep detector clean. Wipe housing after each use; wash coil when necessary. Protect from dust and sand as much as possible. Disassemble stem and clean after use in sandy areas, especially after working in or near salt water. ˙

For storage periods longer than one month, remove batteries from detector and/or battery tray.

Never use spray cleaners or lubricants on the printed circuit board or controls. Such materials leave harmful residues. Never use any petroleum product on or in your detector.

And, again, don't forget to check the headphones. Headphones have been known to fail, especially the connecting wires where they are soldered to the earphone plug. With the detector turned on and operating, wiggle the headphone wires. Pull on them gently where they go into the headphone pieces and where the wires go into the plug. Detectors have been returned to repair stations when the only problem was faulty headphones.

If all of the above procedures fail and your detector will not operate, you may require repairs that must be performed at a factory or service center. If away from home for an extended period, perhaps you can locate a local dealer to examine your detector. Many dealers are factory-trained in detector repair. Some may charge a small service fee. Don't overlook this possibility as one way of getting back into the field.

If the detector must be shipped to a service center, pack the detector carefully and use lots of insulation. It is not necessary in most cases to return stems, headphones, etc. Do not pack digging tools which add weight and increase postage cost. Enclose a letter with your name and address and a brief yet complete description of the problem; i.e., how often it occurs and the special conditions that seem to cause it.

Let's hope your detector never fails in the field, but don't baby it to protect it. USE IT! Garrett detectors are built to stand up in the field during many years of hard use.

Glossary

(See also Chapters 5–11 for additional metal detector terminology)

ADMIRALTY LAWS — Those rules that relate to the rights and conduct of property and persons on the high seas. So called, because in England trial of such cases is held in an admiralty court or court of admiralty. In the United States Federal district courts are invested with admiralty powers.

AIR TEST — A method to determine the detection distance and sensitivity of a metal detector. The test is performed in air. Depending upon the type detector and soil conditions, actual depth performance can be more or less than air tests.

AMPERE — A unit of electrical current or rate of flow of electrons in a conductor.

AMPLIFIER — An electrical circuit which draws its power from a source other than the input signal and which produces an output voltage/current that is an enlarged reproduction of the essential features of the input signal.

ANTENNA — The component of a transmitter or receiver that actually radiates or receives the electromagnetic energy. (see SEARCHCOIL)

AUDIO ADJUST — The control used to adjust the metal detector to the desired audio "threshold" or "silent" audio level settings. Also designated as TUNING.

AUTOMATIC (AUDIO) TUNING — A circuit incorporated in some detectors which keeps the AUDIO level at a predetermined level by automatically compensating for detector drift and changing environmental conditions that affect detector AUDIO tuning. Do not confuse with AUTOMATIC VLF GROUND ELIMINATING (CANCELING).

AUTOMATIC VLF GROUND ELIMINATION (CANCELING) — A type metal detector circuit that requires no manual adjustments to achieve iron earth mineral elimination (canceling). Circuits continually analyze the soil beneath the searchcoil and automatically adjust the detector circuitry to "ignore" minerals. Do not confuse Automatic VLF Ground Elimination with Automatic (Audio) Tuning, as they have two entirely different characteristics.

BEAT — The periodic variations that result when energy waves of two different frequencies are superimposed upon each other.

BEAT FREQUENCY — Also called heterodyne, it is one of the two different resultant frequencies produced when energy waves of two frequencies are superimposed upon each other.

BLACK SAND — See Magnetic Black Sand.

BODY MOUNT—A detector configuration in which the control housing is strapped to the body, used often by surf hunters.

CALIBRATION—This generally refers to the "zero" rejection calibration setting of the Ground or Target Eliminator control. Some manufacturers calibrate their prospecting detectors so that persons using the detectors for ore sampling (a form of electronic prospecting—also called High Grading) can readily and accurately "set" the controls when it is desired to check ore samples for conductive metal content. Certain models are permanently calibrated and require no adjustment.

CIRCUIT—an electrical or electronic network providing one or more closed electrical paths. More specifically, it is a grouping of components and wiring in devices designed to perform some particular function or group of functions. Examples of circuits are the transmitter circuit, receiver circuit, antenna circuit and audio amplifier circuit.

CIRCUIT BOARD—The thin sheet of material upon which components are mounted and, generally, the wiring and components themselves. If the circuit board is completely self-contained, with wires to and from it only for power (input and output), it is usually referred to as a module. Circuit boards may be hand-wired or have the interconnectors printed electrochemically upon them. They are abbreviated "PCB" (printed circuit board).

CLASSIFICATION, AUDIO—An audio method (or methods) of classifying detected targets into conductivity classes or categories.

CLASSIFICATION, VISUAL—A visual (metered or light) method (or methods) of classifying detected targets into conductivity classes or categories. See also COIN ALERT.

COIL—See SEARCHCOIL.

COIN ALERT (TONE)—An audio method of producing a special tone whenever coins (or silver or high conductivity gold items) are detected. All other detected targets produce normal accept/reject audio sounds.

COMPONENT, CIRCUIT—An essential part of a circuit; i.e., resistor, capacitor, coil, tube, transistor, etc. Or, complete, functional units of a system; i.e., transmitter component, receiver component, searchcoil component, etc.

CONDUCTANCE—The ability of an element, component or device to permit the passage of an electrical current, i.e., eddy currents. It is the reciprocal function of resistance.

CONDUCTOR—A wire, bar or metal mass (coin, hull, cannon, etc.) capable of conducting electric current.

CONTROL HOUSING—The box or container in which is placed all or most of the electronics assemblies, batteries, etc., of a metal detector. On a land detector the control housing must be protected from water.

CRYSTAL-CONTROLLED OSCILLATOR—An oscillator which employs a crystal to determine its output frequency.

384

CYCLE — One complete alternation or cycle of an AC voltage source.

DEPTH DETECTION — A term often used to decribe the ability of a detector to detect metal objects to certain or given depths.

DEPTH PENETRATION — Applied specifically to electronic metal detectors, the term means the distance into a given medium that the instrument is capable of satisfactorily illuminating, or how deep into a matrix the unit will sense targets and produce a detection signal.

DETECTION PATTERN — See SEARCHCOIL DETECTION PATTERN.

DETUNING — A term used to describe when an instrument is "down tuned" in order to more precisely pinpoint, etc. Audio threshold is achieved while the instrument is detecting the target. Ground minerals can also "detune" an instrument, but, generally, in an adverse or undesirable manner.

DISCRIMINATOR — An expression used to describe the capability of a detector to more or less identify ranges of detected targets. See ELIMINATION.

DRIFT — An expression used to describe the ability of an instrument to remain tuned at a preset tuning point. Causes of DRIFT: temperature, battery condition, faulty components, poor design. See STABILITY.

EDDY CURRENTS — Also called Foucault currents, they are induced in a conductive mass by the variations of electromagnetic energy radiated from the detector, and tend to flow in the surface layers of the target mass. Flow is directly proportional to frequency, the density of the electromagnetic field and the conductivity of metal. Eddy currents flowing in a target produce the same effect as that of a shorted-turn secondary and reflect a resistive load back into the antenna circuit of beat frequency detectors, which lowers the effective inductance of the antenna and raises transmitter frequency. Eddy current generation is also a main electrical phenomenon that produces metal detection signals in TR, VLF and Pulse Induction metal detectors.

ELECTROMAGNETIC FIELD — An invisible field which surrounds the transmitter winding. Generated by the alternating radio frequency current which circulates in the transmitter antenna windings.

ELECTROMAGNETIC INDUCTION — The voltage induced in a coil (or object, as a conductive target) due to changes in electromagnetic lines of force which pass through the coil or object.

ELECTRONIC CIRCUIT — A circuit wherein current flows through wires, resistances, inductances, capacitances, transistors and other components.

ELECTRONIC PINPOINTING — A detector mode to cause a "sharpening" of detector signals when objects are detected. An electronic aid to precise target location.

ELIMINATION—There are two forms: Ground Eliminating (also called Ground Canceling) and Target (Trash) Eliminating (also called Discriminating). Detector circuits eliminate the earth's IRON MINERALS from detection. Other circuits eliminate SELECTED UNDESIRABLE METAL OBJECTS from detection. "Elimination" accurately describes these functions.

FALSE DETECTION—Responses to objects or anomalies other than sought targets.

FARADAY-SHIELD—The metal foil wrapping, metal tube, metallic paint, or other metallic cover surrounding the searchcoil antenna wires (or other components) of a metal detector. Its purpose is to provide electrostatic shielding and reduce ground and wet grass capacitance effects and "false" detection signals.

FERROUS—Pertains to iron and iron compounds such as cannons or ships' hulls.

FERROUS, NON—Pertains to non-iron metals and compounds, i.e., brass, silver, lead, alumininum, etc.

FIRMWARE—Computer programs contained permanently as memory in a computerized microprocessor metal detector.

FREQUENCY—As applied to alternating current or voltage. The term means the number of periodic recurrences of a complete alternation or cycle Zero, plus-maximum, zero, negative-maximum, zero, current or voltage levels that occur within one second.

FREQUENCY DESIGNATIONS—

Very Low	VLF	3-30	kHz. (cycles or Hertz)
Low	LF	30-300	kHz.
Medium	MF	300-3000	kHz.
High	HF	3-30	mHz.
Very High	VHF	30-300	mHz.
Ultra High	UHF	300-3000	mHz.
Super High	SHF	3000-30,000	mHz.

GAIN—An increase in voltage, current power with respect to a previous quantity or a standard reference. Gain occurs in vacuum tubes, transistors, transformers, etc., as gain per component, gain per stage and gain per assembly. Such gain can be measured in terms of voltage, current, power or decibels.

GROUND ELIMINATION (ALSO CANCELING)—The ability of a metal detector to eliminate (ignore or cancel) the detection effect of iron minerals or wetted salt.

HEADPHONES—A device that converts electrical energy waves into audible waves of identical form. For metal detector users working in noisy or windy locations. They will do everything loudspeakers will do, and most of the time they do it better. In addition, they are less susceptible to damage by rain, and require much less power than a speaker.

HERTZ (Hz)—A unit of frequency equal to one cycle per second.

HOT ROCK—A mineralized rock that produces a positive signal in a metal detector.

INDUCED CURRENT—The current that flows in a conductor or conductive mass when a varying electromagnetic field is present. Except for eddy currents, induced or secondary currents flow only when there is a complete circuit or closed loop. Eddy currents are, in themselves, closed loops.

MAGNETIC BLACK SAND—Magnetite, a magnetic oxide of iron and, in a lesser degree, hematite. Also contains titanium and other rare-earth minerals but serves mainly as an indicator of the possible presence of placer gold.

MAGNETOMETER—Not a metal detector even though the term is often used interchangeably, especially when walk-through (doorway) type metal detectors are discussed. An instrument for measuring magnetic intensity, especially the earth's magnetic field. Treasure hunters, searching for a metal ship, will use a magnetometer to locate increased earth's magnetic field density caused by the hull.

MATRIX—The entire area below a searchcoil and being illuminated by the transmitted electromagnetic field. A matrix may wholly, partially or intermittently contain conductive and/or non-conductive and/or ferrous and/or non ferrous materials. The matrix may contain moisture, sulfides, metallic ores, etc. The detection pattern is only a portion of the matrix.

METAL DETECTOR—An electronic instrument or device capable of sensing the presence of conductive objects lying within the earth, in its waters or otherwise out of sight, and of providing the operator with an audible or visual indication of that presence.

METAL/MINERAL—Meaning primarily that a given metal detector has metal/mineral detection characteristics and/or the ability to distinguish between the two.

MODE—A manner of operating, generally controllable at the operator's option, i.e., search modes, metal or mineral modes, VLF all metal mode, trash elimination, etc.

NARROW SCAN—A scan width less than full searchcoil diameter. In earlier days, TR detector searchcoils scanned an effective area equivalent to about thirty to forty percent of the diameter of the searchcoil being used.

NULL—A tuning or audio adjustment condition that results in "quiet" or zero audio operation.

OSCILLATOR—The variation of an observable or otherwise detectable quantity of motion about a mean value.

OVERSHOOT—A metal detector "false" signal characteristic. When the searchcoil is passed over a junk metal target, the detector audio will be pulled down into the null (quiet) zone. The automatic tuning circuitry senses the change and immediately starts to push the audio back up to where it can be heard. As soon as the searchcoil passes the target, the junk metal releases its negative effect on the detector and the sound is momentarily pushed up to an audible overshoot level before it returns to normal threshold sound. This generally occurs in TR discriminating/automatic mode detectors.

PENETRATION—The ability of a detector to penetrate earth material, air, wood, rock, and water to locate metal targets. Penetration is a function of detector design and type of detector, material being penetrated, etc.

PERFORMANCE—The ability of a detector to perform the functions which the manufacturer claims his detectors will perform.

PERMEABILITY—The measure of how a material performs as a path for magnetic lines of force as measured against the permeability standard, air. Air is rated as 1 on the permeability scale, diamagnetic materials less than 1, paramagnetic materials slightly more than 1 and ferromagnetic materials much more than 1.

PHASE—The angular (mathematical or time concept) relationship that exists between current and voltage in all AC circuits...regardless of type. When both voltage and current cycles rise and fall in exact unison, voltage and current are said to be in phase. When the rise of current flow lags behind the rise of voltage, the circuit is said to be inductive. Conversely, when the rise of current leads the rise of voltage, the circuit is said to be capacitive.

PHASE ANGLE—The number of angular (mathematical concept) degrees that AC current and voltage peaks are out of phase—or out of step with each other.

PINPOINTING—The art of determining exactly where a detected target is located.

PLACER—This is pronounced plas-er. It sounds like plaster with the "t" removed. In prospecting, an accumulation of gold, black magnetic sand and other elements of specific gravity higher then sand, rock, etc., found in same area.

PUSHBUTTON—A retuning and mode change feature incorporated in certain metal detectors.

RECEIVER—That portion of the instrument circuitry of a metal detector which receives the information created by the presence of targets, acts upon that information and processes it according to design intentions, and then activates the readout system in proportion to the nature of the received information.

RECEIVER GAIN—The amplification of input signals to whatever extent required.

RESPONSE TIME—This indicates in a general sense, the presence (or absence) of time delay in the audio section of a detector that describes the interval between target-sensing and audio and/or meter indication.

RETUNING — The retuning (restoring) of a detector's audio sound (threshold) to a predetermined level. This is accomplished by pushing a button, flipping a switch, adjusting a knob, etc.

REVERSE DISCRIMINATION — A technique whereby targets can be classified as "good" or "bad", "hot" rocks indentified, etc. Performed only in TR discriminate manual mode.

SCANNING — The actual scanning or movement of the detector search-coil over the ground or other objects being searched.

SCRUBBING — A method used to achieve maximum depth detection in the TR DISCRIMINATE MODE. Also, it minimizes earth mineralization disturbance.

SCUBA — (Self-Contained Underwater Breathing Apparatus); a system of equipment used for breathing while swimming under water; usually consists of an air intake device, storage tanks, regulator and necessary hoses.

SEARCHCOIL — The component of the detector which houses the transmitter and receiver antennas. The searchcoil is usually attached to the control housing by way of an adjustable connecting stem. The searchcoil is scanned over the ground or other surface.

SEARCHCOIL DETECTION PATTERN — That portion of the electromagnetic field where metal detection takes place. It is located out from and along the axis of the searchcoil generally starting at full searchcoil width and tapering to a point at some distance from the searchcoil. Its actual width and depth depends upon the size and nature of any given target.

SENSITIVITY — The ability to sense conductivity changes in the detection pattern. Sensitivity is one of the most important operational characteristics of an electronic metal detector. The smaller the changes in conductivity that will produce a meaningful readout, the more sensitive the instrument. The greater a detector's sensitivity, the smaller the target that the detector will detect.

SIGNAL — That received, electromagnetically created, intelligence that produces target responses.

SILENT AUDIO — The tuning of the audio in the "silent" (just below threshold) zone. There is no audio sound heard except when a target is detected.

SPLASHPROOF — See WATERPROOF also. Minor wetting of housing and/or searchcoil (light spray, dew, etc) will not affect detector operation.

STABILITY — The ability of metal detector circuits to remain tuned to the predetermined operating point (threshold).

SUBMERSIBLE — This generally refers to the ability of a detector to be submerged a certain distance under water and still continue operating perfectly. All Garrett searchcoils can be submerged to the connector.

SUPER-SNIPPING—A trademarked detecting method, using a small (three-inch-to-four-inch diameter) searchcoil, that enhances individual target detection. Nearby target influence is minimized. Especially of value in trashy areas.

SURFACE AREA—That surface area of a target lying hoizontal with the plane of the detector searchcoil. In other words, the amount of surface area that is "looking" at the underside of the searchcoil. This is the area through which the electromagnetic field lines pass and on which eddy currents are generated.

SWEEPING—See SCANNING.

TARGET—A sought-for object distinct and apart from matrix conductivity anomalies. A coin is a target but a wad of discarded chewing gum wrapper is not. Junk iron is not normally a target but for bottle hounds who use detectors to locate old trash pits, it is. A target is any sought object lying within a matrix that may or may not contain other but unsought conductive objects and which, by virtue of its materials makeup, is capable of being located with an electronic metal detector. Also used to describe all detectable metal or mineral targets.

TH-ing—An abbreviation for Treasure Hunting.

THRESHOLD—Refers to the low level audio sound achieved when a metal detector is tuned.

TR—The abbreviation for TRANSMITTER-RECEIVER, which is a type of metal detector circuit.

TR MODE—The term which identifies the TR operational setting on a TR and VLF/TR metal detector.

TUNING—The manual adjustment that an operator makes to bring the detector audio sound to an audible, silent or other preferred audio level threshold.

UNIVERSAL CAPABILITIES—A statement or claim that a given metal detector is capable of performing most metal detecting tasks, such as coin, cache and relic hunting; ghost towning; nugget hunting; vein locating, etc.

VERSATILITY—A measure of many applications to which a metal detector can be applied. In other words, how many ways can a particular metal detector be used? See, also, UNIVERSAL CAPABILITIES.

VISUAL INDICATOR—Generally means meter indication. It is possible to design a system using only visual indicators (light, for example).

VLF—Initials that stand for Very Low Frequency, which is a segment of the RF spectrum that includes frequencies from 3 kHz to 30 kHz. It is also a detector type.

VLF MODE—The term which identifies the VLF operational setting on a VLF and VLF/TR metal detector.

VOLUME CONTROL—A control, generally resistance, used to limit voltage and/or current in an audio amplifier and, thereby, control volume of sound or "loudness" of maximum sound when a target is detected. Is is not to be confused with tuning or audio adjustment controls.

WATERPROOF—Generally refers to waterproofing of control housings that allows operation in rain or splashing surf. Waterproof does not necessarily mean submersible.

WETTED SALT—The most prevalent mineral encountered in beach and ocean hunting. Is ignored by Pulse Induction and VLF detectors with ground canceling, which are thus ideal for such hunting.

WIDE SCAN—Generally implies that the scanning width (detection pattern) of a detector, as the searchcoil passes over the ground, is equal to the full width (or wider) of the diameter of the searchcoil being used.

APPENDIX 1:

RAM Publications

MODERN METAL DETECTORS. Charles Garrett. This advanced handbook explains simply yet fully how to succeed with your metal detector. Written for home, field, and classroom study, MMD provides the expertise you need for success in any metal detecting situation, hobby or professional. Easily understood chapters on specifications, components, capabilities, selecting and operating a detector, choosing searchcoils and accessories, and more—increase your understanding of the fascinating, rewarding fields of metal detector use. 524 pages. 56 Illustrations, 150 photos.

DETECTOR OWNER'S FIELD MANUAL. Roy Lagal. Nowhere else will you find the detector operating instructions that Mr. Lagal has put into this book. He shows in detail how to treasure hunt, cache hunt, prospect, search for nuggets, black sand deposits...in short, how to use your detector exactly as it should be used. Covers completely BFO-TR-VLF/TR types, P.I.s, P.R.G's, P.I.P.'s, etc. Explains precious metals, minerals, ground conditions, and gives proof that treasure exists because it has been found and that more exists than you can find! Fully illustrated. 236 pages.

ELECTRONIC PROSPECTING. Charles Garrett, Bob Grant, Roy Lagal. A tremendous upswing in electronic prospecting for gold and other precious metals has recently occurred. High gold prices and unlimited capabilities of VLF/TR metal detectors have led to many fantastic discoveries. Gold is there to be found. If you have the desire to search for it and want to be successful, then this book will show you how to select (and use) from the many brands of VLF/TR's those that are correctly calibrated to produce accurate metal vs. mineral identification which is so vitally necessary in prospecting. Illustrated. 96 pages.

GOLD PANNING IS EASY. Roy Lagal. The author doesn't introduce a new method; he removes confusion surrounding old established methods. A refreshing NEW LOOK guaranteed to produce results with the "Gravity Trap" or any other pan. Special metal detector instructions that show you how to nugget shoot, find gold and silver veins, and check ore samples for precious metal. This HOW, WHERE and WHEN gold panning book is a must for everyone, beginner or professional! Fully illustrated. 112 pages.

392

THE COMPLETE VLF-TR METAL DETECTOR HANDBOOK (All About Ground Canceling Metal Detectors). Roy Lagal, Charles Garrett. The unparalleled capabilities of VLF/TR Ground Canceling metal detectors have made them the number one choice of treasure hunters and prospectors. From History, Theory, and Development to Coin, Cache and Relic Hunting, as well as Prospecting, the authors have explained in detail the capabilities of VLF/TR detectors and how they are used. Learn the new ground canceling detectors for the greatest possible success. Illustrated. 200 pages.

TREASURE HUNTER'S MANUAL #6. Karl von Mueller. The original material in this book was written for the professional treasure hunter. Hundreds of copies were paid for in advance by professionals who knew the value of Karl's writing and wanted no delays in receiving their copies. The THM #6 completely describes fulltime treasure hunting and explains the mysteries surrounding this intriguing and rewarding field of endeavor. You'll read this fascinating book several times. Each time you will discover you have gained greater in-depth knowledge. Thousands of ideas, tips and other valuable information. Illustrated. 318 pages.

TREASURE HUNTER'S MANUAL #7. Karl von Mueller. The classic! The most complete, up-to-date guide to America's fastest growing activity, written by the old master of treasure hunting. This is *the* book that fully describes professional methods of RESEARCH, RECOVERY, and TREASURE DISPOSITION. Includes a full range of treasure hunting methods from research techniques to detector operation, from legality to gold dredging. Don't worry that this material overlaps THM #6...both of Karl's MANUALS are 100% different from each other yet are crammed with information you should know about treasure hunting. Illustrated. 334 pages.

SUCCESSFUL COIN HUNTING. Charles Garrett. The best and most complete guide to successful coin hunting, this book explains fully the how's, where's, and when's of searching for coins and related objects. It also includes a complete explanation of how to select and use various types of coin hunting metal detectors. Based on more than 20 years of actual in-the-field experience by the author, this volume contains a great amount of practical coin hunting information that will not be found elsewhere. Profusely illustrated with over 100 photographs. 248 pages.

TREASURE HUNTING PAYS OFF. Charles Garrett. This book will give you an excellent introduction to all facets of treasure hunting. It tells you how to begin and be successful in general treasure hunting; coin hunting; relic, cache, and bottle seeking; and prospecting. It describes the various kinds of metal/mineral detectors and tells you how to go about selecting the correct type for all kinds of searching. This is an excellent guidebook for the beginner, yet contains tips and ideas for the experienced TH'er. Illustrated. 92 pages.

BURIED TREASURE OF THE UNITED STATES. Robert F. Marx. The author shares several "lifetimes" of acquired knowledge in a complete how-to-locate-treasure field guide which presents new and innovative ideas about what "treasure" is and where to find it. He tells what coin hunting is all about and points out lucrative fields that are often overlooked. Treasure hunters are also given a state-by-state listing of sites where treasure can be found. Illustrated. 284 pages.

WEEKEND PROSPECTING. Roy Lagal. The authoratitive guide for finding gold tells how to locate the precious metal and how to recover it, using language that a hobbyist can understand. Yet the book also presents ideas that will interest the veteran prospector. Includes chapters on panning, dredging, and nugget hunting as well as offering simple instructions on recovering gold from black sand. Tells how to search old mines and dredged locations. Illustrated. 104 pages.

Sources, Magazines

AMERICAN WEST
7000 E. Tanque Verde Rd.
Tucson, Arizona 85715

AQUA FIELD
PUBLICATIONS, INC.
One East/Suite 1191
500 Eastern By-Pass
Montgomery, Alabama 36117

CALIFORNIA DIVER
P.O. Box 7260
Huntington Beach, California
92615-7260

CALIFORNIA MINING
JOURNAL
P.O. Drawer 628
Santa Cruz, California 95061

CARSON ENTERPRISES
Drawer 71
Deming, New Mexico 88031

DIVING RETAILER
P.O. Box 17067
Long Beach, California 90807

EXANIMO PRESS
P.O. Box CGI
Segundo, Colorado 81070

FINS AND FEATHERS
401 No. Third Street
Minneapolis, Minnesota 55401

GOLD NUGGET
PUBLISHING CO.
P.O. Box 268
Willow, Alaska 99688

GOLD PROSPECTORS
P.O. Box 507
Bonsall, California 92003

JESS PUBLISHING CO., INC.
6745 Adobe Road
Twentynine Palms, California
92277

LOST TREASURE
P.O. Box 937
Bixby, Oklahoma 74008

MIDWEST OUTDOORS
111 Shore Drive
Hinsdale, Illinois 60521

OCEAN REALM
4505 Lexington Avenue
Jackson, Florida 32210

PADI
1243 East Warner Avenue
Santa Ana, California 92705

PEOPLE'S PUBLISHING CO.
P.O. Box 1095
Arcata, California 95521

PUBLISHER'S WEEKLY
205 East 42nd St.,
New York, N.Y. 10017

RAM PUBLISHING COMPANY
P.O. Box 38649
Dallas, Texas 75238

RESEARCH UNLIMITED
P.O. Box 448
Freemont, Nebraska 68025

SCUBA PRO
3105 E. Harcourt/ Rancho
Dominguez, California 90221

SCUBA TIMES
147 Drew Circle
Pensacola, Florida 32503

SKIN DIVER
8490 Sunset Boulevard
Los Angeles, California 90069

K.B. SLOCUM-BOOKS
P.O. Box 10998 #620
Austin, Texas 78766

SOVEREIGN PUBLICATIONS
Sovereign House
Brentwood
Essex, CM14 4SE England

THOUSAND TRAILS, INC.
15325 S.E. 30th Place
Bellevue, Washington 98007

TL ENTERPRISES, INC.
2300 Middlebury
Elkhart, Indiana 46516-5598

TOKEN PUBLICATION, LTD.
Crossways Road
Grayshot, Hindead
Surrey GU26 6HF England

TREASURE
6745 Adobe Road
Twentynine Palms, California 92277

UNDERWATER U.S.A.
P.O. Box 705
Bloomsburg, Pennsylvania 17815

WESTERN & EASTERN
  TREASURES
P.O. Box 1095
Arcata, California 95521

WESTERN OUTDOORS
3197-E Airport Loop Dr.
Costa Mesa, California 92626

METAL DETECTION EQUIPMENT

For further information on all metal detection equipment as described in this book, write:

GARRETT METAL DETECTORS
2814 National Drive
Garland, Texas 75041
214 278 6151

Toll Free for literature and/or the name of your nearest dealer:
1-800-527-4011

In Texas, call:

1-800-442-4889

FREE PUBLICATION: To receive this free publication relating to treasure hunting, prospecting and metal detectors, write, sending your name and address to:

The SEARCHER
2814 National Drive
Garland, Texas 75041

APPENDIX 3:

The Garrett Film/Video Library

Outdoor Family Entertainment and Instructional Programs. Available in video cassette. Some available in 16mm, write for details.

No. 16701 "Treasures of Mexico" and "Gold and Treasure Adventures" $24.95 Copyright 1980. Also available in 16mm.

"Treasures of Mexcio"   Running time 18:48 min.

Host Charles Garrett invites us along with the Garrett field team on an outing to the fabulous Canyon de Cobre, near Batopilas. Mexico. The team searches a beautiful old city, silver-laden rivers, and finally, an old mine. As you will see when you take this journey, electronic prospecting in these areas is very productive.

"Gold and Treasure Adventures"   Running time 28:45 min.

Charles Garrett, President of Garrett Metal Detectors, takes us on a visit to a competition treasure hunt in the California desert and on a treasure hunting trip to Europe. While in the desert, Charles and a field team hunt an old mining area where many good recoveries are made. Actor John Quade is featured and narrates part of the film.

No. 16702 "The Silent Past" and "Treasures of the Indian Ocean" $24.95 Copyright 1980. Also available in 16mm.

"The Silent Past"   Running time 26:23 min.

An old prospector, killed by hostile Indians after he discovers a silver mine, is transformed into a ghost whose destiny is to roam the Big Bend area of West Texas until one of his descendants comes to the area. His great-great-grandson and parents travel to the area and discover many artifacts buried during the passage of time.

"Treasures of the Indian Ocean"   Running time 26:30 min.

Robert Marx, internationally known American underwater archaeologist and treasure salvor, leads a team of professionals on a search for the 18th century wreck site of the French merchant ship, *St. Geran,* wrecked in 1744 off Mauritius, which is an island about 500 miles east of Madagascar. This color and sound film has great historical interest which shows many different methods of recovery, as well as touching on research and archaeological procedures.

No. 16703 "Castle Treasures"
$19.95 Copyright 1986

"Castle Treasures"   Running time 12:00 min.

A treasure hunter inherits a castle in Austria. This slide presentation on video is not only an interesting study of a castle, but the found treasures dramatically give us a glimpse of an exciting, eventful segment of history. Narrated by Jack Lowry.

No. 16704 "Gold Panning is Easy"
$29.95 Copyright 1987

"Gold Panning is Easy"   Running time 25:00 min.

The program illustrates methods of using the GRAVITY TRAP and other pans in both wet and dry panning for gold and other materials of high specific gravity. You'll learn where and how to locate gold. Roy Lagal's techniques are demonstrated by Virgil Hutton. It is taped in Arizona and introduced by Charles Garrett.

No. 16706 "Weekend Prospecting"
$39.95 Copyright 1987

"Weekend Prospecting"   Running time 50 min.

This production was filmed while Charles Garrett, Roy Lagal, Tommie T. Long and Virgil Hutton were on a gold hunting expedition in the Northwest country of the United States. It accurately depicts "weekend prospecting," gold locating and recovery techniques that all family members can put to productive use during vacations and weekend trips to the gold country. Electronic prospecting with metal detectors and both wet and dry gold panning and recovery techniques are fully illustrated. Very informative, instructional and interesting with outstanding Northwest United States scenery. Roy Lagal's book, WEEKEND PROSPECTING, published by RAM Books, is a "companion piece" as the book covers in greater detail everything presented in this video production. Introduced by Charles Garrett.

APPENDIX 4:

Books

Adventure Series Productions, *Diver's Almanac,* 1984.

Allen, Joan, *Glittering Prospects,* Elm Tree Books, London, 1975.

American Red Cross, *Lifesaving and Water Safety,* Doubleday & Co., Inc., NY, 1937.

American National Red Cross, *First Aid,* Doubleday & Co., Inc. NY, 1973.

Andrews, Evangeline Walker, *Jonathan Dickinson's Journal,* Florida Classics Library, 1983.

Australian Art Exhibitors Corp. Ltd., *Eldorado Colombian Gold,* Australia, 1978.

Bascom, Willard, *Deep Water, Ancient Ships,* Doubleday & Co., Inc. NY, 1976.

Bascom, Willard, *Waves and Beaches,* Doubleday & Co., NY, 1964.

Boehler, Ted, *Divemaster Manual 2, The Deepstar,* Crestline, CA, 1981.

Brady, Edward, M., *Marine Salvage Operations,* Cornell, 1960.

Bridges, Lloyd, *Mask and Flippers, The Story of Skindiving,* Cornerstone Library, NY, 1960.

Bryfonski, Dedra, *New England Beach Book, The,*Walker & Co., NY, 1975.

Burgess, Robert F., *They Found Treasure,* Dodd, Mead & Co., NY, 1977.

Carrier, Rick & Barbara, *Dive,* Funk & Wagnalls, NY, 1973.

Coffman, F. L. *1001 Lost, Buried or Sunken Treasures,* Thomas Nelson & Sons, NY, 1957.

DeLoach, Ned, *Diving Guide to Underwater Florida,* New World Publications, Jacksonville, FL, 1980.

Dixon, Sarah & Peter, *West Coast Beaches,* Sunrise Books, NY, 1978.

Erickson, Ralph D., *Search and Recovery,* PADI, Santa Ana, CA, 1983.

Fine, John Christopher, *Sunken Ships and Treasure,* Atheneum, NY, 1986.

Fletcher, E., *Treasure Hunting on the Coast,* Fletcher Publications, Redcar, Cleveland, England, 1977.

Frederick, James, *Diver's Guide to River Wrecks,* Rowe Publishing, Milwaukee, Wl, 1982.

Garrett, Charles, L., *Modern Metal Detectors,* RAM Books, Dallas, 1985.

Garrett, Charles L., Tudor, Jim, *Research Methods and Sources for the Treasure Hunter,* RAM Books, Dallas, 1988.

Garrett, Charles L., *Successful Coin Hunting,* RAM Books, Dallas, 1984.

Gibbs, Jim, *Disaster Log of Ships,* Bonaza Books, NY, 1971.

Giguere, John-Paul, *Make Money in Diving,* Rowe Publications, Milwaukee, Wl, 1981.

Giguere, John-Paul, *Salvage Laws for Weekend Divers,* Rowe Publications, Milwaukee, Wl, 1981.

Golden, Hands, *Buried and Sunken Treasure,* Marshall Cavendish, London, 1974.

Granville, Robert, *Shallow Water Treasure Hunting Manual, The,* Conestoga Printing, Sacramento, CA, 1984.

Hamilton, D. L., *Conservation of Metal Objects from Underwater Sites: A Study in Methods,* Texas Memorial Museum, Austin, TX, 1976.

Hammes, Richard B., Zimos, Anthony G., *Safe Scuba,* NASDS, Long Beach, CA, 1979.

Helm Associates, *Treasure Lead Generation,* Austin, TX, 1986.

Hetherington, Keith, *Beachcombing with a Metal Detector,* Gemcraft, Australia, 1980.

H.D.L. Communications, *Diver's Almanac-Guide to the West Coast from Baja to British Columbia,* Costa Mesa, CA, 1985.

Hudson, L. Frank, *Lost Treasures of Florida's West Coast,* St. Petersburg, FL, 1983.

Humphries, Lund, *Treasure of the Spanish Main,* London.

Jenney, James, *Advanced Wreck Diver's Manual,* Rowe Publishing, Milwaukee, Wl, 1983.

Jenny, James, *Diver's Directory of Shipwreck Research,* Rowe Publications, Milwaukee, Wl, 1982.

Jenney, James, *In Search of Shipwrecks,* A.S. Barnes & Co., NY, 1980.

Kelley, Kate, Shobe, John, *Diver's Guide to Underwater America,* Dive Sport Publishing, Branson, MO, 1982.

Lagal, Roy, *Detector Owner's Field Manual,* RAM Books, Dallas, 1981.

Lagal, Roy, Garrett, Charles L., *Electronic Prospecting,* RAM Books, Dallas, 1983.

Lagal, Roy, *Gold Panning is Easy,* RAM Books, Dallas, 1984.

Lagal, Roy, Garrett, Charles L., *Complete VLF-TR Metal Detector Handbook,* RAM Books, Dallas, 1984.

Lagal, Roy, *Weekend Prospecting,* RAM Books, Dallas, 1987.

Lyon, Eugene, *The Search for the Atocha,* Harper & Row, NY, 1979.

Martin, Robert C., *The Deep Sea Diver,* Cornell Maritime Press, Cambridge, 1978.

Marx, Robert F., *Quest for Treasure,* RAM Books, Dallas, 1982; *Buried Treasures of the United States,* RAM Books, Dallas, 1987; *The Lure of Sunken Treasure,* The David McKay Company, NY,

1973; *Underwater Dig,* Henry Z. Walck, Inc., NY, 1975; *Into the Deep,* Van Nostrand Reinhold, NY, 1978; *Shipwrecks of the Western Hemisphere,* David McKay Co., NY, 1971; *Still More Adventures,* Mason/Charter, NY, 1976; *Port Royal Rediscovered,* Doubleday & Co., NY, 1973; *Sea Fever: Famous Underwater Explorers,* Doubleday & Co., NY, 1972. *Shipwrecks in Mexican Waters; Shipwrecks in Florida Waters; Always Another Advanture; They Dared the Deep; A History of Diving; Following Columbus: The Voyage of the Nina 2, The Capture of the Treasure Fleet.*

McAllister, Evelyn Ditton, *Easy Steps to Safe Swimming,* A.S. Barnes & Co., NY, 1973.

Mueller, Karl von, *Treasure Hunter's Manual No. 6,* RAM Books, Dallas, 1977.

Mueller, Karl von, *Treasure Hunter's Manual No. 7,* RAM Books, Dallas, 1979.

Mroczkowski, George, *Professional Treasure Hunter,* RAM Books, Dallas, 1981.

Merkitch, Warren, *Beachcomber's Handbook,* Exanimo Press, Segundo, Co, 1976.

Nannetti, Ettore and Diana, *New York Treasures and Metal Detecting Sites,* Metal Detector Distributors, Brooklyn, NY, 1985.

Ohrellus, Bengt, *Vasa, The King's Ship,* Chilton, Philadelphia, PA, 1959.

National Geographic Society, *Exploring the Deep Frontier,* 1980.

National Geographic Society, *Treasures in the Sea,* 1972.

PADI, *PADI Dive Manual.*

PADI, *Divemaster Manual.*

Pattee, Gerald, *Metal Detecting in Water,* Found Enterprises, 1974.

Patterson, T.W., *British Columbia Shipwrecks,* Stagecoach Publishing, Langley, BC, Canada, 1976.

Potter, John S. Jr., *Treasure Diver's Guide,* Bonanza Books, NY, 1972.

Rieseberg, Lieutenant Harry E., *The Sea of Treasure,* Frederick Fell, NY, 1956.

Rieseberg, Lieutenant Harry E., *I Dive for Treasure,* Frederick Fell, NY, 1970.

Rowe, Alan R., *Relics, Water and the Kitchen Sink,* Rowe Publications, Milwaukee, Wl, 1979.

Sedwick, Frank, *Practical Book of Coins,* Author, Maitland, FL, 1987.

Shiloh Publishing Co., *Who's Buying and Selling Guide,* Staunton, VA, 1976.

Springer, Robert R., *Skin and Scuba Diver's Digest,* Follette Publishing, Chicago, IL, 1975.

Sullivan, George, *Discover Archaeology,* Doubleday & Co., Garden City, NY, 1980.

Sullivan, George, *Treasure Hunt, The 16-Year Search for the Lost*

Treasure Ship Atocha, Henry Holt & Co., New York, NY, 1987.

Time-Life Books, *Atlantic Beaches,* Alexandria, VA, 1972.

Trevillian, Bob, and Carter, Frank, *Diamonds in the Surf,* Spyglass Enterprises, Glenburnie, MD, 1982.

Trevillian, Bob, and Carter, Frank, *Diamonds in the Surf: The Second Adventure,* Spyglass Enterprises, Glenburnie, MD, 1983.

Trevillian, Bob, and Carter, Frank, *The Poor Man's Treasure Hunter,* Spyglass Enterprises, Glenburnie, MD, 1985.

Throckmorton, Peter, *Diving for Treasure,* The Viking Press, NY, 1977.

Voynick, Stephen M., *In Search of Gold,* Paladin Press, Boulder, Co, 1982.

Voynick, Stephen M., *The Mid-Atlantic Treasure Coast,* The Middle Atlantic Press, Wallingford, PA, 1984.

Volker, Roy, Richmond, Dick, *In the Wake of the Golden Galleons,* Oro Quest Press, St. Louis, MO, 1976.

Wilkes, Bill St. John, *Nautical Archaeology,* Stein and Day, NY, 1971.

Wilson, Derek, *The World Atlas of Treasure,* William Collinsons, London 1981.

Index

408

BOOK ORDER BLANK

See your detector dealer or bookstore or send check or money order directly to Ram for prompt, postage paid shipping. If not completely satisfied return book(s) within 10 days for a full refund.

____WEEKEND PROSPECTING $6.95
____MODERN METAL DETECTORS $9.95
____DETECTOR OWNER'S MANUAL $8.95
____ELECTRONIC PROSPECTING $4.95
____GOLD PANNING IS EASY $6.95
____COMPLETE VLF-TR METAL
    DETECTOR HANDBOOK (THE) (ALL
    ABOUT GROUND CANCELING
    METAL DETECTORS) $8.95

____ROBERT MARX. QUEST FOR
    TREASURE $11.95
____TREASURE HUNTER'S MANUAL #6 $9.95
____TREASURE HUNTER'S MANUAL #7 $9.95
____SUCCESSFUL COIN HUNTING $8.95
____TREASURE HUNTING PAYS OFF. $4.95
____TREASURE RECOVERY FROM
    SAND AND SEA $12.95

Please add 50¢ for each book ordered (to a maximum of $2) for handling charges.

Total for Items	$ _____
Texas Residents Add 8% State Tax	_____
Handling Charge	_____
Total of Above	$ _____

ENCLOSED IS MY CHECK OR MONEY ORDER $ _____
I prefer to purchase through my MasterCard ( ) or Visa ( ) account. (Check one.)

_____
Card Number

_____
Bank Identifier Number

_____
Expiration Date

_____
Signature (Order must be signed.)

NAME _____

ADDRESS _____

CITY _____

STATE _____ ZIP _____

PLACE MY NAME ON YOUR MAILING LIST ☐

Ram Publishing Company
P.O. Drawer 38649, Dallas, Texas 75238
214-278-8439
DEALER INQUIRIES WELCOME

BOOK ORDER BLANK

See your detector dealer or bookstore or send check or money order directly to Ram for prompt, postage paid shipping. If not completely satisfied return book(s) within 10 days for a full refund.

_____WEEKEND PROSPECTING $6.95
_____MODERN METAL DETECTORS $9.95
_____DETECTOR OWNER'S MANUAL $8.95
_____ELECTRONIC PROSPECTING $4.95
_____GOLD PANNING IS EASY $6.95
_____COMPLETE VLF-TR METAL
    DETECTOR HANDBOOK (THE) (ALL
    ABOUT GROUND CANCELING
    METAL DETECTORS) $8.95

_____ROBERT MARX. QUEST FOR
    TREASURE $11 95
_____TREASURE HUNTER'S MANUAL #6 $9.95
_____TREASURE HUNTER'S MANUAL #7 $9.95
_____SUCCESSFUL COIN HUNTING $8.95
_____TREASURE HUNTING PAYS OFF. $4.95
_____TREASURE RECOVERY FROM
    SAND AND SEA $12.95

Please add 50¢ for each book ordered (to a maximum of $2) for handling charges.

Total for Items	$ _____
Texas Residents Add 8% State Tax	_____
Handling Charge	_____
Total of Above	$ _____

ENCLOSED IS MY CHECK OR MONEY ORDER $ _____
I prefer to purchase through my MasterCard (   ) or Visa (   ) account. (Check one.)

_____   _____
Card Number   Bank Identifier Number

_____   _____
Expiration Date   Signature (Order must be signed.)

NAME _____

ADDRESS _____

CITY _____

STATE _____ ZIP _____

PLACE MY NAME ON YOUR MAILING LIST ☐

Ram Publishing Company
P.O. Drawer 38649, Dallas, Texas 75238
214-278-8439
DEALER INQUIRIES WELCOME

NOTES

NOTES

NOTES

NOTES

NOTES